OFFICE FOR STANDARDS
IN EDUCATION

The Annual Report
of Her Majesty's
Chief Inspector of Schools

**Standards and
Quality in Education
1998/99**

Laid before Parliament by the Secretary of State for Education
and Employment pursuant to Section 2(7)(a) of the School Inspections Act 1996

Ordered by the House of Commons to be printed 8 February 2000

157   London: The Stationery Office   £13.15

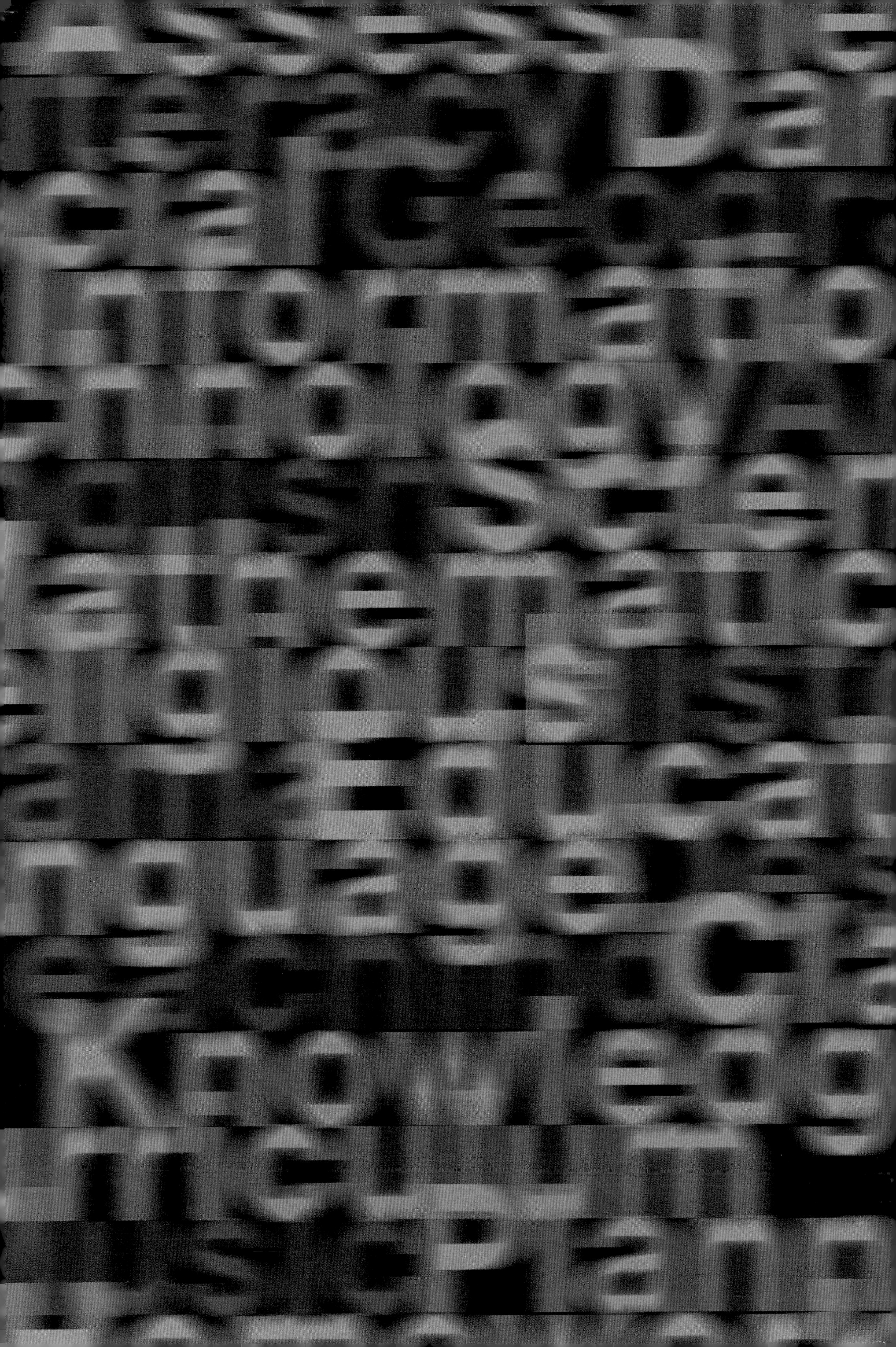

Alexandra House
33 Kingsway
London WC2B 6SE

Tel 0171-421 6800 (Switchboard)

Fax 0171-421 6546   GTN-3066

Chris Woodhead
Her Majesty's
Chief Inspector of Schools

OFFICE FOR STANDARDS IN EDUCATION

The Rt Hon David Blunkett MP
Secretary of State
Department for Education and Employment
Sanctuary Buildings
Great Smith Street
London SW1P 3BT

February 2000

Dear David,

I have pleasure in submitting to you my Annual Report as required by the School Inspections Act 1996.

The report begins, as usual, with a commentary on some of the issues of importance. The second section contains the evidence from the year's inspections across the range of matters which fall within my remit.

I hope the report will be of interest to parents, teachers, headteachers, governors and policymakers, as well as contributing to the public debate on standards and quality of education.

As last year I am arranging for a copy of the report to be sent to every maintained school in England.

Yours ever,

CHRIS WOODHEAD

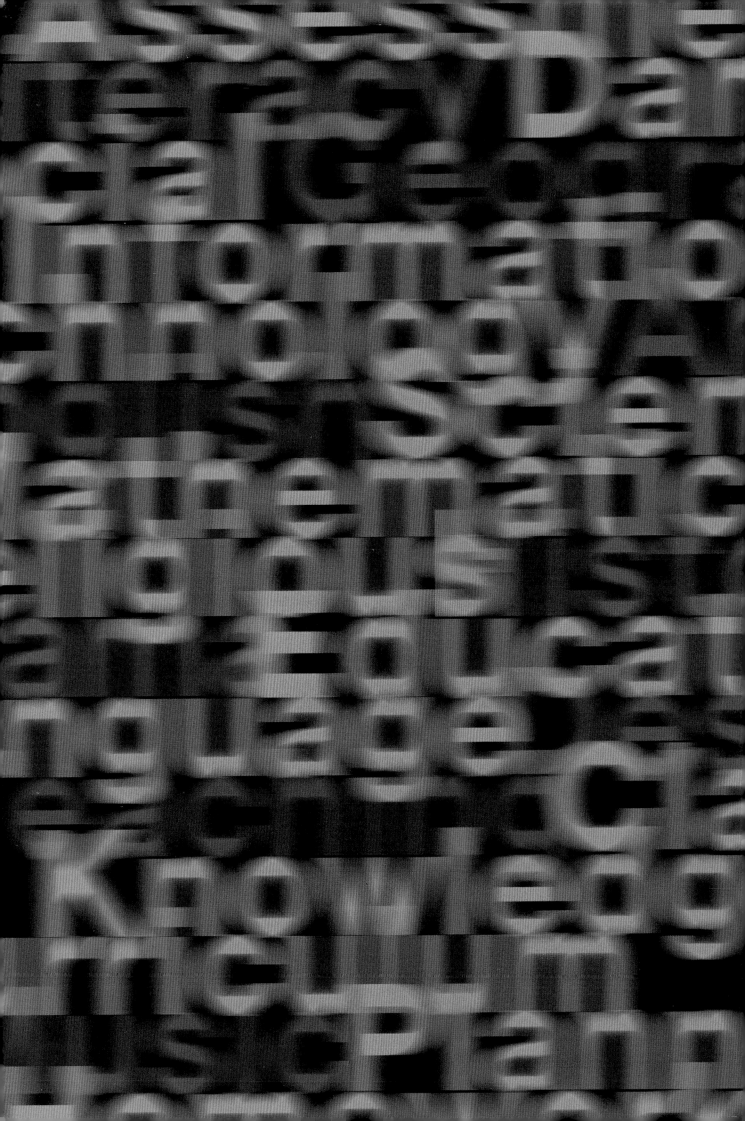

Contents

Preface

This Report draws on three sources of evidence:

- **Section 10 inspections carried out by registered inspectors;**

- **Section 5 inspections carried out by registered nursery inspectors;**

- **inspections carried out by Her Majesty's Inspectors of Schools (HMI).**

The 1998/99 Section 10 inspections provide evidence on the standards, quality and efficiency of one-sixth of secondary, primary and special schools. This year was the second year of re-inspection of secondary schools and the first year of re-inspection of primary and special schools.

HMI have focused their inspections on the work of local education authorities, teacher education and training, adult education and youth work. HMI have also inspected important developments such as the National Literacy Strategy and General National Vocational Qualifications (GNVQs).

Full details of the evidence base are given in Annex 1.

As in previous years, I am identifying a number of schools which are shown by inspection to be providing a good quality of education and achieving high standards. All the SECONDARY SCHOOLS listed have received outstanding inspection reports. In addition, some have excellent General Certificate of Secondary Education (GCSE) results which they have sustained over a number of years. Others have GCSE results which are good, given the circumstances of the particular school.

School Name	Postal Town	LEA
All Hallows RC High School	PRESTON	Lancashire
All Saints RC High School	SHEFFIELD	Sheffield
Anglo-European School	INGATESTONE	Essex
Arden School	SOLIHULL	Solihull
Benton Park School	LEEDS	Leeds
Blessed Thomas Holford Catholic High School	ALTRINCHAM	Trafford
Brannel School	ST AUSTELL	Cornwall
Brookfield Community School	CHESTERFIELD	Derbyshire
Bullers Wood School	CHISLEHURST	Bromley
Canon Slade CE School	BOLTON	Bolton
Chorley Southlands High School	CHORLEY	Lancashire
Cirencester Kingshill School	CIRENCESTER	Gloucestershire
City of Portsmouth Girls' School	PORTSMOUTH	Portsmouth
Comberton Village College	CAMBRIDGE	Cambridgeshire
Coundon Court School and Community College	COVENTRY	Coventry
Dartford Grammar School	DARTFORD	Kent
Dartford Grammar School for Girls	DARTFORD	Kent
Elliott School	WANDSWORTH	Wandsworth
Fairfield High School for Girls	DROYLESDEN	Tameside
Falinge Park High School	ROCHDALE	Rochdale
Fernwood School	NOTTINGHAM	Nottingham, City of
Fulford School	YORK	York, City of
Garforth Community College	LEEDS	Leeds
Hall Mead School	UPMINSTER	Havering
Heckmondwike Grammar School	HECKMONDWIKE	Kirklees
Jews' Free School	CAMDEN TOWN	Camden
John Hampden Grammar School	HIGH WYCOMBE	Buckinghamshire
King Edward VI Aston School	ASTON	Birmingham
King Edward VI Handsworth School	BIRMINGHAM	Birmingham
Lady Manners School	BAKEWELL	Derbyshire
Lampton School	HOUNSLOW	Hounslow
Long Stratton High School	NORWICH	Norfolk
Lordswood Girls' School and Sixth-Form Centre	HARBORNE	Birmingham
Macmillan College	MIDDLESBROUGH	Middlesbrough
Manor CE School	YORK	York, City of
Marlwood School	ALVESTON	South Gloucester
Matthew Moss High School	ROCHDALE	Rochdale
Nonsuch High School for Girls	SUTTON	Sutton
Northgate High School	IPSWICH	Suffolk
Nunthorpe School	MIDDLESBROUGH	Redcar and Cleveland
Oathall Community College	HAYWARDS HEATH	West Sussex
Old Hall Comprehensive School	ROTHERHAM	Rotherham
Ousedale School	NEWPORT PAGNELL	Milton Keynes
Plashet School	NEWHAM	Newham

Presdales School	WARE	Hertfordshire
Queen Elizabeth's School	BARNET	Barnet
Rainford High School	ST HELENS	St Helens
Ripley St Thomas Church of England High School	LANCASTER	Lancashire
Salendine Nook High School	HUDDERSFIELD	Kirklees
Sarah Bonnell School	NEWHAM	Newham
Sheldon School	CHIPPENHAM	Wiltshire
Skegness Grammar School	SKEGNESS	Lincolnshire
St John Fisher Catholic High School	WIGAN	Wigan
St Martin's School	BRENTWOOD	Essex
St Michael's Catholic Grammar School	FINCHLEY	Barnet
St Thomas More Roman Catholic High School	NORTH SHIELDS	North Tyneside
Sutton Coldfield Grammar School for Girls	SUTTON COLDFIELD	Birmingham
Tabor High School	BRAINTREE	Essex
The Ashcombe School	DORKING	Surrey
The Blue Coat CE School	OLDHAM	Oldham
The Camden School for Girls	CAMDEN TOWN	Camden
The City Technology College	KINGSHURST	Solihull
The Douay Martyrs Roman Catholic School	UXBRIDGE	Hillingdon
The Gilberd School	COLCHESTER	Essex
The John Fisher School	PURLEY	Sutton
The King's School	GRANTHAM	Lincolnshire
The King's School	PETERBOROUGH	Peterborough, City of
The Latymer School	ENFIELD	Enfield
The Magna Carta School	EGHAM	Surrey
The North Halifax Grammar School	HALIFAX	Calderdale
The Snaith School	GOOLE	East Riding of Yorkshire
The Westgate School	WINCHESTER	Hampshire
Therfield School	LEATHERHEAD	Surrey
Thomas Alleyne's High School	UTTOXETER	Staffordshire
Wallington High School for Girls	WALLINGTON	Sutton
Westcliff High School for Boys	WESTCLIFF-ON-SEA	Southend-on-Sea
Westcliff High School for Girls	WESTCLIFF-ON-SEA	Southend-on-Sea
Wigmore High School	LEOMINSTER	Herefordshire
William Ellis School	HIGHGATE	Camden
Woodchurch High School	BIRKENHEAD	Wirral

The re-inspection of secondary schools enables me to identify those schools that have achieved EXCELLENT IMPROVEMENT since their first inspection. The schools below stand out amongst the many that have improved their quality of education and the standards achieved by pupils since the previous inspection.

School Name	Postal Town	LEA
Archbishop Tenison's School	KENNINGTON	Lambeth
Brixham Community College	BRIXHAM	Torbay
Claverham Community College	BATTLE	East Sussex
Coombe Girls' School	NEW MALDEN	Kingston upon Thames
Counthill School	OLDHAM	Oldham
Djanogly City Technology College	NOTTINGHAM	Nottingham, City of
Dormers Wells High School	SOUTHALL	Ealing
Fair Oak High School	RUGELEY	Staffordshire

School Name	Postal Town	LEA
Greenford High School	GREENFORD	Ealing
Honley High School and College	HUDDERSFIELD	Kirklees
Huxlow School	WELLINGBOROUGH	Northamptonshire
Kings Norton Girls' School	BIRMINGHAM	Birmingham
Lawrence Sheriff School	RUGBY	Warwickshire
Litcham High School	KING'S LYNN	Norfolk
Nidderdale High School and Community College	HARROGATE	North Yorkshire
Ravens Wood School for Boys	BROMLEY	Bromley
Rosecroft School	SALTBURN-BY-THE-SEA	Redcar and Cleveland
Rushey Mead School	LEICESTER	Leicester City
Sir John Cass Foundation and Redcoat CE School	STEPNEY	Tower Hamlets
St John the Baptist Catholic Comprehensive School	WOKING	Surrey
Stoke Newington School	HACKNEY	Hackney
Stopsley High School	LUTON	Luton
The Charles Dickens School	BROADSTAIRS	Kent
The Hermitage School	CHESTER-LE-STREET	Durham
The King David High School	CRUMSALL	Manchester
The Netherhall School	CAMBRIDGE	Cambridgeshire
The Sacred Heart Roman Catholic High School	HARROW	Harrow
Turves Green Girls' School and Technology College	NORTHFIELD	Birmingham
Westhoughton High School	BOLTON	Bolton

I am also pleased to be able to identify particularly successful PRIMARY, MIDDLE AND NURSERY SCHOOLS. In these schools pupils achieve high standards in literacy and numeracy and make an excellent start to their education.

School Name	Postal Town	LEA
Alexandra Infant School	KINGSTON UPON THAMES	Kingston upon Thames
All Saints CE Infant School	STAFFORD	Staffordshire
Ardleigh Green Junior School	HORNCHURCH	Havering
Avonmore Primary School	WEST KENSINGTON	Hammersmith and Fulham
Axbridge Church of England First School	AXBRIDGE	Somerset
Bailey Green First School	WEST BAILEY	North Tyneside
Balfour Junior School	CHATHAM	Medway
Bathford CE Primary School	BATH	Bath and North East Somerset
Broad Chalke CE First School	SALISBURY	Wiltshire
Catfield CE First School	GREAT YARMOUTH	Norfolk
Charles Kingsley's CE Primary School	HOOK	Hampshire
Church Aston Infant School	NEWPORT	Telford and Wrekin
Cirencester Infant School	CIRENCESTER	Gloucestershire
Clara Grant Primary School	BOW	Tower Hamlets
Crosshall Infant School	ST NEOTS	Cambridgeshire
Dinton CE First School	AYLESBURY	Buckinghamshire
Dorridge Nursery and Infant School	SOLIHULL	Solihull
Easington Lane Primary School	HOUGHTON-LE-SPRING	Sunderland
East Boldon County Infants' School	EAST BOLDON	South Tyneside

Fordingbridge Infant School	FORDINGBRIDGE	Hampshire
Gorse Ride Junior School	WOKINGHAM	Wokingham
Gorsey Bank Primary School	WILMSLOW	Cheshire
Gravenhurst Lower School	BEDFORD	Bedfordshire
Halam CE Primary School	NEWARK	Nottinghamshire
Halterworth Community Primary School	ROMSEY	Hampshire
Hartford Manor Community Primary School	NORTHWICH	Cheshire
Hatfield Crookesbroom Primary School	DONCASTER	Doncaster
Heigham Park First School	NORWICH	Norfolk
High Down Infant School	PORTISHEAD	North Somerset
Highnam Church of England Primary School	GLOUCESTER	Gloucestershire
Hunter's Bar Infant School	SHEFFIELD	Sheffield
Husborne Crawley Lower School	BEDFORD	Bedfordshire
Ingoldsby Primary School	GRANTHAM	Lincolnshire
John Keble Church of England Primary School	WINCHESTER	Hampshire
Langdale Infant School	NEWCASTLE UNDER LYME	Staffordshire
Leadgate Junior School	CONSETT	Durham
Lowther Endowed School	PENRITH	Cumbria
Manor Green Primary School	DENTON	Tameside
Marldon Church of England Primary School	PAIGNTON	Devon
Murton Jubilee Primary School	SEAHAM	Durham
Newbarns Primary School	BARROW-IN-FURNESS	Cumbria
Newchurch-in-Pendle St Mary's CE Primary School	BURNLEY	Lancashire
Nine Acres Primary School	NEWPORT	Isle of Wight
Oakway Infant School	WELLINGBOROUGH	Northamptonshire
Oatlands Infant School	HARROGATE	North Yorkshire
Overleigh St Mary's CE Primary School	CHESTER	Cheshire
Polebrook Church of England Primary School	OUNDLE	Northamptonshire
Poplars Community Primary School	LOWESTOFT	Suffolk
Roecliffe Church of England Primary School	YORK	North Yorkshire
Rowlands Gill Junior School	ROWLANDS GILL	Gateshead
Rumboldswhyke CE Infants' School	CHICHESTER	West Sussex
Saint Charles RC Primary School	NORTH KENSINGTON	Kensington and Chelsea
Seaton Sluice First School	SEATON SLUICE	Northumberland
Shiremoor First School	SHIREMOOR	North Tyneside
Simonside First School	NEWCASTLE UPON TYNE	Newcastle upon Tyne
Skelmersdale Holland Moor Primary School	SKELMERSDALE	Lancashire
Southbourne Infant School	EMSWORTH	West Sussex
Southwater Infant School	HORSHAM	West Sussex
St Alban and St Stephen RC Infant School	ST ALBANS	Hertfordshire
St Bede's Catholic Infant School	WIDNES	Halton
St Elphege's RC Infants' School	WALLINGTON	Sutton
St James' CE Junior School	TUNBRIDGE WELLS	Kent
St John the Divine CE Primary School	CAMBERWELL	Lambeth
St John's Catholic Infant School	BEBINGTON	Wirral
St Marie's Catholic Primary School	STANDISH	Wigan

School Name	Postal Town	LEA
St Mark's CE Primary School	BROMLEY	Bromley
St Mary and St Pancras CE Primary School	EUSTON	Camden
St Mary's Catholic Primary School	ELTHAM	Greenwich
St Monica's Catholic Primary School	BOOTLE	Sefton
St Sebastian's Catholic Junior, Mixed and Infant School	LIVERPOOL	Liverpool
St Stephen's CE Primary School	LADBROKE GROVE	Westminster
St Teresa's RC Primary School	BOLTON	Bolton
Stanley Junior School	TEDDINGTON	Richmond upon Thames
Sudbourne Primary School	LAMBETH	Lambeth
The Cathedral School of St Saviour and St Mary Overie	SOUTHWARK	Southwark
Valley Primary School	BROMLEY	Bromley
Wellfield Infant and Nursery School	SALE	Trafford
Westfield Junior School	ST IVES	Cambridgeshire
Westmoor First School	KILLINGWORTH	North Tyneside
William Gilbert Endowed CE Primary School	BELPER	Derbyshire
Wood End School	HARPENDEN	Hertfordshire
Wordsworth Infant School	SOUTHAMPTON	Southampton
Seria Service Children's School	BRUNEI	Service Children's Education

School Name	Postal Town	LEA
Middle Schools		
Elangeni School	AMERSHAM	Buckinghamshire
Limehurst High School	LOUGHBOROUGH	Leicestershire
Pinner Wood Middle School	PINNER	Harrow
Thomas Harding School	CHESHAM	Buckinghamshire
Woodside School	AMERSHAM	Buckinghamshire

School Name	Postal Town	LEA
Nursery Schools		
Bognor Regis Nursery School	BOGNOR REGIS	West Sussex
Caverstede Nursery School	PETERBOROUGH	Peterborough, City of
Childhaven Nursery School	SCARBOROUGH	North Yorkshire
Clervaux Nursery School	JARROW	South Tyneside
Millfields Nursery School	WALSALL	Walsall
Rosemary Lane Nursery School	PETERLEE	Durham
Sir James Knott Memorial Nursery School	NORTH SHIELDS	North Tyneside
Walbrook Nursery School	DERBY	Derby, City of
Wall Hall Nursery School	WATFORD	Hertfordshire
Walton Lane Nursery School	NELSON	Lancashire
Woodfield Nursery School	BRIERFIELD	Lancashire

The re-inspection of primary schools enables me to identify those schools that have achieved EXCELLENT IMPROVEMENT since their first inspection. The schools below stand out amongst the many that have improved their quality of education and the standards achieved by pupils since the previous inspection.

School Name	Postal Town	LEA
Allanson Street Primary School	ST HELENS	St Helens
Berkley Church of England First School	FROME	Somerset
Castle Hill Junior School	BASINGSTOKE	Hampshire
Cherry Orchard Primary School	BIRMINGHAM	Birmingham

School Name	Postal Town	LEA
Cragside First School	CRAMLINGTON	Northumberland
Crowle Primary School	SCUNTHORPE	North Lincolnshire
Elsworth CE Primary School	CAMBRIDGE	Cambridgeshire
Freemantle CE Infant School	SOUTHAMPTON	Southampton
Gomer Infant School	GOSPORT	Hampshire
Harlow Green Junior School	GATESHEAD	Gateshead
Haslemere First School	MITCHAM	Merton
Higher Bebington Junior School	WIRRAL	Wirral
Hobletts Manor Junior School	HEMEL HEMPSTEAD	Hertfordshire
Holy Family Catholic Primary School	ADDLESTONE	Surrey
Icknield Lower School	DUNSTABLE	Bedfordshire
John Rankin Infant and Nursery School	NEWBURY	West Berkshire
Katherine Semar Infant School	SAFFRON WALDEN	Essex
Lanner Primary School	REDRUTH	Cornwall
Lark Rise Lower School	DUNSTABLE	Bedfordshire
Lumley Medway Infant School	CHESTER-LE-STREET	Durham
Nettlestone Primary School	SEAVIEW	Isle of Wight
Newall Green Infant School	WHYTHENSHAWE	Manchester
Oakwood Infant School	BASINGSTOKE	Hampshire
Park Farm Primary School	FOLKESTONE	Kent
Parson Street Primary School	BRISTOL	Bristol, City of
Poulton-le-Fylde The Breck Primary School	POULTON-LE-FYLDE	Lancashire
Prees CE Primary School	WHITCHURCH	Shropshire
Princess Frederica CE Primary School	KENSALL GREEN	Brent
South Stanley Infant School	STANLEY	Durham
Sparrow Farm Junior School	FELTHAM	Hounslow
St Brigid's Catholic Primary School	NORTHFIELD	Birmingham
St John's CE Infant School	DEWSBURY	Kirklees
St Joseph's RC Primary School	MAIDA VALE	Westminster
St Peter's CE Primary School	NEWPORT	Telford and Wrekin
Stanley Park Junior School	CARSHALTON	Sutton
Strand-on-the-Green Junior School	HOUNSLOW	Hounslow
Throckley First School	NEWCASTLE UPON TYNE	Newcastle upon Tyne
West Hill Primary School	WANDSWORTH	Wandsworth
Weston Shore Infant School	SOUTHAMPTON	Southampton
Woodlands Junior School	TONBRIDGE	Kent

I am also pleased to name highly effective SPECIAL SCHOOLS this year. In similar terms to the schools named above, they demonstrate the best in this highly diverse and important sector of education. Included, for the first time this year, I am pleased to be able to name three highly effective pupil referral units.

School Name	Postal Town	LEA
Ash Field School	LEICESTER	Leicester City
Elms School	PRESTON	Lancashire
Hedgewood School	HAYES	Hillingdon
Leyland School	NUNEATON	Warwickshire
Linwood School	BOURNEMOUTH	Bournemouth
Lister Lane School	BRADFORD	Bradford
Marjorie McClure School	CHISLEHURST	Bromley
Marshfields School	PETERBOROUGH	Peterborough, City of
Mary Hare Grammar School	NEWBURY	West Berkshire

School Name	Postal Town	LEA
Netherlands Avenue School and Community Nursery	BRADFORD	Bradford
Newfield School	LIVERPOOL	Sefton
Ravenscliffe High School	HALIFAX	Calderdale
Redgate School	MANSFIELD	Nottinghamshire
Rosehill School	NOTTINGHAM	Nottingham, City of
Selly Oak Special School	BIRMINGHAM	Birmingham
Southlands School	NORTH SHIELDS	North Tyneside
The Children's Hospital School	LEICESTER	Leicester City
The Foreland School	BROADSTAIRS	Kent
Westlands School	STOCKTON ON TEES	Stockton on Tees
Woodlands Special School	BLACKPOOL	Blackpool
Woodlawn School	WHITLEY BAY	North Tyneside
Woolgrove School	LETCHWORTH	Hertfordshire

School Name	Postal Town	LEA
Pupil Referral Units		
Phil Edwards Centre	CROYDON	Croydon
The Pendlebury Centre	STOCKPORT	Stockport
West Cumbria Learning Centre	DISTINGTON	Cumbria

As last year, OFSTED is delighted to recognise the very substantial improvement in schools that have been REMOVED FROM SPECIAL MEASURES during the year covered by this Report.

School Name	Postal Town	LEA
Abbots Hall Junior School	STANFORD-LE-HOPE	Thurrock
Amberley Ridge School (Special)	STROUD	Gloucestershire
Amy Johnson School	HULL	Kingston upon Hull
Annie Osborn Primary School	COVENTRY	Coventry
Archbishop Sumner's CE Primary School	LAMBETH	Lambeth
Arundale County Primary and Nursery School	HYDE	Tameside
Ashburton High School	CROYDON	Croydon
Aylesham County Primary School	CANTERBURY	Kent
Badocks Wood Primary School	BRISTOL	Bristol, City of
Barlaston CE (C) First School	STOKE-ON-TRENT	Staffordshire
Barley Lane School (Special)	EXETER	Devon
Barton St Lawrence CE Primary School	PRESTON	Lancashire
Battersea Technology College	WANDSWORTH	Wandsworth
Beaufort School (Special)	BIRMINGHAM	Birmingham
Beechwood School	SLOUGH	Slough
Belgrave CE Primary School	LEICESTER	Leicester City
Bellfield First School	HIGH WYCOMBE	Buckinghamshire
Berger Primary School	HACKNEY	Hackney
Bevois Town Primary School	SOUTHAMPTON	Southampton
Bosvigo Primary School	TRURO	Cornwall
Bramfield House School (Special)	HALESWORTH	Suffolk
Brickhouse Junior and Infant School	WARLEY	Sandwell
Brompton and Sawdon County Primary School	SCARBOROUGH	North Yorkshire
Caldecote Community Primary School	CAMBRIDGE	Cambridgeshire
Cam House School (Special)	DURSLEY	Gloucestershire
Canterbury First School	THETFORD	Norfolk
Captain Shaw's CE Primary School	MILLOM	Cumbria

Castle Gresley Infant School	SWADLINCOTE	Derbyshire
Cavalry Primary School	MARCH	Cambridgeshire
Cavendish School (Special)	EALING	Ealing
Caversham Park Primary School	READING	Reading
Central Park Primary School	NEWHAM	Newham
Chace Primary School	COVENTRY	Coventry
Chantry Junior School	LUTON	Luton
Chantry Primary School	GRAVESEND	Kent
Charles Darwin School (Special)	TELFORD	Telford and Wrekin
Chislet CE Primary School	CANTERBURY	Kent
Combe Mead Primary School	TIVERTON	Devon
Cotsbrook School (Special)	SHIFNAL	Shropshire
Creswell Junior School	WORKSOP	Derbyshire
Cribden House School (Special)	RAWTENSTALL	Lancashire
Cuckoo Hall Primary School	EDMONTON	Enfield
Darley Churchtown CE Primary School	MATLOCK	Derbyshire
Darley County Primary School	HARROGATE	North Yorkshire
De La Salle School	BASILDON	Essex
Deansfield High School	WOLVERHAMPTON	Wolverhampton
Dinnington Junior School	SHEFFIELD	Rotherham
Down Lane Junior School	TOTTENHAM	Haringey
Downhill Primary School	SUNDERLAND	Sunderland
Downside Lower School	DUNSTABLE	Bedfordshire
Dunstall Hill Primary School	WOLVERHAMPTON	Wolverhampton
East Bridgwater Community School	BRIDGWATER	Somerset
Eldon County Primary School	PRESTON	Lancashire
Elm Hall County Primary School	WITHAM	Essex
Elphinstone Primary School	HASTINGS	East Sussex
English Martyrs' RC Primary School	STOCKTON ON TEES	Stockton on Tees
Ettingshall Primary School	BILSTON	Wolverhampton
Fagley First School	BRADFORD	Bradford
Fenstanton Junior School	TULSE HILL	Lambeth
Ferrars Infant and Nursery School	LUTON	Luton
Finmere CE Primary School	BUCKINGHAM	Oxfordshire
Fourfields CE Primary School	BOSTON	Lincolnshire
Friary RC Primary School	LIVERPOOL	Liverpool
Great Horton Middle School	BRADFORD	Bradford
Greenlands County Primary School	PRESTON	Lancashire
Hackbridge Infant School	WALLINGTON	Sutton
Halberton Primary School	TIVERTON	Devon
Hallbankgate Village Primary School	BRAMPTON	Cumbria
Hare Street Junior School	HARLOW	Essex
Harry Gosling Primary School	WHITECHAPEL	Tower Hamlets
Hatherden Primary School	ANDOVER	Hampshire
Hayes Primary School	PAIGNTON	Torbay
Hemswell County Primary School	GAINSBOROUGH	Lincolnshire
Henry Compton School	FULHAM	Hammersmith and Fulham
Highwood JMI and Nursery School	WATFORD	Hertfordshire
Hill Top Primary School	BURSLEM	Stoke-on-Trent
Hillcrest Primary School	CHAPELTOWN	Leeds
Hillocks Primary and Nursery School	SUTTON-IN-ASHFIELD	Nottinghamshire
Holloway School	HOLLOWAY	Islington
Howbridge CE Junior School	WITHAM	Essex

Huntington Primary School	CANNOCK	Staffordshire
Inglesea School (Special)	ST LEONARDS-ON-SEA	East Sussex
Intack Primary School	BLACKBURN	Blackburn with Darwen
Jack Taylor School (Special)	MAIDA VALE	Camden
Jeffries Primary School	KIRKBY-IN-ASHFIELD	Nottinghamshire
John F Kennedy School (Special)	STRATFORD	Newham
John Stainer Primary School	BROCKLEY	Lewisham
Jubilee Park Primary School	TIPTON	Sandwell
Kelsey Park School	BECKENHAM	Bromley
Kensington Avenue Junior School	CROYDON	Croydon
Ketton CE Primary School	STAMFORD	Rutland
Kingsmead County Primary School	CANTERBURY	Kent
Lakenham First School	NORWICH	Norfolk
Langley Mill Junior School	LANGLEY MILL	Derbyshire
Lankhills School (Special)	WINCHESTER	Hampshire
Lathom St James CE Primary School	ORMSKIRK	Lancashire
Linden Grove County Primary School	ASHFORD	Kent
Llangrove CE Primary School	ROSS-ON-WYE	Herefordshire
Lordsgate Township CE Primary School	ORMSKIRK	Lancashire
Loughborough Junior School	LAMBETH	Lambeth
Lucas Vale Primary School	LEWISHAM	Lewisham
Lyng Hall School	COVENTRY	Coventry
Manor Court Primary School	CHARD	Somerset
Manor Park Community School	NUNEATON	Warwickshire
Mansel County Primary School	SHEFFIELD	Sheffield
Margaret Sutton School (Special)	SOUTH SHIELDS	South Tyneside
Marston Green Junior School	MARSTON GREEN	Solihull
Melbourne County Primary School	DOVER	Kent
Milefield Primary School	BARNSLEY	Barnsley
Milton Court County Primary School	SITTINGBOURNE	Kent
Nenthead Primary School	ALSTON	Cumbria
Newport Primary School	MIDDLESBROUGH	Middlesbrough
Newry Junior School	LEICESTER	Leicester City
Newstead Primary School	STOKE-ON-TRENT	Stoke-on-Trent
Nields Junior, Infant and Nursery School	HUDDERSFIELD	Kirklees
Nine Acres School (Special)	PLUMSTEAD	Greenwich
North Manchester High School for Boys	MANCHESTER	Manchester
Northiam CE Primary School	RYE	East Sussex
Old Ford Junior School	BOW	Tower Hamlets
Osmani Primary School	BETHNAL GREEN	Tower Hamlets
Our Lady and St Anselm's RC Primary School	ROCHDALE	Lancashire
Our Lady of Grace RC Primary School	CHARLTON	Greenwich
Our Lady's RC High School	LIVERPOOL	Liverpool
Oxley Junior and Infant School	WOLVERHAMPTON	Wolverhampton
Park Community School	HAVANT	Hampshire
Park Lane Primary School	WEMBLEY	Brent
Park View Academy (formerly The Langham School)	TOTTENHAM	Haringey
Park View School	BIRMINGHAM	Birmingham
Parkinson Lane Primary School	HALIFAX	Calderdale
Pear Tree County Primary School	RUGELEY	Staffordshire
Pebble Brook Primary School	CREWE	Cheshire
Pen Park School	BRISTOL	Bristol, City of

Prince Rock Primary School	PLYMOUTH	Plymouth
Priory Lane Junior School	SCUNTHORPE	North Lincolnshire
Pyrgo Priory Primary School	ROMFORD	Havering
Rachel McMillan Nursery School	DEPTFORD	Greenwich
Redcastle Furze First and Middle School	THETFORD	Norfolk
Redwood Park School (Special)	PORTSMOUTH	Portsmouth
Ridge Meadow County Primary School	CHATHAM	Medway Towns
Ringway Primary School (formerly Woodhouse Park Primary School	MANCHESTER	Manchester
Ripplevale School (Special)	DEAL	Kent
Riverside Community College (formerly Rowley Fields School and Community College)	LEICESTER	Leicester City
Riverside Junior School	HEBDEN BRIDGE	Calderdale
Rookery Junior School	BIRMINGHAM	Birmingham
Rose Street County Primary School	SHEERNESS	Kent
Royal Free Hospital Children's School (Special)	HAMPSTEAD	Camden
Saviour CE Primary School	MANCHESTER	Manchester
Scott Wilkie Primary School	NEWHAM	Newham
Seely CE Primary School	ARNOLD	Nottinghamshire
Silkmore Primary School	STAFFORD	Staffordshire
Sir Theodore Pritchett Primary School	BIRMINGHAM	Birmingham
South Benwell Primary School	NEWCASTLE UPON TYNE	Newcastle upon Tyne
Southern Road Primary School	PLAISTOW	Newham
Southfields Infant School	LEICESTER	Leicester City
Springfield Middle School	MILTON KEYNES	Milton Keynes
Spring Hill Primary School	ACCRINGTON	Lancashire
St Andrew's CE Primary School	STOCKWELL	Lambeth
St Anne's RC Primary School	ANCOATS	Manchester
St Bernadette's RC Primary School	HILLINGDON	Hillingdon
St Bernard's RC Primary School	BOLTON	Bolton
St Francis RC Primary School	NAILSEA	North Somerset
St Francis Xavier RC Primary School	WARLEY	Sandwell
St Gabriel's RC Primary School	ROCHDALE	Rochdale
St John's (Park) CE Primary School	SHEFFIELD	Sheffield
St Joseph's Academy	BLACKHEATH	Lewisham
St Joseph's RC Primary School	BANBURY	Oxfordshire
St Joseph's RC Primary School	BERMONDSEY	Southwark
St Joseph's RC Primary School	KINGSTON UPON THAMES	Kingston upon Thames
St Jude and St Paul's CE Primary School	ISLINGTON	Islington
St Mark's CE Primary School	BRIGHTON	Brighton and Hove
St Mark's CE Primary School	GODALMING	Surrey
St Mary's CE Primary School	HANDSWORTH	Birmingham
St Mary's CE Primary School	BURNHAM-ON-CROUCH	Essex
St Mary's Priory RC Infant School	TOTTENHAM	Haringey
St Mary's RC Primary School	BRIDLINGTON	East Riding of Yorkshire
St Matthew's CE Primary School	PRESTON	Lancashire
St Matthew's Junior School	LUTON	Luton
St Michael's CE Infant School	ALDERSHOT	Hampshire
St Peter's CE VA Primary School	WALWORTH	Southwark
St Peter's RC Primary School	ROSSENDALE	Lancashire

St Philip's RC Junior, Infant and Nursery School	SMETHWICK	Sandwell
St Winefride's Catholic Primary School	MANOR PARK	Newham
Stamford Green Primary School	EPSOM	Surrey
Stanley Road Primary School	OLDHAM	Oldham
Staunton Park Community School	HAVANT	Hampshire
Stepgates Primary School	CHERTSEY	Surrey
Stoke Hill Primary School	GUILDFORD	Surrey
Stoneydown Park Primary School	WALTHAMSTOW	Waltham Forest
Summerbank Central Primary School	STOKE-ON-TRENT	Stoke-on-Trent
Summervale Primary School	OLDHAM	Oldham
Symondsbury CE (VA) Primary School	BRIDPORT	Dorset
Syon Park School (formerly John Busch School) (Special)	ISLEWORTH	Hounslow
Tewin Water School (Special)	WELWYN GARDEN CITY	Hertfordshire
The Forest School	NOTTINGHAM	Nottingham, City of
The Grove Primary School	CAMBRIDGE	Cambridgeshire
The Hatherley Centre (Special)	GLOUCESTER	Gloucestershire
The Hayes Manor School	HAYES	Hillingdon
The Mead School (Special) (Now amalgamated and part of Harlow Fields School)	HARLOW	Essex
The Queen Mary School	LIVERPOOL	Liverpool
The Ridgeway School (Special)	FARNHAM	Surrey
The Ridings School	HALIFAX	Calderdale
The Straits Primary School	DUDLEY	Dudley
Thurnby Lodge Primary School	LEICESTER	Leicester City
Tithe Farm Lower School	DUNSTABLE	Bedfordshire
Tuxford Primary and Nursery School	NEWARK	Nottinghamshire
Tweeddale Junior School	CARSHALTON	Sutton
Vange County Primary School and Nursery	BASILDON	Essex
Waltham Holy Cross Infant School	WALTHAM ABBEY	Essex
Wansdyke Primary School	BRISTOL	Bristol, City of
Warbreck High School	BLACKPOOL	Blackpool
Wensley Fold CE Primary School	BLACKBURN	Blackburn with Darwen
Westcourt Primary School	GRAVESEND	Kent
Westlands First School	DROITWICH	Worcestershire
Westminster City School	WESTMINSTER	Westminster
Westmoor Junior School	DEWSBURY	Kirklees
Westwood Park Community School	MANCHESTER	Salford
Whitebridge Primary School	LEEDS	Leeds
Whitton County Primary School	IPSWICH	Suffolk
Windlehurst School (formerly Thornfield School) (Special)	MARPLE	Stockport
Windsor High School	SALFORD	Salford
Winterbourne Junior Boys' School	THORNTON HEATH	Croydon
Woodingdean Primary School	BRIGHTON	Brighton and Hove
Woodlands Primary School (formerly Bradley Park Junior School	GRIMSBY	North East Lincolnshire
Woodside Nursery and Infant School	WALTHAMSTOW	Waltham Forest
Woodside Centre Pupil Referral Unit (Special)	WINCHESTER	Hampshire
Wootton Primary School	RYDE	Isle of Wight

Commentary

The steady improvements that I described in my last Annual Report have continued. Standards of pupil achievement have risen slightly in secondary and special schools, and in sixth forms. The quality of teaching has improved in all types of school, in all subjects and in all year groups. More headteachers are raising expectations and challenging and supporting their staff; more are monitoring teaching in a systematic and rigorous way. Pupils' behaviour has improved and is good in most schools. The exception to this picture of steady, if unspectacular, improvement is the sharp rise in pupil achievement in the Key Stage 2 English and mathematics tests. Seventy per cent and 69 per cent of pupils achieved Level 4 in English and mathematics respectively. Last year the figures were 65 and 59 per cent. In that the drive to raise standards depends above all else on raising standards in the basic skills, this is a very significant and promising development, which is directly linked to the National Literacy and Numeracy strategies.

Almost all primary schools were teaching the Literacy Hour by the end of the autumn term 1998, and many of them anticipated the national timetable and began to implement the Numeracy Strategy a year early. Encouragingly, the quality of teaching of the Literacy Hour has improved throughout the year. Teachers are no longer simply listening to children read: they are teaching the skills upon which progress in reading depends. There is, however, no room for complacency. Phonics is still taught badly in too many lessons, particularly in Years 3 and 4. The teaching of writing is weaker than that of reading, and, not surprisingly, standards of pupil achievement in writing are not rising as quickly as they are in reading. Wide variations, moreover, exist in the performance of pupils and rates of improvement in different local education authorities.

More generally, the quality of teaching in primary schools continues to improve. In part this is because the National Literacy and Numeracy Strategies are beginning to influence teaching in other curriculum areas such as science. Teaching in well over half of primary schools is now good. Eight in ten schools inspected had a higher proportion of good lessons than in their previous inspection. There is a growing recognition that the success of a lesson depends crucially upon the clarity of planning and the identification of clear learning objectives. Whole-class teaching is both more common and more skilful than it once was. Assessment has improved, but remains weak in about one-fifth of schools. In addition, a significant number of schools need to raise their expectations of what their pupils can achieve. The more confident teachers are in their own subject knowledge, the higher their expectations tend to be. Nowhere is this more clearly illustrated than in information technology where expectations are far too low in about a quarter of primary schools. The overall message must be that of my earlier reports: if standards are to rise further in primary schools, then primary teachers must have better access to high-quality training designed to deepen their own subject knowledge.

There is little inspection evidence to support the concern that the Literacy and Numeracy Strategies are undermining standards in other subjects. Most primary schools continue to provide a broad and balanced curriculum. A considerable number find time for subjects, like a modern foreign language, which are not part of the National Curriculum. There is, however, some evidence that an increased emphasis upon study support is reducing the time given to traditional after-school activities such as team games. The two activities ought not to be mutually exclusive, and future developments will need to be monitored carefully.

Turning to secondary schools, it is disappointing to report that there has been relatively little change in National Curriculum test results in English and mathematics at Key Stage 3 over the last five years. After three years at secondary school, one-third of pupils still fail to achieve Level 5. It is not perhaps surprising, given these results, that the long tail of underachievement at Key Stage 4 remains. Thirteen per cent of all pupils fail to gain a GCSE qualification in both English and mathematics and 6.1 per cent fail to gain any GCSE qualification at all. These are deeply disturbing statistics. They confirm the need to build better foundations in literacy and numeracy at primary school, to improve the transition from primary to secondary schools, to raise the quality of teaching in Key Stage 3, and, as the Government intends, to pursue vocational and work-based training options in Key Stage 4 for those students who are unlikely to make a great deal of progress if they continue to study an exclusively academic curriculum.

Despite some improvement this year, particularly in primary schools, pupils' progress in information technology is unsatisfactory in over one-third of schools at Key Stage 2 and over four in ten at Key Stage 4. The overall quality of teaching in both primary and secondary schools remains significantly weaker than that of other subjects. Teachers often expect too little of pupils and too much time is spent practising low-level skills. The in-service training for teachers – especially those who lead the work in schools – has not kept pace with developments in the subject. Carefully targeted, high quality in-service training is urgently needed if pupils are to gain real benefit across the curriculum from the rapid expansion of information and communications technology in schools.

In both primary and secondary schools, the gap between the standards achieved by pupils in the best and worst schools remains too wide. Some schools will always be more successful than others, but the gap must be narrowed. We cannot tolerate a situation where standards in some schools are being allowed to decline. Too many schools are failing their second inspection. Too many are being found to have serious weaknesses. It is true that the numbers, relative to the total number of schools inspected, are small. Most schools have tackled the issues identified in their first inspection, and, as a consequence, have improved. But the fact that the overall situation is positive does not help those children who have the misfortune to attend schools where things have been allowed to slip. If the headteacher and governing body cannot secure progress, then the LEA must. If the LEA cannot discharge this most fundamental of its responsibilities, then the Secretary of State has no option but to intervene so as to ensure that these schools receive the challenge and support they need.

The number of schools serving disadvantaged communities that achieve good results for their pupils continues to increase. It remains, however, small. Looking to the future, Government initiatives such as Education Action Zones and Excellence in Cities may have a profound impact. We do not, as yet, have the inspection evidence to know. Two things are, however, already obvious. The first is that the schools which are bucking the trend are invariably led and staffed by highly effective headteachers and teachers. It is vital, therefore, that action is taken to attract the best-quality staff to work in such schools and to remunerate them properly for the difficult and immensely important work they do so well. The second is that the Literacy Strategy is, it seems, a real ray of hope. The children who leave primary school unable to read and write are the children who will be unable to cope with the demands of the secondary school curriculum, who are likely to truant, and who, as 16-year-olds, will end up with little or nothing in the way of examination qualifications: unemployed and unemployable. The key lies, therefore, in the primary school. If the Literacy Strategy continues to deliver we shall at last have a solution to a deeply intractable problem which has resisted every attempt in recent years to find more immediate remedies.

Most primary and secondary headteachers lead their schools well; one in ten and one in 12 respectively do not. Good headteachers have a clear educational vision and a strong sense of purpose. As a consequence, staff morale in their schools is high. When, conversely, headteachers do not establish clear priorities and, for whatever reason, fail to focus attention on the core task of raising standards of pupil achievement, their teachers, unsurprisingly, become disillusioned and defeated. The best headteachers know what is happening (and not happening) in the classrooms of their schools. The weak ones do not. They are too preoccupied to monitor teaching and evaluate curriculum development in a systematic and rigorous fashion. If they monitor at all, they do so in an *ad hoc* way that causes anxiety amongst staff and has little positive impact on standards. The position with regard to appraisal is equally worrying. It is rare for appraisal to be linked to the monitoring of a teacher's classroom performance. Worse, in many schools appraisal of any kind has stalled. A great deal of work will, therefore, be needed if the Government's drive to introduce performance management is to have any real impact.

Problems with the recruitment of teachers continue in some areas, but we are not experiencing the crisis some commentators have predicted. The match of the number, qualifications and experience to the demands of the curriculum is at least adequate in all but a small minority of primary schools. Inspectors judge the match to be good in about six out of ten secondary schools. Problems do, predictably enough, occur when supply teachers have to be used too often. It is, moreover, disturbing to note that a quarter of the lessons taught by supply teachers are found to be unsatisfactory.

Some, particularly urban, areas do not at present have a range of post-16 provision that meets the needs of potential students. As a consequence, individuals are having to make difficult and expensive journeys to attend the courses they want to follow. The Government's decision to initiate a series of area reviews of post-16 provision is, therefore, timely. My next Annual

Report will summarise the results of the initial reviews that we undertake.

Most schools, primary and secondary, are adequately resourced. About one in 20 primary and one in five secondary schools were, however, judged to have inadequate books, materials and equipment for effective teaching of the curriculum. Some primary schools have found it difficult to purchase the texts they need to teach the Literacy Hour, but these problems should ease in coming years. Most primary schools have sufficient accommodation to teach the National Curriculum. Open plan areas are, however, proving far from ideal for direct whole-class teaching. The situation with regard to accommodation is worse in secondary schools, where it is inadequate in one school in five and inspectors report on problems with buildings such as leaking roofs, broken windows and poor-quality classrooms with inadequate ventilation and lighting.

Two more general points about resourcing need to be made. The first is that the extra £19 billion the Government has pledged to invest in education over the course of this Parliament ought, obviously enough, to solve many of the problems touched upon in preceding paragraphs. Many headteachers worry, however, at the fact that this money is being used to fund local and national initiatives that do not always meet the particular priorities that they have identified for their schools. Some initiatives (like the National Literacy Strategy) do represent excellent value for money. The general principle ought, however, to be crystal clear: extra funding should be used to attract and remunerate successful teachers, buy more books and mend leaking roofs. Each and every penny spent outside the school needs to be scrutinised and each new administrative post challenged. The fact that some schools in the past have not used the money devolved to them to the best effect is no reason now to hold back money from the majority that use it well and have defined and costed a sensible programme of development. The second general point is that the funding of both primary and secondary schools varies too much from school to school according to where the school is situated. Some schools clearly need more resources than others to help deal with the problems they face. Some primary schools have an income, however, of around £1,300 per pupil, others over £2,500 per pupil. The figures for secondary schools range from £1,900 to over £3,000. I do not believe that in every case these variations can be justified. We have a national curriculum and national expectations of how standards should rise. We do not, as yet, have a transparent and educationally defensible mechanism for the equitable devolution of resources from central government to LEAs and from LEAs to schools. We should.

The performance of LEAs, like that of schools, is too variable. Nine of the 41 LEAs inspected so far were found to be giving effective support to their schools. The performance of others, following political change or the appointment of new officers, was judged to be improving. The overall situation is, nonetheless, bleak. Twelve LEAs have received critical reports that require urgent action on many fronts. A further four have been found to be failing to such a degree that the Secretary of State has intervened. These LEAs were adding little or no value to the work of their schools. Their elected members had often lost the trust of their schools by failing to take decisions in a timely and open way. The work of their inspection and advice service was, typically, found to be weak, sometimes because the staff employed were not up to the job, often because the LEA had failed to focus its efforts on the schools which needed support. It makes no sense whatsoever for LEAs to replicate OFSTED's work. The necessary data is available and their role ought to be one of helping weaker schools to improve, not wasting public money and headteachers' time through an indiscriminate pattern of routine and largely ineffective monitoring visits. If all LEAs were to intervene in inverse proportion to success, standards in fewer schools would deteriorate between inspections. Problems begin when the rhetoric of school improvement spawns a plethora of ineffective and often unwelcome initiatives which, more often than not, waste money and confuse and irritate schools.

A substantial number of the English and mathematics primary initial teacher training courses visited this year were identified for inspection because their previous inspection had found room for considerable improvement. The evidence base is not, therefore, representative. The key issue which emerged in English is nonetheless disturbing: trainees' subject knowledge required significant improvement in over three-quarters of the courses inspected. Students simply do not know enough about how English as a language works. Only a minority of trainees were judged, moreover, to have a good understanding of progression across the full primary age-range. As a consequence, too many students arrive in schools insufficiently prepared to teach the National Literacy Strategy . The position with regard to mathematics is, perhaps surprisingly, much better, with nearly 90 per cent of students demonstrating good subject knowledge. The majority of secondary provision was found to be good, but there are wide variations between subjects and training providers and over 20 per cent of the work seen was judged to be in need of significant improvement. Two weaknesses stand out. The first is the assessment of students against the new standards for qualified teacher status. Well over a quarter of the courses were found to be only adequate in this respect. Then, second, in one course in three inspectors identified weaknesses in the students' ability to monitor, assess, record and report on pupils' progress.

Most independent schools provide a good-quality education and pupils achieve good or, in the majority of Independent Schools Council schools, excellent standards. However, the sector is very diverse, and there is a small minority of schools that gives rise to serious concern. The fact that an independent school can register without evidence of a suitable curriculum development plan or financial security is a cause for concern. In the worst examples, pupils have been admitted to sites which represent serious health hazards. The Government's plans to consult on reforms to the registration and monitoring systems are, therefore, welcome.

I wrote last year that "we have a new and rigorous focus on what actually works". We do. But it remains a critical time. The agenda is, or ought to be, obvious. We know what constitutes good teaching and we know what needs to be done to tackle weaknesses: we must strengthen subject knowledge, raise expectations, and hone the pedagogic skills upon which the craft of the classroom depends. We know, too, a great deal about leadership skills and why it is that our best headteachers are so effective. Why, then, is so much time and energy wasted in research that complicates what ought to be straightforward, in expensive initiatives that distract teachers and headteachers from their real responsibilities, in administration and bureaucracy that render the simplest of tasks labyrinthine in their demands? Why indeed? If standards are to continue to rise we need decisive management action, locally and nationally, that concentrates attention on the two imperatives that really matter: the drive to improve teaching and strengthen leadership. We now need, as so many headteachers have said to me in recent months, to focus relentlessly on these essential tasks. We need to ensure that headteachers have the freedom to determine the priorities for development in their schools and the resource to fund the necessary action. The challenge now is to expose the emptiness of education theorising that obfuscates the classroom realities that really matter, to tackle bureaucratic excess and financial waste, and, last but not least, to continue to raise our expectations of what is possible.

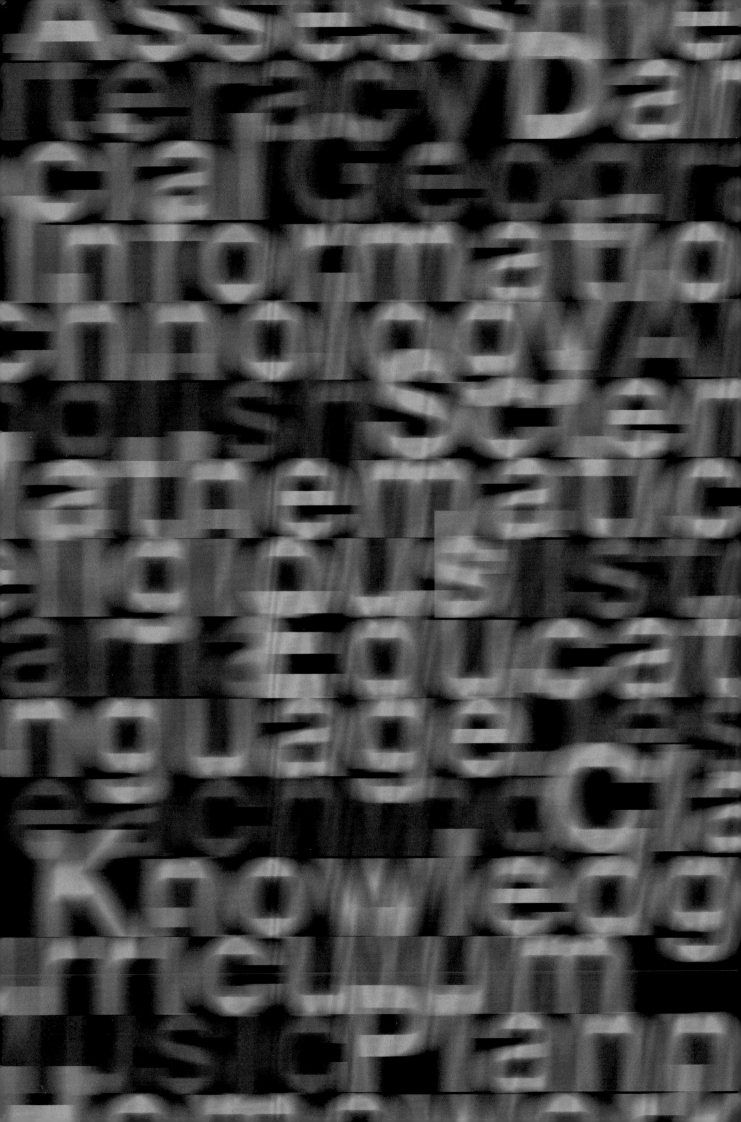

Primary schools

Educational standards achieved

Overview of attainment and progress

1. English primary schools have continued to improve. There is better teaching and, as a consequence, pupils are learning more. Standards achieved by pupils in English and mathematics have, in particular, risen significantly. The school year 1998/99 saw the introduction of the National Literacy Strategy and preparation for the introduction of the National Numeracy Strategy in September 1999. This is the first time in England that detailed frameworks have been established, on a term by term basis, for the teaching of the essential skills of literacy and numeracy. These initiatives have resulted in better teaching and better achievement in English and mathematics. There are, moreover, clear signs that this more structured teaching is having a positive effect in other curriculum areas such as science.

2. Inspection shows that pupils are making greater gains in knowledge, skills and understanding than in previous years. Improvements in progress are seen throughout primary schools, including classes with pupils under the age of five. The chart below shows that the strengths and weaknesses are much the same as in previous years: pupils make a good start in their nursery or reception class; progress is weakest in Year 3 and Year 4, where it is unsatisfactory in nearly one in ten lessons; and best in Year 6, where it is good or better in over half of lessons.[1]

Percentage of pupils achieving Level 4 and above for English at Key Stage 2 1995-99

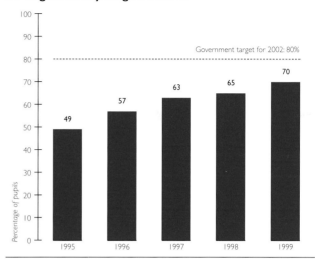

Percentage of pupils achieving Level 4 and above for mathematics at Key Stage 2 1995-99

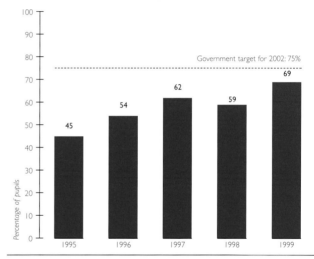

3. NATIONAL CURRICULUM TEST RESULTS[2] are encouraging, especially at KEY STAGE 2 where there has been significant improvement in all three core subjects. The charts above show that the percentage of pupils achieving Level 4 or above has risen to 70 per cent in English and 69 per cent in mathematics.

4. At KEY STAGE 1 improvements have been less. Nevertheless, the proportion of pupils reaching Level 2 in reading and writing has risen by two percentage points to 82 per cent and 83 per cent respectively; in mathematics there has been a three percentage point rise to 87 per cent.

Lessons in primary schools: progress *(percentage of lessons)*

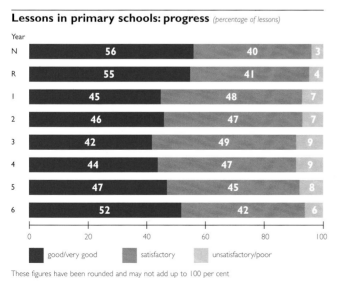

These figures have been rounded and may not add up to 100 per cent

---

1   *See Annex 2 for an interpretation of inspection data.*
2   Provisional Department for Education and Employment (DfEE) data, 1999.

5. These are significant achievements. Inspection evidence and key stage test results, however, show that further improvement is needed in three important areas. First, progress in writing still lags worryingly behind reading at Key Stage 2. In reading 81 per cent of pupils achieved Level 4 or above. The comparable figure for writing was only 56 per cent. Too many pupils are unable to produce sustained accurate writing by the time they leave primary schools. Improving the quality and quantity of the teaching of writing must now be seen as a priority for schools, literacy consultants, and local education authorities.

6. Second, although over four in five pupils reach Level 2[3] in Key Stage 1, this level covers a wide range of attainment. It is a considerable challenge to take pupils from Level 2C at the age of seven to Level 4 by the age of 11. The number of pupils reaching the more demanding Level 2B has increased this year, but still remains too low at 66 per cent in reading, 53 per cent in writing and 64 per cent in mathematics.

7. Third, the performance of boys in English continues to give concern; although the gap between boys' reading and girls' reading has reduced, the difference between the quality of boys' writing and that of girls remains as great as ever. The only area of the curriculum where boys do better than girls is in mental arithmetic. Boys respond particularly well to direct interactive teaching and enjoy the challenge of quickfire question and answer sessions. There are important implications here for raising the achievement of boys in other curriculum areas.

Attainment and progress in the National Curriculum subjects and religious education

8. The charts opposite illustrate inspectors' judgements of the gains in knowledge, understanding and skills made by pupils in the subjects of the National Curriculum. A number of key points stand out:

- progress in the core subjects is now good in about half of the schools at Key Stage 2, but remains weak in about one school in ten;

- the improvement in the core subjects has been much greater than improvement seen in any of the foundation subjects;

- there are now four subjects at Key Stage 2 in which progress lags significantly behind that in all other subjects: religious education, information technology, geography and design and technology.

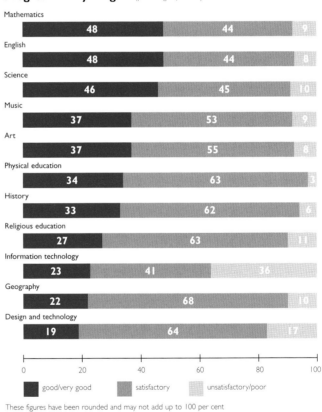

Progress in Key Stage 1 (percentage of schools)

	good/very good	satisfactory	unsatisfactory/poor
English	46	48	6
Mathematics	46	48	6
Science	41	52	7
Art	37	58	5
Music	35	60	5
Physical education	28	69	3
Religious education	24	68	7
History	24	71	5
Geography	20	74	6
Design and technology	20	69	11
Information technology	20	54	26

Progress in Key Stage 2 (percentage of schools)

	good/very good	satisfactory	unsatisfactory/poor
Mathematics	48	44	9
English	48	44	8
Science	46	45	10
Music	37	53	9
Art	37	55	8
Physical education	34	63	3
History	33	62	6
Religious education	27	63	11
Information technology	23	41	36
Geography	22	68	10
Design and technology	19	64	17

These figures have been rounded and may not add up to 100 per cent

9. Standards achieved by pupils in ENGLISH have improved, especially at Key Stage 2. In READING inspection of the implementation of the Strategy showed that there were weaknesses in the teaching of word-level work, and that too many pupils still lacked a good grounding in phonics. Teachers need to make better use of guided reading sessions, where pupils often lack opportunities to reinforce learning or acquire advanced

---

3   Level 2 is subdivided into grades C, B and A. Grade A is the most demanding.

reading skills. Nevertheless, more pupils are becoming confident users of phonic skills. The Literacy Hour introduces pupils to a good range of stories, poems and information books, and is helping pupils to become independent and enthusiastic readers with the ability to explain their preferences, make better use of libraries and understand information presented in a variety of ways.

10. Achievement in WRITING remains significantly lower than in reading or speaking and listening. The Government's targets for the year 2002 will not be met unless there is a significant improvement in the quality of pupils' writing over the next three years. Successful writers use their phonic knowledge and phonemic awareness to spell accurately. They build up a good vocabulary, develop handwriting skills, and most importantly, become fluent in many types of writing. However, writing is less well taught in literacy hours than reading. Teachers are giving insufficient attention to guided writing. Too much writing is low level, consisting of undemanding tasks involving little more than copying out simple text or filling in gaps in worksheets. Too many pupils, especially boys, are unable to produce accurate, grammatically correct writing by the time they leave their primary schools.

11. The Literacy Strategy aims to provide good opportunities for the development of SPEAKING AND LISTENING skills, and many pupils become confident in class and group discussions, adapting their speech for different purposes, reading aloud fluently and accurately, and answering questions fully. Drama features less often in the English curriculum, and there is a widening gap between good and poor practice. Role play and improvisation are underused as ways of strengthening pupils' skills in speaking, listening and working collaboratively.

12. In MATHEMATICS there has been a big improvement in pupils' achievements at Key Stage 2. Achievement in NUMBER has continued to improve, markedly so in some schools, with pupils better able to recall number facts, to apply mental calculation strategies and to explain how they arrive at their solution. Many schools have already introduced a daily mathematics lesson in anticipation of the National Numeracy Strategy. Many teachers used the draft Framework to inform their planning and teaching, and introduced a strong element of oral and mental arithmetic at the start of their lessons. Pupils are now more confident and skilled at manipulating whole numbers in their heads. However, pupils' written methods of calculation are not as well developed. They are not shown how to refine their informal methods to make them more efficient.

13. During Key Stage 1 pupils acquire a range of counting skills and a good knowledge of number properties they can use in making calculations. More pupils can successfully add, subtract and multiply one- and some two-digit numbers quickly and accurately. Pupils are weaker at division. Over Key Stage 2 the increasing attention to oral and mental work and whole class discussion has improved standards. Pupils are more confident at solving problems that require them to determine which operation to use. Pupils' understanding of decimal numbers and fractions has improved, together with their ability to solve problems that involve finding simple fractional parts and percentages, though use of ratio and proportion remains a weakness.

14. Attainment in SHAPE, SPACE AND MEASURES has shown little change overall. Pupils are familiar with the names and basic characteristics of shape. They can use these to sort and classify simple shapes. Pupils' knowledge of angular properties is weak, and many have difficulty measuring angles accurately. They understand and successfully use most common metric units to measure length and weight, but are less confident when measuring capacity. Over Key Stage 1 when HANDLING DATA, most pupils make good use of basic pictograms and block graphs. Pupils' ability to interpret data from a variety of tables and graphs is not developed sufficiently through Key Stage 2. Consequently, they make too little progress in solving problems that require an analysis of data. Key Stage 2 pupils' knowledge of ALGEBRA and their use of symbols to construct simple formulae are weak.

15. In SCIENCE inspection and national assessment provide evidence of continued gradual improvement. Although progress is often slow at the start of Key Stage 2, by the end of the key stage nearly four out of five pupils now reach Level 4 in science tests, a considerable improvement on last year. This reflects the increased attention given to revision towards the end of the key stage, and improvements in the teaching, stemming to some extent from teachers' experiences of the National Literacy Strategy. Science lessons are shorter but objectives are clearer, the use of time has improved and there is a better mix of class teaching and group work.

16. The use of accurate terminology when talking about science has improved, but written work often demands too little of more able and older pupils. The excessive use of worksheets and recording forms limits pupils' responses and prevents them thinking about what should be recorded. Gains have been smallest where the few teachers who continue to lack confidence in science have relied on merely giving information and have not

engaged the interest of pupils through lively exposition or stimulating practical work.

17. Standards in experimental and investigative science continue to be much more variable than other areas of the curriculum. Most pupils can use simple apparatus, make observations and record them, but fewer are able to contribute to planning their own experiments or use their knowledge to explain conclusions, often because they are given insufficient opportunity to do so.

18. In ART the quality of the teaching has improved again, leading to better standards of achievement at both key stages. Teachers raised the level of challenge in the basic skills of art, introducing new techniques and concepts, often through the appreciation and understanding of the work of well-known artists. In the third of schools where pupils made good progress, teachers knew about and built on what pupils had learned in previous years while still allowing and encouraging pupils to express themselves imaginatively. Where schools lack a proper scheme of work, activities are sometimes repeated without any increase in expectation and with little improvement in refinement or sophistication. In some schools pupils make progress in one area, such as drawing with pens, but lack other experience, such as painting on a large scale or using clay.

19. DESIGN AND TECHNOLOGY remains weaker than most other subjects in all aspects of provision and response, mainly because of teachers' weaker subject knowledge and experience. Despite this, there are signs that there has been a marked drop in the incidence of poor teaching. Where in-service training opportunities are taken up, improvements are quickly apparent. The reduction in the National Curriculum requirements has led to a reduction of the amount of time for the subject in some schools, particularly where teachers have been uncertain what to do in design and technology. Despite reductions in time, pupils' making skills continue to be better than their designing skills. Pupils do particularly well when they are engaged in designing and making "real" products, such as musical instruments for specific composition, rather than just models.

20. Despite some small improvement in the number of schools in which pupils make good progress, GEOGRAPHY remains weak relative to other subjects. Much is satisfactory, but insufficient is good. The best work is often based on pupils' practical experiences in the local area where enthusiasm and interest result in work of quality and depth. Knowledge and understanding of themes such as weather and rivers are improving and a

wider range of distant places is being studied. Weaknesses are evident where pupils are insufficiently challenged, resulting in superficial knowledge and insufficient opportunities to compare their own area with a different location. In both key stages the more able are not given tasks to stretch them, such as extended writing or moving from description to explanation.

21. Many pupils are making good progress in HISTORY. They often demonstrate good knowledge of the material they are studying. However, where links are not made between events, people and themes, pupils fail to develop their overview knowledge and understanding of the past. In historical enquiry they are able to ask questions of evidence and draw conclusions. Where there is underachievement it is owing to lack of opportunity or time wasted in unguided "research". Too many pupils do not extend their communication skills because of poor tasks which fail to exploit what they have learned. Despite the suspension of National Curriculum requirements, more schools (well over nine in ten) provide a curriculum that is at least satisfactory. Many schools recognise the possibility of productively linking history with the Literacy Strategy. The use of texts related to concurrent work in history helps to deepen pupils' knowledge, and word-level work improves their understanding of historical terms.

22. Progress in INFORMATION TECHNOLOGY at Key Stage 1 remains at the low level reported last year. In Key Stage 2, however, more pupils are now making good or satisfactory progress, although not as rapidly as in the three core subjects. The breadth of experiences pupils have of information technology and its applications has again widened, and much of the improvement in pupils' progress may be traced to the increasing access pupils have to computers both at home and at school. The work produced by many pupils in communicating information is increasingly sophisticated. Pupils are more aware of, and competent in, control, but in this aspect of the National Curriculum, as well as in modelling, pupils' skills are not generally well developed. The difference between the highest and lowest information technology attainment in a school is often unacceptably large, and has less to do with pupils' ability than with the extent of their exposure to challenging information technology tasks.

23. Although generally the quality of work in information technology is lower than in other subjects, where an inspection identified information technology as a "Key Issue for Action" this has usually been acted upon successfully. Schools increasingly have schemes of work, some of them based on the DfEE/Qualifications and Curriculum Authority (QCA) materials published in 1998, and more schools reserve time for information technology. Arrangements for staff development have improved and information technology features more strongly in schools' development plans. The growth in the number of schools with information technology rooms has also helped to develop good quality work and much improved teaching.

24. The proportion of pupils making good progress in MUSIC at Key Stage 1 and 2 has increased again this year. Pupils' achievements in performing, composing, listening and appraising have improved in both key stages, as schools have become more effective at teaching listening and appraising partly through music making. The introduction of the National Literacy Strategy has not had the negative impact on standards in music predicted by some commentators. The reductions in time for music made by some schools have mainly been balanced by increased efficiency in teaching. It is now rare for pupils to take part in activities, for example some massed sing-songs that fill time rather than promote progress. However, there remain some schools that have taught very little music for several years. Many of these schools neglect imaginative work, including composing, particularly in Key Stage 1.

25. In PHYSICAL EDUCATION overall progress is less than satisfactory in only three per cent of schools. In about a third of schools progress is good. Games account for a good proportion of time in physical education lessons, and the skills are generally well taught. However, the emphasis is too often on the full-scale form of the adult game, rarely appropriate in Key Stage 2 lessons. Swimming is well taught. Most pupils reach the National Curriculum expectation of swimming 25 metres unaided, and know about important aspects of safety by the end of Key Stage 2. However, National Curriculum requirements for outdoor and adventurous activities are only rarely covered within the planned curriculum, although some schools provide these through optional residential experiences for older pupils.

26. In RELIGIOUS EDUCATION there has been little change in pupils' achievements. In the quarter of schools where pupils make good progress, their knowledge of religion is a particular strength. By the end of Key Stage 2 they can identify some of the similarities and differences between religions and understand some of the symbolism. In the one in ten schools where pupils make unsatisfactory progress, they generally have little knowledge or

understanding of religions other than Christianity. There are indications, however, that teachers are becoming more confident in teaching about other religions.

Under-fives in maintained schools

27. In virtually every school most pupils make at least satisfactory progress towards achieving the Desirable Outcomes for Children's Learning.[4] The NATIONAL LITERACY STRATEGY has been successful in early years classes in the great majority of schools. From about the age of four and a half, most pupils are able to concentrate for the full 30 minutes of the whole-class text and word-level work. They respond positively to the Literacy Hour and adapt well to its structure. Most pupils of reception age are working beyond the Desirable Learning Outcomes. Pupils quickly pick up a technical vocabulary about language, for example recognising punctuation marks such as exclamation and question marks. Many reception-age pupils are writing sentences and reading complex words. While some skilled and demanding teaching of phonics was seen in reception classes, too often it was limited to the teaching of initial letter sounds, rather than the more complex blends of letters and whole words, focusing on the initial and final letter. Pupils' progress in letter/sound correspondence was, therefore, often too slow.

28. The MATHEMATICAL SKILLS of under-fives in reception classes are generally sound. They learn to chant number rhymes and to count; they recognise the digits and begin to record their observations, informally at first but later by using the correct number symbols. The more confident pupils can count to 100; they understand basic addition and subtraction and can sequence and order numbers. The National Numeracy Strategy's Framework clarifies expectations about the teaching of number to young children and schools should look at how both strategies can support pupils' language development across the mathematics curriculum, to help pupils understand key ideas needed to make progress.

29. KNOWLEDGE AND UNDERSTANDING OF THE WORLD was the area that was least well taught, but it is still satisfactory in the majority of cases. Almost all under-fives have experience of using a computer. Early scientific awareness, based on observing the germination and growth of seeds or changing weather, for example, is usually well developed and frequently linked to the use of a non-fiction "big book" in the Literacy Hour.

---

4   Nursery Education: Desirable Outcomes for Learning on Entry to Compulsory Education. SCAA, 1995. These are not a statutory requirement.

30. CREATIVE DEVELOPMENT is usually at least satisfactory, with an emphasis on close observation leading to art work. Good work is frequently seen in model-making and music, although in some schools insufficient opportunity is provided for pupils to work imaginatively with sound. Few reports refer to dance and movement, although role play remains a positive feature of good early years provision, and is especially successful when supported by an adult. PHYSICAL DEVELOPMENT is frequently good. However occasional weaknesses exist, including a lack of a designated area for under fives' play, poor indoor space, and, in a minority of schools, insufficient attention to the planning of outdoor physical activity.

The achievement of different groups of pupils

31. The standards achieved by pupils vary quite considerably from school to school. Despite general improvement, schools serving areas of SOCIO-ECONOMIC DISADVANTAGE still have a long way to go before their pupils achieve the national expectations in literacy and numeracy. Some schools with the most disadvantaged intakes are, however, overcoming the very considerable challenges they face and are achieving standards at least equal to the national averages. No single factor accounts for their success, but most display some, if not all, of the following features:

- strong and effective leadership: headteachers who can review and evaluate their schools with rigour and determination, analyse and reflect upon the impact of initiatives, and pursue improvements by insisting on excellence in all aspects of the school's work;

- teachers who bring real commitment to the school, the pupils and the community;

- a very strong emphasis on the development of pupils' knowledge and skills in literacy and numeracy, while at the same time sustaining a broad curriculum in which the arts, in particular, are given a high status;

- a high priority given to provision for pupils with special educational needs, stressing the importance of early identification of such pupils;

- a positive ethos, in which poor behaviour is not tolerated, and levels of fixed-term or permanent exclusions are low or non-existent.

32. The attainment of ETHNIC MINORITY GROUPS as a whole is improving, but some groups continue to underachieve. Although Bangladeshi and Pakistani pupils make good progress once they become fluent in English, the average attainment at the end of Key Stage 2 remains below the national average. Black Caribbean pupils achieve in line with national averages but are generally under-represented in the higher levels of Key Stages 1 and 2. The low attainment of Gypsy Traveller pupils is a cause for concern. The use of ethnic monitoring as part of the school strategy for raising attainment has barely begun in primary schools. Too many schools use general impressions about the performance of different groups which can reinforce unhelpful stereotypes.

33. Many schools have commented on the positive impact of the Literacy Strategy on the response and progress of PUPILS FOR WHOM ENGLISH IS AN ADDITIONAL LANGUAGE (EAL). However, schools rarely have data to support these claims, and more systematic tracking of the progress of EAL pupils is needed before the impact of the Literacy Strategy on EAL pupils can be fully evaluated.

Attitudes and behaviour

34. The ATTITUDES of pupils to their primary schooling are good or very good in over four in five schools. Most pupils co-operate well with each other and concentrate well in lessons; they listen carefully to their teachers and show interest and enjoyment in their lessons. The BEHAVIOUR of pupils is good in most schools: inspectors judged it to be unsatisfactory overall in only two per cent of the schools. Establishing good behaviour is a considerable challenge in some schools and classes, especially those in areas of socio-economic disadvantage. Those that succeed have clear and high expectations of pupils' behaviour, apply rules consistently throughout the school and often involve pupils in considering what is unacceptable behaviour and how such behaviour should be tackled.

35. Permanent EXCLUSIONS from primary schools occur very infrequently. For primary schools as a whole the permanent exclusion rate is one in 24,000 pupils,[5] with boys over ten times more likely to be excluded than girls.

Attendance

36. Attendance in the great majority of schools is good. In 1998/99, 88.31 per cent of schools achieved attendance levels of over 92 per cent.[6] In only three per cent of schools did attendance fall below 90 per cent. The average attendance level is 94.1 per cent, with unauthorised absences running at less than one per cent. Nevertheless, inspectors raised concerns about the attendance of pupils in just over one in ten schools. Apart from unacceptable levels of unauthorised absence (in just over five per cent of schools unauthorised absences run at two per cent or more) the most frequently reported problems with a failure to comply with the statutory requirements relating to the completion of attendance registers and problems with punctuality.

---

5   Provisional DfEE data, 1999.
6   Provisional DfEE data, 1999.

Quality of education

The quality of teaching

37. The quality of teaching continues to improve. In well over half of the schools, teaching is now good; in only one school in 20 is the overall quality of the teaching unsatisfactory. Eight in ten schools inspected had a higher proportion of good lessons than in their previous inspection. The chart below shows the quality of the teaching throughout the primary years. There has been an overall improvement in the quality of the teaching in every year group. However, the dip in the quality of teaching in Years 3 and 4 remains.

Lessons in primary schools: teaching *(percentage of lessons)*

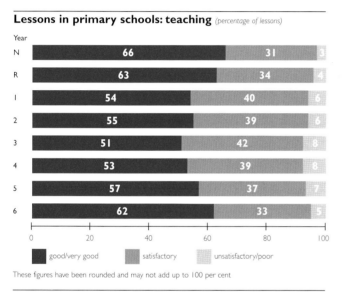

These figures have been rounded and may not add up to 100 per cent

38. The chart opposite shows inspectors' judgements of different aspects of teaching. Most aspects of teaching continue to improve. PLANNING is becoming better, reflecting a growing recognition of the importance of setting clear learning objectives for lessons. More appropriate METHODS OF TEACHING and ways of organising pupils are being employed, and the MANAGEMENT OF PUPILS is good in most schools. Although progress is being made in the quality of DAY-TO-DAY ASSESSMENT, this is still weak in about one school in five.

39. EXPECTATIONS are still too low in too many schools. The drive for higher expectations has been supported by the increased attention given to setting targets for attainment, and by the clarity with which the teaching objectives have been set out in the literacy and numeracy frameworks, term by term and year by year. There is still some way to go, however; expectations are unsatisfactory in one in eight schools at Key Stage 2. Expectations are closely related to teachers' subject knowledge, and vary considerably between subjects. It is no surprise, therefore, to see that expectations are far

too low in information technology in about one-quarter of schools.

40. The Numeracy and Literacy Strategies are influential in the teaching of subjects other than English and mathematics. There is now more DIRECT, WHOLE CLASS TEACHING, in which features of the best practice include clear instruction and skilled questioning. The NATIONAL NUMERACY PROJECT, for example, revealed how successful the oral and mental "starters" could be at the beginning of each mathematics lesson: brisk, challenging and interactive, and having a rapid impact on pupils' mental calculating skills and recall of number facts. The project also revealed weaknesses in direct teaching where weak exposition and too much closed questioning failed to engage the interest and involvement of the pupils.

41. In an inspection of the National Literacy Strategy by HMI in over 300 primary schools, the most successful element of the Literacy Hour has been the initial whole class work using a shared text. This element was well taught in over half of the lessons. The least effective element of the Literacy Hour has been the whole class word-level teaching, especially to pupils in Key Stage 1 and in Years 3 and 4. In too many of these lessons insufficient attention has been given to the teaching of phonics, in many instances revealing a lack of confidence or a lack of subject knowledge of many teachers in the basic skills of teaching reading and writing.

42. Good, direct teaching clearly requires teachers to have a good KNOWLEDGE AND UNDERSTANDING of the subjects they teach, not just in terms of the content but also a knowledge of the incremental steps underpinning progress. There have been significant gains in teachers'

Quality of teaching: Key Stage 1 and 2 *(percentage of schools)*

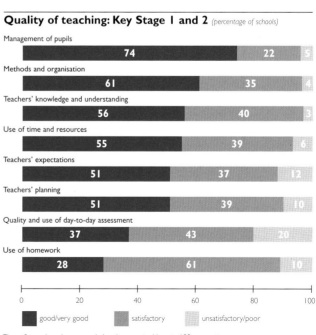

These figures have been rounded and may not add up to 100 per cent

knowledge and understanding, especially in English, during the year. There remain, however, many teachers with insufficient knowledge and understanding to teach information technology, and to a lesser extent design and technology, effectively: in less than one-third of schools is there good subject knowledge in these subjects.

43. In the overwhelming majority of Literacy Hours, EAL pupils were fully integrated into the lesson. The SPECIALIST OR BILINGUAL SUPPORT PROVIDED FOR EAL PUPILS during the Literacy Hour is generally effective, and ensured that the focus on reading and writing did not restrict basic language acquisition and progress in speaking and listening. At best, the EAL specialist staff contributed effectively to planning and provided advice on resources, text selection and training. Not all schools have yet made effective decisions about how to deploy EAL support staff during the Literacy Hour, and in some schools such staff are underused, both during the Literacy Hour and in the school's own training and staff development programme. There were some examples of withdrawal groups, often of pupils at an early stage in their learning of English, in which the pace of the work was slower and there was little challenge to produce either spoken or written English.

44. Only about three in ten schools make good use of HOMEWORK. Nevertheless, there has been a significant growth in the number of schools providing after school study support or "homework clubs" in which pupils can complete homework, receive additional teaching (usually in English, mathematics or information technology) or revise for the National Curriculum tests. Some schools are now focusing their attentions on particular pupils or groups of pupils in these after school sessions, for example helping pupils on the borderline between Level 3 and Level 4 to achieve Level 4 in the Year 6 National Curriculum tests.

45. Many headteachers reported concerns about the haste with which the induction on BOOSTER CLASSES was organised in the period immediately preceding the Key Stage 2 National Curriculum test in the summer of 1999. Nevertheless, most schools also reported that their impact, especially on those pupils that the school felt were "borderline" Level 3/4 pupils, had been positive. Schools chose to use the funds available in a range of ways, some focusing on particular groups of pupils during the Literacy Hour, others providing the booster classes at another time in the school day, or after school. Inspection evidence shows that the classes were having a good effect on attainment, and that they were popular with pupils and their parents.

46. There are signs that the National Literacy Strategy is having a positive impact on the provision for PUPILS WITH SPECIAL NEEDS, although in many schools there has been a debate about the relative merits of withdrawing special needs pupils from the Literacy Hour rather than including them within it. Most schools, on balance, rightly prefer to include pupils in the Literacy Hour, and are making good use of support staff to help the lowest-attaining groups of pupils during the independent and group work elements of the Literacy Hour. Schools are also making good use of support staff to provide individual support within the shared text element of the hour, for example by preparing enlarged texts for visually impaired pupils. This support is most effective when the staff have been involved in the school's literacy training programme and have been carefully briefed by the class teacher.

47. Features of the best provision for special needs pupils have been: the involvement of the special needs co-ordinator in the planning of work and the monitoring of progress; provision of intensive phonic work for particular pupils, sometimes immediately prior to a literacy lesson; and the adaptation of individual education plans to take account of the objectives of the National Literacy Strategy, although this is an issue on which schools would welcome further guidance.

The curriculum and assessment

48. Most schools provide an appropriate BROAD AND BALANCED curriculum, although about one school in ten is failing to do so. Successful schools generally manage to give sufficient attention to the essential skills of literacy and numeracy, while providing sufficient time for worthwhile study of the other foundation subjects and religious education, and often include other curriculum areas such as a modern foreign language.

49. While schools are clearly focusing more closely on the teaching of English and mathematics, there is little evidence to suggest that successful schools are abandoning a broad curriculum. Schools now teach most of their English and mathematics in the mornings, leaving work in most other subjects to the afternoons. Many schools are experiencing difficulties in making the best use of the time available in the mornings. The inclusion of a Literacy Hour, a mathematics lesson, the act of collective worship and a breaktime typically occupy about two-and-a-half hours, leaving around 30 minutes spread throughout the morning, which is often wasted.

50. Weaknesses in the breadth and balance of the curriculum remain in a small minority of schools. Insufficient time for information technology is the principal weakness. However, there are signs that the relaxation of the National Curriculum requirements is leading to some schools reducing the time given to subjects or aspects of subjects in which they lack expertise or confidence: design and technology falls into this category.

51. Although almost all schools have a policy for SEX EDUCATION, the extent to which the programme meets the needs of pupils varies. Some primary schools have elected not to include sex education in the curriculum; others fail to discuss issues such as puberty, ignoring the physical and emotional changes that are taking place in many of the pupils.

52. Many schools are engaged in a wide variety of initiatives to raise the attainment of pupils from ETHNIC MINORITIES, but few monitor the impact of these activities systematically. Most schools have equal opportunities policies and, especially in inner-city areas, policies on education for diversity. Sound intentions are not always translated into effective practice; saying that prejudice is unacceptable is not helpful unless it is backed up by agreed procedures for dealing with racist behaviour, for example. Schools with Gypsy Traveller or Pakistani pupils seem particularly slow to underpin policies with systems to translate them into action.

53. PLANNING for continuity and progression has improved, again supported by the two national strategies, which not only offer widely adopted approaches to medium-term (half-termly) and short-term (weekly) planning, but also identify clearly and helpfully the precise learning objectives on which the teaching can focus. Most schools now have schemes of work for most subjects, although they rarely have such detailed objectives in areas other than literacy and numeracy.

54. Procedures for ASSESSING PUPILS' ATTAINMENT have continued to improve, with an increasing number of schools using the non-statutory National Curriculum tests in the core subjects for Years 3, 4 and 5. Almost eight in ten schools used the Year 3 and 5 tests and almost nine in ten used the Year 4 tests, which provide an important indication of pupils' progress halfway through the key stage. The recent TARGET-SETTING exercise encouraged schools to look closely at the attainment of each year group and to predict how this would change as the pupils moved through school. However, schools and local education authorities are still some way from identifying achievable, realistic targets for each school.

55. If schools are finding it difficult to establish NUMERICAL TARGETS for pupils' attainment which are both realistic and challenging, they are finding it even harder to set targets for improving the curriculum. For too many schools such targets are little more than vague exhortations to do better. Only in a minority of schools are the targets based on a weakness identified through assessment, and leading to a carefully articulated strategy to overcome the weakness. There are signs, however, that this issue is being addressed, with LEAs increasingly contributing through their programmes of school visits to the setting of curricular targets for literacy and numeracy.

56. There remain some confusion and very different practices regarding the administration of BASELINE ASSESSMENT. Some schools make baseline assessment of children when they enter the nursery age, perhaps at the age of three-and-a-half. Others undertake baseline assessment when pupils transfer to the reception class. Still others are "letting the children settle" in their reception class, and then administering a baseline assessment prior to embarking on the Literacy Strategy. Some schools, therefore, operate a system of two "baseline" assessments, thus missing the point that a baseline assessment is an initial assessment of a pupil against which subsequent progress can be monitored.

57. While most schools, especially at Key Stage 2, continue to provide a traditional range of sporting, and, to a lesser extent, cultural EXTRA-CURRICULAR ACTIVITIES after school, there has been more unsatisfactory practice reported this year than in previous years. At the same time, there has been an increase in the number of schools offering after-school study support, especially at Key Stage 2, in English, mathematics and sometimes in information technology. This increased emphasis on academic subject-based study support is reducing the emphasis given to more established after-school activities such as team games, especially in the summer term as the National Curriculum tests approach.

Support, guidance and pupils' welfare

58. As in previous years, the judgements on the quality of the provision for pupils' support, guidance and welfare are overwhelmingly positive. In the vast majority of schools, headteachers, teachers and other adults give the welfare and safety of the pupils the highest priority. Most pupils feel able to report concerns to their teachers and know that these will be taken seriously, for example about bullying.

59. There is still a small number of schools that lack adequate CHILD PROTECTION PROCEDURES; concerns about child protection procedures were raised in eight per cent of schools. This is not to say that the pupils were not well known to the staff in these schools, nor that on a day-to-day basis the pupils' welfare did not receive a high priority. But there were several schools which had no child protection policy, and in others the designated child protection officers were unsure of their duties. In some schools, training in the child protection procedures had not been undertaken, usually because of staff changes.

Partnership with parents and the community

60. The quality of the information provided for parents by schools is now good in almost two-thirds of schools. Most schools now inform parents clearly and regularly about what is taught and about their children's progress. Reports to parents are increasingly well written and free from jargon. Prospectuses and the annual report to parents from governors generally include all the required information. Regular newsletters and other written communications are usually found to be helpful by parents.

61. Almost all schools enrich pupils' experiences through the involvement of the local community, but the range of these contacts and the extent of the partnership vary from school to school. Links are often extensive and include charity work, the provision of adult education facilities, and working with local industry. For example, following a visit to a local engineering company, pupils from a primary school designed a working press and conveyor belt. A growing feature in recent years has been the development of links with schools abroad through the use of email or the Internet. When carefully planned, these enrich and extend the curriculum and provide pupils with useful links with the world beyond their school.

Pupils' spiritual, moral, social and cultural development

62. The quality of schools' support for pupils' spiritual, moral, social and cultural development has changed very little since 1997/98. Of the four elements, provision for pupils' spiritual and cultural development is weaker than that for moral and social development. SPIRITUAL DEVELOPMENT is fostered principally through acts of collective worship and religious education, which provide opportunities for reflection on significant issues, and for pupils to consider how Christians and people from other faiths respond to these issues. Provision for spiritual development is good in one-half of schools. These schools provide opportunities across the curriculum for pupils to consider, for example, the wonders of creation, the importance of relationships and the worth of each individual.

63. The proportion of schools failing to provide a daily act of collective worship continues to fall, and is now well below 10 per cent. Most acts of worship are held for groups of pupils, typically by key stage or year groupings. In most schools teachers work hard to make collective worship a meaningful experience which provides pupils with a chance to reflect on important issues and builds a sense of community. In a minority of schools, assemblies contain no element of worship, the whole time being used for notices and awards. Assemblies based on explicitly religious themes are most frequently found in church schools, and are often led by priests or ministers. Examples of such themes include Christian perspectives on right and wrong, forgiveness and repentance, stories about saints, and teaching about the core events of the Christian year. Occasionally, acts of worship focus on other religions, such as stories about a boy's bar mitzvah or the theme of the Buddhist wheel.

64. Most schools have good provision for pupils' moral development. These schools see MORAL DEVELOPMENT as much more than the establishment of good behaviour; for example pupils are encouraged to consider what distinguishes right from wrong. Values such as fairness, honesty and respect for others are promoted, and opportunities are found across a range of subjects to consider moral issues.

65. SOCIAL DEVELOPMENT is also good in most schools. Pupils are encouraged to accept responsibilities and to contribute to the life of the school, and older pupils are encouraged to look after younger pupils. Pupils respond well to duties such as running the school library, selling snacks at the tuck shop and ensuring the grounds are free from litter. Many schools also have a tradition of raising funds for charities, often selected by pupils.

66. Provision for CULTURAL DEVELOPMENT is good in half the schools. The challenge for schools is to establish an appropriate balance between ensuring pupils understand the cultural traditions of the United Kingdom and preparing them for life in multicultural Britain. The best provision forms part of a planned programme that includes visits and visitors covering a broad range of cultural experiences and supported by work in subjects such as religious education, history and geography. The main weakness identified by inspectors is the limited emphasis given to non-Western cultures. On the other hand, the range of provision for cultural provision in some schools is outstanding, and includes dance, drama, music and poetry from a range of cultural perspectives, often linked to work undertaken in other subjects.

The management and efficiency of the school

Leadership and management

Leadership and management: primary schools *(percentage of schools)*

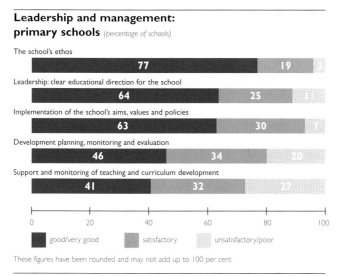

The school's ethos
77 | 19

Leadership: clear educational direction for the school
64 | 25

Implementation of the school's aims, values and policies
63 | 30

Development planning, monitoring and evaluation
46 | 34 | 20

Support and monitoring of teaching and curriculum development
41 | 32

0   20   40   60   80   100

■ good/very good   ■ satisfactory   □ unsatisfactory/poor

These figures have been rounded and may not add up to 100 per cent

67. Most schools are well led. Clear educational direction is now provided in almost two-thirds of schools, an improvement on previous years. These schools have responded positively to the previous inspection, and the vision and sense of purpose of the headteacher sustain high morale amongst the staff. By contrast, one in ten schools still has weak overall leadership. These schools typically have not tackled the weaknesses identified in the previous inspection, they are unable to prioritise their work and give insufficient attention to raising standards achieved by pupils.

68. Headteachers' success at establishing a strong and positive ethos in their schools remains one of the most successful aspects of English primary schools. The MONITORING OF TEACHING AND CURRICULUM DEVELOPMENT have improved considerably, but remain the weakest aspects of management. There are schools in which monitoring and evaluation are tackled capably, systematically and productively. There are others in which if they happen at all it is on an *ad hoc* basis which causes anxiety among staff and has little impact on the work of the school. Four in ten schools now fall into the former category, about a quarter in the latter.

69. The role of the headteacher in successfully implementing the Literacy and Numeracy Strategies has been highlighted in the reports on the Literacy and Numeracy Projects and in the interim reports on the implementation of the National Literacy Strategy.[7] Part of that role has been to monitor the implementation of the

project or strategy by observing teachers at work and providing feedback. Increasingly, headteachers are realising that providing the most effective feedback requires not just an understanding of the features of good teaching but also a detailed knowledge of the literacy framework and of how reading and writing are best taught.

70. While an increasing number of co-ordinators monitor the quality of the teaching effectively, it is usually only the headteacher who has sufficient non-teaching time to provide systematic coverage of all classes. Nevertheless, co-ordinators need a clear view of how work in their subject progresses as pupils move through the school, and many headteachers are seeking to release their subject co-ordinators for just this purpose.

71. In almost four-fifths of schools, FINANCIAL CONTROL AND ADMINISTRATION are good or very good. DAY-TO-DAY ORGANISATION AND ROUTINE ADMINISTRATIVE PROCEDURES are mostly efficient and effective. Finance sub-committees of GOVERNING BODIES are increasingly helping schools to set priorities and reduce expenditure. Governors who receive detailed advice from headteachers increasingly take part in planning, setting the annual budget, and targeting areas for improvement. Financial planning is good or very good in three-fifths of schools, but unsatisfactory in one school in ten.

72. Schools generally use the resources available to them well. However, there are unacceptably wide variations in the income that schools receive. This is shown in the charts on the following page. Primary schools receive from as little as £1,300 to over £2,500 per pupil. Some variation is inevitable. For example, those schools with a higher proportion of pupils with special educational needs will need higher funding. However, when schools with similar proportions of pupils with special educational needs and similar levels of disadvantage are compared the variation is still very wide. On average primary schools receive about two-thirds of the income per pupil that secondary schools receive.

73. The Literacy and Numeracy Strategies have raised some issues related to the use of resources. For example, while many schools choose to deploy teaching assistants to support the group work element of the Literacy Hour, it is not always clear how these assistants can be used most effectively during other parts of the lesson. With mornings generally taken up by literacy and numeracy, some schools are finding facilities for subjects such as physical education, art and music under pressure during the rest of the school day.

---

7   *The National Literacy Strategy - an interim evaluation.* OFSTED 1999.

Distributions of income per pupil for primary schools inspected - 1998/99

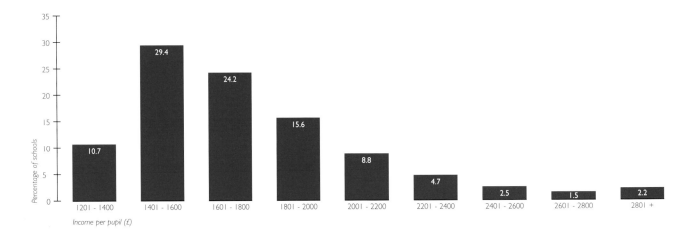

Income per pupil (£)

Distributions of income per pupil for primary schools inspected - 1998/99. Selection of similarly disadvantaged schools

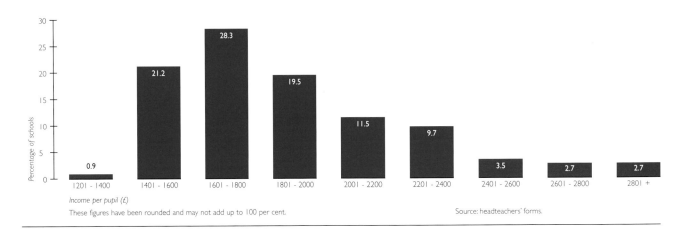

Income per pupil (£)

These figures have been rounded and may not add up to 100 per cent.

Source: headteachers' forms.

Staffing, accommodation and learning resources

74. The match of the NUMBER, QUALIFICATIONS AND EXPERIENCE OF TEACHERS to the demands of the curriculum is at least adequate in all but a small minority of schools. Problems with the recruitment of teachers continue in the south east and in inner cities, particularly inner London, where about three per cent of posts[8] have been advertised but remain unfilled. There are also some difficulties in the recruitment of headteachers and deputies, where there were about 450 unfilled vacancies across the country. The trend to increase the number of support staff continues. The quality of their work is usually good, particularly where additional training has been provided. They provide particularly valuable support for pupils with special needs or for whom English is an additional language.

75. Most schools have sufficient ACCOMMODATION to teach the National Curriculum, and most make good use of what facilities they have. Open plan areas are proving far from ideal, however, for the direct whole class teaching which is now being employed to a greater extent; such teaching is most effective in a quiet environment.

76. The QUANTITY AND QUALITY OF LEARNING RESOURCES for the effective teaching of the curriculum are good in three schools in ten. They are inadequate in 5 per cent of schools, a lower proportion than last year. Virtually all schools have concentrated their spending on the provision of books to support the literacy teaching: "big books" for the shared reading sessions, and sets of books for the "guided reading" sessions. There are signs that publishers are responding rapidly to the requirements of the Literacy Strategy in providing schemes that are designed to match the learning objectives, and a range of texts to match the different genres of writing the Strategy expects pupils to encounter.

8   Provisional DfEE data, 1999.

77. Initial government and local education authority funding for the National Grid for Learning has often been targeted at primary schools, especially those with little information technology provision. These funds, along with supermarket vouchers, special parent and teacher association collections, and donations from industry, have enabled most schools to improve their equipment.

Nursery education in the private, voluntary and independent sector

78. In 1998 OFSTED published a report on nursery education based on inspections of all institutions receiving funding.[9] In just under 60 per cent of these institutions the provision was acceptable in promoting the desirable learning outcomes, and there were no serious weaknesses. The following judgements are drawn from the re-inspection of those nursery settings that had some weaknesses in provision – mainly for literacy and numeracy – and that were judged to require a second inspection within one to two years of their first inspection.

79. There has been a marked improvement in the quality of provision in what were the weaker institutions 12 months previously. In almost 70 per cent of these nursery settings the provision is now acceptable; in only 1 per cent is provision unacceptable. In 29 per cent of settings the provision was broadly acceptable but requiring further inspection within two years. Particularly significant has been the improvement in playgroups and pre-schools since the 1997/98 inspection. Three things have led to improvements: the provision of a common curriculum based on the desirable learning outcomes; partnership working between local authorities, providers and their organisations; and inspection and public reporting by OFSTED.

80. The quality of provision has improved in all types of institution for each of the six areas of learning. Personal and social development is now a considerable strength. The increased emphasis on a planned curriculum, giving priority to language and literacy and mathematics, has not been at the expense of pupils' personal and social development. Some differences between the provision remain. For example, children in almost all playgroups and local authority day nurseries are generally good at using their initiative, such as choosing activities and selecting appropriate resources. However, these aspects are well developed in only three-quarters of the independent schools in the cohort.

81. There has been an important improvement in the quality of the provision for LANGUAGE AND LITERACY, especially in playgroups and local authority day nurseries. The best provision is found in independent schools, where over 93 per cent of institutions promote language and literacy at least acceptably, compared with 66.4 per cent of playgroups. Most institutions in this cohort made progress, but about one-third, while having broadly acceptable provision, continue to have some weaknesses in promoting early reading and writing skills and will require re-inspection in one to two years. Almost half of local authority day nurseries need to do more to develop early reading, and a quarter of playgroups do little to encourage children to recognise letters of the alphabet or to write their own names.

82. Although most institutions have made progress in their provision for MATHEMATICS, weaknesses persist in all types of institution. Children generally use mathematical language well to identify and describe shapes and objects; they enjoy counting games and number rhymes, and almost all children (especially those in independent and private nursery schools) can recognise numbers up to ten. However, children are given insufficient opportunities to solve mathematical problems and to apply mathematics in everyday practical situations; this weakness is most apparent in playgroups and local authority day nurseries.

83. All types of institutions found it challenging to provide well for the wide-ranging and complex area of KNOWLEDGE AND UNDERSTANDING OF THE WORLD. Although there have been some improvements in all settings, many institutions continue to have difficulties in supplying a range of technological resources such as tape recorders, programmable toys or computers. However, eight in ten local authority day nurseries are now doing so.

84. All types of institution improved the quality of their provision for PHYSICAL DEVELOPMENT, although poor provision remains in some institutions and a lack of suitable accommodation hampers progress. There is some way to go before the quality of the provision for practical work and climbing apparatus in independent schools, private day nurseries and private nursery schools is similar to that usually found in local authority nurseries.

85. All types of institution have improved their provision for CREATIVE DEVELOPMENT. In almost all playgroups, children have the opportunity to work with colour, shape

9   *The quality of education in institutions inspected under the nursery funding arrangements.* OFSTED, 1998.

and texture and to produce art work in two or three dimensions. This compares favourably with the lack of appropriate provision still found in one in six independent schools. Provision for drama, dance, imaginative play, and making and performing music is weakest in independent schools, where weaknesses in one-third were reported.

86. Many nursery institutions are now better at PLANNING, although half of them continue to have weaknesses, mainly because of a lack of clarity about what the institution is trying to achieve. Many staff are still unclear about: the purpose of the activities mentioned in the plans; the best way to organise children and deploy adults; and how staff would know whether the children have learned what is intended.

87. The QUALITY OF TEACHING has improved over the past year, and is now effective in more than three-fifths of local authority day nurseries and independent schools and about half of private nursery schools, private day nurseries and playgroups. Staff's knowledge of the desirable learning outcomes is now better; it is secure in about 70 per cent of local authority day nurseries and independent schools, but is insecure in 40 per cent of other institutions.

88. In some institutions, the teaching methods chosen by staff lack variety. At one extreme, children are free to choose activities for most of the time; at the other extreme, especially in some independent schools and private day nurseries, staff overdirect children's work.

89. The findings related to the quality of work in the private, voluntary and independent sector suggest three main lines of action:

- continue to promote, with a sense of priority, language and literacy and mathematics, in order to help children make the best possible start on the National Curriculum.

- nursery staff need to be better trained to assess children's learning in accordance with the desirable learning outcomes, and to use assessment more effectively to prepare work which builds on existing knowledge, skills and understanding;

- all institutions need to keep their curricular provision under review to make sure that children have good access to all six areas of learning.

Secondary schools

Educational standards achieved

Overview of attainment and progress

90. Standards achieved by pupils in secondary schools continue to improve gradually. The average GCSE point scores per pupil in maintained secondary schools has risen from 36.8 in 1998 to 37.8 in 1999.[10] The proportion of pupils gaining five or more A*–C grades has risen from 44.6 per cent to 46.3 per cent. The proportion of pupils gaining five GCSEs at grade G or above has also improved slightly.

91. Evidence from secondary schools inspected for the second time shows that they have generally responded positively to the previous inspection and that key areas of teaching, management and assessment have improved. Pupils are, on the whole, making greater gains in knowledge, understanding and skills.[11] The chart below shows inspectors' judgements of the progress pupils made in lessons. There have been improvements in each year group. Pupils make a sound start to secondary education, but progress is weakest in Years 8 and 9.

Lessons in secondary schools: progress *(percentage of lessons)*

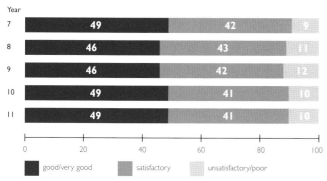

These figures have been rounded and may not add up to 100 per cent

92. Despite these gradual improvements, six key concerns remain. First, NATIONAL CURRICULUM TEST RESULTS AT KEY STAGE 3 remain too low. There has been some improvement in the mathematics results and a slight decline in English, but overall there has been relatively little change over the last five years. One-third of pupils still lack the literacy and numeracy skills to reach Level 5. The pupils who took Key Stage 3 tests this year had taken Key Stage 2 tests in 1996. After three years in secondary schools these pupils have, on average, increased their attainment by only just over one

level. Moreover, the significant improvements in the 1996 Key Stage 2 results have not carried through to an improvement in 1999 Key Stage 3 results.

93. Second, the long tail of underachievement at the end of Key Stage 4 remains. This is shown in the chart below. Pupils' GCSE point scores have been ranked and divided into quarters.[12] The highest attaining quarter of pupils score almost six times the average GCSE point scores of the lowest quarter. It remains a concern that 13 per cent of all pupils fail to gain a GCSE qualification in both English and mathematics and 6.1 per cent fail to gain any GCSE at all.

Average GCSE point scores of 15-year-old pupils by quarters: girls and boys 1997/98 - all maintained schools

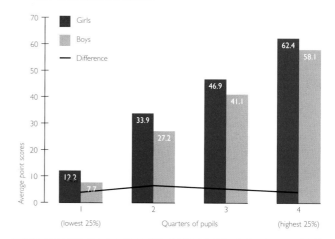

94. Third, the DIFFERENCE IN THE ACHIEVEMENT OF BOYS AND GIRLS shows no signs of narrowing. Girls achieve better than boys across the whole attainment range, as shown in the chart above. The difference is least amongst the high-attaining pupils and particularly large in the second quarter of the attainment range at GCSE. Girls achieve better than boys across all subjects, although differences vary considerably, as shown in the chart on the next page.[13] In addition to achieving better in the subjects they are entered for, on average girls are also entered for more subjects. This further increases the difference between boys' and girls' overall achievement.

95. Fourth, the achievement of pupils from particular minority ethnic groups is complex and variable but overall a matter for concern. Black Caribbean pupils often underachieve after a generally sound start in primary school. Pakistani and Bangladeshi pupils generally make reasonable progress but performance

10 OFSTED analysis of provisional DfEE data 1999. The point scores per pupil is calculated by allocating one point for a G; two points for an F up to eight points for an A*, for each subject taken.
11 *See Annex 2 for an interpretation of inspection data.*
12 OFSTED analysis of DfEE data, 1998.
13 OFSTED analysis of provisional DfEE data, 1999.

Difference in average GCSE points per entry between boys and girls by subject 1999 (Girls - Boys) - all maintained schools

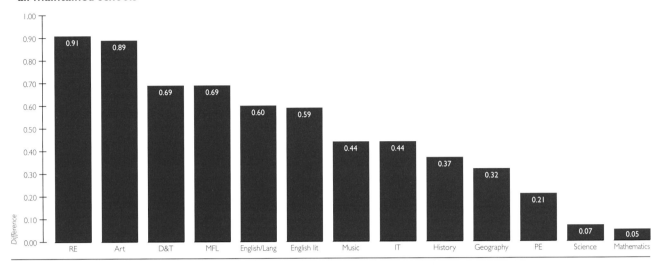

remains below the national average, particularly at the high grades. The low attainment of Gypsy Traveller pupils is also a matter for concern.

96. Fifth, the range of attainment scores for schools remains too wide. Seven in ten schools have an upward trend in results since their previous inspection. Despite the fact that low-attaining schools have improved by more than the national average, the high-attaining schools have an even greater improvement and the gap therefore continues to widen. The range of scores achieved by schools with pupils from broadly similar backgrounds is also too wide – typically about 13 GCSE points.

Finally, overall attainment of pupils in INNER CITY SCHOOLS continues to be too low. The link between social disadvantage and educational attainment is complex and longstanding. Nevertheless, two important points stand out. There is evidence that the most disadvantaged schools are improving more rapidly than schools overall. Second, there is clear evidence that schools can and do make a difference and can achieve relatively good results against the odds.

One in six non-selective schools has 35 per cent or more pupils eligible for free school meals. Ninety-five per cent of these schools are located in urban areas. They have a high proportion of families on low incomes, in poor housing with little experience of education beyond compulsory schooling. Following inspection they are more likely to be judged to have serious weaknesses or to require special measures. Few have GCSE scores in line with the national average.

However, over one-third of these schools have results at GCSE level that are well above average in comparison with other schools with pupils from similar backgrounds.

These more effective schools tend to have a higher proportion of pupils from minority ethnic backgrounds than less effective schools. Girls' schools are also better represented in the effective group.

100. Schools in disadvantaged areas need to be able to operate more effectively in all key areas if they are to succeed. The more effective schools are distinctive in the clarity, consistency and persistence of their work and the rigour with which they keep it under review. In the key areas of leadership, teaching – particularly of English, management of behaviour and use of resources, these more effective schools do as well as or better than the average of all schools nationally.

Attainment and progress in National Curriculum subjects and religious education

101. The charts on the next page show pupils' gains in knowledge, understanding and skills across the subjects of the National Curriculum. Two key points stand out:

- pupils are making better progress compared with last year across all subjects except information technology;

- particular weaknesses remain in information technology, and – despite some improvements – in religious education, music and modern foreign languages.

102. Achievement in ENGLISH has improved slightly, and this is reflected in GCSE results and in the progress made by pupils. Schools in 22 pilot local education authorities and elsewhere have implemented strategies to improve the LITERACY SKILLS of pupils at Key Stage 3. These initiatives and Summer Literacy Schools have encouraged English teachers to plan, with other subject specialists, ways of building on the literacy work in primary schools to help pupils transfer effectively to Year 7.

103. Skills in SPEAKING AND LISTENING are generally good. Pupils often speak fluently and confidently in a wide range of situations, presenting their views clearly and cogently and showing good communication skills in group work. However, there still remain too many pupils who are unable to sustain a discussion or to listen with concentration.

104. In READING AND WRITING the majority of pupils achieve adequate standards. The majority of pupils become independent readers, understand the normal range of texts and write in a variety of forms. However, some fail to build on these basic skills and rarely read or write at length, find it difficult to vary their style and use a limited vocabulary. Their understanding remains at the literal level and they find it difficult to use reference materials. They seldom turn to books for enjoyment or as a way of improving their work in other subjects. Weaknesses in writing persist; even fluent writers make errors in spelling, punctuation and syntax. Particular weaknesses include attempts at long sentences without appropriate punctuation and poor agreement of nouns with verbs. Too much writing is left unfinished. It remains a concern that one in ten pupils reaches the end of compulsory education without at least a grade G in GCSE English. Where it features in mainstream English, DRAMA makes a positive contribution to the development of pupils' communication skills but provision and standards are variable. When taught as a separate subject, standards are often high.

105. Standards of achievement in MATHEMATICS have shown some improvements but these do not yet reflect the gains made in primary schools. At Key Stage 3 pupils spend too much time on work they can already cope with. Consequently more able pupils fail to make sufficient progress. Initiatives to identify and pay particular attention to Year 7 pupils who do not reach Level 4 by the end of Key Stage 2 are not yet sufficiently well established in secondary schools. By the end of Key Stage 4 the gap in attainment continues to be unacceptably wide. There is still a core of pupils which reaches the end of compulsory education with poor numeracy skills, and about one in ten pupils does not achieve even a grade G in GCSE. Too many pupils, particularly boys, present their work poorly. Consequently basic mistakes are made which are difficult to identify and remain uncorrected.

106. In number pupils' mental calculation strategies are improving slowly as more attention is given to sharpening these skills. Increasingly schools are restricting pupils' access to calculators when the work involves only straightforward calculations that pupils should be able to do quickly in their heads. Written calculation methods involving fractions, ratio and division are less secure. In SHAPE, SPACE AND MEASURES, while pupils generally have a sound knowledge of

Progress in Key Stage 3 *(percentage of schools)*

Physical education
| 54 | 43 | |

English
| 53 | 43 | 5 |

History
| 49 | 46 | 5 |

Art
| 48 | 44 | 8 |

Design and technology
| 47 | 46 | 7 |

Mathematics
| 45 | 48 | 6 |

Geography
| 45 | 47 | 8 |

Music
| 45 | 40 | 15 |

Science
| 44 | 47 | 9 |

Religious education
| 43 | 46 | 11 |

Modern languages
| 39 | 52 | 9 |

Information technology
| 35 | 38 | 27 |

Progress in Key Stage 4 *(percentage of schools)*

Art
| 61 | 32 | 7 |

Music
| 59 | 35 | 6 |

History
| 58 | 36 | 6 |

English
| 56 | 41 | 3 |

Geography
| 50 | 45 | 5 |

Physical education
| 49 | 45 | 6 |

Design and technology
| 49 | 43 | 8 |

Science
| 48 | 41 | 11 |

Mathematics
| 43 | 49 | 8 |

Religious education
| 39 | 39 | 21 |

Modern languages
| 36 | 52 | 12 |

Information technology
| 24 | 34 | 43 |

| 0 | 20 | 40 | 60 | 80 | 100 |

■ good/very good   ■ satisfactory   ■ unsatisfactory/poor

These figures have been rounded and may not add up to 100 per cent

shapes and their properties, they are often unable to use these properties to reason and prove results. Pupils are generally able to measure and to record their results accurately. They have difficulty converting between units, particularly those relating to volume and capacity, and between metric and imperial measures. Manipulative skills in ALGEBRA have improved, but the use of algebraic techniques to model and to solve problems is given too little attention; pupils lack confidence in tackling more complex problems involving unfamiliar contexts. Data handling skills are often good, particularly where information and communications technology has been used to analyse data and to draw inferences from graphs and charts.

107. Progress in SCIENCE at the start of Key Stage 3 has improved, though this is not, as yet, reflected in test results at the end of the key stage, which show no consistent pattern of improvement. Achievement at Key Stage 4 has improved as a result of the more detailed preparation for GCSE. At the start of Key Stage 3 pupils have a much better grasp of basic science than previously and secondary departments are beginning to take account of this in their planning. However, insufficient use is made of data from primary schools to ensure that all pupils in Year 7 build on what they already know. Teachers spend a considerable amount of time on assessment throughout the key stage, but they make insufficient use of this to aid planning, set individual targets for pupils or track their progress. Where this does happen it has been effective in raising standards. Although practical work continues to be prominent, too few pupils attain high levels because experimental and investigative science is often neglected until Year 9 and features largely as an assessment activity carried out to a prescribed pattern. Opportunities for using practical work to consolidate understanding are being missed. Despite these weaknesses in practical work, thorough and well-structured teaching has led overall to improved attainment, particularly by those pupils in the middle range of ability.

108. The progress made by pupils in INFORMATION TECHNOLOGY remains unsatisfactory overall. In only one-third and one-quarter of schools at Key Stages 3 and 4 respectively do pupils make good progress in information technology. Most pupils are adept at handling text and graphics and acquire reasonable skills in presenting information graphically. While many pupils are not yet fluent in keyboard use, the range of applications and facilities which they experience continues to grow. Many pupils are able to transfer skills

readily between applications and between different types of computer. The majority of pupils in both key stages spends too much time practising low-level information technology skills. This involves manipulation of text, graphics and even moving images, but does not often result in high-quality informative or sufficiently attractive outcomes. Only a small proportion of pupils reaches higher levels of attainment, mainly those studying for examination courses in information technology. Some interesting and relevant approaches have been used in schools to teach information technology skills and knowledge in sensible subject contexts, but the quality of teaching remains weak too often, and is overall significantly below that of other subjects. Teachers often expect too little of pupils given their technical skills and the facilities available. Good work often occurs in designated information technology lessons, but it is insufficiently integrated with applications of information technology in other subjects. The in-service training of information technology teachers, especially of those who lead information technology work in secondary schools, has not kept pace with developments in the subject. Given the low base of information technology, the dearth of targeted professional in-service training gives cause for concern.

109. There are consistent improvements from last year in nearly all aspects of DESIGN AND TECHNOLOGY. Pupils' skills in making are generally sound. Designing skills are weaker, often because teachers are unsure how to structure the work so that pupils develop the complex skills of investigation, developing design specifications and reconciling the conflicting requirements of the products they are designing. Pupils' knowledge and understanding are improving as teachers become more familiar with increased expectations and demands of new syllabuses. Overall, although there are wide variations, the use of information and communication technology has increased. Where resources are good and teachers have benefited from focused In-Service Training (INSET), pupils make impressive use of computer-aided design and manufacture, particularly in technology colleges where resources are generally of high quality.

110. Standards in MODERN FOREIGN LANGUAGES are slowly rising but the improvement is uneven. Some familiar problems remain. The progress of pupils at Key Stage 4 has improved but is held back where sufficient momentum for learning has not been generated in Year 8 and Year 9. Some aspects of the programme of study, such as those requiring pupils to take the initiative or cope with the unfamiliar, remain underdeveloped, and many pupils lack confidence in speaking the target

language. The ability of many pupils at Key Stage 4 to manipulate language is limited, partly because their retention is weak. Boys' underachievement is marked, though the gap between boys' and girls' performance in the subject varies greatly between schools. The quality of the teaching shows similar variation between and within schools. Better-led departments are addressing these variations through closer teamwork and monitoring of teaching and learning. Assessment is not used sufficiently in planning: more specific feedback and guidance to pupils are needed if speaking skills in particular are to be improved.

111. The progress made by pupils in GEOGRAPHY continues to improve. Where underachievement remains, expectations are at times too low, and time is often wasted on undemanding worksheets. In the half of schools where progress is good, pupils have a sound knowledge and understanding of places and themes. They can offer explanations and apply these to new geographical contexts and show improving locational knowledge and specialist vocabulary and an increasing understanding of more complex environmental issues. By the end of Key Stage 4 they have good investigative skills and some produce excellent extended studies. Schemes of work have improved and often include practical work and fieldwork which have enthused pupils and led to better achievement. In public examinations girls continue to outperform boys in the higher grades, and the gap shows no signs of lessening.

112. Continued improvement in pupils' progress in HISTORY is reflected in National Curriculum assessments and public examination results. Many pupils have a good working knowledge of this subject. However, a continuing weakness is in the development of overview knowledge and understanding, with pupils lacking a context for their work and unable to make relevant connections. Most pupils demonstrate the skills of historical enquiry, although some still underachieve because they lack critical skills in use of evidence. Many pupils have little opportunity to understand, evaluate and compare interpretations of history. Pupils' organisation and communication are often good, particularly as they develop their ideas through extended writing. There has been a further improvement in the quality of teaching. Dullness and poor match of work to the attainment levels of pupils are the main characteristics of weak teaching in the small minority of schools where pupils make unsatisfactory progress. Almost all schools meet the requirements of National Curriculum history, although some do not give sufficient emphasis to non-European history.

113. In PHYSICAL EDUCATION pupils make good progress in most schools in Key Stage 3. The performance of skills and their application in games are usually satisfactory or better. By Key Stage 4 most pupils know the rules of the games they play and demonstrate some tactical awareness. Boys tend to perform better than girls in games, but girls' achievements in gymnastics and dance tend to be better. Where swimming is chosen as an optional activity by a school, attainment across both key stages is reported as good; pupils show good techniques in the three strokes, and possess good knowledge of personal survival techniques. Most pupils understand the long- and short-term effects of exercise on body systems and how to prepare for and recover from strenuous activity. In Key Stage 4 increasing numbers of pupils are following GCSE examination courses and results continue to improve.

114. Pupils' achievements in ART continue to improve. At Key Stage 3 pupils make good gains in knowledge, understanding and skills in about half of schools. In these schools, pupils have a grasp of observational and imaginative drawing, understand basic composition and colour handling, can work in a variety of two- and three-dimensional media and know how to use sketchbooks for developing ideas. They often incorporate techniques and ideas from other artists into their own work, but still include elements of personal expression. The poorer work often reflects weak planning, which fails to ensure the progressive acquisition of basic skills such as drawing, composition and colour work. There is overreliance on copying, so that, for example, pupils replicate the work of artists but gain no real understanding of their style, genre or chronology. Pupils are asked to do low-level tasks, which are often poorly differentiated between year and ability groups.

115. Pupils' achievements in MUSIC at Key Stage 3 has improved, but remains lower than in most other subjects, particularly among boys. Music teachers have worked hard to improve their teaching, so that it builds more effectively on pupils' prior learning at school, at home and in the community, and pupils have improved accordingly in performing, composing and appraising. Teaching which assumes that pupils learnt very little in their primary schools has all but disappeared, although there are still some examples of pupils undertaking oversimplified tasks that have no intrinsic musical interest and which lead to pupils making little progress. Improvements in teaching have led to improvements in pupils' attitudes, and many schools are finding that more pupils wish to continue music in Key Stage 4.

116. The continuing weakness in pupils' achievements in RELIGIOUS EDUCATION reflects the unevenness of provision. In many schools, insufficient time is being given to the subject for an Agreed Syllabus to be covered. The quality of the teaching has improved, but low expectations, poor use of resources and poor planning are the main weaknesses in the schools where pupils make unsatisfactory progress. While statutory requirements for religious education are not met in about a third of schools, there has been a significant increase in the proportion of schools introducing GCSE full and short courses for religious education. These accredited courses have improved the quality of planning and teaching and have resulted in improved achievement by pupils.

Vocational courses

117. Just over 20 per cent of secondary schools are now offering PART ONE GNVQ courses. The strongest feature of the courses continues to be the opportunity they offer students to learn in a vocational context and develop their capacity for independent study. Achievement is highest in business and health and social care courses, where it was satisfactory or better in about 80 per cent of Intermediate courses, and lowest in the more recently established art and design, where only 55 per cent of courses came into this category. Achievement is less satisfactory on Foundation courses.

118. In the KEY SKILLS[14] communication skills and information technology were at least satisfactory in the large majority of Intermediate courses. However, number work was only satisfactory in about 65 per cent of courses; it was often limited in scope and poorly represented in many portfolios. In communication oral work was often good, but Foundation students often failed to complete the requirements of the course because of their poor command of English.

Attitudes and behaviour

119. The proportion of schools where BEHAVIOUR is good has increased. In the majority of schools pupils have positive ATTITUDES to their lessons and to school. In an increasing number of schools pupils' responses to target setting and associated monitoring and review are resulting in improved attitudes to learning. In a minority of schools pupils' attitudes to learning are particularly poor in Year 9, though the most significant decline in attitudes occurs between Year 7 and Year 8. In too many of these schools not enough is done to respond to such early indicators of pupil disaffection.

120. Procedures for monitoring and promoting discipline and good behaviour are in place in the majority of schools. The latest available figures (1997/98) show that there has been a small decrease in the number of pupils permanently excluded from schools. Schools are increasingly alert to racist behaviour or bullying and generally have appropriate policies. However, the monitoring of the consistency of their implementation is often weak. Though serious incidents involving violence are rare, too many potentially harmful incidents involving name calling or taunting go unchallenged, even when they occur in lessons.

Attendance

121. While there has been some improvement, attendance is still below 90 per cent in just over one-quarter of schools. A minority of parents contribute to poor attendance by being too casual about absence, and in some cases colluding with truancy. Changes in the patterns of attendance of pupils are not always detected early enough or linked to other indicators of disaffection. The result is that while attendance may be improved by the action of the school, this often occurs too late to make a significant impact on the pupils' attainment. Procedures for monitoring and promoting good attendance continue to improve, with nine out of ten schools now having adequate or better systems in place. Where weaknesses remain, schools lack a consistent approach to recording, monitoring and acting on pupils' absence.

Quality of education

The quality of teaching

122. The quality of teaching has continued to improve and is good in over half of lessons. At Key Stage 3 the quality of teaching is marginally lower than at Key Stage 4. Nearly nine in ten of the schools inspected had a higher proportion of good teaching compared with the previous inspection.

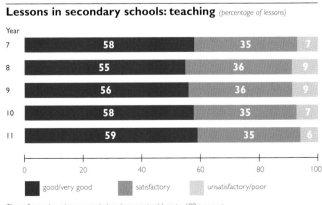

Lessons in secondary schools: teaching *(percentage of lessons)*

Year	good/very good	satisfactory	unsatisfactory/poor
7	58	35	7
8	55	36	9
9	56	36	9
10	58	35	7
11	59	35	6

These figures have been rounded and may not add up to 100 per cent

---

14 The three mandatory key skills are communication, the application of number and information technology.

123. The chart shows inspectors' overall judgements of the different aspects of teaching. There have been particular improvements in areas that have been highlighted as in need of improvement in previous annual reports: teachers' expectations, the quality of day-to-day assessment and the use of homework in Key Stage 3.

Quality of teaching: Key Stages 3 and 4 *(percentage of schools)*

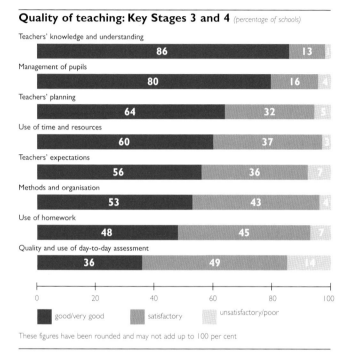

Teachers' knowledge and understanding
86 | 13

Management of pupils
80 | 16 | 4

Teachers' planning
64 | 32 | 5

Use of time and resources
60 | 37 | 3

Teachers' expectations
56 | 36 | 7

Methods and organisation
53 | 43 | 4

Use of homework
48 | 45 | 7

Quality and use of day-to-day assessment
36 | 49 | 14

0   20   40   60   80   100

■ good/very good   ▨ satisfactory   ▦ unsatisfactory/poor

These figures have been rounded and may not add up to 100 per cent

124. Procedures for assessing pupils' attainment are good in about half of schools. The subsequent use of assessment in curriculum planning continues to be a weakness, with few schools adopting consistent practice across the subjects of the curriculum. Nevertheless, information from careful and regular marking of work is increasingly influencing teachers' planning, particularly in improving literacy. One of the features of the more effective schools in disadvantaged areas is the close attention they give to setting targets and working on them with individual pupils.

125. Many schools are taking steps to improve the literacy skills of low-attaining pupils. A range of strategies is used, including withdrawal groups, paired reading schemes where older pupils support less advanced younger pupils, and frameworks to assist writing in different subjects. Subject teachers are increasingly recognising the need to teach, explicitly and systematically, the specialist language of their subject, thereby reinforcing the subject's important concepts. Such work is especially valuable for pupils who are learning English as an additional language.

126. The quality of teaching in personal, social and health education has improved at Key Stage 3. More specialist teaching is used and there is with less reliance on form tutors to teach these topics. This shift reflects the greater awareness that if teachers are to be more successful in this area they need clearly defined curriculum objectives, a core of up-to-date specialist knowledge and the ability to communicate it effectively.

127. Provision for pupils with special educational needs is good in about a half of schools. In these schools, there is effective co-operation between special needs departments, learning support assistants and subject teachers. In the best instances, teachers across a school are aware of assessment information concerning pupils who have specific learning difficulties, and they work hard to match teaching and learning resources to pupils' needs. Pupils with special educational needs often respond very well to short-term targets resulting from careful diagnosis of strengths and weaknesses, which point clearly to what they have to do in order to improve.

The curriculum and assessment

128. The quality of curriculum planning has improved since last year: it is good in four out of ten schools but remains weak in about one school in ten. Forty per cent of schools have increased the amount of taught time since the previous inspection. Sixty per cent of schools now have 25 hours of taught time compared with 40 per cent at the previous inspection. However, there is no clear link between increased taught time and improved standards. Other factors such as the quality of teaching, the impact of homework and changes in cohorts of pupils are likely to obscure any improvement brought about by increasing taught time by relatively small amounts. The available time needs to be used effectively before benefits will be derived from simply increasing the amount of taught time. Most schools provide a broad, balanced and relevant curriculum, with equality of access and opportunity to all pupils. In the main, statutory requirements are met, although there are some deficiencies in about half the schools for religious education and information technology and in a minority of schools for design and technology and modern foreign languages.

129. Foundation subjects at Key Stage 3 sometimes receive too little attention. The time allocated to teach music and art is occasionally insufficient to cover the full programmes of study. Some schools expect all pupils to study two modern foreign languages for part, or the whole, of Key Stage 3. This can severely restrict the time available for each language. Regular exposure to the foreign language is needed to consolidate learning and less-able linguists struggle to make satisfactory progress where such arrangements require them to divide their efforts between two modern foreign languages.

130. At Key Stage 4 the curriculum is generally sufficiently broad and most schools offer at least adequate guidance to enable pupils to choose sensible programmes. Some schools fail to offer enough choice to pupils, especially as many continue with full GCSE courses in humanities and design and technology for all pupils. In many schools minority subjects, such as a second modern language, are increasingly being offered only after school; these are popular and of benefit to the more able pupils.

131. Few schools have made use of the opportunity of disapplication: some disapply the National Curriculum for one or two pupils and less commonly for whole groups. The relaxing of the National Curriculum regulations is leading to some experimentation but not a radical change to the curriculum. The majority of schools provide well-organised work experience for all pupils. In a significant minority of schools, disaffected pupils undertake extended or concentrated periods of work experience. While pupils often benefit from this, the schools need to ensure that it does not adversely affect the development of their literacy and numeracy skills. Courses at Key Stage 4, run in conjunction with the further education sector, are limited to relatively few schools, though where they do exist they have a positive motivating effect on disaffected pupils. Effective links were seen with NVQ level 1 courses in the bakery and building trades and other links enabled pupils to work on practical-based skills such as brickwork and construction, vehicle maintenance and catering.

132. Planning for Part One **GNVQ** courses was handled well in about two-thirds of the pilot schools. In the remaining third, however, ineffective long-term planning often contributed to low completion rates. In general, planning was better for the vocational units than for the key skills units, and more confidently organised in Phase 1 schools (those starting in 1995) than in schools which joined the pilot at a later stage. Over nine in ten schools allocate the recommended 20 per cent of Key Stage 4 curriculum time to Part One GNVQ courses. The requirement for students to be registered at Foundation or Intermediate level at too early a stage in the course is a significant factor in the failure of some students to complete the course. A persistent weakness in the assessment of Part One GNVQ portfolio work is the emphasis given exclusively to coverage of the specifications rather than the quality of the work produced.

133. Almost three-quarters of Foundation pupils who have completed all or part of the first Part One GNVQ courses have enrolled on well-established post-16 programmes of education or training, or are in employment. The experience of Part One GNVQ courses has had a beneficial impact on these pupils' ability to cope with the demands of working independently in post-16 education and provided them with a wide range of study options.

134. Inspectors report that about one-third of secondary schools have introduced the Certificate of Achievement for low-attaining pupils across a range of subjects. Pupils have generally responded well. The courses have increased motivation and enabled these pupils to gain recognition for their efforts. However, their value as a qualification is not always clear enough to employers or to the pupils themselves, especially since no equivalence to GCSE grades has been established.

135. The quality of curriculum planning for PERSONAL, SOCIAL AND HEALTH EDUCATION is satisfactory or better in nine out of ten schools but good in only one school in six. Where planning is weak the elements of the programme were not well balanced. Schools need to give more thought to distinguishing personal, social and health education from the tutorial programme so that the roles of personal, social and health education teacher and tutor can be more clearly defined. The large majority of schools have policies on sex and relationships education and drug education. While the quality of policies is often adequate, there is a minority of secondary schools that does not review its provision in order to determine whether it continues to meet the needs of the pupils.

136. Key Stage 4 CAREERS EDUCATION modules in schools generally provide students with up-to-date information about the further education, training and employment opportunities available to them. In a significant minority of schools, however, careers work is not planned in sufficient detail, there is some duplication of provision, and some important topics are not covered. Links between schools and careers services are generally good, although more work is needed on linking action plans which have been agreed between pupils and careers advisers to the schools' assessment and recording of pupils' progress.

137. STUDY SUPPORT is a strength of many schools. A few schools, particularly those in rural areas, of necessity restrict many clubs and activities to lunchtimes, which limits their impact. A minority of schools also provide further support for pupils through homework clubs; the

best of these offer special interest clubs, continuous access to the library or information and communication technology, or Saturday morning revision sessions for Year 11. In the more effective schools in disadvantaged areas well-structured study support before and after school, including holiday clubs and holiday revision classes, had a significant beneficial impact on overall achievement.

Spiritual, moral, social and cultural development

138. Provision for pupils' SPIRITUAL DEVELOPMENT has improved significantly and is now good or better in about one-third of schools but unsatisfactory in a similar proportion of schools. Good schools do much to enable pupils to gain insights into matters of faith and belief. The notion of spirituality is taken seriously and schools generate a respect for people's spiritual perceptions that are encountered through fiction and through living examples. Where provision is poor schools typically offer little reflective, open-minded examination of questions of belief or faith. Collective worship is often poorly planned and hurried so that there is little of substance to cause other than superficial attention. Many teachers fail to cope satisfactorily with the "Thought for the Day" that typically passes for the spiritual element in tutor periods.

139. Provision for pupils' MORAL DEVELOPMENT also continues to improve; it is now good in almost nine out of ten schools and unsatisfactory in very few. Schools with a strong moral emphasis promote good behaviour through clear policies and referral systems which reward the good, strongly discourage the bad, and which are implemented at all levels. Within such systems the pupils themselves have responsibilities for ensuring that the school community is civilised and well-run.

140. Provision for pupils' SOCIAL DEVELOPMENT is also much improved this year and is good or very good in almost nine out of ten schools and unsatisfactory in only one school in 100. Older pupils often take a measure of responsibility for younger pupils. This might mean a pairing arrangement whereby the older pupil acts as a friend and guide, or assists with paired reading. Many schools emphasise the importance of teamwork and mutual support amongst all members of the school community.

141. Provision for pupils' CULTURAL DEVELOPMENT is good in just over half the schools. Pupils' understanding of their own and other cultures is fostered more explicitly in some schools than others, for example by the existence of a range of high-quality visits and cultural activities, especially where these are linked closely to the subjects that pupils are studying. For example, foreign language exchanges and visits to sites, museums and galleries can support pupils' classroom work effectively and extend their horizons. Similarly, within schools, dramatic or musical productions are sometimes valuably augmented by bringing in professional dancers, theatre groups, storytellers or artists. Where schools exploit such opportunities less effectively, they often fail to make pupils sufficiently aware of the wider community or to enable them to explore a variety of traditions, attitudes and beliefs.

Support, guidance and pupil welfare

142. In three-quarters of schools, the provision for pupils' support, guidance and welfare is good: an improvement on last year. Often, effective pastoral systems are a strength of schools: tutors and co-ordinators provide a strong, firmly-established climate of expectation for how pupils are to work and behave; they use disciplinary measures consistently; and they help pupils to become better at planning their time and developing good habits of work, behaviour and attitudes. This focused support for personal development is less well maintained in a minority of schools, where form tutors and others with pastoral responsibilities lack on occasion clear definition of their roles or a shared understanding of how best to use their time with individuals or classes.

143. Schools are making increasingly effective use of baseline data to monitor the progress of pupils and often use predicted GCSE performance based on this data in setting departmental and individual targets. Many schools rely more heavily on standardised tests on or soon after entry than they do on Key Stage 2 data, which is not always readily available.

144. Tutors have a key role in monitoring the progress and personal development of their pupils. In two-thirds of schools such monitoring is good. Academic monitoring has improved considerably. Specific performance-based targets at subject level are increasingly being used, making target setting more effective and measurable. This process is having a positive effect on the attitudes, progress and attainment of pupils.

145. The overwhelming majority of schools have appropriate child protection procedures. In over a quarter of schools inspectors identified health and safety issues that needed to be addressed. In about one in ten schools there were a significant number of such problems. Over one-quarter of schools are not carrying out risk assessment procedures on a sufficiently regular basis.

Partnership with parents and community

146. Partnerships with parents have been strengthened in the majority of schools. Most annual reports to parents continue to provide clear information about pupils' attainment and progress. Some reports, compiled from a centrally-held computerised phrase bank, fail to convey an accurate picture of the progress of individual pupils.

147. Effective home–school agreements provide clear expectations for each of the partners. As a consequence, parents feel more confident about what is expected of them. Equally, such an agreement provides a good starting point in discussion with pupils, parents or staff when difficulties arise. It also provides a regular method for reinforcing agreed good behaviour and attitudes, and consistent use of the agreement as part of the school's approach includes behaviour and gains greater commitment from pupils.

148. The majority of schools are strengthening their links with local communities. An increasing number of schools use business mentors to work with Key Stage 4 pupils in order to improve their self-esteem and self-confidence, to increase motivation to learn and to improve personal and social skills.

Management and efficiency of the school

Leadership and management

149. There have been significant improvements in the quality of leadership and management. One in 12 schools, however, is still judged to lack clear educational direction and purpose. In these schools staff morale is often low and the schools have often been unable to tackle the weaknesses identified in the previous inspection. Where leadership is good, the headteacher gets the best out of staff by establishing clear priorities, developing effective teamwork amongst senior staff and motivating and enabling teachers to teach well.

Leadership and management:
secondary schools *(percentage of schools)*

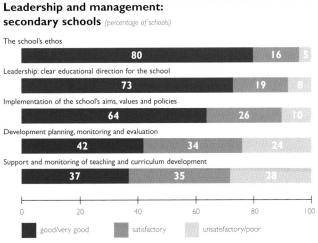

These figures have been rounded and may not add up to 100 per cent

150. Despite the broadly encouraging picture in the important areas of leadership and ethos, other areas of management remain significantly weaker. Although there has been some improvement, it remains a concern that in about one-quarter of schools the monitoring and evaluation of the quality of teaching and the standards achieved by pupils are judged to be weak, since these tasks are central to a school's effective running. Without these securely in place it is difficult to see how a headteacher, even with the strong support of a governing body and of senior managers, can demonstrate a firm focus on the prerequisites for raising standards.

151. In all but a small minority of schools, ethos is sound or better. In most schools the leadership and management create a positive and caring ethos where pupils are ready to learn and can develop into well-rounded and capable members of the community. In the one in 20 schools where the ethos is unsatisfactory, pupils are not given the opportunity to offer their views or contribute to the life of the school and have limited access to the school buildings.

152. The most effective governing bodies were involved in the strategic management of schools, encompassing all aspects of development planning and management of resources. They took part in decision making, linking the distribution of resources to the priorities set out in the development plan. There were, though, many governing bodies that were not involved at this strategic level and not all schools have governors with an adequate level of financial expertise. However, most governing bodies are effective at ensuring that expenditure is appropriate and properly recorded. Governors also had an acute awareness of the importance of pupils' personal and social development and of the school's engagement with the community.

153. Reviews of responsibilities, sometimes brought about by financial considerations, have led to a reduction in the size of senior management teams in many schools. In consequence, increased expectations are being placed on middle management. In six out of ten subject departments the quality of leadership and management is good: it remains weak in about one in ten. Heads of subject departments are often more effective in organisation and routine administration than strategic leadership. Departmental development planning, monitoring and evaluation have improved slightly and are now good in four out of ten schools. Weak departmental plans often gave insufficient attention to financial details or made bids for funding based on historical allowances rather than future needs.

154. The cross-curricular nature of information technology places particular demands on departmental management. Over three in ten schools have weak leadership in information technology, and staff, especially co-ordinators, require clearer role definitions. School management teams and governors are beginning to respond positively when information technology is raised as a key issue for action during inspection. In particular, schools are investing in technical support and staff training. One in five teachers of information technology is not qualified to teach the subject but staff development continues to show little sign of improvement.

Efficiency

155. Financial planning is good in almost two-thirds of schools, an improvement on last year. In these schools, development plans include priorities, costs and timescales that are manageable. In the one in nine schools where financial planning is weak, three factors can be identified:

- in some schools a large amount of money is held in reserve, despite evident shortages in resources that affect the quality of learning in many subject areas;

- not all aspects of the development plan are costed;

- subject departments vary in the effectiveness with which they plan their contribution to the school priorities and allocate departmental budgets to achieve them.

156. The efficiency of financial control and school administration continues to improve and is good in over eight out of ten schools and rarely unsatisfactory. Routine administration is efficient, and systems of accounting and financial control are good.

157. Schools generally make good use of the money that they have. However, there are unacceptably wide variations in the income that schools receive. This is shown in the chart below. Schools without sixth forms receive as little as £1,900 to over £3,000 per pupil. Typically the range is from £2,100 to £2,500. Some variation is inevitable, for example as a result of differences in numbers of pupils with special educational needs. However, when schools in similar circumstances are compared, the variations in income are still large, as shown below.

Distributions of income per pupil for secondary schools without sixth forms inspected - 1998/99

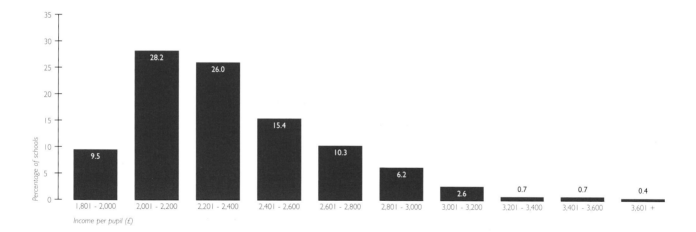

Distributions of income per pupil for secondary schools without sixth forms inspected - 1998/99
Selection of 115 schools with similar proportions of pupils eligible for free school meals and with Statement of SEN

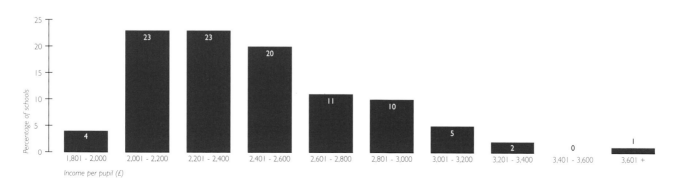

Staffing, accommodation and resources

158. The match of number, qualifications and experience of teachers to the demands of the subject curriculum is good in about six out of ten schools. It is unsatisfactory overall in one school in 20. Teachers are appropriately deployed in the majority of schools, but in a minority of cases rapid turnover of staff and heavy use of SUPPLY TEACHERS have had an adverse effect upon standards. One-quarter of lessons taught by supply teachers are unsatisfactory: the quality of teaching by supply teachers is weaker than for all other groups of teacher including newly qualified and trainee teachers.

159. Long-term absences are often the reason for the employment of supply teachers. Too often supply teachers receive insufficient guidance and support, and schools fail to provide them with adequate information about the attainment of the pupils they are teaching. The frequent use of supply teachers often disrupts regular routines, unsettles pupils and adversely affects their attitudes to work. In some schools, non-specialist supply teachers are used to cover specialist staff absence as some schools find it difficult to recruit temporary teachers of sufficient quality and expertise to cover for some subjects, especially in shortage areas.

160. LEARNING RESOURCES have improved since last year, particularly in terms of the availability of computers. Libraries continue to be better resourced and many have been turned successfully into learning centres, combining access to books and computers on the same site. Nevertheless, about one in five schools has inadequate books, materials and equipment for effective teaching of the curriculum. The main weaknesses were a lack of textbooks for pupils to take home and a lack of up-to-date library books. There were also shortages in art and science equipment. Visual aids, such as overhead projectors, were often of poor quality.

161. The quality of ACCOMMODATION is worsening. It is inadequate in one in five schools. In almost a third of these cases the fabric was poor with leaking roofs, crumbling walls or broken windows. Poor-quality classrooms with inadequate ventilation and insufficient lighting had an adverse effect on teaching and learning. A quarter of these schools lacked access to classrooms for disabled pupils. Specialist accommodation was mostly adequate and good in about one-third of schools. The main weakness was in physical education where accommodation was unsatisfactory in one in eight schools.

Sixth forms in schools

Educational standards achieved

Overview of attainment and progress

162. There are over 1,800 maintained schools with sixth forms. They provide for about 30 per cent of the 16–19 cohort. Just over half have more than 150 students and about 120 have 50 or fewer. Just over three-quarters of students in sixth forms in England are following GCE A-level courses, a tenth are studying Intermediate GNVQ and a tenth Advanced GNVQ. In the last decade participation in full-time education and the achievements of 16–19 years old have risen steadily. The proportion of students achieving Level 3 (two GCE A-levels or equivalent) qualifications has risen from 25 per cent to 37 per cent between 1987 and 1997; more than two-thirds of these qualifications have been achieved in school sixth forms. Evidence from inspection and from national examinations shows continued gradual improvements in the achievements of sixth-form students.

163. The average point score per student entered for two or more GCE A-levels was 17.9 compared with 17.6 in 1998.[15] The average point score per student entered for Advanced GNVQ was 10.2 compared with 9.5 in 1998. The percentage of those entered achieving at least one pass at GCE A-level was 91 per cent, the same as last year. The percentage entered achieving an Advanced GNVQ rose from 78 per cent in 1998 to 82 per cent in 1999. The girls entered for two or more A-levels gained an average point score of 18.1, compared with 17.7 for boys. This is a significantly smaller difference than at GCSE, indicating that boys make greater progress overall in sixth forms.

164. The chart opposite shows inspectors' judgements of progress made by students in A-level lessons. There has been a slightly lower proportion of good and very good progress made this year compared with last year, but the overall proportion of satisfactory or better work remains the same. Progress is noticeably less good in religious studies and information technology than in the other A-level subjects.

165. The first chart on the next page shows the very wide variation in the average point scores of students in different schools.[16] Small sixth forms tend to recruit students with lower levels of prior attainment and these pupils tend to achieve lower point scores than those in schools with large sixth forms. Inspection evidence shows that progress tends to be slower in small sixth forms. This is confirmed by the second chart on the next page. The average A-level point score per candidate in each school in 1998 has been plotted against the GCSE scores for the same candidates two years earlier.[17] This shows that larger sixth forms tend to achieve greater progress. There are a number of reasons for this. Small sixth forms tend to have a limited range of teaching expertise, and are more likely to have inadequate teaching time and often have to co-teach different year groups or courses. However, both inspection and the evidence from the chart indicate that there are examples of successful small sixth forms. Effective collaborative links with other schools and colleges, a curriculum closely matched to the needs of the students and well-planned teaching have resulted in students making good progress and achieving high standards.

GCE A-level courses

166. Students on **GCE A-LEVEL** courses generally make good progress. It is usually best in classes of between 11 and 16 students and weakest in very small classes, or in classes containing more than 20 students. Many students respond to effective teaching and guidance by producing coursework assignments which are thoughtful, well reasoned and, at their best, scholarly. More of them would be challenged to reach the highest standards if the criteria were more stringent. The overall standard of work by the highest achieving A-level students, on both linear and modular courses, is outstanding: it is marked by such qualities as penetrating analysis and perception, and convincing argument, based securely on a good grasp of the fundamental subject matter. Those who do less well are

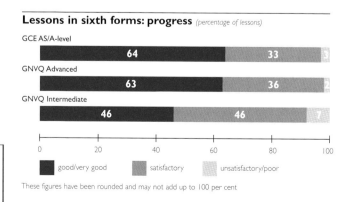

Lessons in sixth forms: progress *(percentage of lessons)*

GCE AS/A-level

GNVQ Advanced

GNVQ Intermediate

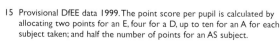
good/very good   satisfactory   unsatisfactory/poor

These figures have been rounded and may not add up to 100 per cent

---

15 Provisional DfEE data 1999. The point score per pupil is calculated by allocating two points for an E, four for a D, up to ten for an A for each subject taken; and half the number of points for an AS subject.

16 OFSTED analysis of provisional DfEE data, 1999.

17 DfEE data, 1998. General studies is excluded.

**1999 GCE/GNVQ average point scores per pupil
(pupils taking two or more A levels or equivalent) against size of sixth form**

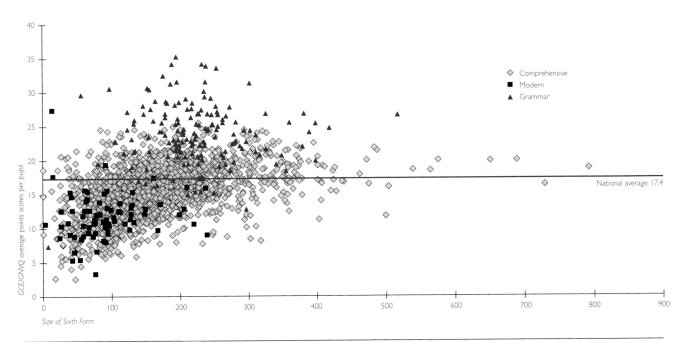

Performance of candidates attempting two or more GCE A/AS by school

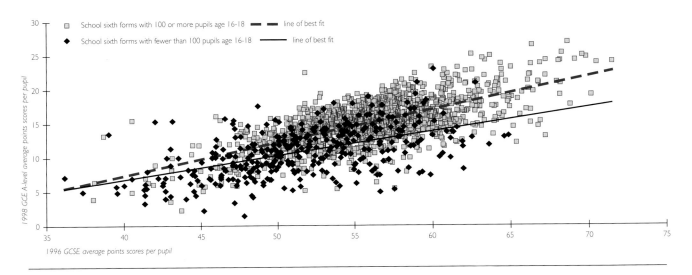

less certain in their own knowledge and hence less able to construct work which goes beyond the basic requirements.

GNVQ courses

167. The best Advanced GNVQ distinction portfolios match A-level grade A performance, and provide evidence of mature work of impressive range and depth. Work at this level is characterised by students' ability to synthesise material from a range of sources and analyse complex ideas. By contrast, students achieving pass and merit grades are often insufficiently critical of the evidence they collect and sometimes fail to draw sound conclusions from this evidence. The revised unit structure of the NEW **GNVQ ASSESSMENT MODEL,** piloted

between 1997 and 1999, led to more rigorous teaching and improved standards in the vocational areas. **ADVANCED WORK** in all subjects other than information technology is at least satisfactory overall: there have been examples of some very good work in most subject areas, but particularly in art and design and business studies.

168. The standards achieved by **INTERMEDIATE GNVQ** students are generally satisfactory, and in art and design there is a high proportion of good work. The new assessment model has improved standards on **INTERMEDIATE COURSES,** and, apart from in information technology, a level of performance commensurate with comparable GCSE courses. The main weakness at this level is a tendency for students to copy routinely from secondary sources. The new specifications have encouraged students to gain a better knowledge and understanding of the subjects and developed their ability to analyse and synthesise material, particularly when they are given the opportunity to work on assignments in realistic vocational contexts.

169. Students on FOUNDATION AND ENTRY-LEVEL vocational courses generally make satisfactory progress, better than when they are inappropriately placed in Intermediate level groups, where they are unable to cope with the demand and pace of the work. The achievement of students on lower-level sixth-form courses is often limited by poor attendance records and lack of motivation.

Key skills

170. In KEY SKILLS[18] in Advanced GNVQ students' competence in using INFORMATION AND COMMUNICATIONS TECHNOLOGY varies greatly between schools and between subjects within schools. In some classes students make good use of up-to-date technology for research and the interrogation of databases; elsewhere there is little evidence of technology being used to develop ideas and follow up lines of enquiry. Students on vocational courses are generally more confident in their use of information and communications technology than those on GCE A-level courses. In COMMUNICATION most sixth-form students on Advanced GNVQ courses can write reports in an organised and logical fashion, with appropriate analysis of data. They can make effective presentations and give convincing accounts of their assignments. A minority write descriptions or transcribe data without relating it closely to their field of study. The synthesis and analysis of complex material drawn from a variety of sources is the weakest aspect of communication. Number work is generally the least satisfactory of the three main key skills.

171. Standards in the PILOT KEY SKILLS QUALIFICATION have been satisfactory for GNVQ students. However, only a small proportion of GCE A-level students starting the pilot completed either the full qualification or individual key skills units; the work of those who did so was good. Other than in the development of oral presentations in some sixth forms and more comprehensive information technology capability in others, there is little evidence of the key skills qualification having an impact on the performance of students in their A-level studies.

Attitudes and attendance

172. The great majority of sixth-form students are very positive about their work. Well-motivated sixth-form students are universally regarded as an asset to their schools. However, with more lower-attaining students staying on into post-16 education, some schools are finding that attendance is becoming more irregular and that coursework and other deadlines are more frequently missed. It is also becoming increasingly rare for sixth-form students not to have some form of part-time employment. While this can be good for their independence, self-esteem and social confidence, it usually makes heavy demands on them and reduces the time they have to devote to their academic work.

Quality of education
The quality of teaching

173. The quality of sixth-form teaching continues to improve. The proportion of lessons judged to be very good or excellent has risen by about four per cent from 22 per cent to 26 per cent and there has been a slight reduction in the already small proportion judged to be unsatisfactory, from three per cent to two per cent.

174. The chart below shows inspectors' judgements of the different aspects of teaching. Compared with last year, there have been improvements in all categories. Overall, the proportion of good and very good teaching was highest in music and English (83 per cent). It was noticeably lower in modern languages and mathematics (73 and 71 per cent respectively), and lowest of all in information technology (53 per cent). The highest proportion of unsatisfactory teaching was in religious education (two per cent), science (three per cent) and information technology (four per cent).

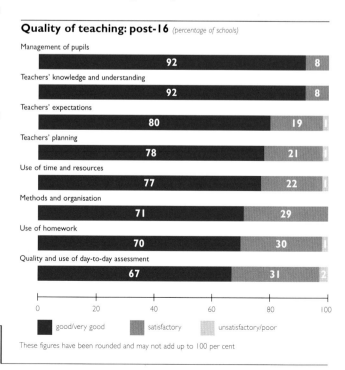

Quality of teaching: post-16 *(percentage of schools)*

Management of pupils
92 | 8

Teachers' knowledge and understanding
92 | 8

Teachers' expectations
80 | 19 |

Teachers' planning
78 | 21 |

Use of time and resources
77 | 22 |

Methods and organisation
71 | 29

Use of homework
70 | 30 |

Quality and use of day-to-day assessment
67 | 31 | 2

0   20   40   60   80   100

■ good/very good   ■ satisfactory   ■ unsatisfactory/poor

These figures have been rounded and may not add up to 100 per cent

---

18 The three mandatory key skills are communication, the application of number and information technology.

175. Most sixth form A-level teachers are highly committed to their work: their planning and organisation are usually good, they assess students' work regularly, and they comment in detail on their progress. Good A-level teaching is characterised by stimulating exchanges of ideas between teachers and students and the detailed exploration of key concepts underpinning the subject. In the very small number of lessons where the teaching was poor, teachers were under-prepared and students were often insufficiently challenged to think for themselves. Where students from Year 12 and Year 13 were taught together in the same class, teachers frequently found it difficult to meet the widely varying needs of the group. The most skilled **GNVQ** teaching was characterised by a combination of direct instruction from the teacher, independent research on the part of the students, and good links with the vocational sector.

Curriculum and assessment

176. The curriculum in schools with small sixth forms can be as limited as seven GCE A-levels, or, in a small number of cases, restricted to vocational courses alone. The cost-effectiveness of such provision is often questionable, particularly where numbers on courses are small and students are constrained into choosing combinations of courses that limit access to careers or higher education. It can work, however, where the subjects available fully meet the students' needs or where consortium arrangements provide them with additional courses to choose from. Some larger sixth forms are able to offer well in excess of 20 A-level courses and occasionally as many as ten free-standing advanced supplementary (AS) courses. An increasing number of sixth forms are admitting students of relatively low prior attainment for the first time. Where these students are few in number and the provision of additional, lower-level courses for them would not be financially viable, they are sometimes advised to join courses that are inappropriate and where they inevitably struggle.

177. The take-up of modular GCE A-level courses has increased to some 60 per cent of A-level entries in schools. In March 1999 OFSTED published the findings of a two-year scrutiny of modular syllabuses and their impact on teaching and examining – *Modular GCE AS and A-level examinations 1996–1998*. The report confirmed that subjects such as English, modern languages and geography were less suited to modular forms of assessment than mathematics and science subjects. The reason for this is that progress in the former group of subjects depends heavily on the growing maturity and experience of the students and few will make sufficient progress in the early stages to enable them to take modules early in the course. In mathematics and science, on the other hand, students can acquire the knowledge and understanding more rapidly by taking modules at an earlier stage.

178. Modular syllabuses are as demanding as linear syllabuses, and in addition offer the flexibility for students to improve their performance over the period of the course. There are drawbacks, however. For example, there is the risk of students – and sometimes teachers – developing a fragmented view of their subject, and of learning and teaching programmes being disturbed by students revising to re-take module tests while at the same time working on new modules. It is vital that sufficiently rigorous questions are set for synoptic assessment so that students can be tested on their command of the A-level syllabus as a whole, not just its component modules. The inspection of modular syllabuses revealed that practice in this respect was inconsistent and was managed better by some examiners than others. The examining of modular syllabuses caused particular problems for geography and, to a lesser extent, business studies. In these subjects, new modular syllabuses were being examined for the first time, and there were difficulties in achieving a proper balance between the professional judgement of the examiners and the statistical evidence used to ensure consistency with previous linear courses.

179. Teachers have a generally good knowledge of the assessment criteria associated with the courses they teach and feedback to students is frequently well-focused on potential examination performance. Teachers are increasingly making good use of the greater refinement in the GCSE grades afforded by the A* grade to set ambitious targets for higher-attaining students. Good A-level teachers have always set regular tests for students and adjusted their teaching according to the outcomes. However, modular courses provide teachers with clear additional evidence of the effectiveness of their teaching for the early module tests and this helps them to take corrective action in time to improve students' performance in later modules. The analysis of students' performance is developing in GNVQ courses, but it is not fully effective or consistent across the different vocational areas, nor is it used to review and evaluate all aspects of courses.

180. Well-balanced enrichment programmes are on offer to about 70 per cent of school sixth-form students, providing the opportunity for them to follow their own interests and contribute to the wider life of the school and the community. Students in about three in ten sixth forms, however, are provided with very little beyond their main academic courses. About one student in 20 in school sixth forms takes AS general studies and nearly two-fifths take A-level general studies; the average point score achieved (4.84) is significantly lower than the overall average for GCE A levels. At their most extensive enrichment programmes or complementary studies courses can occupy students for four or five hours a week. Only about half of all sixth formers take part in any physical activity or sport. Occasionally this is because the school lacks the facilities, but it can also reflect the fact that physical activity for sixth-form students may not be seen as a priority for the school or the students. The quality of enrichment programmes is highly variable. Despite the considerable resources often allocated to them, their effectiveness is rarely evaluated and there is no clearly established consensus on their scope, content and structure.

181. There is little effective teaching of RELIGIOUS EDUCATION except for students on examination courses and, except in church schools, there is rarely any requirement for students to participate in a daily act of worship. Since the first cycle of school inspections, some schools have incorporated an identifiable element of religious education within the sixth-form curriculum, usually as part of a wider programme of personal and social education. However, such provision is characterised by a number of weaknesses: lack of learning objectives, little, if any, continuity with the curriculum in earlier key stages, and the small amount of teaching time usually made available.

182. The provision of COLLABORATIVE ARRANGEMENTS for post-16 students was inspected jointly with the Further Education Funding Council inspectorate. The extent of collaboration varies in scale from two schools sharing the teaching of just one minority subject, to large, well-established consortia in which all examination courses are planned and provided jointly. Some of the consortia are restricted to school sixth forms, while others operate in partnership with further education colleges. Such arrangements broaden the range of subjects offered to students to some degree, and in most cases they do so economically, but there is inevitably some loss of autonomy for individual institutions.

183. New specifications for the PILOT KEY SKILLS QUALIFICATION have clarified the level of demand required for key skills. The introduction of an external assessment component and more thorough portfolio moderation have increased the rigour with which they are assessed. Almost all schools involved in the pilot have encountered substantial difficulties in implementing key skills with GCE A-level students, and relatively few students achieved either the full qualification or accreditation for individual units. There have been uncertainties about the role of teaching staff, the nature and sufficiency of portfolio evidence, and the standards of work expected. It has proved to be extremely difficult for teachers to plan for students whose existing competence in key skills varies widely and who are studying different combinations of A-level subjects. Many staff and students are unconvinced of the value of this initiative and are sceptical about the level of public awareness of the qualification.

Support and guidance for students

184. Schools usually offer good general INDUCTION programmes to students joining their sixth form from elsewhere, but their induction in subject areas can be highly variable. For example, science teachers do not always take sufficient account of the different GCSE backgrounds of their Year 12 students, some of whom may have studied three separate sciences, while others have followed a modular balanced science course. Recruitment and induction to vocational courses in the sixth form are smoothest when students have had some experience of such courses in Key Stage 4.

185. Although form tutors are generally efficient in monitoring ATTENDANCE, there are some schools where this is not followed through as consistently as it should be. Sixth-form students usually appreciate close supervision of their workload and guidance to help them meet targets for course modules and units and prepare for end-of-course examinations.

186. Specific CAREERS ADVICE is stronger than systematic careers education. External events – for example, careers and industry fairs – play a useful part in providing sixth form students with realistic information about the options available to them. Most schools routinely offer work experience in the sixth form for vocational students, and work experience for students on other courses is becoming increasingly common in Year 12. Careers specialists in schools could do more to make subject teachers aware of the diverse qualification and career pathways for which they can be preparing students.

Management and efficiency

187. The great majority of sixth forms are well managed. Most successful sixth forms have a head of sixth form who is also part of the school's senior management team. There is an increasing tendency for schools to create separate sixth-form base areas. This encourages the development of a more distinct and independent character for the sixth form and gives students more freedom and privileges than they would otherwise enjoy.

188. Although development planning for the sixth form overall is generally satisfactory, the quality of planning at subject level is much more varied. Many schools – probably the majority – are now using value added measures to set targets for their sixth-form students.

189. There is generally now much greater awareness of the need to have reliable information on how much sixth-form provision in schools costs. In many schools, senior staff analyse sixth-form costs much more closely than was previously the case. Those manage to strike the balance between keeping within budget and at the same time protecting those courses which are often under-subscribed but which nonetheless make an important contribution to the life of the school. Sometimes, for example, overall teaching time is reduced or Year 12 and Year 13 classes are taught together. Such solutions can be superficially attractive, and skilled, well-organised teaching can often achieve good results under less than ideal conditions. However, they can also increase pressures on both teachers and students, and make the courses concerned less effective. Some schools are attempting to operate more economically by establishing links with sixth forms in neighbouring schools or colleges.

190. The proposals for post-16 developments, which include key skills, revised A and AS levels, modular A levels, vocational courses, and potential changes in funding arrangements, will lead to a further reconsideration of the sixth-form curriculum and the way in which subjects have traditionally been taught. It will also be necessary to review the amount of time students spend on their post-16 courses, which is generally less than in other European countries. The resource implications of these impending changes are considerable and will need careful consideration.

Special schools

191. As in previous years, the predominant types of school inspected are for pupils with moderate learning difficulties (MLD), severe learning difficulties (SLD) and emotional and behavioural difficulties (EBD), but the sample also includes schools for pupils with sensory and language impairment, for pupils with less common disabilities such as autism, schools which meet a variety of needs, and hospital schools.

Educational standards achieved

Overview of attainment and progress

192. Pupils' achievement in special schools continues to improve. The proportion of schools where pupils make good or very good progress has increased considerably. Pupils under five years of age and those over 16 make particularly good progress. This is against a background, in many schools, of an increase in the range and complexity of disabilities since their first inspection. Schools for pupils with EBD are taking an increased proportion of pupils with very difficult behaviour, while the population of many schools for pupils with MLD includes a higher proportion of pupils with behavioural problems and pupils who would formerly have attended schools for SLD.

Progress in special schools *(percentage of schools)*

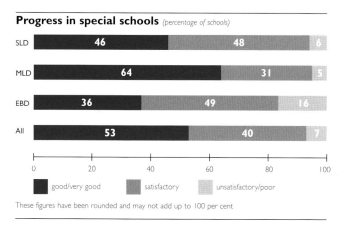

These figures have been rounded and may not add up to 100 per cent

193. There is evidence that most schools have used the findings from their first inspection as a basis for improving quality and raising achievement. A significant proportion has done so successfully, through better teaching and monitoring of performance, and through more extensive use of accredited courses, together with clear targets for individuals. A substantial minority, however, have made no discernible progress in response to inspection recommendations, and consequently identified weaknesses still exist.

194. Pupils' progress in English is at least satisfactory in almost all schools for pupils with MLD and SLD, and is good or very good in half. In schools for pupils with EBD, progress in English is satisfactory or better in eight out of ten schools, and good or very good in a third. In many schools for SLD, attention given to the consistency of use of signing and symbols is helping pupils' progress.

195. In all types of school, pupils have responded well to the National Literacy Strategy and their reading skills have improved as a result. Pupils' knowledge of punctuation and spelling has been strengthened, although their increased confidence is only now beginning to be reflected in writing of greater length and in a wider variety of styles. Some schools are trialling the Strategy with pupils beyond Year 6 and the early evidence is that pupils are responding positively.

196. The success of the introduction of the Strategy into schools for pupils with SLD has surprised many teachers. Pupils across the ability range including many with profound and multiple learning difficulties (PMLD) enjoy the sessions and concentrate on group reading activities for longer periods than anticipated. The stronger focus on literacy, and pupils' greater access to books, are increasing the interest of the full range of pupils in books and improving the reading skills of the more able pupils.

197. Schools for pupils with EBD which have pupils at Key Stages 1 and 2 have found that pupils respond well to the regular structure of the Literacy Hour and to the variety of activity, often behaving particularly well during this period. However, in many of these schools, pupils' lack of confidence in writing remains a barrier to progress.

198. More pupils in Key Stage 4 and post-16 have access to nationally recognised qualifications in English through Associated Examining Board Basic Skills Tests, Certificates of Achievement and GCSE. This is improving their motivation and achievement.

199. Pupils make good progress in MATHEMATICS in half of the special schools, and unsatisfactory progress in only a small proportion. Achievement is high in many schools for MLD, but unsatisfactory in one in five schools for EBD pupils. In all kinds of school, more of the older pupils are achieving nationally recognised accreditation, most often in basic numeracy. Progress in numeracy is often a strength, but in some schools too little attention is given to other aspects of mathematics. The most frequently reported weakness is a lack of practical applications for numeracy and other aspects of mathematics. However, in many schools, particularly those for pupils with SLD, pupils make good progress in lively mathematics sessions that are practical and relate to real-life situations. Most pupils have positive attitudes to mathematics and are well motivated in lessons.

200. Pupils make satisfactory or better progress in SCIENCE in the majority of schools, with the exception of those for pupils with EBD where difficulties in recruiting specialised science teachers results in widespread weaknesses in teaching. A lack of time for the subject and inadequate accommodation and resources also limit progress at Key Stage 4 and after the age of 16. The best progress by older pupils is associated strongly with courses leading to external accreditation.

201. Despite some improvement, information technology remains the weakest subject, with pupils failing to progress satisfactorily in almost a third of schools. Pupils' progress continues to be restricted by schools' lack of planned progression and breadth of activities and by the under-use of equipment across the curriculum. Achievement is best in schools for pupils with physical disabilities, where intensive use is made of information and communications technology to support pupils' communication and access to the curriculum, and technician support is more frequently available than in other special schools.

202. Pupils' achievements in modern foreign languages have improved significantly. Whereas in the previous cycle of inspections, pupils made satisfactory progress in only a third of schools, in the re-inspected schools their progress is satisfactory or better in nine in ten schools. While pupils make satisfactory or better progress in geography and history in nine out of ten schools (a slight increase on last year), the proportion of schools promoting good progress has remained disappointingly low at about a third. Progress in design and technology has improved slightly. In physical education and art, two-thirds of pupils are making good or very good progress. Pupils make good progress more often in art and in design and technology in schools for pupils with MLD and for those with sensory disabilities than in other special schools, which largely reflects their greater access to specialist teaching and facilities in these schools.

203. In music, pupils with SLD generally make good progress. In contrast, the absence of specialist teaching in schools for pupils with EBD, particularly for older pupils, leads to good progress in fewer than a third of these schools. Achievement in religious education is also often weak in schools for pupils with EBD. This reflects

a shortfall in the amount of time spent on religious education and diffidence amongst staff toward teaching the subject to EBD pupils.

204. Pupils' progress in PERSONAL, SOCIAL AND HEALTH EDUCATION is improving as schools plan and document their curriculum for this element of their work and implement systems for assessing and recording pupils' strengths and weaknesses. Achievement is satisfactory in almost all schools. Personal, social and health education continues to be a strength within provision for under-fives and for pupils post-16, and standards are good for these groups in the majority of schools. In schools for pupils with impairments of sight or hearing, personal, social and health education programmes are usually highly individualised to develop key areas such as study skills and mobility, and progress is often closely monitored. As a result, pupils make good progress.

205. Behaviour remains good in the great majority of schools. The use of fixed-period and permanent exclusion of pupils for unacceptable behaviour in this first cohort of re-inspected schools is similar to patterns in earlier years, with the encouraging exception of a slight reduction in the rate of exclusion in schools for pupils with EBD. This reverses a strong and consistent upward trend in such schools over the previous four years.

Quality of education

The quality of teaching

206. The quality of teaching has improved in almost all schools since their first inspection and is good overall in two-thirds of schools. Although lower in schools for pupils with EBD, the quality of teaching is improving in these schools. A number of schools for pupils with EBD have improved the quality of teaching by recruiting teachers (both full- and part-time) with particular subject expertise where this has been missing. However, the recruitment of specialist subject staff remains a problem for many of these schools.

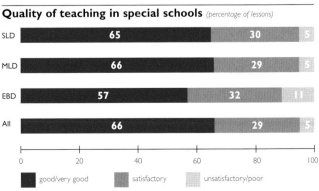

Quality of teaching in special schools *(percentage of lessons)*

	good/very good	satisfactory	unsatisfactory/poor
SLD	65	30	5
MLD	66	29	5
EBD	57	32	11
All	66	29	5

These figures have been rounded and may not add up to 100 per cent

207. The introduction of the Literacy Hour has improved the quality of teaching in English in all types of special school. The discussion of teaching strategies for literacy, the observation of colleagues' teaching by co-ordinators, the long-term planning for pupils' progression in skills and knowledge, and the careful briefing (and occasionally the training) of learning support assistants have all contributed to these improvements. The reading and discussion together of large texts, often supported by real objects and models, have carried over as a teaching strategy into other subjects. In schools for SLD specific attention to pupils' verbal and non-verbal communication skills, the setting of challenging targets and the increasing involvement of speech and language therapists in planning and team teaching have enhanced the quality of teaching in English. Teachers are making increasingly effective use of video, for example to give more pupils access to the works of such authors as Shakespeare. There is still some overuse of worksheets, limiting the range of pupils' writing.

208. The quality of teaching in mathematics is good in six out of ten schools overall, and is highest in schools for pupils with MLD and SLD. A small number of schools have applied the structure and approach of the National Literacy Strategy to mathematics lessons in advance of detailed guidance on the National Numeracy Strategy, and this has enhanced pupils' understanding of mathematical processes and vocabulary. Schools are making increasing use of pupils' individual education plans to identify personal targets in mathematics for pupils and to highlight their progress. Features of the best lessons include the careful planning and preparation of resources, a practical approach, the briefing of support assistants as to their role, keeping pupils informed of their progress, and giving praise for success. In science, teaching that encourages pupils to investigate and experiment in practical activities is particularly effective.

209. The quality of teaching is lowest in information technology lessons, even within the narrow range of activities undertaken within the subject in most schools, and in the use of information and communications technology in other subjects. The weakness reflects a continuing lack of confidence and of awareness amongst teachers of the potential use of cross-curricular information and communications technology across the curriculum.

210. Schools are responding successfully in two main ways to earlier recommendations that teachers should improve their knowledge of National Curriculum subject programmes of study. Teachers have attended in-service training or undertaken self-study to improve their personal knowledge, and subject co-ordinators have supported non-specialist colleagues through advice and the provision of detailed schemes of work, and increasingly through their monitoring of colleagues' teaching.

211. Teachers continue to make insufficient use of assessment information on pupils in planning lessons. This use is less than satisfactory in four in ten schools. The (usually wide) range of individual needs within classes is, therefore, not as well met as it should be. Information from assessment is used most successfully with under-fives and with pupils post-16. Baseline assessments are used, as intended, in planning for the youngest pupils. With older pupils, published schemes of work associated with nationally accredited courses are often based upon continuous assessment by the teacher and self-assessment by the pupil, so that the link between assessment and planning is firmly established.

212. Given the nature of the pupils, the control of their behaviour in schools for those with EBD is especially important. In almost half of schools weaknesses in behaviour management lower the quality of some lessons, reflecting variations between the skills of individual members of staff. Most schools now have agreed guidelines for behaviour management, but few have introduced the necessary monitoring by senior staff to ensure that the guidelines are effective and are being followed by all staff.

Curriculum

213. Half of schools re-inspected have improved their coverage of the National Curriculum. Nevertheless, a third of schools need to make further improvements to ensure that all pupils have access to the full National Curriculum and religious education and that programmes of study for subjects are in place. This affects schools for pupils with EBD and SLD in particular. The desirable learning outcomes have helped to sharpen objectives for the teaching of under-fives. At post-16 the adoption of courses leading to nationally recognised accreditation has raised expectations and standards in many schools.

214. A third of schools have significantly improved their curriculum planning since the first inspection, mainly by producing schemes of work for subjects. However, a key issue is to ensure that sufficiently detailed schemes of work are in place for all subjects. About half of the schools for SLD had yet to establish clear roles for subject co-ordinators. Not surprisingly, therefore, these schools found greatest difficulty in producing schemes of work.

215. Provision for pupils' moral and social development is good in about nine in ten schools. It is usually promoted effectively by the day-to-day interactions within the school and by the example set by staff. That for spiritual and for cultural development is weaker; it is good in about half of schools and unsatisfactory in one in ten. Spiritual development is promoted directly through assemblies, which vary greatly in quality, and by lessons in religious education, which is one of the weaker subjects. In the best practice opportunities to develop pupils' spiritual awareness are planned explicitly into lessons in subjects such as science, geography, history, art and music. An aspect of pupils' cultural development which is often neglected is their insight into other cultures.

216. Most mixed-sex schools for pupils with EBD have a significant majority of boys. In previous years the number of schools with inappropriately small numbers of girls amongst large groups of boys has been falling, as "mixed" schools have decided increasingly not to admit any girls so as to avoid the problems created. However, amongst the schools inspected this year, there is an increased number with very small numbers of girls, for example one girl amongst 44 boys. Although curricular access (except in physical education) is usually not a great problem, the social and emotional needs of the very small numbers of girls are not met well in such schools.

Assessment and recording

217. The assessment and recording of pupils' progress are improving only slowly. They are good in only a quarter of schools and unsatisfactory in one-third. While the first round of inspections made it clear to many schools that their existing practice was weak, few have improved significantly. Assessment and recording are rather better with pre-school and with post-16 pupils where schools have specific systems for these age groups.

218. Assessment and recording are particularly weak in schools for pupils with EBD, where only one school in ten has good practice, and assessment in half of schools is unsatisfactory or poor. The lack of an agreed policy and clear system for monitoring implementation leads to inconsistency in practice in many schools. The records focus on experiences or attitudes rather than what pupils can do and are poorly linked to target setting. New systems are run alongside existing systems, so that teachers are overburdened and messages are obscured.

The management and efficiency of the school

Leadership and management

219. The majority of special schools are well led, but the quality of leadership is unsatisfactory or poor in a third of schools for pupils with EBD. In this type of school, the challenges of day-to-day management often divert the senior staff from taking a strategic view of the school's development. Across all types of special schools some aspects of leadership are significantly stronger than others. Weaknesses occur most often in the direction and oversight of curriculum development and in strategic planning. Where curricular leadership is underdeveloped the governing body, headteacher and curriculum co-ordinators do not provide sufficiently clear guidance for teachers as to what to teach and how to teach it, for example through a coherent set of schemes of work and through advice and monitoring.

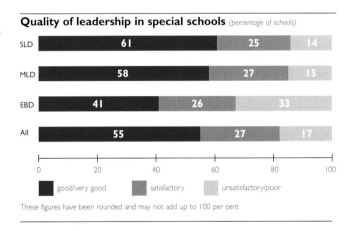

Quality of leadership in special schools *(percentage of schools)*

	good/very good	satisfactory	unsatisfactory/poor
SLD	61	25	14
MLD	58	27	15
EBD	41	26	33
All	55	27	17

These figures have been rounded and may not add up to 100 per cent

220. The quality of strategic planning is sufficiently weak in a quarter of schools for this to be a key issue in the inspection report. Similarly, a quarter of special schools and half of schools for pupils with SLD need more detailed development plans. In a quarter of schools of all kinds the governing body needs to take on a strategic role.

221. The lack of monitoring of the performance of the school by the governing body, senior management team and subject co-ordinators is an issue to be addressed urgently in half of the schools. Schools are increasingly aware of the value of monitoring and evaluating quality of teaching and the impact of initiatives, but have difficulty in putting these into practice. Most governing bodies have yet to establish a means of evaluating value for money and enhanced progress (not least because many schools are still developing their systems for pupil assessment). Despite the fact that in many schools, classroom observation by other teachers has become a familiar part of internal evaluation, too many senior managers either are reluctant to observe colleagues or do so in ways which are perceived as a threat. The monitoring roles of curriculum co-ordinators are undeveloped in many schools, and co-ordinators often lack timetabled opportunities during taught time to observe colleagues at work and to advise them, so that there is little prospect of developing the role.

222. Schools which have established effective monitoring systems generally find that the time invested in these is well spent since it can improve the quality of teaching and rates of pupils' progress. Concerns about the threatening nature of the monitoring process, particularly the observation of classroom practice, have been dispelled as staff have experienced and benefited from effective monitoring.

Accommodation and resources

223. The amount of classroom space and quality of specialist subject accommodation have improved significantly in a quarter of schools since their first inspection. Further upgrading is urgently required in specialist subject accommodation (particularly for science, design and technology, music and physical education) in one school in five overall, and in a third of schools for pupils with SLD. Library facilities are unsatisfactory in a quarter of all schools. Most accommodation for under-fives is satisfactory, but some provision lacks such features as outdoor play space and suitable lavatory and hygiene/changing facilities.

224. Schools have continued to acquire further resources for teaching and learning to support the National Curriculum. The most significant developments have been associated with the National Literacy Strategy. Schools have reviewed existing book stocks and have purchased sets of books for group reading and also large text books for whole-class reading and discussion. The success of work with large texts has led schools to seek (and sometimes to make) similar books for use in other subjects, particularly science, geography and history.

Residential education

225. Of the 20 residential special schools inspected this year, 18 have improved their residential provision since their first inspection. Most of the schools had addressed all the key issues raised in inspection reports. The two schools that made little or no improvement had failed to tackle deficiencies in accommodation and weaknesses in the planning of the residential curriculum.

226. Increasing numbers of schools have satisfactory systems for staff induction and training. Staff, including care managers, are being encouraged to acquire relevant specialist qualifications. Fewer than half of schools have adequate arrangements for the professional appraisal of care staff.

227. Significant improvements have been made to the contribution by care teams. Staff provide appropriate role models for pupils' social and personal development, and an increasing variety of appropriate and purposeful extra-curricular activities is being provided. Progress is slower in the development of effective liaison between care staff and teachers. Care staff do not consistently contribute to pupils' annual reviews and to the setting of pupils' personal targets, nor do they always attend annual review meetings. Many schools have yet to establish a system for monitoring and evaluating the quality of the curriculum in order to ensure its effective contribution to the development of pupils' independent living skills.

228. Most schools have effective child protection procedures but a small minority lack regular staff training on child protection and do not clearly communicate procedures to all staff concerned. Health and safety audits take place regularly in only just over half of schools. Fire protection procedures remain unsatisfactory in over a third, in that fire practices are not conducted appropriately and fire equipment is not inspected regularly.

229. Parents in half of residential schools report limitations in both informal and formal liaison procedures with the school. The lack of provision of homework is of concern to parents in seven out of ten schools. Residential schools' liaison with their local communities has improved, especially in localities where there is a business partnership or an Education Action Zone. Liaison with agencies including health and therapy services and social services is less effective, with unsatisfactory links in six out of ten schools.

Schools requiring special measures and schools with serious weaknesses

230. The picture is very mixed. The 230 schools that improved sufficiently to be removed from special measures during this year demonstrate that considerable improvement is possible given the right conditions. However, the number of schools failing their second inspection and being put into special measures is a significant cause for concern. During the year all schools, except a very few new schools, were being inspected for the second time. A little over a quarter of these schools had been brought forward in the inspection programme because of their previous weak performance. A total of 193 schools were put into special measures either as a result of a Section 10 inspection or a follow-up inspection by HMI.

231. As in previous years, the primary schools requiring special measures differ in size, type and socio-economic circumstances. Many were found to have unacceptably low standards of achievement, with pupils attaining lower levels in National Curriculum tests than those found in schools in similar socio-economic circumstances. Almost all of the primary schools which were put into special measures had poor progress by pupils, serious shortcomings in teaching and weak leadership. These schools had not remedied the weaknesses exposed at the time of their first inspection. Some had declined further. In about one-third of schools the pupils' behaviour had deteriorated. Although some schools had declined rapidly, others had drifted into special measures because managers and governors had failed to take decisive action on key issues.

232. In most cases, the schools which had previously been placed in special measures made rapid progress. The OFSTED report *Lessons Learned from Special Measures* identified the key features behind the improvement in the schools removed from special measures. Above all, these schools faced up to their shortcomings and kept their eyes firmly on improving achievement. Two-thirds of the primary schools removed from special measures during 1998/99 had achieved this improvement within two years of the initial inspection. Of the remaining third there were delays in appointing headteachers or teaching staff in some cases, so the improvements took longer to secure. All these schools had improved the levels of pupils' attainment by the time special measures were removed, but the need for further improvement remained a key issue in many schools, especially at Key Stage 2. Most schools had successfully concentrated on raising pupils' skills and competences in English, especially reading, and in mathematics, with particular emphasis on mental arithmetic and numeracy. Many primary schools taught the pupils in sets according to their attainment and often established additional study groups for pupils in Years 2 and 6. These strategies were especially effective in raising the pupils' fluency and accuracy in reading.

233. Secondary schools that were placed in special measures this year had similarly made too little progress on the key issues from their first inspection. They often had very significant weaknesses to deal with and had not taken sufficient, rigorous action. The reasons for failure included significant weaknesses in the quality of teaching, low standards – with pupils making unsatisfactory progress – and, in half of the schools, regular disruptive behaviour and poor quality leadership and management. In the middle deemed secondary schools the most common reasons for being placed in special measures were poor progress in improving the curriculum and inadequacies in teachers' subject knowledge.

234. The shortcomings in the quality of teaching were widespread and included low expectations of what pupils could achieve, inadequate lesson planning and too limited a range of classroom activities. In those schools with unsatisfactory leadership, there was no clear direction to the work of the school, work was not monitored effectively and there was too little, if any, evaluation of the impact of any changes that had been implemented. Having been placed just above the threshold for special measures at the time of their first inspection, too many of the schools gave insufficient attention to tackling key weaknesses and failed to demonstrate a commitment to improvement. Where the quality of leadership was not a major reason for failure, the headteacher was usually new in post and had not yet dealt with the weaknesses left by the previous regime.

235. One secondary school remained in special measures for less than two years, but most take a little more time to reach an acceptable standard of education. The size and complexity of many secondary schools slow the rate of progress compared to most primary schools. Almost all the secondary schools made progress in raising some pupils' levels of attainment, but were still not reaching national levels, nor was there a significant improvement in the percentage of pupils achieving five or more A*–C grades. The percentage of pupils gaining one or more A*–G and five or more grades in GCSE improved during the period of special measures. Most schools had used a variety of measures to improve pupils' basic approaches to learning, often through homework and study groups held after the school day. To bring about improvement in Key Stage 4, schools appointed mentors for pupils in Year 11, who were responsible for strengthening the pupils' study skills and commitment to work and ensuring that coursework and homework were completed on time. However, pupils' poor reading skills, coupled with a backlog of underachievement over several years, had prevented the schools from making significant improvements in the levels of achievement in the upper ability range.

236. Some schools have introduced planning diaries for pupils' use and encouraged the pupils to develop independent working habits. To improve literacy, many have concentrated on the younger pupils, introducing reading partners, computer programs, additional literacy time in Year 7 and a focus on key words in all subjects. Some have taken part in summer schools with the local primary schools for pupils in Year 6 who were thought to need particular improvement. These measures have generally helped the pupils who attend school regularly. On removal of special measures, most of the schools still had a disaffected minority of pupils who had been excluded from one or more other schools, and continued to have a hard core of truants. However, all schools had made at least satisfactory progress in improving the levels of attendance, although in two-thirds of the secondary schools, attendance remained below 90 per cent.

237. Special schools that were placed in special measures during the year showed similar weaknesses to primary and secondary schools, poor progress by pupils, unsatisfactory teaching and weak leadership being key factors. A fall in the standard of behaviour was noted in a small number of schools. Far too little action had been taken since the first inspection. The schools' action plans had often covered all the key issues but the action to be taken was superficial and the timescales lacked urgency. The criteria for measuring success were poorly defined and the procedures for monitoring and evaluating improvements were weak.

238. On average, special schools remained in special measures for slightly under two years. In most of these schools, the progress made by the pupils had improved and was satisfactory or better in between 90 and 100 per cent of lessons. In almost all the schools a weak or inadequate curriculum had been a key issue in the initial inspection. Schools had claimed to be providing full coverage of the National Curriculum but were not, and there were limited opportunities for the pupils to take accredited courses. Too often, planned teaching time was insufficient to deliver a broad curriculum. Improving the curriculum in these special schools was a significant factor in the increased rate of pupils' progress and in raising their levels of achievement.

239. The role of governors is critical when a school is placed in special measures. Governors in most of these schools have had additional training, emphasising their part in monitoring and evaluating progress. This has often led to their becoming more effective. Governing bodies have also been strengthened by the appointment of additional governors, some with particular expertise in areas such as finance. The governors' ability to probe and support the headteacher's efforts to raise standards was at times a significant factor in effecting the required improvement.

240. While schools are in special measures they usually receive well-focused support. They typically have a link adviser who has an important role in providing or organising appropriate training for staff, including the managers. In schools where there is an initial high level of consistent, well-directed support from the same advisers, progress is generally secured. But not all schools receive the support they need. Progress is slow when local education authority staff do not ensure that schools prioritise what needs to be done and then concentrate on those priorities. Too often the local education authority does not take swift enough action when the leadership of the school is weak. A further weakness is excessive monitoring, for example of the quality of teaching, without providing any help that results in better practice in the classroom.

241. Some schools, mostly primary schools, successfully involve parents in helping the school to improve. They have played an important part in improving the appearance of the school and have helped in the classroom. However, some schools have an uphill struggle to encourage parents to ensure that their children attend regularly and punctually and complete homework. For many primary and secondary schools, there remain parents who continue to take term-time holidays and condone regular absence; this was a constant problem for those schools which still had poor levels of attendance when special measures were removed.

242. Schools formally designated in 1997/98 as having serious weaknesses have been monitored by HMI during 1998/99. Most of the schools visited were making satisfactory progress in addressing their weaknesses. In the schools that had made most progress the headteacher, senior managers and governors improved communication within the school, clarified staff roles, identified training needs, used test data to monitor pupils' progress, and planned appropriate programmes of work for pupils who were underachieving. As with schools in special measures, deficiencies in curricular provision were remedied. Many schools had weaknesses in the provision for the pupils' spiritual development and also for their cultural development. The provision was strengthened through the content of subjects taught and visits and visitors to the school, for example using art, music and literature from a wide range of cultures in assemblies. In many of these schools, the parents are active in supporting the school and staff in implementing new policies. The schools keep parents involved through curriculum meetings and regular newsletters.

243. About 10 per cent of the schools with serious weaknesses made too little progress in addressing their weaknesses and were made subject to special measures. Sometimes the headteacher, senior managers and governors failed to establish a clear direction and priorities for action. Staff training was not linked to the priorities for the school, teachers' planning for lessons lacked consistency and the curriculum had continuing weaknesses. Attendance in secondary schools was often too low, and the provision for pupils with special educational needs was often poor. The schools had not tackled the matters for improvement with sufficient urgency or rigour. Neither had the local education authorities responsible for such schools ensured that effective action was taken, for example to improve the quality of teaching or of leadership and management. Such a lack of rigorous action stopped pupils making satisfactory progress.

244. Since September 1998, the action plans of schools with serious weaknesses and the statements of action written by local education authorities have been scrutinised and comments provided for the schools and local education authorities. The good plans and statements set demanding but achievable targets and are costed in terms of finance and time. The school and local education authority are both clear about what help is needed and what support will be provided. In the weak plans (about 15 per cent) and statements (about 10 per cent) it is not clear who will do what, by when or how, and in some cases there is no clear statement of how the School Improvement Grant of the Standards Fund will be used. As has been reported previously, the existence of a good plan does not guarantee success, but a poor plan almost always hinders progress.

The education of young people who have disengaged from mainstream education

New Start

245. The first phase of the New Start initiative, which has run from 1997 to 1999, is designed to help disaffected and underachieving 14- to 16-year-olds back into the educational mainstream. The majority of New Start students have responded positively to the opportunity to learn in a wider range of contexts, both in and out of school, and their attitudes towards learning and their willingness to participate have often improved. Although few schools or other institutions have developed detailed evaluation procedures, the small number that have can point to general improvements made by students across the curriculum, including their achievements in literacy and numeracy. A key feature of New Start has been the use of vocational and work-related experience to motivate students. Standards of achievement were generally high in projects where aims had been clearly defined and shared, trainers and advisers well briefed, and where achievement was linked to recognised, national qualifications. However, in a significant minority of cases insufficient preparation and weak lines of communication between the different partners led to disappointing experiences for students.

246. While some New Start students have achieved reasonable standards, most have become disengaged from full-time education and have a poor command of basic skills. It has been a prime aim of many projects to repair this weakness. In only about a quarter of the basic skills sessions seen0 was good teaching helping young people to overcome their lack of confidence in their ability to manipulate language and number. In many of the remaining sessions the teaching had been entrusted to staff who were unqualified and inadequately prepared for the task, and the students' progress was correspondingly slow. The assessment and tracking of students' progress were often haphazard, although they were generally more effective when students were following courses leading to recognised, national qualifications.

247. The young people on New Start have benefited greatly from enhanced careers education and guidance support. They have also responded well to some well-organised mentoring schemes, although these have not always been effective. Finding suitable mentors has proved difficult and they need to be suitably screened and trained before they can fulfil this role. Despite the shortcomings in basic skills teaching, about 90 per cent of the remaining work – including the general advisory and counselling sessions, for example youth award schemes, youth challenge and achievement projects, vocational courses in schools and further education, and work experience placements – was satisfactory or better, and about a fifth was good, with high-quality planning and use of specialist staff who were clear about the aims of the initiative. Conversely, unsatisfactory teaching was often found when staff were operating outside their expertise or were ill-prepared to cope with the behaviour of some uncooperative students.

248. Partnerships between different agencies have been at the heart of many of the projects. They have been responsible for some imaginative and innovative developments. They are not, however, without some problems. In many projects, co-ordination between the different partners was underdeveloped and lines of communication were poorly defined. Project co-ordinators in schools were often devoting considerable time to managing the scheme, but the irregular flow of information between the different partners made it difficult to monitor closely the nature and quality of the programme being followed by young people, some of whom were still occupied for only a small portion of the week.

249. Many of the projects have used New Start money to expand schemes that were already in existence, many of which are likely to endure beyond the end of this first phase. However, it is unlikely that those projects specifically developed for New Start will have reached sufficient numbers of young people to make a significant difference to the number of pupils disengaging from education. In addition, New Start's chances of success have been seriously affected by the late start to many of the projects and the short-term funding arrangements.

Pupil referral units

250. Almost all pupils attending pupil referral units have been excluded from other schools or are awaiting placements in special schools, often for pupils with emotional or behavioural difficulties. Not surprisingly, their attainments are below those expected for pupils of their ages, often significantly so. The exception is in the pupil referral units which cater for schoolgirl mothers, where attainment is often in line with or approaching national expectations. In nine-tenths of the units, pupils who attend regularly make satisfactory or better progress, including one-third where it is good. Progress is generally better in English and mathematics than in science, where there is often a lack of specialist teaching, accommodation and resources. The majority of units are successful in improving pupils' behaviour and contribute effectively to their personal development.

251. The quality of teaching was satisfactory or better in nine out of ten pupil referral units, with almost half being good or very good. It was often more successful when the teachers were members of a behaviour support team and the subject specialisms of the members of the team were used on a part-time basis, rather than one or two teachers teaching all the subjects offered.

252. Most pupil referral units provide part-time education only. About 7 per cent provide less than the minimum ten hours per week expected and teach a curriculum restricted to the core subjects and a few of the foundation subjects. Those pupil referral units offering full-time education are able to offer a wider curriculum, covering the whole of the National Curriculum. An increasing number of pupil referral units are providing opportunities for pupils to achieve external accreditation through the Basic Skills Certificate of Achievement and, in a small number of cases, GCSE. A small but significant number of local education authorities have not yet met the requirement to publish a curriculum statement in respect of their pupil referral units.

253. Attendance in pupil referral units remains a problem, even though many pupil referral units have adopted strategies to improve attendance. Although the impact of these strategies is often limited, pupils in pupil referral units frequently attend better than they had in mainstream schools.

254. The accommodation used by the units varies considerably. Some have plentiful space and specialist facilities in premises previously used as a school; others are housed unsatisfactorily in one room, sometimes with more than one group being taught at the same time. Specialist accommodation for science and for design and technology is lacking in many pupil referral units and is reflected in the unsatisfactory progress made in these subjects. In a number of referral units there are no toilet facilities on the premises or staff and pupils have to share the same toilet. These arrangements are unacceptable and need urgent attention.

255. Resources for learning are generally satisfactory for the curriculum offered, with the exception of science and design and technology. Overall, one pupil referral unit in

five had shortages of resources. There is a particularly wide variation in the quality of resources available for information and communications technology. While one in ten pupil referral units had good resources for information and communications technology, a similar proportion had little or outdated equipment and software.

256. Day-to-day management by the headteacher or teacher in charge is satisfactory in most pupil referral units, although occasionally headteachers have insufficient time for management and planning because of heavy, or even full-time, teaching commitments. Overall management and evaluation of the pupil referral units by the local education authorities are much more variable. In about a third of the units inspected, inspectors were critical of the local education authority's management. They are better where the units are part of a wider behaviour support service and the head or deputy head of the service has direct management responsibility for one or more units. Where the management is by an officer of the local education authority, the role is frequently poorly developed, particularly in terms of monitoring and evaluating the effectiveness of the provision.

Young people in secure accommodation

257. There has been continued growth in the number of places available to young people in secure accommodation during the year, as local authorities complete their adaptation of existing accommodation and extend into new buildings. The secure units managed by local authorities and a further secure unit managed by the Home Office provide beds for up to 480 young people, ranging in age from 10 years to 16+ years. Most young people are aged 11–16. In 1998/99 two secure training centres opened. These provide places for 120 young people from the age of 12 years, who are sentenced under the Secure Training Order, which came into force in April 1998. A new Detention and Training Order, within the Crime and Disorder Act 1998, will bring in custodial sentences to replace the sentence of detention in young offender institutions and Secure Training Orders. The secure training centres, as well as secure units, will then make provision for young people up to the age of 15 years, who are sentenced under a Detention and Training Order.

258. HMI have inspected education in six secure units and one secure training centre during 1998/99. Although education is being given higher status in secure accommodation, there is still evidence that education and care staff could work more co-operatively to ensure regular attendance, fewer withdrawals from lessons and more regular and consistent support in lessons. Two secure units which have been revisited a year after the previous inspection had identified serious weaknesses have improved significantly.

259. There are still serious problems in gaining information about young people and their educational experiences and achievements before admission. Attainment is almost invariably below that which is expected for their age, because of periods of missed education. Assessments on entry are helping teachers to plan their work more effectively and are beginning to be used to record progress made within the secure unit or secure training centre.

260. As staff in secure accommodation raise their expectations of what young people can achieve, more opportunities are being provided for entry to courses leading to GCSE, Certificates of Achievement and other forms of accreditation. Some units are making commendable attempts to allow young people to continue with courses begun in the unit at colleges of further education when they leave, or to return to the unit to sit GCSE exams after they have left.

261. Young people's attitudes to learning generally become more positive during their stay in secure accommodation. In four of the six secure units inspected recently, the quality of teaching is at least satisfactory, and sometimes good or very good, in all lessons. In these units, teachers have high expectations and the work is similar to that expected in mainstream schools.

262. All secure units and secure training centres aim to provide a broad and balanced curriculum, which includes the National Curriculum and religious education. There are still difficulties in covering the range of subjects, particularly music, a modern foreign language and design and technology, because of a lack of specialist teachers and accommodation. Schemes of work often need to be reviewed and improved to ensure that all young people, whatever their length of stay, have work which is matched to age and ability.

263. A few secure units provide specialist help for students with learning difficulties, but most are having difficulty in addressing the young peoples' reading and writing problems owing to a lack of skilled teaching in these areas, as well as deficits in the areas of numeracy and information and communications technology. This remains a serious issue which must be addressed if these young people are not to remain disadvantaged and excluded from society in the future.

264. Assessment, recording and reporting are still generally weak. Effective monitoring of progress by teachers, which leads on to the review of targets and which aids future planning, is rare. Teachers need to build assessment into their curricular planning and ensure that progress is clearly recorded and that detailed reports move on with young people as they proceed to the next stage of their education.

265. The difficulties of providing positive educational experiences for the young people when teachers are on leave are being overcome very effectively by some units which divide the school year into more than three terms with shorter breaks. Artists, drama specialists and other professionals are invited to work with the young people while teachers take leave during the shortened holiday breaks, and activities provide some exciting and different educational experiences. Better-planned liaison between care and education staff is needed to ensure that educational programmes are not needlessly interrupted.

266. Management of education in secure units and secure training centres is generally sound and leadership is usually strong. It is particularly helpful when the head of education is a member of the senior management team of the unit. Several secure units are finding it difficult to recruit and retain staff. Strong links with the local education authority for professional advice and in-service training lead to good support for teachers. Development plans often focus on resources and would benefit from a greater emphasis on identifying curricular issues in order to act as a basis for planning.

Education and training in prisons and young offender institutions

267. During 1998/99, HMI inspected education and training in 15 prisons and young offender institutions (YOIs) as part of the Prison Inspectorate's full inspection programme. They also undertook three unannounced inspections and made 17 short visits to YOIs to inspect the provision made for the support of young offenders' career aspirations.

268. Despite some improvements in prisoners achieving accreditation, particularly in basic literacy and numeracy, standards overall remain poor. This is due to lack of resources, insufficient provision, inadequate needs analysis, and the narrow curriculum on offer in many establishments. The core curriculum for the prison service and regular inspection have improved the situation in some establishments, but many have eliminated creative subjects such as art and music in order to meet requirements for basic education. Although there are one or two notable exceptions, this narrowing of the curriculum has usually had a detrimental effect. Few establishments are reinforcing basic skills through the teaching of other subjects or in

workshops, where many prisoners are motivated to learn to read and write. One-to-one sessions on basic skills with adults and with young prisoners are successful, but this success would be greater if prisoners were able to learn, use and improve these skills in other learning contexts.

269. The quality of education is frequently marred by lack of appropriate needs analysis. The education department is rarely allocated the opportunity to interview every prisoner on induction, and as a result has to rely on results of basic tests and word of mouth to identify prisoners' specific needs. It is rare for prisoners who have experienced little but failure in schools to opt for education, or for those who cannot read or write to volunteer for a written test.

270. The quality of teaching is on the whole good, but value for money is often unsatisfactory because of low numbers in classes and continual disruption to lessons; this might sometimes be unavoidable but it is often for trivial reasons beyond the control of the education department. The situation has improved little since last year. There has, however, been a marked improvement in the development and use of learning plans by teachers and students. Both adults and young prisoners found these plans motivating, whether or not they were used for accreditation purposes. In establishments where education staff were involved in sentence planning, sentence plans were well linked to learning plans, but such establishments were in the minority.

271. Remand prisoners rarely had sufficient, appropriate education and training provision. Short courses, individual teaching, and roll-on, roll-off programmes, should be provided. At present the situation for prisoners on remand, even for juveniles, is unacceptable.

272. Many prisons and YOIs have workshops, but few of these provide adequate training and accreditation. This situation has grown worse over the past year, with very few institutions now offering NVQs or other qualifications. This is due to the lack of resources for courses leading to accreditation, and to the fact that prisoners are frequently moved to other establishments before they can complete courses. The problem is compounded by the incomplete nature of prisoners' records and their slow transfer between prison establishments.

273. In the best practice, education and training were carefully integrated. In some establishments prisoners spent half of the day in education and half in the workshop. Equally successful was the policy of incorporating education into workplace activities, particularly basic and key skills and English as an additional language. On occasions, evening classes in key skills supported

workshops. This enabled prisoners who wished to work full-time to improve their key skills and gain qualifications. However, the situation in relation to evening classes has generally deteriorated, and few establishments now run any, even in recreational and arts subjects.

274. Provision made for the support of young offenders' career aspirations is highly variable. Many YOIs had no meaningful link with their local Careers Service Company, and careers education and guidance is not part of a coherent package offered to all young offenders. The concept of appropriate careers education and vocational guidance for prisoners is at an early stage of development, despite the importance of employment in helping to prevent re-offending. Welfare to work programmes are just becoming established in a number of YOIs, and so far involve a relatively small number of young offenders. Few establishments have a policy, practice is piecemeal, communication between careers service, prison staff, and the education staff is frequently poor, and few establishments have taken advantage of the careers library initiative. There are, however, notable exceptions: at HMYOI Wetherby, for example, where there was good support from the careers service and a YMCA project, effective links had been established between the education and prison staff, aimed at helping young offenders to develop useful and successful lives on release. However, even here many programmes reached only a small number of those who could benefit from them.

275. If the rate of re-offending is to be reduced, particularly among young offenders, education and training should be given much higher status in establishments. Young people might then return to the community with improved educational qualifications and an improved confidence in their skills and ability to succeed that can help open the door to further education, training, or employment. This will only happen when the resources for education are based on the needs of the prisoners and protected from arbitrary financial cuts, often imposed by individual establishments at short notice.

Youth work

276. During 1998/99 HMI, assisted by additional inspectors who were senior youth work professionals, carried out full inspections of a sample of nine local education authority youth services. More than 360 youth work sessions were observed and 320 units or projects visited. Of the nine services inspected, the quality of provision and value for money were very good in one, good in one other, satisfactory in three and less than satisfactory in four.

277. In addition, HMI made monitoring inspection visits to more than 50 voluntary youth organisations funded by the DfEE under its scheme of grants to National Voluntary Youth Organisations (NVYOs). 1998/99 was the final year of the three-year scheme which allocated funding specifically to work with disadvantaged young people in the DfEE's priority groups: young women, those at risk of becoming involved in criminal behaviour or drug misuse, those with learning or physical difficulties, and young people from minority ethnic groups, inner cities and rural areas. Funding was also directed at increasing participation in youth work and improving its efficiency. Generally, this work maintained the steady improvement noted last year and organisations have learned from each other's expertise through effective co-operation and some dissemination of good practice. This latter aspect, however, now needs more attention if the most is to be made of the programme's achievements.

Educational standards achieved

278. As in 1997/98, the achievement of young people who took part in local education authority youth service provision was good in just over half the sessions inspected. However, the number of unsatisfactory sessions has increased from one in eight to one in six. Many of these poor sessions were in centre-based work, frequently in general youth work or activity sessions. Too often an unvarying programme of recreational activities did little to challenge young people; low expectations resulted in low levels of achievement. Although a small proportion of excellent work was seen which encouraged the active involvement of young people, there were in general too few planned opportunities for young people to participate in decision-making.

279. Young people often did well in arts-related work. Through international exchanges they were able to gain a better knowledge and understanding of other countries, improve the quality of their relationships with others, develop the skill of team-working, and increase their awareness of social issues. Individual counselling and group work made an important contribution to young people's understanding of issues important to their lives and personal development. The small proportion of youth work undertaken in schools was usually of a high standard. Achievement was often high where the work was carefully directed at, for example, those from minority ethnic groups, those with learning or physical difficulties, or those who were frequently excluded socially from the majority of youth provision. This was particularly true of the NVYOs, some of which achieved high standards of work with disaffected young people. A few organisations worked very successfully with those held in young offender establishments.

280. Too often the activities provided for young people did not match their needs because of an inadequate needs analysis. It was frequently impressionistic and failed to provide sufficient information to allow resources and enough provision to be directed to where they would be most effectively deployed. This was true of both the voluntary and statutory sectors, although targeting is a particular strength of a number of the NVYOs in the DfEE scheme. By contrast, some organisations, although they have a clear view of their target groups, have difficulty in reaching them. Some NVYOs have been particularly successful in group work and work specifically aimed at conflict resolution, and in dealing with those who have failed in the statutory sector, either in school, youth club or sometimes custody.

Quality of education

281. Although much of the youth work observed was of good quality, some was not sufficiently linked to the service's priorities. Some youth workers were not dealing with contemporary youth work issues, but providing a simple diet of general youth work, too often dependent on repetitive, recreational activities. This is partly due to the high number of unqualified part-time youth workers who are expected to take on roles for which they have insufficient knowledge and skills. These workers are often isolated and the system for identifying their training needs is frequently unsatisfactory.

282. In some cases, workers were not clear about the purpose, principles or practices of youth work. The best work was undertaken by full-time qualified youth workers and was often in contracted-out partnership projects. It focused on specific groups where staff could make the best use of their specialist knowledge.

283. On the whole the quality of youth work in the NVYOs was good. Some of the more tightly structured organisations are gradually adopting a more informal approach towards youth work, creating the conditions where young people can be more involved in influencing the pattern of provision. Some extremely effective work is being done by this sector with the most difficult young people. In this work, the high priority given to the training, support and development of staff has helped to produce sustained improvement. More organisations are paying serious attention to improving the professional youth work element of their schemes.

Management and efficiency

284. The quality of management across the nine maintained services varied considerably. In a few services there was no strategic planning or clear sense of purpose. They lacked effective co-ordination, and communication was frequently weak. Monitoring and evaluation were at an early stage of development in a number of services and there were no effective management information systems. The most marked weakness was in quality assurance. Although some authorities had sophisticated data collection procedures, others were unable to provide even the most basic statistics.

285. Several of the local education authority youth services inspected were undergoing reorganisation and were not managing change well. A number of services – frequently those where the level of political support was high – had made good use of demographic data in planning reorganisations, so that resources could be targeted at the areas of greatest need. Others, however, were uncertain about the future direction of their service. In a number of them, senior staff were remote from the youth work practitioners and had little experience or understanding of youth work. This often led to a lack of corporate identity for the youth work and the service at times became fragmented.

286. DfEE funding has encouraged NVYOs to develop partnership projects, and joint working has led to improved quality through a variety of innovative projects which have made use of the skills and expertise of different organisations. Joint working has not always been effective because responsibilities have not been made clear at the outset and because insufficient time has been allocated to the initial planning of the work and to developing monitoring and evaluation processes. There was little joint work with schools, but where this took place, often in personal and social education lessons, the contribution was much valued and of good quality.

287. Most services inspected were well-managed financially and had adopted sensible administrative procedures. In a few instances, however, services have failed to gain access to relevant data, particularly when they are trying to work with other departments of an authority and where cooperation is poor. They have therefore been unable to evaluate their own cost-effectiveness. The picture in NVYOs is similar; data collection is a particular problem for autonomous groups.

Adult education

Educational standards achieved

288. During 1998/99 HMI, assisted by additional inspectors, carried out full inspections of three local education authority adult services. HMI also inspected access to adult learning by disadvantaged groups in 13 local authorities and family learning in 28 local authorities. The standards of achievement of students participating in adult education in the three services inspected since the publication of the last Annual Report were good or very good in eight out of ten sessions, and were satisfactory in all but a very small proportion of the rest. Adult learners are highly committed to their courses and many make disciplined independent learners.

289. The work seen in the exercises with disadvantaged groups showed that, in all areas visited, there were projects that had successfully increased participation in education and provided disadvantaged people with good opportunities to learn in convenient locations. The adult participants in family learning schemes generally achieved high standards, but their children were too often provided with lower-level activities, inappropriate for their age and levels of previous attainment. The adults taking part in these schemes were motivated by a wide range of factors: for example, the desire to raise their level of basic skills, or to contribute to community life, or to support their children's learning. Those seeking employment or ambitious to proceed to higher education particularly valued courses which provided them with suitable accreditation.

Quality of education

290. The quality of the teaching seen on the three full service inspections was good or very good in about eight out of ten sessions. The number of sessions with unsatisfactory teaching was negligible. The great majority of adult education tutors have a good grasp of their subject areas and respond well to the opportunity to teach well motivated adults. Many bring with them extensive professional experience of, for example, business, information technology or the creative arts. There has been an increase in basic skills teaching, family learning, information technology and vocational courses. The best sessions were well planned, varied in content and conducted at a brisk pace; they were well matched to the diverse needs and levels of attainment of adult learners. Tutors in these sessions kept detailed records, monitored students' progress regularly, and provided them with an objective view of their attainment. They encouraged their students to take full responsibility for managing their own learning.

291. Successful teaching of adults from disadvantaged groups also possessed such characteristics; however, teaching was made more difficult where authorities had not obtained a sufficiently detailed and reliable audit of local needs, often owing to lack of resources or expertise. Family literacy and numeracy programmes were particularly successful when parents could see how they could become active partners in their children's schooling, but the advances made by children were not systematically recorded and reports produced at the end of projects were largely anecdotal. In projects of this nature, joint planning of the curriculum by the school teachers and adult education staff is still a prerequisite for the development of effective programmes. However, such coordinated approaches were relatively unusual and the link between curriculum planning and successful practice was too often weakly established.

Access and participation

292. The three services inspected as part of the full inspection programme had developed effective strategies for ensuring access to education for a wide range of adult learners. They had, for example, commissioned detailed research, undertaken an analysis of particular needs, developed outreach work, or set up satellite basic education centres. They had all managed to increase participation from disadvantaged communities. There continues to be a large imbalance in the numbers of male and female learners. Women outnumber men by about three to one overall, although there are differences within individual courses. A large number of students in the services inspected were entitled to concessionary fees – over 60 per cent in one service, and about half in the others. A significant barrier to participation was often the low level of childcare facilities.

293. The best adult education services are successful in motivating and encouraging adult learners, many of whom may have had negative experiences of education in the past. In order to make access easier and broaden participation, services that were previously highly centralised are sometimes being recast to make them more responsive to local needs. There is also a consistent trend towards partnership working, which goes beyond a concern with details of funding to reach potential students wherever they might be.

Management and efficiency

294. The way in which local authorities manage their responsibility to secure certain aspects of adult learning still varies too much. Whilst the individual services inspected were all well managed and gave good value for money, some services have to operate against a background of funding uncertainties and at arm's length from the local authority, with only light supervision.

295. Some authorities have continued to devolve responsibility for adult education to community schools or further education colleges. These need to accept responsibility for monitoring closely the quality of work. Although the evaluation of the quality of teaching and learning has improved in mainstream provision, it was the weakest aspect of the adult and family learning projects, and in some authorities there was little attention paid to whether the activity represented good value or not. There was instead an assumption that it was bound to be of benefit to all those taking part in it.

296. The growth in partnerships has sometimes resulted in additional sources of funding, but they can be time-consuming and, where interests overlap or are in conflict, they are not without their problems. Many services are well-run, efficient operations that continue to provide crucial support for many of the most disadvantaged adult members of our society, while also providing high quality education for some able and talented learners, a number of whom will go on to higher education.

Independent schools

Background

297. The independent sector provides education for about 500,000 children, or seven per cent of the school population. The majority of these (80 per cent) go to schools that are members of the Independent Schools Council (ISC).

298. This is the first year in which most of the inspection of ISC schools has been taken over by its own inspection agencies. Consequently, most of HMIs' work in relation to that part of the independent sector has concentrated on monitoring these inspections.

299. In the first six months, the new arrangements for the inspection of ISC schools have generally started well. The main weaknesses identified in the OFSTED report of 1997 on inspection quality have been addressed, although there is still room for improvement in a number of areas. The inspection bodies have made improvements both in their inspections and in the reports they produce. Of the 12 inspections so far monitored, over a third were high quality and only one was poor. A similar picture emerges from the 20 reports checked.

300. HMI also carried out monitoring visits to 457 schools: 91 ISC schools and 366 non-ISC schools. Of these, 64 visits were to provisionally or newly registered schools, 67 were to follow up concerns arising out of previous visiting, while the remainder were routine five-yearly visits. HMI published reports on six schools. This means that the sample of schools directly inspected by OFSTED was by no means representative of independent schools nationally.

Statutory requirements

301. Most schools inspected meet the minimum requirements of the 1996 Act in most respects. At the start of the academic year there were 60 schools causing serious concern in one or more respects, ranging from the quality of the education provided to welfare and the quality of the accommodation. Of the 156 ISC schools inspected by HMI or ISC inspection agencies only five failed to meet all the requirements. Among non-ISC schools, the corresponding figure was 116. The vast majority of these are either too small to possess sufficient resources, or occupy cramped, unsuitable or ill-adapted premises, or fail to pay proper regard to health and

safety. ISC inspectors also identify a substantial number of their schools with shortcomings in arrangements for health and safety, though these are rarely as serious as in the rest of the sector. The number of non-ISC schools with unacceptable quality of teaching or curriculum is increasing. Notice of Complaint action has been begun in relation to five schools.

302. Of 65 schools newly registered this year, four have achieved final registration. The others still have improvements to make.

303. Provision for the welfare of pupils in boarding schools continues to improve in many areas. The greatest improvement has been in the levels of supervision of boarding pupils. The most common deficiency is the lack of an up-to-date and effective child protection policy familiar to all staff. There is an acute need for induction and training for boarding staff on welfare issues.

304. Overall, schools in the ISC perform substantially better than schools outside its membership. In a significant minority of schools outside the ISC, partly because of inexperience and inadequate finance, the educational provision is very poor. There is no requirement under the 1996 Act for schools to have any documentation, including a prospectus. The fact that they can register without evidence of a suitable curriculum, development plans or accounts is a major cause for concern. A number of schools have been started in sites, such as disused hospitals, which require a major commitment of capital expenditure before they can be safely used for school accommodation. In the worst examples, pupils have been admitted before this work has been done, and the Secretary of State has issued a Notice of Complaint. In one boarding school, for example, little had been done at the time of the inspection to render an abandoned, vandalised and dangerous former hospital safe and suitable for pupils.

305. In some other schools the curriculum is not suited to the ages and needs of the pupils. Some tutorial colleges, for example, provide well for their traditional clientele of pupils over 16, but also admit younger pupils for the whole of Key Stage 4, putting them into the existing one-year repeat GCSE courses, rather than laying on a proper broad and balanced course to meet their needs.

306. The Government's plans to consult on reforms to the registration and monitoring system to tackle the problems identified in this section are welcome.

Standards of achievement and the quality of teaching

307. Most of the ISC schools inspected provide a good, in many cases excellent, education. The teaching is generally of high quality and pupils achieve good standards. There are examples of non-ISC schools where challenging and enthusiastic teaching engages pupils and leads to high attainment, but among non-ISC schools the difference between the best and the worst is very great.

308. In independent secondary schools overall 86 per cent of pupils achieved five or more grades A*– C in GCSE, 91 per cent obtained five or more grades A*– G. A significantly higher proportion of pupils in independent schools achieved five or more grades A*– C than in maintained schools. The proportion of pupils gaining five or more grades A*– G and one or more A*– G is similar in maintained and independent schools. The ISC schools achieve significantly better than the non-ISC schools on all measures. Perhaps not surprisingly, the rate of improvement is higher in non-ISC schools, but they also have a greater variability in their results.

309. The gap between boys and girls at GCSE level is less in independent schools than in maintained schools. Performance in single-sex schools is considerably higher than in mixed schools, where there is also much more variation in performance.[19]

310. The 421 non-boarding schools do better on average than the 367 boarding schools on all measures, but there is less variation in the results of boarding schools and a few of the very best independent boarding schools frequently outperform all other schools.

311. A large number of independent schools (634) have a wide age-range of pupils; only 154 independent schools now admit pupils only from the age of 11. The GCSE scores of schools with a wide age-range of pupils are significantly better than those schools covering only the secondary age-range. This in part reflects the number of major ISC senior schools that have in recent years extended their age-range or absorbed primary schools.

312. There are 97 independent schools with no sixth form. Whilst their GCSE average point scores are slightly lower than those with a sixth form, slightly more of their pupils obtain at least one graded result. This suggests that schools without sixth forms do slightly better at GCSE for their less able pupils.

313. Although the evidence is limited, it suggests that the quality of teaching in ISC schools is very much better than it is in other independent schools. For ISC schools, teaching was judged good in 74 per cent of schools and in 65 per cent of lessons. The findings of ISC inspections are broadly consistent with HMI evidence. By comparison, in non-ISC schools, teaching was good in only 36 per cent of schools and 49 per cent of lessons. In non-ISC schools 16 per cent of all lessons were judged unsatisfactory, compared with only one per cent in ISC schools.

19 OFSTED analysis of 1998 DfEE data.

Teacher education and training

Primary initial teacher training

Introduction

314. A new round of primary initial teacher training (ITT) inspections began in the autumn term 1998. Each inspection focused on either English or mathematics and a specialist subject, either core or non-core. The courses inspected were three-year or four-year undergraduate programmes, except where the only provision was a one-year postgraduate course. During this first year of a two-year cycle, 29 (of approximately 80) providers were inspected. A substantial proportion of these were selected because some or all areas of their work inspected in the previous year were graded adequate but with room for significant improvement. Four of these providers had been judged to offer poor provision in one area, that is, failing to reach the Secretary of State's requirements, during the 1997/98 primary follow-up survey (PFUS) inspections. As a consequence, they were the subject of re-inspections. The quality of provision inspected in this year was not, for the above reasons, likely to be fully representative, but to have a downwards skew.

315. Inspectors reported on two aspects of quality and three sets of standards agreed between OFSTED and the Teacher Training Agency (TTA) on the basis of their joint *Framework for the Assessment of Quality and Standards in Initial Teacher Training*. The areas reported on were:

- the quality of the training process;
- the accuracy and consistency of the assessment of trainees against the standards for the award of Qualified Teacher Status (QTS);
- the trainees' knowledge and understanding;
- the trainees' planning, teaching and classroom management;
- the trainees' monitoring, assessment, recording, reporting and accountability.

316. Only two providers had very good provision in all areas inspected. This was not surprising in view of the decision not to inspect, in this first year of the cycle,

courses which had been graded as very good in the PFUS. Although 11 of the 29 providers inspected were good in all aspects of either English or mathematics, 18 fell below this level. However, all four of the re-inspected providers improved to at least an adequate level and two of them made excellent progress to achieve good quality in all the areas inspected. One was judged to be very good in two areas.

English

317. The English courses of 17 providers of primary ITT were inspected, including two providing training for the first time. Nine providers, including four scheduled for re-inspection, offered postgraduate courses. The other eight providers offered undergraduate teacher training. Two courses were judged non-compliant with regard to the accuracy and consistency of the assessment of trainees against the standards for the award of QTS. One of these providers was also judged to be non-compliant in a second area – the trainees' knowledge and understanding of English.

318. Most providers had revised the content of courses to meet the new requirements of the National Curriculum for ITT in English. Slightly over half of the training inspected was of good quality. On these courses, provider-based and school-based training were closely linked and course documentation set out roles and responsibilities clearly. The majority of providers experienced difficulties in combining the audit of subject knowledge with rigorous and successful follow-up. The lack of provision for trainees to teach across the full primary age-range continues to be a significant weakness in much of the training.

319. The quality of the ASSESSMENT OF TRAINEES against the standards was good in just over a third of courses and needed significant improvement in over half the courses inspected. Most providers tend to overestimate their trainees' subject knowledge in English, especially where excessive reliance is placed on initial audits of subject knowledge. Furthermore, staff in schools are often reluctant to make judgements on subject knowledge. A minority of assignments provide insufficient breadth of evidence of the trainees' knowledge of language. Too often, additional sources of evidence, such as trainees' own spelling, punctuation and grammar, are overlooked.

320. The TRAINEES' SUBJECT KNOWLEDGE requires significant improvement in over three-quarters of courses inspected if it is to meet fully the requirements of the National Curriculum for ITT in English. Although the majority of trainees have a good knowledge of the schools' National Curriculum programmes of study and level descriptions in English for the key stage in which they specialise, their knowledge of those for their non-specialist key stage is often limited. Only a minority of the trainees seen have a good knowledge and understanding of progression across the full primary age-range.

321. The great majority of the trainees PREPARE THEIR LESSONS thoroughly and possess a good knowledge of what needs to be taught to the year group(s) with whom they work. They have also acquired a good knowledge of the National Literacy Strategy framework for teaching, which has provided them with valuable insights into how to structure the teaching of reading, including phonics. Some weaknesses remain, nevertheless, in the trainees' knowledge of phonics, especially for those specialising in Key Stage 2.

322. Most trainees have at least an adequate grasp of aspects of the National Curriculum for ITT such as word-level and sentence-level features and linguistic terminology. However, a substantial minority of trainees continue to make significant numbers of spelling and punctuation errors in their own writing and have weaknesses in their knowledge of grammar. While the majority are familiar with texts suitable for the year group or key stage in which they are teaching, only a minority demonstrate a reasonable knowledge of suitable texts for the full primary age-range.

323. The quality of TRAINEES' PLANNING, TEACHING AND CLASSROOM MANAGEMENT is good in just under three-quarters of courses. The implementation of the National Literacy Strategy in primary schools has helped trainees who are using the structure of the Literacy Hour to plan their teaching. Trainees follow the National Literacy Strategy framework closely and know it well, ensuring comprehensive coverage of the programmes of study for reading and writing. Less attention is paid, however, to explicit planning for speaking and listening. Trainees generally plan clear structures for lessons and for sequences of lessons. However, the majority have few opportunities to undertake medium-term planning independently because they understandably are required to follow schools' closely-focused planning for the National Literacy Strategy. Although there has been some improvement in trainees' ability to set clear objectives for their teaching, further work is still needed to ensure that the objectives they set can be assessed.

324. Most trainees use appropriate TEACHING METHODS successfully, especially whole-class questioning and demonstration. They create a purposeful working atmosphere and manage the classes well, even when these include pupils who are badly behaved. They are often skilled in listening carefully to pupils' responses and building successfully on them.

325. Weaknesses remain in the quality of TRAINEES' ASSESSMENT, RECORDING AND REPORTING and, in almost half of the courses inspected, significant improvements are needed. Trainees mark pupils' written work conscientiously and offer frequent praise to pupils, but they do not always give them enough guidance on how to improve their work. Their marking tends to focus on the surface features of spelling and punctuation rather than on the content and effectiveness of the writing. Trainees know how to use different kinds of assessment for different purposes and the majority maintain detailed records and profiles on small groups of pupils. Too often, record-keeping for whole classes is more likely to note the work covered than to contain any diagnostic analysis that might be used in future planning and teaching. The recording of pupils' progress in speaking and listening is generally a neglected area.

326. Trainees have at least adequate knowledge of national testing procedures at both key stages, but they have not always observed the tests in action, even when they are teaching classes at the end of a key stage. Trainees have made progress in understanding how various test data can be used to set targets for pupils' achievements, especially where schools have involved them in their own discussion of school target setting.

Mathematics

327. The mathematics courses of 15 primary ITT providers were inspected during 1998/99. Although nine out of 15 were judged to be good or very good in all five areas that were inspected, one course was judged to have poor provision in four areas out of five. The proportions of courses reaching only an adequate standard (with room for significant improvement) in particular areas were as follows: one in three in trainees' monitoring, assessment, recording and reporting; one in four in trainees' planning, teaching and class management, and one in five in the accuracy and consistency of the assessment of trainees.

328. Twelve out of 15 of the courses inspected provided good quality training. These courses had been adapted to meet the requirements of the National Curriculum for

ITT in mathematics and increased attention had been given to auditing, developing and assessing trainees' subject knowledge. However, trainees are still not being provided consistently with experience across the full primary age-range. Failure to provide early years experience for upper primary trainees and Year 5 and 6 experience for lower primary trainees is weakening their understanding of progression in pupils' learning of mathematics. The accuracy and consistency of the ASSESSMENT OF TRAINEES against the standards have improved and are mostly good or better. However, there is still some uncertainty about the assessment of trainees against the additional requirements for early years courses. Trainees receive regular feedback from school-based staff but this is still not sufficiently subject-focused.

329. TRAINEES' SUBJECT KNOWLEDGE in mathematics is similar to that for number in the earlier PFUS, with nearly 90 per cent of the trainees seen demonstrating good subject knowledge. Trainees' knowledge of the mathematics curriculum for ITT is generally good and their knowledge of pupils' common errors and mistakes is improving.

330. Two-thirds of courses produced trainees whose TEACHING AND CLASSROOM MANAGEMENT were good. Trainees' planning of lessons is broadly good but they sometimes pay insufficient attention to planning productive plenary sessions. Weak planning for progression over time was a significant factor where trainees' teaching was only adequate.

331. Most trainees are able to teach whole-class lessons well and they often give purposeful introductions to lessons which focus upon mental and oral mathematics. They are mostly enthusiastic about teaching mathematics and are imaginative in their choice of activities. However, while aware of the importance of questioning, significant numbers of trainees do not understand sufficiently how to build on and extend pupils' responses to questions. They often give insufficient time to pupils to think things through before answering, and some ask an excessive number of closed questions.

332. The quality of trainees' ASSESSMENT, RECORDING AND REPORTING remains the weakest aspect of their performance. Only two-thirds of providers were judged good in this respect. Not enough is done to familiarise trainees with national tests and the levels of attainment expected of pupils across the full primary age-range.

Specialist subjects

333. Each inspection also focused on training in one specialist subject, either core or non-core. In this first year of the cycle, the numbers of courses inspected in each subject were low, and at this stage do not permit analyses of particular subject strengths and weaknesses. Few providers offer a full range of specialist subjects and the number of students taking a particular specialism, especially on postgraduate courses, can be very small. The time devoted to specialist subject studies on postgraduate courses is very limited. Consequently, the quality of the trainees' subject knowledge usually reflects their first degrees rather than what they acquire through their training course. It is a matter of concern that a minority of trainees, whose degree does not match a National Curriculum subject, can find themselves following a specialism which they have not previously studied beyond GCSE level. Although undergraduate courses generally devote more time to training in the specialist subject, this time is under pressure from competing demands. Undergraduate trainees mostly demonstrate at least sound and often better levels of subject knowledge and an ability to teach their specialist subject effectively.

Secondary initial teacher training

Introduction

334. In 1999 OFSTED published *Secondary Initial Teacher Training,* an overview of 513 secondary subject inspections carried out between November 1996 and July 1998. Almost all of this training was on a one-year route to QTS for graduates, leading to the award of a Postgraduate Certificate in Education (PGCE). This cycle of inspections was completed in 1998/99. Over the three years a total of 577 inspections have been carried out of the initial training of secondary teachers in 13 different subjects. The 1998/99 programme also included 26 re-inspections. In addition, 12 courses were inspected in information technology, the most substantial inspection to date of this relatively new specialist subject. The findings and issues outlined below interpret this year's inspection evidence against the background of the overview report. In each subject, inspectors reported on three aspects of quality and three sets of standards agreed between OFSTED and the TTA on the basis of their joint *Framework for the Assessment of Quality and Standards in Initial Teacher Training.* The areas reported on were as for primary providers plus the quality of admissions policy and the selection procedures.

Quality and standards

335. In all six areas assessed, the majority of the provision is good, but there are significant shortcomings in two of them. By the end of their training, the majority of the trainees meet the national standards for QTS at a good level. Nevertheless, there are wide variations between subjects and between training providers in all the areas assessed, and a significant proportion of the work inspected falls short of the aspiration in the framework that all initial teacher training should be of good quality. Poor provision and poor teaching which fail to meet the required standard are rare (under one per cent), but over 20 per cent of the work inspected was in need of significant improvement.

336. There are two persistent areas of weakness across all subjects. The first is assessing all trainees accurately and consistently against the new standards for QTS – well over a quarter of the courses are only adequate in this respect. The second weakness is the trainees' competence in monitoring, assessing, recording and reporting on pupils' progress. In one course in three, inspectors identify a considerable need for improvement in this aspect, especially in the skills of assessing and recording.

337. Twenty-six courses at 21 providers were re-inspected in 1998/99 either because none of the provision had been found to be better than adequate in the previous inspection, or because some of it was poor. In the great majority of these courses and providers, substantial improvements were found in the quality of the provision and in the standards achieved by trainees.

338. More than one course in four has very good admissions policies and selection procedures. Almost all providers promote their courses actively and have devised thorough selection interviews and practical tasks to probe the applicant's subject knowledge, suitability and any experience relevant to teaching. Most providers now include in the initial interviews a formal check on candidates' ability to communicate well in spoken and written English.

339. The calibre of applicants varies markedly between subjects. Many subjects recruit a significant proportion of mature trainees who have already worked in business, the arts or teaching and this contributes strongly to the quality of recruitment. However, concerns remain over the numbers of applicants in many subjects, and there are particular recruitment problems in some, such as design and technology and modern foreign languages. There has been an encouraging increase in the number of applications in mathematics and science where financial incentives have been made available. In design and technology and physical education, the procedures by which candidates are selected are less effective than in other subjects in assessing candidates' subject knowledge and its relevance to the National Curriculum.

340. Much of the training is good and some courses are outstanding. Trainers are responding to the need to provide opportunities for trainees to update their subject knowledge in the light of an initial audit, though the role of school-based trainers in contributing to this needs to be planned more thoroughly. Trainers at times give insufficient attention to planning for progression, and school mentors do not always focus systematically enough on the standards relating to assessment and recording.

341. The training in art, economics and business education, music and history is good or very good in almost every course. At the other end of the scale, one in three physical education and design and technology courses require significant improvement. Physical education trainees, for example, frequently do not have the opportunity to teach and assess pupils in all six areas of the physical education National Curriculum. In design and technology, there is often too little training in specialist fields, especially in food and textile technology.

342. In INFORMATION TECHNOLOGY, over nine in ten higher education institution-based training sessions were good, but four in ten school-based sessions led by mentors had major shortcomings. The main information technology teachers often have many responsibilities in school and many are unable to dedicate time to support information technology trainees. Although the best school placements provided trainees with good training in information technology across a wide age-range, a significant minority of trainees had a restricted experience because they were required to teach identical material to several classes each week. This often contributed to underachievement by information technology trainees. Higher education institutions face the fact that many of the school partners with whom they have developed good working relationships are amongst the half of secondary schools which are non-compliant in information technology provision or where information technology teaching is no more than adequate. Therefore, ways need to be found of offering all the trainees enough opportunity to see good teaching, for example by making more intensive use of those schools where information technology is very well taught.

343. In all subjects the assessment of trainees needed to be more accurate and more consistent in about one-third of the courses inspected. A small number of courses failed to make secure decisions on whether trainees had reached the QTS standards and for this reason were judged to be non-compliant. The great majority of providers are reasonably accurate in judging standards achieved, but a number assessed trainees too favourably, especially in relation to subject knowledge and understanding, and trainees' assessment, recording and reporting of pupils' progress. This weakness was marked in physical education.

344. In their assessment of information technology trainees, one in three providers graded the trainees' knowledge too high because they failed to consider properly all the standards or used too little evidence. This occurred most often in relation to trainees' use of assessment, recording and reporting, where many trainees had insufficient practical experience of assessing pupils' work against national standards for information technology and lacked confidence in their ability to do so reliably.

345. Nevertheless, most providers now have in place good systems to track trainees' progress in relation to the QTS standards. There are regular progress reviews, and individual target setting is an increasingly effective element in the majority of courses. Profiles are often sophisticated and well constructed and a number of subject courses have devised good exemplification of the standards in subject terms, so that tutors and mentors can assess trainees more consistently on the basis of evidence from lesson observation and subject assignments.

346. The trainees generally demonstrate good standards of subject knowledge and understanding by the end of their training. In art, economics and business education, history and geography trainees achieve good or very good standards of subject knowledge on one course in three. In science, where trainees must apply their subject knowledge across the broad range of subjects covered by Attainment Targets 2, 3 and 4, prospective science teachers reach a very good standard on only one course in 12. In information technology few trainees started with a good understanding of key information technology skills and concepts, but the training was in most cases effective in remedying this. Because of the nature of the degree courses they have done, trainees in physical education and in design and technology often have significant gaps in their knowledge and experience, and providers are not always successful in bringing them up to the required level on a 36-week PGCE course.

347. Trainees generally achieve good standards of class management. Most organise their time and resources well and they manage and motivate pupils effectively. The best communicate enthusiasm for their subject, draw impressively on their subject expertise in devising activities for pupils, and present their material in a clear and stimulating manner. The majority of trainees have a good general understanding of the Code of Practice for special educational needs and take account of it in their planning, teaching and assessment.

348. On one course in five a significant minority of the trainees is unclear about lesson objectives and insecure about planning assessment opportunities within lessons. Trainees in all subjects find difficulty with planning for progression and with the constructive use of homework to extend pupils' learning. In evaluating their lessons trainees take too little account of pupils' responses, including their errors and misconceptions.

349. In assessment, recording and reporting the majority of trainees perform well, but on one course in three a significant proportion of the trainees achieves only an adequate standard by the end of their training. There are long-standing weaknesses associated with assessment in secondary schools. School mentors frequently do not fully understand what is required of them and lack the confidence and the experience of effective assessment needed to provide effective support. Trainees are aware of statutory requirements and of principles of assessment but often lack a working knowledge of National Curriculum assessment: a substantial minority do not have a secure understanding of level descriptions, mainly through lack of experience in attempting to apply them. On many 11–18 courses trainees' knowledge of GCSE and of post-16 assessment is weak.

Teacher development, appraisal and performance management

350. In December 1998 the Government published a Green Paper, *Teachers: meeting the challenge of change*. This set out a wide-ranging programme to improve the recruitment and retention of good teachers and the leadership qualities of existing and potential headteachers through better training and support, rigorous annual appraisals, and linking pay with performance. Evidence from Section 10 inspections and from a number of small-scale inspection exercises carried out by OFSTED's Teacher Education and Training Division during 1998/99 highlight a number of issues to be addressed through implementing the Green Paper proposals.

Newly qualified teachers and their induction

351. A small-scale survey of 12 LEAs, selected because they were considered to have good practice in induction, found that there was wide variation, even within these LEAs, in their knowledge and understanding of the proposed statutory regulations for induction. Some of these LEAs were building on effective arrangements which already existed and were providing newly qualified teachers with good support and clear guidance. Others had a long way to go. LEAs were beginning to make use of the Career Entry Profile as a means of pinpointing areas for development for newly qualified teachers, but these were not always sufficiently clearly defined. In general, support for primary teachers was better than for secondary. Almost all of the schools visited by HMI in this sample of LEAs provided effective support and were well placed to carry out the roles and responsibilities required under the new statutory induction programme. The planning and content of the induction programme were particular strengths. Very good induction was seen where three strands of induction were firmly in place: a whole-school strand dealing with generic issues such as the behaviour of pupils; a subject strand supported by specialists; and an LEA strand dealing with the relevant local services and resources.

352. The chart opposite shows Section 10 inspectors' judgements of the quality of teaching of newly qualified teachers. Not surprisingly, the experienced teachers teach more good and fewer unsatisfactory lessons. However, the gap in performance, particularly in primary schools, is relatively small. This is in line with the improvements that have taken place in initial teacher training and reflects the fact that there is effective induction in some schools and LEAs, although the proportion of unsatisfactory lessons shows that there is a need for greater consistency, which the Green Paper proposals are designed to address. The teaching of newly qualified teachers in primary schools is strongest in English, where the training for the National Literacy Strategy has clearly paid dividends.

Staff development

353. Section 10 inspectors judged that the arrangements for the professional development of teachers are good in about half of schools but weak in about one in ten primary schools and one in five secondary schools. The main weaknesses in secondary schools are a lack of systematic dissemination of staff development and a lack of evaluation of its impact. In primary schools, the focus of much of the school-based training during 1998/99 has been the teaching of literacy. In-service training has

generally followed a set of videos and training notes specifically prepared to support the implementation of the National Literacy Strategy. While the training materials have been broadly welcomed, it has been a significant and demanding responsibility for English co-ordinators to lead a sustained sequence of training sessions. Many co-ordinators have reported that they would have appreciated training in how to lead these training sessions. It has not been ideal for a major national strategy to rely so much on "twilight" training sessions and on a "cascade" model which depends so heavily on subject co-ordinators who have widely varying degrees of skill and confidence.

354. Despite this mixed picture of staff development, the sections of this report on primary, secondary and special schools have highlighted the continued improvements in the quality of teaching. This year's evidence base

Quality of teaching in secondary schools: qualified teachers with more than one year's experience and newly qualified teachers *(percentage of lessons)*

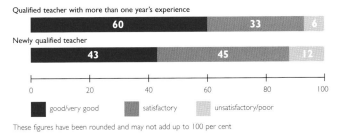

These figures have been rounded and may not add up to 100 per cent

Quality of teaching in primary schools: qualified teachers with more than one year's experience and newly qualified teachers *(percentage of lessons)*

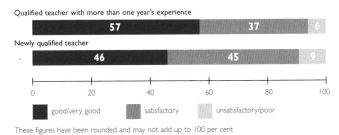

These figures have been rounded and may not add up to 100 per cent

Quality of teaching in lessons by subject for newly qualified teachers in primary schools - 1998/99

(percentage of lessons)

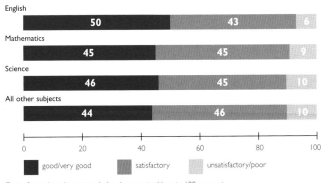

These figures have been rounded and may not add up to 100 per cent

contains a full set of judgements on the teaching of anonymised individual teachers. Of the primary teachers observed on five or more occasions, 52 per cent taught more than half their lessons well. Poor teachers are rare. There were only 2.7 per cent of teachers who taught more than half their lessons unsatisfactorily. Of the secondary teachers observed on three or more occasions, 79 per cent taught no unsatisfactory lessons and 56 per cent taught more than half their lessons well. Again, poor teachers are rare. Only four per cent of teachers taught more than half their lessons unsatisfactorily. While some of these teachers can be helped to improve through support and further training, schools continue to report that the dismissal of incompetent teachers is a difficult and time-consuming process. Award-bearing courses funded by the TTA are increasingly focused on Government priorities, including literacy and numeracy. Preliminary evidence from inspections of these courses indicates that the sharper focusing of such courses in relation to the perceived needs of teachers has already been beneficial, although the effectiveness of the courses in achieving the desired impact on school practice is still to be evaluated.

National Professional Qualification for Headteachers (NPQH)

355. The National Professional Qualification for Headteachers (NPQH) provides a qualification designed to prepare aspiring headteachers for their roles as professional leaders of schools. The national training and assessment programme is based upon the National Standards for Headteachers, which set out the key knowledge, understanding, skills and attributes that are required of headteachers.

356. In the period from October 1998 to March 1999, OFSTED carried out a further study of training for those aspiring to be headteachers. This involved visits to almost 100 candidates. The vast majority of these were NPQH candidates. A few aspiring headteachers who were attending other leadership training courses or who had recently been appointed to headship without the NPQH qualification, were also visited as part of a small-scale comparative study. Inspectors observed a range of NPQH training sessions and also the final assessment arrangements for a small number of candidates.

357. Considerable attention has been given to addressing earlier concerns about the NPQH. Improvements have been made to both the structure of courses and the training process. For example, the newly-established accelerated route is appreciated by candidates and seen as an important means of allowing the accreditation of prior learning and experience. Candidates also welcome the thorough initial assessment for this route, particularly the opportunity for skilled assessors to carry out school-based assessment.

358. NPQH training is helping the majority of candidates to develop a strategic view of the school and an understanding of how to secure school improvement through planning and target setting. Most candidates are more confident to take on headship and have gained a wider perspective of headship. Candidates are supported well by their schools but headteachers could play a more active part in their training.

359. The quality and value of assessment tasks have improved steadily over time. The tasks chosen are now more likely to be drawn from the school development plan, which significantly increases their impact and reduces the burden from conflicting priorities. As a direct result of work undertaken on NPQH tasks, more than half of the candidates visited were seen to be making marked contributions to school developments. However, questions about the basic NPQH training model remain, especially about its capacity, as currently constituted, to respond flexibly to the varied needs of aspiring headteachers in schools with different characteristics and age-ranges.

360. Variations in the quality of training remain both within and across centres. The majority of sessions provide good training but a third were judged to be in need of significant improvement in the presentation and use of training materials. The course gives appropriate emphasis to core tasks common to all headteachers but too few of the tasks and sessions address issues related to particular types of school. Provision for candidates from special schools is especially weak in this respect.

361. Overall there has been an improvement in the quality and value of initial needs assessment, although almost ten per cent of candidates remain highly critical of this element. For many candidates, the relationship between needs assessment and action planning remains tenuous and there is a lack of monitoring, evaluation and review of personal action plans within the training.

362. NPQH represents an important mechanism for preparing for effective leadership. But there are others. Visits to management courses outside the aegis of the NPQH underlined that there is also a range of other valuable training opportunities. At best this training is successful in responding to the needs of a specific known clientele and supporting these with good-quality training.

363. The development of the NPQH has been of particular significance in the context of the Government's declared interest in introducing a mandatory qualification for all aspiring headteachers. The Green Paper *Teachers: meeting the challenge of change* proposes a national training framework for headship and the establishment of a new national college for school leadership to ensure that all heads and aspiring headteachers have access to high-quality training at every stage of their careers. As part of the priorities it is intended to develop the NPQH further, building on its strengths and successes to date.

364. Any future headship strategy will need to review carefully the question of how to undertake realistic and not excessively burdensome or bureaucratic assessments. Assessment of suitability and of readiness for headship continues to pose challenging issues, not least because of the all-embracing nature of the National Standards for Headship as currently conceived. A further important need will be the articulation and coherence of the various strands of leadership training offered to aspiring and serving headteachers, which to some extent have developed along different lines.

Appraisal and performance management

365. HMI have continued to monitor developments in schools' practice in appraisal and performance management. The broad picture in 1998/99 is of a weakening of regular appraisal in schools. While it is clearly cost-effective to link classroom monitoring with staff appraisal, this is very rarely the case at present. In a recent survey of schools reported to have good appraisal arrangements in their last Section 10 inspection, about a quarter were no longer operating an appraisal system, and the headteachers involved had not themselves been appraised for two years. The delay in setting new statutory requirements has meant that an increasing number of schools are failing to meet the existing requirements of Circular 12/91. Evidence from Section 10 inspections indicates that two in five schools are not fully compliant. In many schools, particularly secondary schools, appraisal has simply stalled.

366. A few schools have replaced appraisal with new systems of performance management, with initiatives associated with Investors in People, or with monitoring the curriculum in a way which does not focus on the individual teacher. In the schools where appraisal still operates, there is a trend to adopt a one-year cycle, usually associated with the timetable for school development planning. About half of the secondary

schools in a survey conducted in 1999 had moved towards a line manager system of appraisal.

367. Through involvement in initial teacher training, many schools are increasingly aware of the national standards set for newly qualified teachers. However, there is very little use of these standards in appraising teachers already in post, and little evidence that the Career Entry Profile of new teachers is used as a basis for appraisal and support during their first year of teaching.

368. The objectives set for appraisal purposes in primary schools are rarely linked to targets for the pupils' attainment, or to national priorities. In secondary schools there is evidence that pupil performance data are beginning to be a factor in the appraisal process, but few schools are at the stage where such data can be used for setting objectives for individual teachers.

Performance pay

369. A small-scale survey on the use and effects of the teachers' pay incentives continued through this year. The pay policy of a school is often used as part of a strategy to raise standards across the school. However, headteachers remain reluctant to use pay points to reward excellence in teaching. Instead, points continue to be given for additional management responsibility and for National Curriculum provision. Similarly, pay points are rarely used directly for the retention of staff. However, the award of such points to teachers is frequently based indirectly on a review or estimate of their performance as class and/or subject teachers.

370. There is growing evidence that the planned provision of INSET for individual teachers is linked to a review of their performance and that schools are establishing a structure for staff development. However, there is little direct linking of pay with an annual performance review. Headteachers prefer, where possible, to motivate staff through less direct rewards, such as minor improvements in their conditions of service.

371. Governing bodies are in some respects taking a more positive role in monitoring aspects of the impact of pay policy throughout the school. There is some use of the discretionary powers to increase the pay of the headteacher and the deputy headteachers above the annual pay award, but this is not widespread, and it is often managed unsatisfactorily. In some instances, pay policy is being used successfully to promote improvements in teaching and learning. Overall, steady but rather slow progress is being made.

Local education authority support for school improvement

The performance of local education authorities

372. Between September 1998 and September 1999 OFSTED, with the assistance of the Audit Commission, inspected 29 local education authorities (LEAs), by virtue of HMCI's powers under Section 38 of the Education Act 1997. By 1 September 1999, 25 reports had been issued and four were pending. Two of those inspections were revisits: Calderdale and Hackney LEAs. In addition, an inspection of Rotherham LEA was carried out (largely by Audit Commission staff) which focused wholly on the provision and maintenance of school buildings.

373. Forty-one of the 150 LEAs in England had been inspected by 1 September 1999. They do not represent a balanced sample, in that they include a relatively high proportion of authorities whose schools perform poorly. All LEAs will have been inspected (or their inspections will have begun) by September 2001.

374. Overall, the performance of LEAs as organisations remains too variable. So far four LEAs (Hackney, Islington, Liverpool and Leicester City) have been found to be failing to such a degree in the performance of their functions that the Secretary of State has intervened. A further 12 LEAs have received critical reports, requiring urgent action on many fronts. By contrast, nine LEAs were found to give, to a greater or lesser extent, effective support to their schools: Barking and Dagenham, Cornwall, Birmingham, North Somerset, Brent, Bury, Surrey, Newham and Warwickshire. Like North Somerset, Rutland had made a good start as a unitary authority, and Stoke-on-Trent and Kingston-upon-Hull were making significant inroads into a difficult legacy. Elsewhere, for example in Norfolk, Leicestershire, Sunderland, Nottinghamshire, Sandwell, Tower Hamlets, Lambeth, Kent, Barnsley and Knowsley, there were signs of some recent improvement, often associated with political change or a change in personnel in the professional leadership of the education department. That improvement, however, was not always sufficient or had yet had a discernible impact in the schools.

375. However limited, these signs of improvement are encouraging. It is, nevertheless, unacceptable that almost two in five of the LEAs inspected so far should have been found seriously deficient, often in many respects. Moreover, the gap between the best and the worst is too large.

376. The worst-performing LEAs consume resources to little, and in some cases to negative, effect. In three of the four LEAs in which major intervention has been required, the root cause of failure has been the lack of effective political leadership. In such circumstances, elected members have often forfeited the trust of schools by failing to take reasonable decisions in a timely and open way. Once that trust between LEAs and schools is gone, it requires leadership of an exceptional nature to restore it. Only three re-inspections of LEAs have so far been conducted, two of Calderdale and one of Hackney. In each case there was progress, following intervention and the appointment of competent senior management; but it was slow and insufficient.

School improvement

377. The School Standards and Framework Act 1998 laid on LEAs a duty to discharge their functions "with a view to promoting high standards". This gives legislative force to the Government's intentions for LEAs set out in the White Paper *Excellence in Schools* (1997) and discussed in the last Annual Report. The LEA's role in relation to schools is to challenge and support them in setting and attaining demanding targets.

378. There is, as yet, no sign that LEAs are directly responsible for an overall rise in standards, nor would it be reasonable to expect any such evidence. The principal mechanism for LEAs to contribute directly to raising standards is the education development plan (EDP), implementation of which has only just begun. More fundamentally, there is no straightforward connection between the quality of an LEA as an organisation and the standards achieved in its schools. The work of LEAs is only one possible influence on standards achieved in schools. It will be a much less powerful influence than the leadership of the headteacher. In each LEA inspected, inspectors visited a sample of schools in order to evaluate in detail the effectiveness of the LEA's contribution to improving the quality of teaching, management and governance, literacy and numeracy, the use of performance data and the performance of schools in special measures or with serious weaknesses. Those visits showed, however, that LEAs can and, with some significant exceptions, are making a positive contribution to specific aspects of improvement.

379. The 25 reports issued during the year recorded visits to 549 schools, with HMI and the Audit Commission's judgement on the effectiveness of the LEA contribution in each school. That contribution was judged to be effective in two-thirds of the schools visited. However, effectiveness varied widely. A few LEAs had made effective contributions to improvement in all, or nearly all, their schools, notably: Kingston-upon-Hull, Nottinghamshire, Stoke-on-Trent, Bury, Warwickshire, Brent, and Newham. By contrast, in the following LEAs there was evidence of effectiveness in only half the schools visited, or fewer: Liverpool, Buckinghamshire, Barnsley, Islington, Southwark and Hackney.

380. Generally speaking, LEAs were more effective in support of primary schools, where the demand for support was higher than secondary (though the best were equally effective in both phases). LEAs gave effective support to special schools in half the instances in which a separate judgement was made. In several cases, however, the effectiveness of support to special schools was impaired because of uncertainty over the future of the schools' pending reorganisation.

Inspection and advice

381. The largest single factor influencing the effectiveness of LEAs in support of schools was the variable quality of their inspection and advice services. In half the LEAs inspected the quality of inspection and advice provided was deemed sufficiently weak to justify a specific recommendation. This was true even in some high performing LEAs, such as Newham.

382. In all LEAs the inspection and advisory service has a key role in delivering the EDP. It is largely through advisers, sometimes allied to officers linked to schools, that LEAs fulfil their functions of monitoring, challenging and supporting schools. All the LEAs inspected accepted in principle that support should be directed at schools in greatest need – "intervention in inverse proportion to success". Not all knew which schools those were, and too many, despite the powerful data available to them, believed that they needed to visit all their schools, sometimes undertaking routine inspection visits.

383. Understanding of the notion of challenge and the capacity to apply that understanding in practice are not widely disseminated in the weaker LEAs. This is particularly evident in relation to target-setting. LEAs have a responsibility to persuade schools to set challenging, but realistic, targets for improvement in performance. Usually, this entails an adviser visiting the school and insisting (or attempting to insist) on a target that is no more than an extrapolation from existing data, with the presumption of no significant change in the school's provision. The tasks are to influence the school to set targets whose attainment will require real improvements, usually in teaching, and then subsequently to advise on what those improvements might be. The failure to exert this influence represents, given the number of adviser days involved, a gross waste of public money.

384. In about half the LEAs reported on, there were weaknesses in the capacity of advisers/inspectors to challenge schools in any meaningful way or in the management of advisory teams to support them in doing so. Occasionally, poor relationships between the LEA and schools, as in Calderdale, make it difficult to offer such challenge. More frequently, particularly in secondary schools, advisers lack management experience at a sufficiently senior level to carry conviction. Increasingly, LEAs attempt to compensate by the linking of senior officers to schools or by the attachment of experienced heads to schools in difficulty. Both strategies need to be pursued, but more should be done. The lack of induction and training for performance management for advisory staff needs urgent attention, locally and nationally, but LEAs should also reconsider whether the number of permanent advisory staff needs to be increased still further.

385. There are particular tasks which LEAs generally carry out effectively, and to which advisory services contribute considerably. The use of performance data has already been mentioned as an improving area. Support for literacy and numeracy and school governance are generally favourably reported, and are now significant strengths in about half the LEAs inspected.

Support for schools in special measures and with serious weaknesses

386. None of the LEAs inspected in this year was found to be failing in its statutory duty to support schools in special measures. Even in LEAs that in other respects had considerable weaknesses, such support was often effective. LEAs were increasingly prepared to take steps to tackle schools that failed to improve, including the closure of schools. Leicester City, for example, decided to close five secondary schools in special measures, as part of a city-wide reorganisation. However, the support given was often extremely time-consuming, and could be overwhelming for smaller LEAs. Leicester City estimated that 50 per cent of its advisory staffing went to support schools in special measures. In Stoke, the new LEA's original staffing intentions had been distorted by the need to deal with a large number of primary schools placed in special measures in the first 18 months of the LEA's existence. Despite the effort being made by some LEAs the fact that 193 schools were put into special measures following their second inspection is a cause for concern *(see paragraph 230)*. These schools often had very significant weaknesses to deal with after their first inspection. The fact that they failed to improve, or declined even further, raises serious questions about the quality of LEA support.

387. In relation to schools with serious weaknesses, the position is less clear-cut. In a third of LEAs inspected recommendations were made on the need to improve support for such schools, especially those identified by the LEAs themselves (rather than by OFSTED) as causing concern. Eight LEAs inspected lack a clear definition of levels of concern, with associated criteria set out openly and shared with schools. In such cases, intervention at times appeared arbitrary and the targeting of support haphazard.

The provision of school places

388. The provision of sufficient, suitable school places is a basic task of LEAs. During the course of this year LEAs were formulating School Organisation Plans and setting in place School Organisation Committees, reflecting changes in the statutory framework for planning school places.

389. The LEAs inspected faced many problems in managing the supply of school places, often of their own making. For example, Leicestershire managed well the complexity of a school system with ages of transfer or admission at three, four, five, seven, 10, 11 and 14. Norfolk was reviewing ages of transfer, and Buckinghamshire was suffering the effects of a change that it had managed poorly. In several LEAs, notably Stoke-on-Trent, a problem of excessive surplus places had arisen as a result of local government reorganisation. Finally, LEAs such as Liverpool and Knowsley faced problems of the loss of pupils across LEA boundaries within a large conurbation; Bury had the converse problem. Movement of pupils between LEAs at the age of eleven was a particularly acute difficulty for London LEAs. Lambeth, for example, "lost" half of its pupils at that stage.

390. There were few signs that LEAs were grasping the nettle of school reorganisation more readily than in the past. Eleven reports found some evidence of waste. Warwickshire was a rarity in having carried through a large, and highly effective, reorganisation. Apart from this general problem, there were also particular difficulties, notably patterns of special schools that reflected no clear planning but only a history of expedient decision-making, as in Liverpool, or the historical accident of local government reorganisation, as in Stoke-on-Trent.

391. Except where there were particular complexities, such as a very high population of grant maintained secondary schools or a system of selection at 11, LEA administration of admissions was found to be generally efficient, though several large shire LEAs needed more effective monitoring procedures to ensure equity between local areas. The number of appeals is rising, particularly where schools are attracting admissions from surrounding LEAs.

Provision for special educational needs

392. In relation to special educational needs, LEAs face a particular problem of dealing with limited resources which need to be carefully targeted and, in some areas, with inexorably rising demand. Particularly in London LEAs, expenditure on special educational needs is rising rapidly, both in absolute terms and as a proportion of the overall budget. For example, the report on Tower Hamlets speaks of "a rapid and unchecked growth in statements in the secondary phase", and that growth no doubt reflects the desire of schools to use the statementing process as the key to unlock resources. Dissatisfaction with LEAs' performances in relation to special educational needs remains high, both among schools and parents. That dissatisfaction rarely focuses on the support given to individual pupils: rather, it concentrates on the frequent unavailability of such support, particularly for pupils who have (or whom schools suspect of having) emotional and behavioural difficulties. Particular weaknesses are:

- the speed of compiling and the quality of statements;

- the targeting of special educational needs resources;

- planning for special educational needs;

- monitoring the success of special educational needs provision.

393. In relation to special educational needs provision, LEAs are engaged in a task of necessary discrimination. Some are able to undertake that task with some success. Most cannot. Few, if any, monitor effectively the use schools make of delegated special educational needs funding.

394. Most authorities inspected provided generally effective support to individual pupils, but a third of LEAs failed to convince schools that resources were equitably and accurately allocated. Not all needs were met and the assumption was made that the needs were too great for the resources available. That assumption needed to be re-examined in the light of a clearer specification of criteria for moving between stages of the Code of Practice levels of support and evaluation of the overall effectiveness of support. In few authorities had there been a rigorous audit of the contribution of special educational needs services to raising attainment, and it was rare to find regular review leading to the LEA ceasing to maintain a statement.

395. All the LEAs inspected supported the Government's policy of inclusion of pupils with special educational needs, wherever possible, in mainstream education. However, interpretation of the policy was often unclear, and good intentions were not always matched by precise definition and delivery. Most were devolving, or proposing to devolve, more of the available funding to schools. Where LEAs retained a high proportion of statemented pupils in special schools, plans for reorganisation were either under consideration or actually in the process of implementation. Inevitably that created some uncertainty for both special schools and mainstream schools, particularly where specialist services had a narrow view of their role and gave little advice on the development of provision.

Support for improving attendance

396. Support for improving attendance was evaluated in 12 LEAs. It was effective in only five, including Hackney, where a thorough-going reorganisation of the Education Welfare Service had led to rapid improvement. There was excellent practice in Newham, where a well-managed Education Welfare Service worked effectively with schools to improve attendance. Referral routes were clear and staff precisely deployed to support those schools most in need and the groups of children identified, on the basis of a careful analysis, as being "at risk". Reporting procedures were detailed, and the analysis of attendance rates and patterns in each school was of exemplary quality. Moreover, the Education Welfare Service had

succeeded in communicating to the schools the need for meticulous recording, analysis and follow-up. A wide variety of methods was used in a systematic and determined way to improve attendance, including:

- the issue of school attendance orders;
- frequent and consistent contact between the LEA's education welfare staff;
- home visits to families when a child is absent for more than four days;
- stringent guidelines to deter parents from taking their children on extended holidays abroad;
- the active involvement of other agencies in providing an alternative curriculum for older disaffected pupils;
- frequent use of the Magistrates Court to prosecute parents.

In many LEAs the Education Welfare Service failed to focus sharply enough on attendance, and links with advisory services to address curricular issues relevant to attendance were ineffective. More generally, there had been no strategic attempt to confront poor attendance through an analysis of patterns of absence.

397. A third of the reports make recommendations about support for attendance. This was particularly poor in Liverpool where, despite being very expensive, the Education Welfare Service was poorly managed, undertook little analysis of data on attendance and had no realistic strategy for improving attendance. Effective work in support for attendance depended on good management of education welfare, with clear specifications of caseloads and referral routes, known criteria for prevention, rigorous and rapid follow-up to absence and a willingness to hold parents to account. Schools needed to know what entitlement to Education Welfare Service support they had, and benefited from LEA guidance on how to analyse patterns of non-attendance and produce effective attendance policies.

Support for improving behaviour

398. Behaviour support plans were in place in the LEAs most recently inspected. Even where, as in Barnsley, drafting and consultation over drafts had been somewhat rushed, the plans were beginning to raise awareness of the range of interventions available and of the need for co-ordination between relevant agencies. The danger was that this became solely a paper audit. The plans seen were more specific about achieving greater collaboration than improving standards of behaviour.

399. The effectiveness of the support provided was evaluated in ten of the authorities inspected this year, in eight of which it was generally effective. In four, Bury, Newham, Lambeth and Knowsley, it was a significant strength and had contributed to a reduction in the number of exclusions. Effective intervention to support particular pupils was combined with training that assisted teachers to manage disruptive behaviour better. A further factor contributing to the fall in exclusions was effective liaison with headteachers which persuaded them to seek alternatives to exclusion, wherever possible. The most effective authorities also had clear policies, supported by schools, for the reintegration of excluded pupils. In Newham, the influence of elected members, a panel of whom considered all exclusions, was considerable and beneficial.

The provision of education otherwise than at school

400. All the LEAs inspected this year were taking steps to meet their statutory obligation to provide education for pupils who have no school place. Specific concerns were raised in some about the amount of education provided. For example, two LEAs were providing amounts of home tuition that were clearly insufficient. There were some signs of improvement, for example in tracking the whereabouts of pupils excluded from school. No authority this year was so short of information as to be in no position to discharge its duty of care. Several authorities were working energetically to improve their provision, notably Lambeth, which had commissioned, and rapidly implemented the findings of, an external review. As a result, all pupils for whom it was appropriate were following accredited courses.

401. Problems remained. Virtually all authorities maintained at least one pupil referral unit; the number ranged between one and 11. Where these had been inspected by OFSTED, provision was usually satisfactory. However, the pupil referral unit was one element in what was often an uncertain mixture of various types of provision, instituted ad hoc to deal with particular exigencies, including home and hospital tuition, off-site centres, central support units, social services children resource centres and alternative curricular provision in liaison with further education or the private sector. Achieving coherence and appropriate referral was, in this context, often far from easy. A further difficulty derived from the absence of provision for pupils with EBD or uncertainty about its place in the overall continuum of support, and indeed about the accurate designation of pupils.

402. The concerns expressed in previous reports on looked-after children remain. Effective provision for these children depends crucially on liaison between education and social services. That is still rare, but awareness of the need for it is growing; Knowsley, for example, had appointed teachers jointly funded by education and social services to co-ordinate the education and care of these children.

Support for the attainment of ethnic minority pupils

403. Provision to raise the attainment of ethnic minority pupils received particular attention in seven LEAs, all of whom had either a very large overall proportion of such pupils or large concentrations in particular areas, like Calderdale. In both Hackney and Calderdale, revisits noted modest improvements, following earlier very critical reports. Two LEAs, Brent and Newham, provided generally effective support, and Southwark demonstrated good practice in monitoring the attainment of ethnic minority pupils and in the provision of mentors for underattaining black pupils. In Tower Hamlets, the picture was more mixed, with some schools well supported, particularly those with effective literacy policies and co-ordinators, but also a great deal of variability in practice, insufficient monitoring and a lack of precision in the match of support to need. In Leicester City, as in other LEAs, a major structural review was in process, with funding devolved to schools. The specific support provided was generally good. On the other hand, the LEA's ethnic monitoring was weak and the recording of instances of racial harassment in schools insufficiently meticulous.

Management and support for management

404. Obviously enough, a key task of all LEAs is the allocation of resources to priorities. This process is usually carried out openly, with adequate consultation with schools. The budget information provided to schools is generally timely, accurate and sufficient to enable them to plan their use of resources. Where this is not the case, the effect on relationships between the LEA and schools and on the possibility of improvement is very serious. In Calderdale, for example, continued secrecy over aspects of budget setting undermines much work of quality elsewhere. In Lambeth, the failure of the council to establish consistent, efficient and effective financial systems which schools can trust does nothing to support the LEA's energetic attempts to raise standards. In Islington, a lack of financial discipline across the council was found to have undermined schools' capacity to plan.

405. LEAs also have a duty to monitor the use schools make of their budgets. Generally, this duty is effectively performed, even in weaker LEAs. Only in Lambeth were a significant number of schools experiencing budget deficits or excessive surpluses that resulted, at least in part, from the poor quality of information provided by the LEA.

406. LEAs are generally successful in maintaining or securing, at reasonable cost, the effective provision of financial, legal and personnel advice, payroll administration and the organisation of school meals and transport. Very few instances of inadequate management services were reported. In about half the LEAs inspected the extent and quality of these services were important factors in creating and maintaining good relations between the LEA and the schools. As in other aspects of LEA work, where there is a well-defined job to do, it is usually well done. Personnel services contribute most directly to school improvement through support for staff appointments and for competency proceedings. Usually, the support they receive is good, and schools are satisfied with it.

407. The most common exceptions to this pattern of sound provision are information and communications technology, which is of variable quality, and the maintenance of buildings and grounds, which is a regular cause of dissatisfaction in schools. Rotherham LEA received an inspection that focused wholly on the maintenance of school buildings. Underfunding, inefficient use of resources and inadequate intervention all contributed to the poor condition of school buildings.

Section 10 inspections

The Section 10 inspections of primary, secondary and special schools were carried out by registered inspectors. There were 4,520 such inspections: 3,508 of primary or nursery schools, 704 of secondary schools, 239 of special schools and 69 of pupil referral units.

HMI inspections

During the year HMI made some 4,550 visits to schools. These included more than 1,200 monitoring inspections of schools in special measures and about 400 inspections of schools with serious weaknesses. There were over 450 inspection visits to independent schools. They also included inspection of the implementation of the National Literacy Strategy in 350 primary schools.

The sample of schools inspected by HMI included all types, but the sample was not chosen to be representative of the different types of school in England.

HMI inspected LEA support for school improvement in 29 LEAs, under Section 38 of the Education Act 1997. Two of these were revisits.

HMI inspected a range of initial teacher training, including 82 subjects offered by 48 secondary providers, and English or mathematics and one specialist subject by 29 primary providers.

HMI also inspected a range of youth work and adult education provision: full inspections of adult education in three LEAs; full inspections of youth work in nine LEAs; evaluation of family learning in 28 local authorities and separate inspections to review access to aid participation in adult learning by disadvantaged groups in 13 LEAs.

Annex 2
Interpreting inspection evidence

Evidence from Section 10 inspections for 1998/99 has been compiled from a number of distinct sources:

- judgements on individual lessons – graded on a seven-point scale;

- judgements on features of the school such as the progress made by pupils – also graded on a seven-point scale;

- written evidence supporting these judgements;

- published reports;

- information on the schools provided by the headteacher.

All of these sources of evidence were used to produce this report. The quantitative judgements have been based on grades provided by inspectors which have been checked against supporting textual information. A summary of these grades is contained in the statistical annex.

Standards achieved by pupils

Inspectors make two separate judgements of standards achieved by pupils:

- attainment – how well pupils are achieving in relation to national standards or expectations;

- progress – the gains pupils make in knowledge, skills and understanding.

When judging attainment, inspectors judge whether the proportion of pupils achieving the national expectation is below, broadly in line with or above that which is found nationally. This comparison with norms is a key part of the measurement of standards and provides important information for the school being inspected. However, because the inspection grades for attainment are made in comparison to a national norm, when aggregated nationally they can only produce a distribution about that norm. They cannot produce a measure of the national level of attainment of pupils. In this report, evidence from national tests and examinations is used to provide a quantitative measure of the national level of pupils' attainment. Inspection evidence is used to identify key strengths and weaknesses in pupils' attainment and the school factors contributing to high and low attainment.

While attainment provides an important component of evidence on the achievement of pupils, it provides only a partial picture of the effectiveness of the school. Able pupils who are achieving levels which are above the average could still be underachieving if they do not make the progress that they should. Conversely, pupils of low ability might be doing well if they are making good gains, even though their attainment is below the average for pupils of a similar age. Pupils with moderate or severe learning difficulties in special schools will invariably be attaining at well below the national level, but in effective schools they will make good progress. Progress is, therefore, a valuable indicator of the impact and effectiveness of the school.

Inspectors judge the progress made in individual lessons. They also make overall judgements for each National Curriculum subject and for each key stage and for the schools as a whole. These judgements are based on a range of evidence – lesson observations, written work, pupil interviews and test and examination results – and, therefore, provide a rounded view of achievement. These overall judgements have mainly been used to provide the evidence for the educational standards achieved by pupils in individual subjects and in the school as a whole. Lesson grades have been used occasionally when finer detail is required, for example of variations across years within a key stage.

Interpreting grades

Inspectors use a seven-point scale when grading progress and other features of schools. Grades 1–3 indicate very good or good progress where most pupils achieve better than expected. Grade 4 indicates satisfactory progress where most pupils achieve reasonably well. Grades 5–7 are used where progress is unsatisfactory or poor and most pupils underachieve. For other features of the school, grades 1–3 generally indicate a strength that promotes high standards, grade 4 indicates neither a strength nor a weakness, leading to sound standards. Grades 5–7 indicate a weakness which promotes low standards. In the charts in this report, grades 1–3 are grouped and displayed as good/very good, and grades 5–7 are grouped and displayed as unsatisfactory/poor.

The quality of teaching

Direct observation in lessons provides the clearest view of the quality of teaching. Inspectors use a seven-point scale to judge the quality of teaching. Grades 1–3 indicate very good or good teaching that promotes high standards. Grade 4 is satisfactory teaching that promotes sound standards. Grades 5–7 are unsatisfactory or poor teaching that promote low standards. In this report lesson grades have generally been used to provide quantitative overviews of the quality of teaching.

Annex 3
A balanced sample of schools

HMCI's *Annual Report* gives an evaluation of quality and standards in English schools during the 1998/99 academic year. The main evidence base for this evaluation is inspections carried out under Section 10 of the School Inspections Act 1996.

The schools inspected during the 1998/99 academic year were not, overall, representative of English schools as a whole. This year was the first year of the second cycle of school inspections for primary and special schools, and the second year of the second cycle for secondary schools. In planning the programme for this cycle HMCI ensured that schools to be inspected during each year include:

- a balanced sample, including all relevant types and displaying the full range of performance as judged in previous inspections;

- within the balanced sample, schools which are likely to be models of good practice;

- schools whose performance was weak at the time of the previous inspection or whose performance has declined significantly. These schools are inspected earlier than they would otherwise be.

While this earlier inspection of weak schools means that there was a disproportionate number of these schools inspected in 1998/99, the balanced sample of schools has ensured sufficient evidence to enable a full and representative picture of English schools to be obtained from inspection evidence.

To enable a representative picture to be obtained it has been necessary, in the evaluation of the inspection evidence, to weight data about different types of schools in proportion to their numbers in the total school population. At the same time, the higher rate of inspection of weak schools allows a sharper focus both on quality and standards in the weakest schools and on the weaknesses in the schools that need to be remedied in order to raise standards.

Annex 4: Statistical summary
Progress in primary schools 1998/99
(percentage of schools)

Art

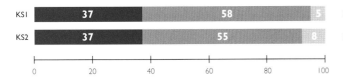

Design and technology

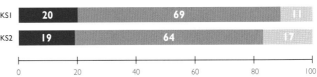

English

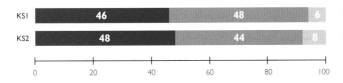

Geography

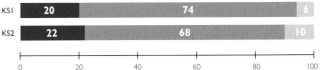

History

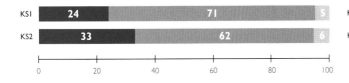

Information technology

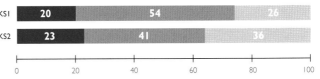

Mathematics

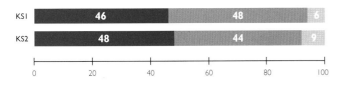

Music

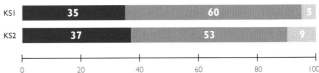

Physical education

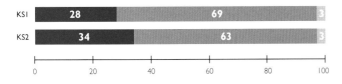

Religious education

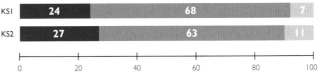

Science

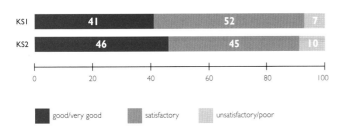

■ good/very good   ■ satisfactory   ▨ unsatisfactory/poor   Figures have been rounded and may not add up to 100 per cent

Annex 4: Statistical summary
Teaching in primary schools 1998/99
(percentage of schools)

Art

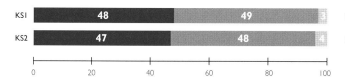

	good/very good	satisfactory	unsatisfactory/poor
KS1	48	49	3
KS2	47	48	4

Design and technology

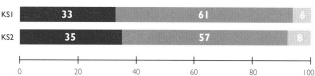

	good/very good	satisfactory	unsatisfactory/poor
KS1	33	61	6
KS2	35	57	8

English

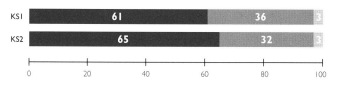

	good/very good	satisfactory	unsatisfactory/poor
KS1	61	36	3
KS2	65	32	3

Geography

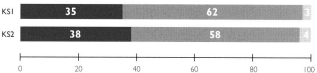

	good/very good	satisfactory	unsatisfactory/poor
KS1	35	62	3
KS2	38	58	4

History

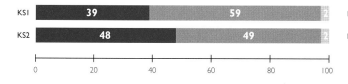

	good/very good	satisfactory	unsatisfactory/poor
KS1	39	59	2
KS2	48	49	2

Information technology

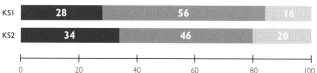

	good/very good	satisfactory	unsatisfactory/poor
KS1	28	56	16
KS2	34	46	20

Mathematics

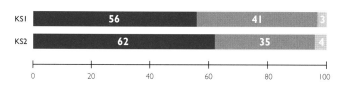

	good/very good	satisfactory	unsatisfactory/poor
KS1	56	41	3
KS2	62	35	4

Music

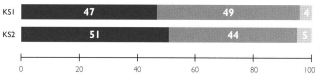

	good/very good	satisfactory	unsatisfactory/poor
KS1	47	49	4
KS2	51	44	5

Physical education

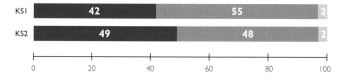

	good/very good	satisfactory	unsatisfactory/poor
KS1	42	55	2
KS2	49	48	2

Religious education

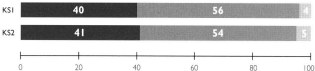

	good/very good	satisfactory	unsatisfactory/poor
KS1	40	56	4
KS2	41	54	5

Science

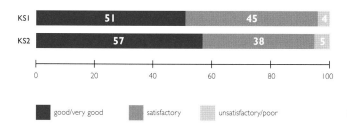

	good/very good	satisfactory	unsatisfactory/poor
KS1	51	45	4
KS2	57	38	5

good/very good   satisfactory   unsatisfactory/poor   Figures have been rounded and may not add up to 100 per cent

Annex 4: Statistical summary
Progress in secondary schools 1998/99
(percentage of schools)

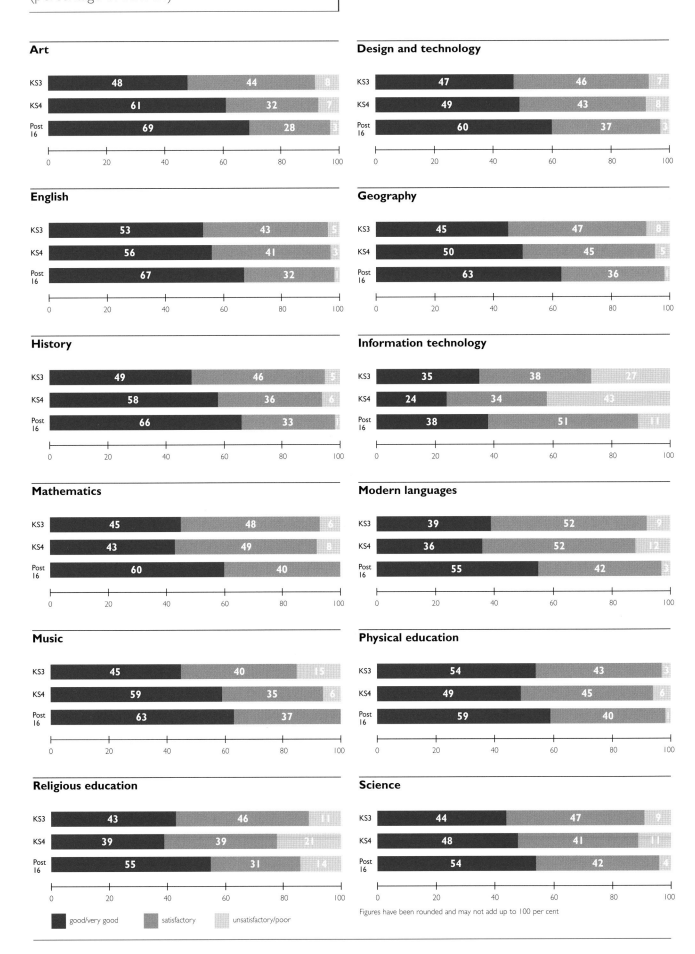

Art

KS3	48	44	8
KS4	61	32	7
Post 16	69	28	3

0   20   40   60   80   100

English

KS3	53	43	5
KS4	56	41	3
Post 16	67	32	1

0   20   40   60   80   100

History

KS3	49	46	5
KS4	58	36	6
Post 16	66	33	1

0   20   40   60   80   100

Mathematics

KS3	45	48	6
KS4	43	49	8
Post 16	60	40	

0   20   40   60   80   100

Music

KS3	45	40	15
KS4	59	35	6
Post 16	63	37	

0   20   40   60   80   100

Religious education

KS3	43	46	11
KS4	39	39	21
Post 16	55	31	14

0   20   40   60   80   100

Design and technology

KS3	47	46	7
KS4	49	43	8
Post 16	60	37	3

0   20   40   60   80   100

Geography

KS3	45	47	8
KS4	50	45	5
Post 16	63	36	1

0   20   40   60   80   100

Information technology

KS3	35	38	27
KS4	24	34	43
Post 16	38	51	11

0   20   40   60   80   100

Modern languages

KS3	39	52	9
KS4	36	52	12
Post 16	55	42	3

0   20   40   60   80   100

Physical education

KS3	54	43	3
KS4	49	45	6
Post 16	59	40	

0   20   40   60   80   100

Science

KS3	44	47	9
KS4	48	41	11
Post 16	54	42	4

0   20   40   60   80   100

Figures have been rounded and may not add up to 100 per cent

■ good/very good   ▨ satisfactory   ▦ unsatisfactory/poor

Annex 4: Statistical summary
Teaching in secondary schools 1998/99
(percentage of schools)

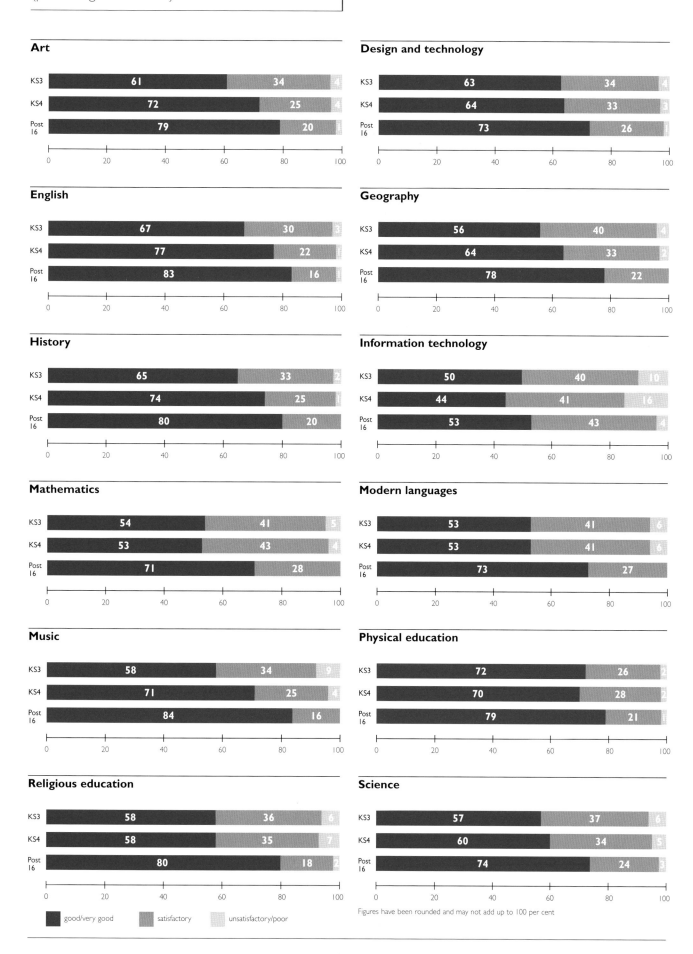

Art

KS3	61	34	4
KS4	72	25	4
Post 16	79	20	1

English

KS3	67	30	3
KS4	77	22	1
Post 16	83	16	1

History

KS3	65	33	2
KS4	74	25	1
Post 16	80	20	

Mathematics

KS3	54	41	5
KS4	53	43	4
Post 16	71	28	1

Music

KS3	58	34	9
KS4	71	25	4
Post 16	84	16	

Religious education

KS3	58	36	6
KS4	58	35	7
Post 16	80	18	2

Design and technology

KS3	63	34	4
KS4	64	33	3
Post 16	73	26	1

Geography

KS3	56	40	4
KS4	64	33	2
Post 16	78	22	

Information technology

KS3	50	40	10
KS4	44	41	16
Post 16	53	43	4

Modern languages

KS3	53	41	6
KS4	53	41	6
Post 16	73	27	

Physical education

KS3	72	26	2
KS4	70	28	2
Post 16	79	21	

Science

KS3	57	37	6
KS4	60	34	5
Post 16	74	24	3

■ good/very good   ■ satisfactory   ☐ unsatisfactory/poor

Figures have been rounded and may not add up to 100 per cent

Annex 4: Statistical summary inspection grades for primary schools - 1998/99

Aspects of the School		Inspection grade*	Percentage of Schools		
			Good/very good	Satisfactory	Unsatisfactory/poor
Educational Standards Achieved					
4.1.2	Progress	Under Five	59	38	3
		Key Stage 1	41	53	6
		Key Stage 2	44	48	8
		School	46	47	7
4.1.3	Progress of pupils with Special Educational Needs	Under Five	61	37	2
		Key Stage 1	59	37	4
		Key Stage 2	58	37	5
		School	60	36	4
4.2.1	Attitude		84	15	1
4.2.2	Behaviour		83	15	2
4.2.3	Relationships		90	10	1
4.2.4	Personal development		66	30	3
4.3	Attendance		47	42	11
Quality of Education					
	Teaching				
5.1	Teaching	Under Five	70	27	3
		Key Stage 1	56	40	4
		Key Stage 2	60	35	5
		School	62	34	4
5.1.1	Teachers' knowledge and understanding	Under Five	70	24	6
		Key Stage 1	55	42	3
		Key Stage 2	58	39	4
5.1.2	Teachers' expectations	Under Five	69	25	6
		Key Stage 1	49	40	11
		Key Stage 2	52	35	13
5.1.3	Teachers' planning	Under Five	62	30	8
		Key Stage 1	51	39	9
		Key Stage 2	50	39	10
5.1.4	Methods and organisation	Under Five	67	26	8
		Key Stage 1	59	36	4
		Key Stage 2	62	34	4
5.1.5	Management of pupils	Under Five	84	14	2
		Key Stage 1	72	23	5
		Key Stage 2	75	21	5
5.1.6	Use of time and resources	Under Five	66	29	5
		Key Stage 1	54	41	6
		Key Stage 2	56	38	6
5.1.7	Quality and use of day-to-day assessment	Under Five	61	30	8
		Key Stage 1	39	43	18
		Key Stage 2	36	42	22

* As explained in Annex 2, Good/very good includes grades 1–3. Satisfactory is grade 4, and Unsatisfactory/poor includes grades 5–7.

Figures have been rounded and may not add up to 100 per cent

Aspects of the School		Percentage of Schools		
	Inspection grade*	Good/very good	Satisfactory	Unsatisfactory/poor
5.1.8 Use of homework	Under Five	41	58	1
	Key Stage 1	26	68	7
	Key Stage 2	31	55	14
Curriculum				
5.2 The curriculum	Under Five	56	36	8
	Key Stage 1	41	51	8
	Key Stage 2	38	52	10
	School	40	51	9
5.2.1 Breadth, balance, relevance of the whole curriculum	Under Five	55	36	9
	Key Stage 1	38	53	8
	Key Stage 2	37	53	10
5.2.2 Equality of access and opportunity	Under Five	55	41	3
	Key Stage 1	46	48	5
	Key Stage 2	44	50	7
5.2.3 Provision for pupils with SEN	Under Five	69	29	2
	Key Stage 1	68	27	4
	Key Stage 2	65	30	5
5.2.4 Planning for progression and continuity	Under Five	53	36	11
	Key Stage 1	38	42	20
	Key Stage 2	36	41	23
5.2.5 Provision for extra-curricular activities, including sport		55	36	9
Assessment				
5.X Assessment	Under Five	54	35	11
	Key Stage 1	34	39	27
	Key Stage 2	31	38	31
	School	33	39	28
5.2.7 Procedures for assessing pupils' attainment	Under Five	62	33	5
	Key Stage 1	46	40	15
	Key Stage 2	43	40	16
5.2.8 Use of assessment to inform curriculum planning	Under Five	51	35	14
	Key Stage 1	32	36	32
	Key Stage 2	30	34	37
Spiritual, Moral, Social, and Cultural Development				
5.3 Provision for pupils' SMSC development		74	24	2
5.3.1 Pupils' spiritual development		50	43	7
5.3.2 Pupils' moral development		86	13	1
5.3.3 Pupils' social development		83	15	1
5.3.4 Pupils' cultural development		53	42	5
Support, Guidance and Pupils' Welfare				
5.4 Support, guidance and pupils' welfare		69	28	3
5.4.1 Procedures for monitoring progress and personal development		54	38	8
5.4.2 Procedures for monitoring and promoting discipline and good behaviour		80	16	3

* As explained in Annex 2, Good/very good includes grades 1–3, Satisfactory is grade 4, and Unsatisfactory/poor includes grades 5–7.

Figures have been rounded and may not add up to 100 per cent

	Aspects of the School		Percentage of Schools		
		Inspection grade*	Good/very good	Satisfactory	Unsatisfactory/poor
5.4.3	Procedures for monitoring and promoting good attendance		64	29	7
5.4.4	Procedures for child protection and promoting pupils' well being, health and safety		59	33	8
	Partnership with Parents and the Community				
5.5	Partnership with parents and the community		68	30	2
5.5.1	Quality of information for parents		61	33	5
5.5.2	Parental involvement in children's learning		62	31	6
5.5.3	Enrichment through links with community		72	26	2
Management and Efficiency					
	Leadership and Management				
6.1	Leadership and management		58	32	10
6.1.1	Leadership: clear educational direction for the school		64	25	11
6.1.2	Support and monitoring of teaching and curriculum development		41	32	27
6.1.3	Implementation of the school's aims, values and policies		63	30	7
6.1.4	Development planning, monitoring and evaluation		46	34	20
6.1.5	The school's ethos		77	19	3
	Staffing, Accommodation and Learning Resources				
6.2	Staffing, accommodation and learning resources		42	56	2
6.2.1	Match of number, qualification and experience of teachers to the demands of the curriculum		41	57	2
6.2.2	Match of number, qualification and experience of support staff to the demands of the curriculum		58	37	5
6.2.3	Arrangements for professional development of all staff		52	38	10
6.2.4	Adequacy of accommodation for effective delivery of the curriculum		45	45	9
6.2.5	Adequacy of resources (including books/materials/equipment) for effective delivery of the curriculum		32	63	5
	Efficiency of the School				
6.3	Efficiency		63	33	4
6.3.1	Financial planning		60	30	10
6.3.2	Use of teaching and support staff		59	36	6
6.3.3	Use of learning resources and accommodation		57	40	3
6.3.4	Efficiency of financial control and school administration		78	20	2
6.4	Value for money		50	43	8

* As explained in Annex 2, Good/very good includes grades 1–3, Satisfactory is grade 4, and Unsatisfactory/poor includes grades 5–7.

Figures have been rounded and may not add up to 100 per cent

Annex 4: Statistical summary Inspection grades for secondary schools - 1998/99

Aspects of the School		Percentage of Schools			
		Inspection grade*	Good/very good	Satisfactory	Unsatisfactory/poor
Educational Standards Achieved					
4.1.2	Progress	Key Stage 3	48	47	5
		Key Stage 4	50	44	6
		Post-16	62	37	1
		School	52	43	5
4.1.3	Progress of pupils with SEN	Key Stage 3	52	43	5
		Key Stage 4	49	46	5
		Post-16	55	44	1
		School	52	44	4
4.2.1	Attitude		79	18	3
4.2.2	Behaviour		74	21	5
4.2.3	Relationships		88	11	1
4.2.4	Personal development		66	29	5
4.3	Attendance		40	35	25
Quality of Education					
	Teaching				
5.1	Teaching	Key Stage 3	67	29	5
		Key Stage 4	71	26	3
		Post-16	89	11	0
		School	71	26	3
5.1.1	Teachers' knowledge and understanding	Key Stage 3	84	16	1
		Key Stage 4	88	11	1
		Post-16	92	8	0
5.1.2	Teachers' expectations	Key Stage 3	52	40	8
		Key Stage 4	61	33	7
		Post-16	80	19	1
5.1.3	Teachers' planning	Key Stage 3	61	34	5
		Key Stage 4	67	30	4
		Post-16	78	21	1
5.1.4	Methods and organisation	Key Stage 3	52	44	5
		Key Stage 4	55	41	4
		Post-16	71	29	0
5.1.5	Management of pupils	Key Stage 3	79	17	4
		Key Stage 4	82	15	4
		Post-16	92	8	0
5.1.6	Use of time and resources	Key Stage 3	59	38	3
		Key Stage 4	61	36	2
		Post-16	77	22	1
5.1.7	Quality and use of day-to-day assessment	Key Stage 3	32	51	17
		Key Stage 4	40	48	11
		Post-16	67	31	2

* As explained in Annex 2, Good/very good includes grades 1–3, Satisfactory is grade 4, and Unsatisfactory/poor includes grades 5–7.

Figures have been rounded and may not add up to 100 per cent

Aspects of the School		Percentage of Schools			
		Inspection grade*	*Good/very good*	*Satisfactory*	*Unsatisfactory/poor*
5.1.8	Use of homework	Key Stage 3	45	47	8
		Key Stage 4	51	42	7
		Post-16	70	30	1
	Curriculum				
5.2	The curriculum	Key Stage 3	39	54	7
		Key Stage 4	34	51	15
		Post-16	59	37	4
		School	38	54	8
5.2.1	Breadth, balance, relevance of the whole curriculum	Key Stage 3	39	52	9
		Key Stage 4	29	49	22
		Post-16	59	30	11
5.2.2	Equality of access and opportunity	Key Stage 3	51	42	7
		Key Stage 4	45	42	13
		Post-16	58	39	3
5.2.3	Provision for pupils with SEN	Key Stage 3	52	36	11
		Key Stage 4	50	39	11
		Post-16	52	44	4
5.2.4	Planning for progression and continuity	Key Stage 3	37	50	13
		Key Stage 4	44	48	8
		Post-16	60	38	2
5.2.5	Provision for extra-curricular activities, including sport		83	15	2
5.2.6	Careers education and guidance		71	26	3
	Assessment				
5.X	Assessment	Key Stage 3	27	47	26
		Key Stage 4	34	51	15
		Post-16	50	45	5
		School	31	50	19
5.2.7	Procedures for assessing pupils' attainment	Key Stage 3	41	45	14
		Key Stage 4	49	46	5
		Post-16	64	35	1
5.2.8	Use of assessment to inform curriculum planning	Key Stage 3	23	43	33
		Key Stage 4	29	48	23
		Post-16	47	48	6
	Spiritual, Moral, Social, and Cultural Development				
5.3	Provision for pupils' SMSC development		66	32	3
5.3.1	Pupils' spiritual development		30	38	32
5.3.2	Pupils' moral development		86	13	1
5.3.3	Pupils' social development		87	12	1
5.3.4	Pupils' cultural development		55	40	6
	Support, Guidance and Pupils' Welfare				
5.4	Support, guidance and pupils' welfare		74	23	3
5.4.1	Procedures for monitoring progress and personal development		64	28	8
5.4.2	Procedures for monitoring and promoting discipline and good behaviour		81	15	4

* As explained in Annex 2, Good/very good includes grades 1–3.
Satisfactory is grade 4, and Unsatisfactory/poor includes grades 5–7.

Figures have been rounded and may not add up to 100 per cent

Aspects of the School		Percentage of Schools		
	Inspection grade*	Good/very good	Satisfactory	Unsatisfactory/poor
5.4.3	Procedures for monitoring and promoting good attendance	71	22	7
5.4.4	Procedures for child protection and promoting pupils' well-being, health and safety	59	31	11
Partnership with Parents and the Community				
5.5	Partnership with parents and the community	66	31	3
5.5.1	Quality of information for parents	55	37	7
5.5.2	Parental involvement in children's learning	49	41	11
5.5.3	Enrichment through links with community	81	17	1
Management and Efficiency				
Leadership and Management				
6.1	Leadership and management	62	29	9
6.1.1	Leadership: clear educational direction for the school	73	19	8
6.1.2	Support and monitoring of teaching and curriculum development	37	35	28
6.1.3	Implementation of the school's aims, values and policies	64	26	10
6.1.4	Development planning, monitoring and evaluation	42	34	24
6.1.5	The school's ethos	80	16	5
Staffing, Accommodation and Learning Resources				
6.2	Staffing, accommodation and learning resources	31	57	12
6.2.1	Match of number, qualification and experience of teachers to the demands of the curriculum	58	37	5
6.2.2	Match of number, qualification and experience of support staff to the demands of the curriculum	44	43	14
6.2.3	Arrangements for professional development of all staff	47	35	18
6.2.4	Adequacy of accommodation for effective delivery of the curriculum	25	53	22
6.2.5	Adequacy of resources (including books/materials/ equipment) for effective delivery of the curriculum	22	60	19
Efficiency of the School				
6.3	Efficiency	65	29	6
6.3.1	Financial planning	62	26	11
6.3.2	se of teaching and support staff	57	33	10
6.3.3	Use of learning resources and accommodation	60	37	3
6.3.4	Efficiency of financial control and school administration	85	13	2
6.4	Value for money	57	35	8

* As explained in Annex 2, Good/very good includes grades 1–3,
Satisfactory is grade 4, and Unsatisfactory/poor includes grades 5–7.

Figures have been rounded and may not add up to 100 per cent

Annex 5
OFSTED publications 1998/99

PRICED PUBLICATIONS

The Annual Report of Her Majesty's Chief Inspectors of Schools 1997/98	0-11-254799-8	£11.90
Modular GCE AS and A-level examinations 1996–1998	0-11-350107-2	£6.95
Primary Education 1994–1998 – A review of Primary Schools in England	0-11-350106 4	£22.95
Special Education 1994–1998 – A review of Special Schools, Secure Units & Pupil Referral Units in England	0-11-350108-0	£14.95
Modular GCE AS and A-level Examinations	0-11-350107 2	£6.95
Inspecting Schools – Handbook for Inspecting Primary & Nursery Schools	0-11-350109 9	£15
Inspecting Schools – Handbook for Inspecting Secondary Schools	0-11-350110 2	£15
Inspecting Schools – Handbook for Inspecting Special Schools and Pupil Referral Units	0-11-350111 0	£15

UNPRICED PUBLICATIONS

Corporate Plan 1997–98 to 1999–2000	HMI 116
Inspecting Schools: The Framework	HMI 214
LEA Support for School Improvement – A Framework for the Inspection of LEAs (revised July 1999)	HMI 121
Lessons Learned from Special Measures	HMI 176
MORI Report – Survey of School Inspection	HMI 165
MORI: The Impact of School Inspections Children's Views	HMI 175
Primary Follow-Up Survey of the Training of Trainee Teachers to Teach Number and Reading	HMI 193
Principles into Practice: Effective Education for Pupils with Emotional and Behavioural Difficulties	HMI 177
Pupils with Specific Learning Difficulties in Mainstream Schools	HMI 208
Quality of Education: Developments Since 1997–99 in the Private, Voluntary & Independent Sector	HMI 178
Raising Attainment of Minority Ethnic Pupils – Schools & LEA Responses	HMI 170
Secondary Initial Teacher Training Secondary Subjects Inspections 96-98 Overview Report	HMI 171
SEN Code of Practice: Three Years On	HMI 211
Standards in the Secondary Curriculum 1997–98 (12 leaflets)	HMI 162

OFSTED COMPLAINTS ADJUDICATOR

Annual Report 1999

The role and functions of the OFSTED Complaints Adjudicator

Priced publications are available from:
The Stationery Office
Publications Centre
PO box 276
London SW8 5DT

or from any Stationery Office bookshop and most other booksellers. The Stationery Office produces a regular catalogue of its education publications including OFSTED titles.

Telephone 0870 600 5522. Fax 0870 600 5533.

Unpriced OFSTED publications are available from:
OFSTED Publications Centre
PO Box 6927
London E3 3NZ

Telephone 020 7510 0180

Reports on individual state-funded schools are available from the schools themselves or on the Internet.
The OFSTED website is at:
http://www.ofsted.gov.uk

The website also carries OFSTED reports on nurseries and playgroups providing funded education for four-year-olds, teacher training institutions, local education authorities, inspection guidance and other publications.

Printed in the UK for
The Stationery Office Limited
on behalf of the Controller of
Her Majesty's Stationery Office
Dd 5067387
2/00
39462
Job No 000052

The Mental Health Act Commission

Ninth
Biennial Report
1999–2001

*Laid before Parliament by the
Secretary of State for Health
pursuant to Section 121 (10)
of the Mental Health Act 1983*

London: The Stationery Office

First Published 2001

ISBN 0 11 322467 2

Mental Health Act Commission,
Maid Marian House,
56 Hounds Gate,
Nottingham,
NG1 6BG

Tel: 0115 943 7100

Email: chief.executive@ms.mhac.trent.nhs.uk

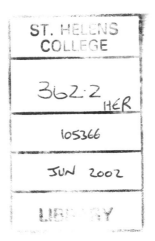
Printed in the United Kingdom for the Stationery Office
TJ5556 C22 11/01 9385 15732

Acknowledgements

The Commission wishes to thank the staff of the Health Authorities, Social Services Departments, NHS Trusts, Private Providers and High Security Hospitals throughout England and Wales who have been so willing to co-operate with Commissioners during their visits and whose Board Members and staff have taken action on Commission Visit Reports in order to improve their service to detained patients. We have greatly appreciated their assistance and courtesy.

This report is based on the knowledge and experience of Commissioners, taken from their visit reports, from contributions from each Commission visiting team and from many individual Commissioners. These major inputs are gratefully acknowledged.

The main writer of this report was the Commission's Communications Manager, Mat Kinton, guided by an editorial board consisting of Margaret Clayton (Commission Chairman), Paul Hampshire (Chief Executive) Dr Geoff Roberts (Medical Director, Warrington Community NHS Trust and Commission Member), and Christopher Heginbotham (Chief Executive, Eastern Region Specialised Commissioning Group) who acted as an independent adviser. We thank Mr Kinton, in particular, for his skill in bringing together the many strands of the Commission's work so effectively.

Farewells

The Commission extends its warmest thanks to the following key members of staff and/or the Board who have already left the Commission or will be leaving this year. All have made considerable contributions to our work and to this report.

William Bingley, who became the Commission's Chief Executive in 1991, left at the end of January 2000 to take up an academic appointment. He is now Professor of Mental Health Law at the University of Central Lancashire.

Jeff Cohen, who was employed by the Commission from 1996, lately as Head of the Policy Unit (and was a Commission member prior to that employment), left at the end of January 2001 to set up his own mental health consultancy service.

Professor Richard Williams, Professor of Mental Health Strategy at the Welsh Institute of Health and Social care in the University of Glamorgan and a Consultant Child and Adolescent Psychiatrist in the Gwent Healthcare NHS Trust, who became Vice-Chairman of the Board in 1996, leaves at the end of his second term of appointment in September 2001.

Gordon Lakes CB MC, ex-Deputy Director-General of the Prison Service, who has been a Commissioner since 1991, led the Visiting Team at Ashworth for three years, and was Acting Chairman from August 1998 to November 1999, will also be leaving at the end of his permitted terms of appointment at the end of December 2001.

Contents

Schedule of Recommendations from this Report

Appendices

Chairman's Foreword

The two years covered by this report have seen significant advances in the framework within which mental health services are provided and a very positive commitment by both the Department of Health and the National Assembly for Wales to the improvement of these services. Nevertheless, the issues raised by my predecessor in his foreword to the Eighth Biennial Report remain substantially unchanged. As this report shows, there are still huge variations in the quality of provision made for detained patients. A high proportion of these patients would not need to be detained if satisfactory health and social care were available for them in the community. Many patients who are detained do not receive care and treatment in accordance with the guidance given in the Code of Practice, and a number are treated unlawfully through inattention to the requirements of the Act. There is often scant regard to the principle of reciprocity in compulsion.

The Commission warmly welcomes the Government's proposals to reform mental health legislation and to strengthen the safeguards available to those who are compelled to accept care and treatment for mental disorder. Neither increased funding nor reforming legislation will, however, achieve the improvements required or tackle inequalities in provision. Both need to be underpinned by a robust infrastructure which ensures that diverse, skilled and dedicated people are available in sufficient numbers to provide the close relational safety and security essential to a therapeutic approach to any kind of mental disorder.

Similarly, providing a better legislative framework and more staff will not ensure improvements unless skilled managers are able to help staff translate policy into practice in relation to each individual patient. The right of every individual patient to be treated as an individual without discrimination, stigma or stereotype must be paramount.

The Department of Health and National Assembly for Wales have recognised these needs in the raft of plans to enhance the recruitment and training of the wide range of professionals involved in mental health and social care, and in the introduction of new regulatory bodies. The main message in this report is that self-regulation and strong systems within mental health care are the key to unlock the potential of all of these initiatives, particularly in relation to detained patients. This is true as much for the existing Act as for future legislation. The comments and recommendations made in this report therefore highlight the Commission's intention to focus on these matters in the current biennial period.

The comments and recommendations of this report are based on the knowledge and experience gained from the two-year rolling programme of visits by Commissioners to all NHS Trusts and Registered Mental Nursing Homes that detain patients under the Act. Our development plans recognise the key importance of these visits and we have no intention of reducing them as a result of our stronger focus on effective systems. I take this opportunity to pay tribute to the skills of the Commissioners and Secretariat who give unstintingly of their time and energy in examining whether the interests and rights of patients are being properly observed.

The development of the detailed legislation necessary to give effect to the broad principles in the White Paper on reforming the Act will provide a more appropriate opportunity than a Biennial Report to pursue issues of concern about how patients are likely to be affected by the proposed changes. The White Paper is not therefore discussed in this report. Preparation of the report has, however, highlighted two points which must be emphasised here. The first is that the drafting and implementation of the new legislation will need a high degree of consultation with practitioners and careful phasing if the gaps between policy and practice that are identified in the report are to be closed. The second is that, although the Commission accepts that national regulatory bodies and local advocacy services may provide an adequate substitute for our current visiting functions, it is essential that Mental Health Act Commissioners continue to visit detained patients until satisfactory alternative arrangements are in place and their knowledge and experience should be utilised in the new arrangements.

Finally, although I am responsible, on behalf of the Commission, for the submission of this report to the Secretary of State, I did not become Chairman until December 1999. Mr Gordon Lakes CB MC was therefore Acting Chairman for the first eight months covered by this report. This was a particularly difficult role because of the significant changes which were taking place both inside and outside the Commission. I cannot speak too highly of the skill and dedication with which Mr Lakes fulfilled the role, nor of the generosity with which he has offered me the benefit of his experience and knowledge in succeeding him. In particular, he has reinforced my own commitment and that of all Commissioners to our Mission Statement *"Safeguarding the interests of all people detained under the Mental Health Act"*. This is what reviewing the implementation of the Act is all about.

M.A.Clayton

Miss M A Clayton

Chairman

Rhagarweiniad y Cadeirydd

Mae'r ddwy flynedd a gwmpesir gan yr Adroddiad hwn wedi gweld cynnydd arwyddocaol yn y fframwaith y darperir gwasanaethau iechyd meddwl o'i fewn ac ymrwymiad cadarnhaol dros ben gan yr Adran Iechyd a Chynulliad Cenedlaethol Cymru fel ei gilydd tuag at welliant yn y gwasanaethau hyn. Er hyn, mae'r materion a godwyd gan fy rhagflaenydd yn ei ragarweiniad i'r Wythfed Adroddiad Dwyflynyddol yn parhau i fod heb eu newid yn sylweddol. Fel y mae'r Adroddiad hwn yn dangos, y mae amrywiadau anferthol yn ansawdd y ddarpariaeth a wneir ar gyfer cleifion dan orchymyn. Ni fyddai cydran uchel o'r cleifion hyn angen eu rhoi dan orchymyn pe byddai gofal iechyd a chymdeithasol boddhaol ar gael ar eu cyfer yn y gymuned. Nid yw llawer o'r cleifion sydd dan orchymyn yn derbyn gofal a thriniaeth yn unol â'r cyfarwyddyd a roddir yn y Côd Ymarfer, ac fe gaiff llawer ohonynt eu trin yn anghyfreithlon drwy ddiffyg talu sylw i ofynion y Ddeddf. Yn aml parch prin a delir i'r egwyddor o gilyddoldeb mewn gorfodaeth.

Mae'r Comisiwn yn croesawu'n gynnes gynigion y Llywodraeth i ddiwygio deddfwriaeth iechyd meddwl a chryfhau'r mesurau diogelwch sydd ar gael i'r rhai hynny a orfodir i dderbyn gofal a thriniaeth ar gyfer anhwylder meddwl. Ni bydd cynnydd mewn cyllid na deddfwriaeth ddiwygiol fodd bynnag, yn cyflawni'r gwelliannau sy'n angenrheidiol nac yn mynd i'r afael â'r anghyfartaledd sy'n y ddarpariaeth. Mae angen i'r deubeth gael eu cynnal gan rwydwaith cryf sy'n sicrhau bod digon o bobl amrywiol, medrus ac ymroddedig ar gael i ddarparu'r diogelwch perthynol clòs a'r diogelwch sy'n hanfodol ar gyfer dull gweithredu therapiwtig at unrhyw fath o anhwylder meddwl.

Yn yr un modd, ni bydd darparu gwell fframwaith deddfwriaethol a rhagor o staff yn sicrhau gwelliannau os na bydd rheolwyr medrus yn gallu cynorthwyo'r staff i drosi polisi yn ymarfer parthed pob un claf unigol. Rhaid i hawl pob un claf unigol i gael ei drin fel unigolyn heb wahaniaethu, stigma na stereoteip fod o'r pwys mwyaf.

Mae'r Adran Iechyd a Chynulliad Cenedlaethol Cymru wedi cydnabod yr anghenion hyn mewn peth wmbredd o gynlluniau i fwyhau recriwtio a hyfforddi ystod eang o bobl broffesiynol sy'n ymwneud â iechyd meddwl a gofal cymdeithasol, ac mewn cyflwyno cyrff rheoleiddiol newydd. Prif neges yr Adroddiad hwn yw mai hunanreoliad a systemau cryfion o fewn gofal iechyd meddwl yw'r allwedd i ddatgloi potensial yr holl fentrau hyn, yn enwedig parthed cleifion dan orchymyn. Mae hyn yr un mor wir am y Ddeddf bresennol ag y mae ar gyfer deddfwriaeth y dyfodol. Mae'r sylwadau a'r argymhellion a wneir yn yr Adroddiad hwn gan hynny'n amlygu bwriad y Comisiwn i ganolbwyntio ar y materion hyn yn y cyfnod dwyflynyddol presennol.

Mae'r sylwadau a'r argymhellion sy'n yr Adroddiad hwn wedi eu sylfaenu ar yr wybodaeth a'r profiad a enillwyd o raglen dreiglol ddwy flynedd o ymweliadau gan y Comisiynwyr a'r holl Ymddiriedolaethau GIG a Chartrefi Ymgeledd Meddwl Cofrestredig sydd â chleifion dan orchymyn yn unol â'r Ddeddf. Mae ein cynlluniau datblygol yn cydnabod pwysigrwydd allweddol yr ymweliadau hyn ac nid oes gennym unrhyw fwriad i'w cwtogi o ganlyniad i'n canolbwyntio cryfach ar systemau effeithiol. Rwyf yn manteisio ar y cyfle hwn i dalu teyrnged i fedrau'r Comisiynwyr a'r ysgrifenyddiaeth sy'n rhoi'n hael o'u hamser a'u hegni mewn archwilio os yw buddiannau a hawliau'r cleifion yn cael eu cadw'n gywir ai peidio.

Fe fydd datblygiad y ddeddfwriaeth fanwl sy'n angenrheidiol i ddwyn i fod yr egwyddorion bras sy'n y Papur Gwyn ar ddiwygio'r Ddeddf yn darparu cyfle mwy priodol nag Adroddiad Dwyflynyddol i fynd ar ôl materion sy'n achosi pryder yngln â sut y mae'r cleifion yn debygol o gael eu heffeithio gan y newidiadau arfaethedig. Nid yw'r Papur Gwyn gan hynny'n cael ei drafod yn yr Adroddiad hwn. Mae'r paratoad ar gyfer yr Adroddiad, fodd bynnag, wedi amlygu dau bwynt y mae'n rhaid eu hamlygu yma. Y cyntaf yw y bydd y drafftio a gweithredu'r ddeddfwriaeth newydd angen graddfa uchel o ymgynghori gyda'r ymarferwyr a chyflwyno cam wrth gam gofalus os yw'r bylchau rhwng polisi ac ymarfer a nodwyd yn yr Adroddiad hwn i gael eu cau. Yr ail yw, er bod y Comisiwn yn derbyn y gall cyrff rheoleiddiol cenedlaethol a gwasanaethau eiriolaeth lleol ddarparu gwasanaeth amgen digonol i'n swyddogaethau ymweld presennol, mae hi'n hanfodol bod y Comisiynwyr Deddf Iechyd Meddwl yn parhau i ymweld â chleifion dan orchymyn hyd nes y bydd trefniadau amgen boddhaol mewn bod ac fe ddylid defnyddio'u gwybodaeth a'u profiad yn y trefniadau newydd.

Yn olaf, er fy mod yn gyfrifol, ar ran y Comisiwn, am gyflwyno'r Adroddiad hwn i'r Ysgrifennydd Gwladol, ni ddeuthum yn Gadeirydd tan fis Rhagfyr 1999. Mr Gordon Lakes CB MC gan hynny oedd y Cadeirydd Dros Dro am yr wyth mis cyntaf a gwmpesir yn yr Adroddiad hwn. Roedd hon yn swyddogaeth neilltuol o anodd oherwydd y newidiadau arwyddocaol a oedd yn digwydd y tu mewn a'r tu allan i'r Comisiwn. Ni allaf roi canmoliaeth rhy uchel i fedr ac ymroddiad Mr Lakes wrth gyflawni'r swydd, na'i haelioni i mi wrth iddo gynnig ffrwyth ei brofiad a'i wybodaeth wrth i mi ei olynu. Yn arbennig, y mae wedi atgyfnerthu f'ymrwymiad i fy hunan ac ymrwymiad yr holl Gomisiynwyr tuag at ein Datganiad Cenhadaeth *"Safeguarding the interests of all people detained under the Mental Health Act"*. Dyma beth yw hanfod adolygu gweithredu'r Ddeddf.

Miss M A Clayton

Cadeirydd.

1   Introduction

1.1   The Mental Health Act Commission (the Commission) is a Special Health Authority whose main role is to keep under review the implementation of the Mental Health Act 1983 (the Act) as it relates to patients who are detained, or liable to be detained, under the Act in England and Wales. In the first issue of its Corporate Strategy and Business Plan, the Commission adopted the mission statement '*Safeguarding the interests of all people detained under the Mental Health Act*' to summarise its own interpretation of its statutory functions.

1.2   The Commission is required to publish a report on its activities every second year. This must be sent to the Secretary of State, who must lay a copy before each House of Parliament. This report relates to the two years from 1st April 1999 to 31st March 2001.

1.3   Because the Commission believes that its focus must be on the implementation of the Act and the patients whose lives are affected by it, the main part of this report (Chapters 2 – 7) concentrates on the findings and implications of our rolling programme of visits to all hospitals and nursing homes which hold detained patients. This programme enables us to meet with detained patients, review patients' records, examine the policies and systems which relate to them, and report to service providers on our findings in relation to the operation of the Act. Detailed information about the organisation of the Commission and its staff, the work we do and the use made of the finance allocated to us as a public body is given in Chapter 8.

Chapters 2 – 7: The Implementation of the Act

1.4   The contents of Chapters 2 – 7 are a distillation of the reports made after each Commission visit in the period under review, and also take account of the work of Second Opinion Appointed Doctors. Our object in these Chapters is not to name and blame but to provide an overview which:

■ shows how the implementation of the Act is affecting the people it aims to protect;

■ helps the facilities visited to improve their own practice;

■ draws attention to general areas of poor practice; and

■ advises on possible remedies for some of the issues raised.

Commissioners see so many individual examples of both good and poor practice that it can be invidious to select any for particular attention. Specific references to individual service providers are therefore limited to a relatively few examples of good practice. In making this extremely selective use of a few specific examples, we hope to avoid an unproductive focus on relative performance. Instead, we aim to encourage all readers to consider how far the issues identified and the recommendations made are relevant to their own working practices and circumstances.

1.5	The way in which the main themes in Chapters 2 – 7 are addressed has enabled us to make specific recommendations on the actions that we believe are needed to ensure that the Act is properly implemented. The Commission is not an inspectoral body, but our very wide knowledge of individual patient experiences under the various provisions of the Act puts us in a unique position to comment on implementation. Most of the comments and recommendations relate to the way in which any legislation needs to be implemented and will therefore be as relevant to new legislation as they are to the 1983 Act. We therefore make no apology for using this report to take the logical step from review to recommendation.

The Commission in Wales

1.6	Chapters 2 – 6 relate, in general, to both England and Wales. Chapter 7 recognises that mental health policy and practice in Wales are largely determined by the National Assembly for Wales and mentions briefly the main differences in strategy and policy. Most of the comments and recommendations in Chapters 2 – 6 apply as much to Wales as to England but Chapter 7 highlights the few areas in which there are significant differences. As the two national healthcare services develop, the Commission hopes that each may learn from the best practice of the other.

Commentary and Schedule of Recommendations

1.7	Chapter 9 sets out the recommendations from Chapters 2 – 7, commenting on the wider mental health environment in which they are set. By ordering the recommendations in relation to those with the primary responsibility for implementing them, it is intended to help everyone concerned to work together to achieve higher levels of compliance with the Act and with any new legislation. We hope that the way in which we have been reviewing and changing our own practices during the past two years will make a significant contribution to better implementation of the Act.

The Organisation and Work of the Mental Health Act Commission

1.8	Chapter 8 sets out the organisational and financial details of the Commission both as the background to and validation of all that precedes it, and also to demonstrate our compliance with the requirements of public sector accountability. In carrying out the functions of the Commission, we are aiming to follow the same principles of self-assessment and self-regulation which we emphasise as essential in Chapter 9.

Conclusion

1.9	In the present transitional period between the 1983 Act and the new legislation which has been promised in the Government's White Paper "Reforming the Mental Health Act"[1], the Mental Health Act Commission believes that it can best serve the interests of detained patients by highlighting in this report those aspects of the 1983 Act which our work suggests most need attention, both now and in future legislation. This is why, although previous Biennial Reports are valuable reference documents because they range widely over issues of interpretation of the Act, (e.g. summarising changes in legislation, significant law cases and differences of view between academics, lawyers and practitioners) we decided that this report should be a more narrowly focused, action-orientated document. We hope that the Secretary of State, to whom the report is submitted in accordance with the Act, will find it a useful contribution to ongoing consideration of how best to meet the interests of patients subject to compulsion under mental health law.

---

1 **Department of Health (2000) Reforming the Mental Health Act.** London, Stationery Office Cm. 5016-11

2   Rights and Respect

Protecting Patients' Rights and Encouraging Autonomy

2.1   All mental health services should be provided within the context of the guiding principles of the Mental Health Act Code of Practice. These include requirements that patients should be treated:

- with respect for their individuality and diversity;

- in the least controlled and segregated manner possible; and

- in such a way as to promote their self-determination to the greatest practicable degree consistent with their own personal needs and wishes[2].

This section focuses on some practical ways in which services can uphold these principles.

Stigma

2.2   Behaviour is determined more by values, ethos and attitudes than by exhortation or examples of good practice. The Commission is convinced that it will not be possible to achieve the quality of services which should be offered to detained or other mentally ill people until there is a fundamental change in attitudes towards such people.

2.3   We warmly welcome the Government's campaign to end discrimination against those with mental health problems[3]. We strongly endorse the Declaration of Intent published by the Royal College of Psychiatrists as part of their "Changing Minds" campaign, which is reproduced in full in **Appendix A** to this report. Everything in this and the following Chapters should be read in the light of our commitment to ensure that detained patients, in particular, are not doubly disadvantaged by the stigma attached to their illness.

> Recommendation 1
>
> The Department of Health and the National Assembly for Wales should take every opportunity to challenge inaccurate representation of mentally ill people, in the media and elsewhere, based on stigmatising attitudes and stereotypes.

---

2 Department of Health and Welsh Office (1999) **Mental Health Act Code of Practice**. London, Stationery Office. see *Chapter One: Guiding Principles*

3 Mind out for mental health – a campaign co-ordinated by the Department of Health to stop discrimination. Mindout@forster.co.uk

Providing Information to Patients and Relatives

2.4   It is a statutory duty on hospital managers to provide certain information to detained patients about their circumstances in relation to detention, consent to treatment, rights of appeal and other matters as soon as they can practicably do so[4]. Detailed guidance on the discharge of this duty is given in Code of Practice (Chapter 14) and the Memorandum to the Act (para 297).

2.5   The Commission recognises the difficulties in explaining legal matters to patients whose mental state may preclude the understanding or retention of such information. It is therefore important that services are sensitive to the capacity of each individual patient and that rights are explained, as far as possible, in a way that the patient understands. It will often be necessary to make repeated attempts to achieve this.

2.6   The Commission's experience shows that, where patients do not understand their legal position and rights, this is often a result of poor practice in providing communication at an appropriate level and checking that this has been understood. Examples of staff being unable to identify when and by whom individual patients' rights were explained, even by reference to the patient's notes, were found in almost a quarter of units visited by Commissioners. The introduction of systems to record and monitor the provision of information to patients has been an important factor in improving performance in this area for many service providers.

Recommendation 2

Service providers should ensure that a system of verification using a standardised form is used to record that information has been given to patients about their legal position and rights under the Act. The form should have space for recording:

- the name of the person giving the information;
- the date that the information was given;
- whether the patient understood the information;
- subsequent attempts to give the information; and
- the planned date for the next attempt.

2.7   Hospital managers have a duty to provide written information to a patient's Nearest Relative, unless that patient objects to them doing so. Guidance on these duties is given at Chapter 14 of the Code of Practice.

Recommendation 3

Hospital Managers should ensure that patients' wishes in relation to Sections 132(4) and 133 are ascertained and recorded, and that information is provided to the Nearest Relative if the patient has not objected.

---

4 **Mental Health Act 1983**, Section 132.

MHAC research on the giving of information on patients' rights

2.8 In 1999/2000 we gave a specific focus on our visits to the ways in which hospital managers were discharging their statutory duty to ensure that detained patients are afforded real opportunities to understand their legal status and rights. One finding of this exercise was the considerable proportion of units that failed to keep records of the communication of patients' rights (see paragraph 2.6 above). Another focus was the provision of such information in appropriate written forms.

2.9 Figure 1 shows the percentage of the 2,193 facilities visited that had available copies of English-language leaflets on Sections 2, 3 and 37. Although the figures are fairly high, it is alarming to reflect that, despite the legal and good practice requirements on units to provide information under Section 132, 180 units could not provide a Section 2 leaflet and 263 had no Section 3 leaflets.

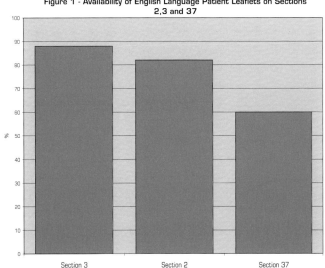

Figure 1 - Availability of English Language Patient Leaflets on Sections 2,3 and 37

2.10 We are also concerned to have found that nearly half of the facilities visited (49%) had no leaflets available in any language other than English, and only 9% were equipped with any information in braille.

> Recommendation 4
>
> Hospital managers should ensure that the Department of Health's patient information leaflets on the Mental Health Act are available on all units in an appropriate range of languages and formats.

2.11 The Commission supports the Law Society's recommendations[5] on the further development of standards in the giving of information, which include the following:

■ The Department of Health's leaflets should be re-designed into a more user-friendly format and should include more specific advice on the procedures for applying to a Tribunal, such as a tear-off application form contained within each leaflet.

---

5 Law Society (2000), **Comments on the Review of Tribunals Consultation Paper.** London, Law Society September 2000

- The leaflets should set out the criteria for compulsory detention and the grounds on which the Tribunal would allow discharge.
- Staff should be trained on how to explain to patients their rights. Merely repeating what is already written on the leaflet is inadequate.
- There must be access to oral explanations through independent interpreters.
- An obligation should be placed on hospital managers to ensure that the information is repeated after a specified period of time (eg. 10 days) has elapsed since admission.

Recommendation 5

The Department of Health should ensure that patient information leaflets on the Mental Health Act 1983 are available in formats appropriate to the following groups of patients:

- children and adolescents;
- deaf patients;
- blind patients;
- deaf/blind patients;
- patients with learning disabilities

see recommendations 67 (paragraph 6.45), 68 (6.54) and 71 (6.64)

2.12   We will be reviewing the Commission's own patient information leaflets over the next reporting period, giving particular attention to whether other formats would be more appropriate for particular groups of patients.

Patients' access to legal advice and Tribunals

2.13   The right of patients to an independent review of their detention by a Mental Health Review Tribunal is an important safeguard. Patients have a right to be legally represented at the Tribunal to ensure that their case is fully and fairly put forward. Appropriately trained solicitors are franchised by the Legal Services Commission, which produces regional lists to publicise the solicitors' availability.

Recommendation 6

Hospital managers should ensure that each ward is issued with a copy of the Legal Services Commission list of franchised solicitors to assist in the process of securing representation at Mental Health Review Tribunals.

Voting rights of patients

2.14   The Commission was pleased to note the changes in law introduced in the Representation of the People Act 2000, which widened the franchise to all patients detained under Part II of the Act or on remand.

2.15 We have previously commented on the need for hospital managers to ensure that detained patients are assisted in exercising their right to vote in elections[6]. We therefore particularly welcome the publication of the Explanatory Notes to the Representation of the People Act 2000, available from the Stationery Office[7], and commend these to hospital managers who are unclear about the current legal position relating to the enfranchisement of detained patients.

Patient Involvement

Capacity and consent to treatment

2.16 The general principle that patients should be treated and cared for in a way that promotes, insofar as is possible, their self-determination and responsibility[8] underlies the Code of Practice's specific recommendations on consent to treatment. All staff working with detained patients should be familiar with the guidance on medical treatment at Chapter 15 of the Code. The GMC, Royal College of Psychiatrists and UKCC have also produced specific good practice guidelines for relevant professionals[9].

2.17 It is of paramount importance that patients are treated lawfully. Common errors in completing authorisations for treatment and the Commission's recommendations for ensuring that these are avoided are given at paragraphs 2.63 – 2.67 below. The following paragraphs deal with the need to ensure that patients' capacity is properly ascertained and that capable patients are given the opportunity to give informed consent.

2.18 For all detained patients, it is the duty of the Responsible Medical Officer (RMO) to evaluate fully whether the patient has the capacity to give informed consent to the treatment. The basic principles of informed consent are defined in the Code of Practice as the voluntary and continuing permission of the patient to receive a particular treatment, based on an adequate knowledge of the purpose, nature, likely effects and risks of that treatment including the likelihood of its success and any alternatives to it. Permission given under any unfair or undue pressure is not 'consent'.

2.19 Commissioners often see patients who are reticent to raise issues of concern about their medication because their only contact with their RMO is at ward rounds with the whole clinical team present. Patients should be offered the opportunity of discussing their medication with their RMO on a one-to-one basis.

2.20 Despite the wide availability of guidance on consent to treatment issues, we remain disappointed at the prevalence of bad practice that we encounter on visits:

  ■ There is often no entry in the medical notes of the discussion during which consent to treatment was sought and obtained, nor any reference to the patient's capacity to consent, as required by the Code of Practice (paragraphs 16.11, 16.13 etc).

6 Mental Health Act Commission (1997) **Seventh Biennial Report**. London, Stationery Office. Paragraph 3.1.3.

7 **Explanatory Notes, Representation of the People Act 2000, Chapter 2** (2000). Stationery Office (ISBN 0-10-560200-0) £5.95.

8 Department of Health and Welsh Office (1999) **Mental Health Act Code of Practice**. London, Stationery Office. paragraph 1.1

9 General Medical Council (1999) **Seeking Patients' Consent: The Ethical Considerations**; Royal College of Psychiatrists (2000) **Council Report CR83: Good Psychiatric Practice 2000**; UKCC (1998) **Guidelines for Mental Health and Learning Disabilities Nursing – a guide to working with vulnerable clients.**

- Where there are such entries, these are frequently insufficient. The General Medical Council's 'Good Medical Practice'[10] states that doctors must " keep clear, accurate and contemporaneous records which report the relevant clinical findings, the decisions made, the information given and any drugs or other treatment provided." Entries such as, "S.... consents to his treatment regime" and "consent to treatment completed" are inadequate.

- Commissioners frequently see patients who are deemed to be consenting but whose medical and nursing notes throw doubt on their capacity to be so. To give one example from many, Commissioners on a visit to an NHS Trust in May 1999 found one patient being given six different forms of medication on the purported authority of a Form 38 (on which his RMO had certified the patient's consent), despite a clear statement by the same doctor on the renewal of detention Form 30, completed days after the Form 38, that the patient had no insight into his condition and despite a number of references in the medical notes to his reluctance and even refusal to take the medication prescribed. Where the Commission finds such practice it draws it to the attention of hospital managers and expects immediate remedial action.

Recommendation 7

Hospital managers should arrange for effective audit, monitoring and flagging systems to be in place to ensure that the capacity of all detained patients to consent to treatment is assessed and reviewed regularly from their admission, that treatment is regularly discussed with patients, that they should be given the opportunity of having those discussions on a one to one basis and that such discussions are recorded, as required by Chapters 15 and 16 of the Code of Practice.

(see also recommendation 22, para 2.67)

2.21   A few service providers have managed to achieve uniformly high standards of practice in the recording of the discussion with the patient concerning capacity and consent. This has been achieved through both the commitment of medical staff to ensuring that patients are treated with respect for their legal and human rights, and the use of audits and clear flagging systems. Many wards at the three High Security Hospitals show excellent practice (see Chapter 5.22) and some other service providers have maintained excellent standards and introduced innovative practices (see paragraph 2.67).

Good Practice Example

Manchester Mental Health Partnership have designed a form to record the determination of each patient's capacity to consent. The form also records the nature of the proposed treatment and reminds staff to record findings separately in the patient's case notes.

Contact Mrs M Worsley, Director of Adult Services, Barlow House, Minshull St, Manchester M1 3DZ Tel :0161 2331627

2.22   Some services do not invite patients to be present at "ward-rounds" and similarly designated interdisciplinary discussions of their treatment. We believe that patients should, as a matter of course, be included in such inter-disciplinary discussions. Paragraph 15.7 of the Code clearly

---

10 General Medical Council (1998) **Good Medical Practice**. London, GMC

states that, wherever possible, patients should be enabled to be involved in their care plan and to express agreement or disagreement with it. Where patients are reluctant to join in such meetings, or it is considered inappropriate for them to do so, every effort should be made to meet with the patient on a one-to-one basis to discuss plans being made. These attempts should be recorded.

Patient advocacy

2.23 We recognise the important role played by advocacy schemes in helping staff and patients communicate more effectively. Representatives of advocacy services often meet with Commissioners on their visits to hospitals and have made an increasingly valuable contribution through sharing their experience of local issues. Nevertheless, while there are clear examples of good practice in the provision of such services across England and Wales, there are problems with the quality of some services, both in defining advocacy and in delivering advocacy services. We continue to note the general lack of access for patients from black and ethnic minority groups to appropriate advocacy service provision (see Chapter 6.31).

2.24 We are glad to record the Commission's representation on the Project Advisory Group for the study of good practice in mental health advocacy, which Durham University is undertaking under contract to the Department of Health. We look forward to discussions on the Government's proposed statutory advocacy service. The establishment of the Royal College of Psychiatrists' Carers and Users Experience Survey (CUES) initiative, which systematically reviews the experience of mental health patients and their carers, is a welcome move. With the pilots at the North Mersey, Warrington Community and Sheffield Trusts complete, the move to patients as participants in their care is set to progress.

> Recommendation 8
>
> The Department of Health should issue guidelines on good practice in the provision of advocacy services as soon as possible, in advance of whatever is decided on the special advocacy service proposed for the forthcoming legislation.

Complaints by patients and other people

2.25 The Commission has a general and discretionary remit to investigate complaints. Our complaints policy provides that, as a general rule, formal complaints should have been considered at a local level through the NHS complaints procedure prior to the Commission undertaking any investigation itself. However, we deal with patients' concerns and complaints in other ways than through formal investigation.

2.26 At the most basic level, Commissioners on a visit to mental health facilities always talk to patients, either at their request or in a general discussion. Relatively minor individual complaints, such as the removal of particular possessions or the refusal of particular requests, are dealt with by negotiation with managers on the spot and the patient is informed of the outcome immediately. Many general complaints and concerns are raised in such discussions, e.g. on access to fresh air, regularity of showers/baths, access to activities, which can both be followed up immediately with local managers and logged for consideration as matters to be raised as of wider concern. Sometimes the volume of complaints on a particular aspect of service reveals very serious shortcomings, e.g. as in the application of the Security Directions in the High Security Hospitals (see Chapter 5), which can be resolved only by changes of policy at a high level.

2.27 The Commission provides some help to patients who make formal complaints through the NHS complaints procedure, by offering advice and guidance on the procedure and, where appropriate, monitoring the complaint's progress through the system (see Chapter 8.24). The use of the NHS complaints procures, introduced in 1996, has made it much easier for patients to have their complaints acknowledged and, in good examples, addressed, but some patients still feel that they are not being listened to. Hospital managers should ensure that staff are alert to this potential problem, and also recognise that the sometimes lengthy and cumbersome processes which have to be followed can cause exceptional stress for patients who are already suffering from a mental illness and may well contribute to deterioration in their condition. We welcome the Department of Health's current intention to reform and strengthen the NHS complaints procedure[11] and have contributed to consultations on this.

Recommendation 9

Hospital managers should closely monitor the handling and outcome of all complaints, both to ensure minimum delay and to note any quality implications arising from the complaint.

Recommendation 10

Complaints managers should ensure that complaints made by detained patients are not regarded less seriously than those from other patients, and should be sensitive to the potentially adverse effects on the progress of such patients of delays in handling complaints.

2.28 We recognise the difficulties posed by vexatious and unreasonably persistent complainants to many hospitals' complaints services, and commend the Health Service Ombudsman's advice and suggestions on local policies to deal with this[12].

2.29 Where the Commission believes that a formal complaint needs an instant reaction which cannot be provided through the NHS complaints process, or where, exceptionally, a complaint is made by a member of staff about the way in which a service is being provided, a Commissioner may investigate the matter immediately and provide a full written report to the Commission and the managers concerned. For example, at the end of this reporting period we intervened in such a way to examine and report on the conditions in which a learning disabled patient with profound behavioural difficulties was being cared for by one NHS Trust. Our report and recommendations were immediately implemented by the hospital managers, ending two months of very unsatisfactory service provision. Fortunately, the number of these exceptional cases is relatively small. They nevertheless highlight the need for a continuing provision for exceptional interventions, both now and under the new mental health legislation.

---

11 Department of Health (2001) **Reforming the NHS Complaints Procedure: a listening document.** www.doh.gov.uk/nhscomplaintsreform

12 Health Service Ombudsman (2001) **Health Service Ombudsman's Annual Report 2000–01**, London, Stationery Office *para 1.4 page 14*

Patient Confidentiality

2.30   In most cases, mental health services' respect for patient confidentiality is exemplary. The extent to which services have embraced the Department of Health's Guidance[13] and the subsequent Caldicott recommendations on patient confidentiality is encouraging. We welcome the development of the Mental Health Minimum Data Set[14], which should ensure that appropriate information is collated in retrievable form for managers and clinicians.

2.31   However, Commissioners do encounter rare examples of poor practice on their visits. One ward was found to use a "patient information whiteboard" in the nursing office, which was clearly visible to the ward through the office window. The Board displayed personal information about patients, including unflattering assessments of their presentation and propensities. Commissioners insisted that this practice be discontinued.

2.32   The Commission urges hospital managers to be continually vigilant to ensure that confidential patient information is handled and stored appropriately.

2.33   It is essential that a holistic approach to responsibility for the welfare of patients is fostered by the judicious sharing of information between agencies. For this reason, we have recommended statutory provision for such information sharing and welcome the Government's commitment to this in the White Paper[15]. We consider that clear protocols (requiring, for example, the transfer of information only to named individuals), proper safeguards and careful monitoring are essential to ensure that the advantages of a holistic approach are not outweighed by abuses of confidence.

Upholding the Safeguards of the Act

2.34   The Mental Health Act's framework for compulsion provides a number of structural safeguards against its powers being used arbitrarily or incorrectly. By ensuring that the Act is administered properly and to the best practice standards attainable, services can not only ensure that they act within the law, but can contribute to the protection of the patients that they deal with.

---

13 Department of Health (1996) **The Protection and use of Patient Information – Guidance from the Department of Health**

14 NHS Information Authority (2000) **Mental Health Minimum Data Set; Using the MHMDS**. London, Stationery Offfice

15 Department of Health (2000) **Reforming the Mental Health Act 1983, Part 1: The new legal framework**. London Stationery Office. Cm 5016-I para 5.33 –5. 34

2.35   The duties of hospital managers under the Act are summarised and discussed at Chapter 22 of the Code of Practice. One vital duty, which hospital managers should delegate to properly trained and competent staff, relates to the receipt and scrutiny of documents. Clear guidance on the actions required of such delegated staff is given at Chapter 12 of the Code. The Commission expects all hospital managers to have suitable systems in place to ensure that the Act is operated lawfully and appropriately at all times.

2.36   The following section considers some of the problem areas in the administration of the Act that have been of concern to the Commission

Concerns over the use of holding powers

2.37   The Commission has expressed its concern in the last three Biennial Reports about the relatively high number of patients who agree to enter hospital on a voluntary basis but then are prevented from leaving under Section 5(2). The purpose of Section 5(2) is to hold a patient whilst a full assessment is made of whether a longer-term detention under the act is appropriate. There continues to be a high use of this power (see figure 2, Chapter 3.2).

2.38   There are a number of reasons for the use of Section 5(2). There is certainly the desire of clinicians to take the views of patients into account; to avoid the use of compulsion at the point of admission when it is possible to do so; and to treat patients, as the Code requires, in the least restrictive way possible. There is also the convenience of avoiding the assessment process required for formal admission under Sections 2 or 3. High use of Section 5(2) may also be an indication that in-patient wards have become places where patients who require treatment have to be coerced to stay.

Recommendation 13

The Department of Health should commission research to examine the possible reasons for the nationally high use of Section 5(2), particularly with a view to investigating whether the physical and / or therapeutic environment is an influencing factor.

2.39   Section 5(2) authorises the detention of the patient for up to 72 hours but should be used for the shortest time possible. Commissioners often find delays in arranging assessments of patients detained under this holding power.

Recommendation 14

Hospital managers should arrange for the routine collation of detailed statistics on the use of Section 5(2), including the time taken to complete assessments, for audit purposes.

2.40   We are also concerned about the practice of keeping the holding power in reserve in case the patient tries to leave the ward. It is not uncommon for a psychiatrist to leave instructions on the ward that a patient should be "put on a 5(2) if he or she attempts to leave". This amounts to de facto detention, where the patient is denied the safeguards of the Act. It also blurs the distinction between informal and detained patients and could lead to all patients feeling under coercion to stay in hospital (see Chapter 4.20).

> **Recommendation 15**
>
> All providers should ensure that risk assessments of informal patients take account of the likelihood of <u>and</u> risks involved in their leaving the ward, and if both are high, an assessment for detention under the Act should be considered.

> **Recommendation 16**
>
> Nursing and medical staff must ensure that all patients who are not detained under the Act should have a clear understanding of their legal status.

The use of Sections 2 and 3

2.41   We welcome the Government's proposal that new legislation should set a single route of entry to the system of compulsion. This will have the advantage of being simpler and more easily understood by both patients and professionals, with all patients being entitled to the same rights of multi-disciplinary assessment and independent review. In the meantime, debates continue as to the appropriate use of the Mental Health Act 1983 powers provided by Sections 2 and 3. In our Eighth Biennial Report, we commented upon debates around whether it was appropriate to use Section 2 or Section 3 when compulsorily admitting patients to hospital, and what the threshold for such admissions should be[16].

2.42   The fundamental criterion for admission under Section 3 is more rigorous than that for Section 2, in that admission to hospital for treatment must be certified as *necessary* for Section 3, whereas a patient can be admitted for assessment under Section 2 on the grounds that such admission is *warranted for at least a limited period*. To meet the stricter criterion for Section 3 admission, the Code of Practice suggests that Section 3 should normally be used for patients already known to and recently assessed by the clinical team, whether or not they have had any previous compulsory admissions to hospital[17].

2.43   The Commission has heard of a number of disputes being raised over the legal interpretation of Sections 2 and 3, particularly since the coming into force of the Human Rights Act. We remain of the view that practitioners should continue to follow the guidance given in Chapter 5 of the Code of Practice in relation to when it is appropriate to use either Section 2 or Section 3 to compulsorily admit a patient to hospital. Although, to date, there have been no legal challenges under the HRA to the use of Sections 2 or 3 *per se*, practitioners should remember that, even if such a challenge were made successfully, domestic law can only be reinterpreted through case law or changed through Parliament. We are alarmed at the proliferation of scare-stories about elements of current legislation being potentially in breach of the ECHR, particularly where these persuade practitioners not to follow the requirements of the current law and Code of Practice.

Extending the detention of Section 2 patients

2.44   Commissioners often find examples where assessments to detain Section 2 patients further under Section 3 are only undertaken at the imminent expiry of the Section 2 detention order. It

---

16 Mental Health Act Commission (1999) **Eighth Biennial Report**. London, Stationery Office. p75–78

17 Department of Health and Welsh Office (1999) **Mental Health Act Code of Practice**. London, Stationery Office. Paragraph 5.3a

is unacceptable that this should occur routinely, as it can prevent full discussion and consultation as required by Chapter 2 of the Code of Practice, and also preclude General Practitioners from being available to carry out the second medical examination.

> Recommendation 17
>
> Hospital and social services managers should ensure, through audit and review, that, if a patient detained under Section 2 appears to require further detention, a Section 3 assessment is arranged at the earliest opportunity and undertaken according to the requirements of the Code of Practice.

Reviewing and discharging detentions under Sections 2 and 3

2.45 Patients should be discharged from civil detention orders as soon as it is clear that detention is no longer justified. This is a requirement of both the Code of Practice (Chapter 1.1) and Article 5 of the ECHR, following the ruling in <u>Winterwerp v Netherlands</u> [1979] that detention must only continue for as long as the persistence of the mental disorder upon which it was based.

> **Recommendation 18**
>
> Hospital managers, through audit and review, should ensure that:
>
> - the detention of each patient is kept under constant review by the clinical team;
> - decisions on the continuation of detention are based upon clinical need and not administrative convenience;
> - detentions are not allowed to lapse, but are actively rescinded unless a decision is made to renew detention; and
> - RMOs have access to a suitable form to rescind detentions, a copy of which is given to the patient upon discharge.

2.46 Hospital managers should ensure that their duties in relation to informing Nearest Relatives of a patient's discharge are met (see paragraph 2.7 above).

Approved Social Worker (ASW) Issues

The important role of ASWs

2.47 The Code of Practice describes the role of ASWs in assessing patients for possible admission under the Act as one of co-ordinating both the assessment itself and the implementation of any decision to admit. The role is also widely seen as providing a safeguard against unnecessary admission by bringing in a balancing, non-medical view of the best interests of the patient[18] and the need to use the least restrictive alternative available to provide care[19].

---

18 see Campbell, Wilson, Britton, Hamilton, Hughes & Manktelow (2001); *The Management of Approved Social Workers: Aspects of law, policy and practice.* **Journal of Social Welfare and Family Law** 23(2)20 for a literature review on the functions of ASWs.

19 Department of Health and Welsh Office (1999) **Mental Health Act Code of Practice**. London, Stationery Office. para 1.1

2.48 The ASW's role is therefore complex and, at times, beset with problems of both practice and principle. However, we continue to believe that ASWs play a vital role in the administration of the Act. If an equivalent role in new legislation is to be undertaken by a wider professional group (such as community-based nurses), we urge the Government to consider how the benefits of the current structure might be protected.

Urgent Admissions where there is no bed

2.49 The common problem of ASWs finding no beds available when conveying a patient to a hospital for urgent compulsory admission was raised in our Eighth Biennial Report[20]. We advised that the ASW should remain with the patient while a bed is organised, taking the view that, where the hospital has been identified by a Health Authority as a place that will admit patients in emergencies, it is reasonable to expect the hospital to find a bed for the patient, even though Section 140 does not place a legal duty on it to do so.

2.50 Some providers have identified strategies to deal with this difficult situation:

Good Practice Example

Following discussions with local social services and consultation with the Commission, Wakefield and Pontefract Community NHS Trust identified a holding area and additional staff cover at Fieldhead Hospital where an ASW can wait with a patient if no bed is immediately available. The patient is formally admitted to the hospital upon arrival at this waiting area, so that nursing staff are able to hold the patient if he or she attempts to leave. If it proves impossible to identify a bed within the hospital, it is then legally possible (although clearly undesirable) to grant Section 17 leave to a temporary bed in another hospital.

Contact: Chief Executive, Wakefield & Pontefract Community NHS Trust, Fieldhead Hosptial, Ouchthorpe Lane, Wakefield WF1 3SP. Tel: 01924 327000

The Commission's ASW report checklist

2.51 When ASWs admit patients to hospital under the Act, they are required to leave an outline report giving reasons for admission, any practical matters about the patient that the hospital should know and, where possible, the telephone number of a social worker who can be contacted for further details[21].

2.52 The Commission has provided all social services departments with a checklist of all issues that we consider should be included in ASW reports, and we use this checklist to scrutinise samples of such reports on our visits. This checklist covers the following areas:

- the patient's spoken language and ethnicity;
- record of interview with the patient;
- name of the person appearing to be the Nearest Relative, and the process of his/her identification;
- whether the Nearest Relative was notified of the application and given information on the patient's rights, with reasons if not notified or consulted;

---

20 Mental Health Act Commission (1999) **Eighth Biennial Report**. London, Stationery Office. p 87

21 Department of Health and Welsh Office (1999) **Mental Health Act Code of Practice**. London, Stationery Office. para 11.13

- records of discussions with the recommending doctors and other parties;

- reasons for the decision to make the application and alternatives considered;

- comments on risk to the patient or other peoples' safety, or to the patient's health;

- comment on any avoidable delay in the assessment/admission process;

- information relating to the possibility of children visiting;

- any other practical matters that the hospital needs to know; and

- the name and number of the Local Authority contact person.

A full copy of the checklist is available upon request from the Commission.

Recommendation 19

Social service authorities should develop forms for ASWs to complete on the admission of a patient to hospital under the Act, to ensure that the above information is left with the receiving hospital.

Nearest Relative issues

2.53 The requirement that ASWs must consult with a patient's Nearest Relative as a part of the statutory assessment process, regardless of the wishes or best interests of the patient[22], was the subject of a legal challenge to the Mental Health Act 1983 in this period[23]. We raised this issue in 1997[24] and welcome the Government's decision to concede that this requirement of the Mental Health Act breached the right to respect for private and family life contained in Article 8 of the ECHR. As part of a 'friendly settlement', the Government agreed to pay JT damages and to make changes in the law.

2.54 At the time of writing, it is unclear whether these changes are to be made as part of the review of the Mental Health Act or whether they are to be introduced beforehand. The outcome of the case has caused some confusion over how to implement the Act's requirements in the meantime.

2.55 Commissioners have noted a number of applications for detention recording that either the patient or the Nearest Relative had objected to the statutory consultation. It was not clear from these comments whether, in some cases, the ASW had actually contacted the Nearest Relative as required by the Act. We advise that such contact should be both made and recorded to ensure the lawfulness of the patient's detention. Neither the wishes of the patient nor of the Nearest Relative can obviate these legal requirements, regardless of the settlement in JT v UK, until and unless domestic law is changed (see paragraph 2.43 above).

2.56 The Commission is aware of the argument proposed in Richard Jones' Mental Health Act Manual (Seventh edition 1–127) that consultation with the Nearest Relative can be avoided if it would be likely to have an adverse effect on the patient's situation, given that the Act only requires such consultation where "practicable". The Code of Practice does not support this interpretation of the Act, despite its attraction and the requirement to interpret legislation in accordance with Convention rights. Unless the code's guidance is changed, 'practicable' should be considered to refer to the availability of the Nearest Relative and not to the repercussions that consultation

---

22 **Mental Health Act 1983** Section 11(3) and (4).

23 *JT v United Kingdom* Application No 26494/95, European Court of Human Rights, 30 March 2000

24 Mental Health Act Commission (1997) **Seventh Biennial Report** London, Stationery Office p 189–90

might have on the patient. The Commission is concerned that the requirement for consultation should not be contingent upon the subjective views of practitioners and that the Government should decide what is the best remedy to this problem.

> Recommendation 20
>
> Standard formats should be developed for ASWs' reports which ensure that details of how the Nearest Relative was identified and consulted are included. This will enable hospital administrators to include these issues in their scrutiny of admission documents and ensure that the papers are legally valid.

GP and Section 12 Approved Doctor Issues

2.57   Standard 3 of the National Service Framework states that any individual with a common mental health problem should be able to make contact round the clock with the local services necessary to meet their needs. This is even more essential for those whose mental illness may make them subject to compulsion. The local milestone: " A duty doctor, Section 12 approved, and approved social worker must always be available for mental health emergencies" is of key significance for such patients.

2.58   We have recorded in several Biennial Reports that the arrangements to secure the services of Section 12 approved doctors are not working satisfactorily[25]. Much time and money is wasted in fruitless attempts to find Section 12 approved doctors who are available and willing to assess patients for compulsory admission to hospital.

2.59   In the Eighth Biennial Report, we called for a national solution which would include making Section 12 duties more financially rewarding and which would build in other incentives around the education and training of GPs to become approved. We welcome the work currently being undertaken by the British Medical Association to survey a large percentage of consultants and other doctors to discover and address the reasons for the shortage and lack of availability of Section 12 doctors. Recent advice on the making of recommendations under the Mental Health Act, issued to GPs by the Department of Health, may also improve the situation.

2.60   We are engaging with the Department of Health, the Royal College of Psychiatrists and the police to ensure that a solution to the lack of availability of Section 12 doctors is positively pursued.

2.61   We have suggested the following specific measures to the Department of Health:

■ inclusion of a clause in the contract of consultant psychiatrists requiring them to be approved under Section 12;

■ ensuring that all medical students involved in training in psychiatry are made aware of the need for and importance of more Section 12 doctors;

■ making the entry requirements for approval more flexible so that GPs who can show that they have sufficient knowledge and experience in treating mental disorder are eligible to apply;

---

25 Mental Health Act Commission (1999) **Eighth Biennial Report**, p 82–4; MHAC (1997) **Seventh Biennial Report**, p 56 –8; MHAC (1995) **Sixth Biennial Report** p 83–4. London, Stationery Office.

- making the Section 12 approval training available to all interested GPs before any commitment to become approved;

- encouraging Primary Care Groups / Trusts to aim to increase the number of GPs in their area who are approved under Section 12;

- similarly to encourage Primary Care Groups / Trusts to require co-operatives operating out-of hours services in their area to guarantee the availability of at least one Section 12 doctor at all times;

- streamlining the system of payment to ensure that fees are paid promptly by the area in which the assessment is carried out, rather than being passed from one health authority to another;

- inviting Chief Constables to require forensic medical examiners to become approved.

Recommendation 21

The lead Health Authority responsible for the approval of doctors under Section 12(2) in each region, in partnership with the other relevant services, should ensure that :

- there is systematic high level collation of data from ASWs on the numbers of telephone calls made, the time taken to locate a Section 12 Approved doctor and the sharing of workload between doctors so that baselines and targets for improvement can be established;

- regular monitoring meetings between Health Authorities, Trusts, Social Services and Police are held to ensure that targets are met;

- intensive, possibly modular, training courses are established to enable a wider range of GPs to carry out the assessment function with confidence; and

- approved training courses are monitored to ensure both quality and consistency.

2.62 There is no reason why increased flexibility in the approval criteria for the appointment of Section 12 Approved Doctors should lead to any diminution in the standard of assessments, provided that the situation is properly monitored and existing inter-regional variations in standards are overcome. There is, however, no doubt that neither Standard 3 of the National Service Framework nor the local milestone mentioned at paragraph 2.57 above will be met unless something positive is done to address the shortage of Section 12 Approved Doctors.

The Administration of Particular Treatments (Part IV of the Act)

2.63 Our concerns over the evaluation of patients' capacity to give informed consent and discussions between RMOs and their patients over proposed treatments are detailed at paragraphs 2.16 – 2.22 above. Concerns over RMOs' completion of statutory forms authorising such treatment, subsequent to their having made an evaluation of patients' capacity and consent status, are also frequently raised on Commission visits. This is disappointing, particularly given the clear guidance provided in Chapters 15 and 16 of the Code of Practice, which should be familiar to any member of staff involved in the operation of Part IV of the Act[26].

---

26 Department of Health and Welsh Office (1999) **Mental Health Act Code of Practice**. London, Stationery Office. para 16.3.

2.64 Commissioners frequently encounter practice that potentially renders the administration of some or all of a patient's prescribed medication unlawful. Where they do so they draw this to the attention of hospital managers, recommending that they take immediate remedial action, inform the patient of the position and assist the patient in obtaining legal advice if he or she wishes to do so.

2.65 Commissioners may question the lawfulness of the administration of treatment when, for example:

■ the medication for mental disorder being administered is different, in relation to type of drug, number of drugs in each BNF category, or upper limit of dosage from that authorised on Form 38 or 39;

■ drugs are described incorrectly on Forms 38 (i.e. with reference to the wrong BNF category);

■ the initial three-month period of detention has expired without a Form 38 or 39 being completed to authorise continued treatment with medication for mental disorder; or

■ patients appear to have withdrawn their consent but are still being treated on the questionable authority of a Form 38.

2.66 Commissioners will raise issues of good practice when, for example:

■ Forms 38 do not state an upper dosage limit, or the number of drugs authorised in any BNF category described;

■ Forms 38 have been completed by a doctor who is neither the current RMO nor a SOAD; or

■ Forms 38 have not been regularly reviewed.

2.67 Where we have noted improvements in the administration of Part IV of the Act, this is usually due to the introduction or refinement of audit tools and flagging systems to record and trigger specific actions ensuring compliance with good practice and the law (see, for example, Chapter 5.22 on High Security Hospitals).

Recommendation 22

All service providers should have adequate audit tools and flagging systems to record and trigger specific actions ensuring compliance with the consent to treatment provisions of the Act.

(see also recommendation 7, para 2.20)

Recommendation 23

A copy of the relevant statutory Form 38 or 39 should be kept attached to patients' medicine charts and pharmacists should be asked to check against this authorisation before dispensing medication for patients.

Compliance with CPA Guidance and Section 117

2.68 Guidance on implementing the Care Programme Approach is given in *Effective Care Co-ordination in Mental Health Services: Modernising the Care Programme Approach*[27]. This builds upon the National Service Framework for Mental Health's specific standards (Standards Four and Five) aimed to ensure that services for people with severe mental illness are effective. These include requirements that patients detained under the Act, as well as informal patients:

- receive care which optimises engagement, anticipates or prevents a crisis, and reduces risk;

- have a copy of a written care plan which is regularly reviewed; and

- have a written aftercare plan agreed on discharge, which sets out the care to be provided, identifies the care co-ordinator, and specifies the action to be taken in a crisis.

2.69 Although the the NSF standards extend the expectation of pre-discharge planning to *all* patients, those subject to Section 117 of the Act have a statutory entitlement to aftercare. Patients with such entitlement should therefore be clearly identified in patient records, particularly as funding questions may arise during discharge planning.

2.70 Clear and detailed guidance on aftercare planning and discharge is given in the Mental Health Act Code of Practice (Chapter 27). Given the frequent failures to comply with aspects of this guidance, the following points are often highlighted by Commissioners on visits:

- The planning arrangements for aftercare should start when the patient is admitted to hospital, rather than only being addressed when imminent discharge is envisaged.

- Some discussion of aftercare needs must take place prior to any Mental Health Review Tribunal or hospital managers' hearing, so that suitable aftercare arrangements can be implemented if the patient is discharged, even if the care-team does not expect discharge to result from the hearing.

- Multi-disciplinary Section 117 meetings should be held and documented before a patient can be granted any substantial period of leave under Section 17.

Recommendation 24

All relevant agencies should take particular note of discharge planning requirements for patients subject to Section 117 of the Act

---

2.71 We still find many examples of poor practice on visits, although examples of the effective use of the Care Programme Approach and fulfillment of statutory duties under Section 117 are increasingly in evidence. Where this is so, marked benefits have been noted in relation to patients' relationship with their RMOs and care-teams. The Commission will continue to check CPA documentation on its visits and to encourage service providers to comply with the Code of Practice's advice.

---

27 Department of Health (2000) **Effective Care Co-ordination: Modernising the Care Programme Approach.** London, Stationery Office. www.doh.gov.uk/pub/docs/doh/polbook/pdf

2.72 In a number of examples encountered on Commission visits, even where high quality Care Programme Approach documentation was evident, the effectiveness of the Care Programme Approach for individual patients' care was hampered by lack of co-operation from outside agencies, or lack of appropriate facilities for patients to go to when discharged from hospital. In particular:

- Some social service authorities seem reluctant to accept their statutory duties in relation to Section 117: the Commission was informed that one authority would only do so after judicial action had been threatened.

- Many care-teams have reported that the transfer or discharge of patients was held back due to lack of social care provision and suitable housing accommodation. A typical example was recorded on a Commission visit to an NHS Trust in March 2000, where managers and staff all reported to Commissioners that the lack of throughput through the unit, a lack of funding for community placements and a shortage of suitable accommodation outlets were a significant and constant problem. Managers suggested that fifteen to twenty of the patients detained in one unit would have been discharged were it not for these difficulties.

- The independent sector has reported difficulties in getting relevant agencies, such as social services or referring hospital consultants for Out of Area Treatments, to attend planning meetings, partly due to the fact that many of its patients are out-of-area placements from NHS facilities. The Commission has encouraged independent sector facilities to seek a rapprochement with such agencies and to allow flexibility over the scheduling of such meetings, but it has been reported that some agencies have indicated that they are too busy even to attend six-monthly meetings. We are very concerned that such attitudes could hamper the transfer or eventual discharge of patients from out-of-area independent sector placements.

2.73 The provisions for new joint health and social care Trusts and for pooled budgeting arrangements under the Health Act 1999 offer the potential for problems of this kind to be minimised. Meanwhile, the Commission condemns the widespread derogatory term of 'bed blockers' to describe patients whose discharge is hindered by a lack of provision over which the patient has absolutely no control.

Monitoring the Independent Sector

2.74 The Commission visits and monitors the application of the Mental Health Act in all Registered Mental Nursing Homes (the term encompasses all hospital provision in the independent sector) that are licensed to detain patients under the Act. In some of the smaller homes that may only occasionally provide care for detained patients, the operation of the Act can be difficult because of lack of administrative support, training and experience, as well as uncertainty over who can fulfil the role of hospital managers under the Act. Many smaller homes' medical cover is also provided part-time by General Practitioners, with psychiatric input being provided on a part-time basis by a psychiatrist, often from a local NHS Trust. The former may not have the necessary experience of the Act, and neither may have sufficient time, to ensure that good practice is always observed. Difficulties in liaison with referral bodies and social services, particularly when patients are received into nursing homes for Out of Area Treatment, continue to be a problem. We discussed these problems in our Seventh and Eighth Biennial Reports[28].

---

28 Mental Health Act Commission (1997) **Seventh Biennial Report** London, Stationery Office p74 – 76. Mental Health Act Commission (1999) **Eighth Biennial Report** London, Stationery Office p106 – 110

2.75 Under current legislation, services in the independent sector that are able to take detained patients must be registered under Part II of the Registered Homes Act 1984 by local Health Authorities. The process of registration itself should be an opportunity to ensure that such homes are able to comply with the requirements of the law and the Mental Health Act Code of Practice. The Commission works alongside local authority registration units providing advice and assistance in this matter, but has repeatedly pointed to the lack of legislative regulations or standards concerning the use of the Mental Health Act that registration units could apply, as well as to the lack of an effective and focussed sanction that could be brought to bear on failing service providers.

2.76 We welcome the Government's acknowledgement that the Registered Homes Act 1984 and the systems established to police it are no longer suited to the patterns of mental healthcare provision. We are therefore pleased that the Care Standards Act 2000 has provided for the establishment of the National Care Standards Commission (NCSC), one of whose duties will be, when it takes up its regulatory work in April 2002, to set standards for registration of private and independent services providing care to patients detained under the Mental Health Act.

2.77 In its response to the House of Commons Health Committee's call for Mental Health Act Commission representation at a national level on the new regulatory body[29], the Government has given assurances that the successor body to the Commission under new mental health legislation will have complementary functions to other bodies, including the NCSC[30]. In the meantime, we hope that the Government will give its full support to collaborative working between the Mental Health Act Commission and NCSC to ensure that the experience of the former informs regulation of the independent sector in both the short and long term.

29 House of Commons Health Committee, **Fifth Report of Session 1998–99 on the Regulation of Private and other Independent Health Care** (HC 281–I), July 1999 (para 75).

30 Department of Health (1999) **The Government's Response to the Health Committee's Fifth Report on the Regulation of Private and other Independent Healthcare**. Cmnd 4540. London, Stationery Office. (Page 6).

3   Quality and Standards of Care

The Infrastructure of Mental Health Services

Admission Trends

3.1   Over the last decade there has been an increase in the numbers of patients detained under the Act (see figure 2 below). This increase has occurred during a time when there has been a reduction in the number of beds and an increase in the use of community-based facilities and outpatient treatment for those patients whose mental disorder can be managed away from an institutional setting. This means, however, that a high proportion of psychiatric in-patients is now detained. In a simultaneous visit to a large representative sample of acute units in 1996[31], the Commission found that nearly one third of the patients in acute units were detained. In some areas this proportion reached over 90%. This makes the role of the Commission, whose remit is limited to monitoring the use of powers and discharge of duties in relation to patients who are liable to be detained, all the more central in the overview of inpatient mental health services.

3.2   Under present legislation, compulsory treatment can only be administered in hospital. It seems likely that this may be a deciding factor in the instigation or continuation of a significant proportion of detentions under the present Act. We welcome, cautiously, the proposal that new legislation will break the link between compulsory treatment and detention in hospital[32], particularly in that it may shorten the time that some patients are required to stay in hospital.

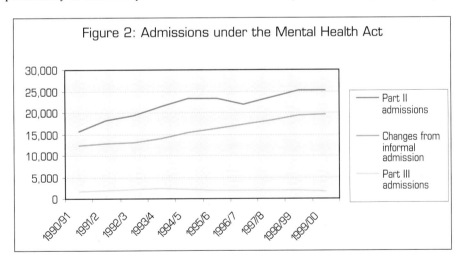

Figure 2: Admissions under the Mental Health Act

(Due to the availability of data, the above table relates to admission in England only. Changes from Places of Safety detentions are not included.)

---

31 Mental Health Act Commission and Sainsbury Centre (1997) **The National Visit. A one-day visit to 309 acute admission wards by the Mental Health Act Commission and Sainsbury Centre for Mental Health**. London, Sainsbury Centre for Mental Health.

32 Department of Health (2000) **Reforming the Mental Health Act**. Part I: The New Legal Framework London, Stationery Office. Cm 5016-I para 2.13 et seq

3.3 A discussion of the use of holding powers (shown as "changes from informal admission" in the above table) can be found at Chapter 2.38. Further discussion of admission data in relation to ethnicity is at Chapter 6.9.

Bed Pressures

3.4 Standard Five of the National Service Framework sets out the expectation that any patient who is assessed as requiring mental health care away from their home should have timely access to an appropriate hospital or alternative bed, in the least restrictive environment and as close to home as is possible.

3.5 We continue to be concerned that the pressures on inpatient beds reported in our last four Biennial Reports continue to hamper achievement of this objective, resulting in:

■ delays in acute admissions;

■ patients being moved during their admission;

■ sending patients on leave, often to poor living environments and with inadequate community support and supervision (sometimes shifting the burden of care and responsibility onto relatives or carers who may be ill-equipped to cope), so as to free beds for other admissions;

■ staff time being diverted from direct patient care to find alternative placements;

■ patients being transferred to expensive and distant out-of-area placements, away from family and other supporters;

■ inappropriate patient mix on admission wards, in that patients of a wide range in age and diagnosis share facilities (e.g. elderly or depressed patients being cared for alongside young men with drug or alcohol problems);

■ and lack of appropriate aftercare planning, both through pressures on staff time and because of logistical problems due to patients' movements within mental health services.

3.6 These pressures, and their effects on patient care, are frequently noted by Commissioners during visits. Many services are operating at well over 100% capacity and sending patients on leave to generate 'free' beds. Our experience is that high bed occupancies and lack of free beds hampers patient movement across all services, from low security to the High Security Hospitals. The National Service Framework for Mental Health recognises that up to a third of all inpatients would be better placed elsewhere and that there are gaps in medium secure and low secure long-stay provision, intensive care and supported community daycare[33]. The Government has accepted that a holistic approach to relieving pressures on such services is needed, but this could be hampered by the extent of the problem not being accurately reflected in national statistics, given that patients who are on leave are not uniformly counted in bed-occupancy figures.

> Recommendation 25
>
> The Department of Health should ensure that national statistics on bed occupancy take account of detained patients who are on leave from inpatient beds, so that available beds and bed occupancy can be monitored more meaningfully.

---

33 Department of Health (1999) **A National Service Framework for Mental Health**. London, Stationery Office, p 49.

3.7 A number of mental health services have attempted to deal proactively with the problem of bed pressures, with some encouraging results. Common to most attempts is an increased focus on community-based and outreach services, so as to reduce the numbers of patients requiring admission to hospital under compulsion and to facilitate the discharge of patients who could leave hospital if appropriate services in the community were available. We welcome the following Government initiatives included within the NHS Plan that should enhance such services.

- Proposals for 50 early intervention teams for the effective support and treatment in the community of young people experiencing the first signs of psychosis.

- The establishment of 335 crisis resolution teams, aimed at providing home-based services to people currently admitted to hospital.

- The establishment of 220 assertive outreach teams across the country to provide active support to people with mental health problems whom traditional services have found hard to engage.

3.8 In the ongoing development of mental health services it is essential that commissioners of health care monitor bed occupancy and ensure that safe standards are applied. We encourage all mental health services to adopt proactive bed management strategies:

Recommendation 26

Where shortage of beds appears to be adversely affecting services, service commissioners and providers should jointly consider and identify within the NSF local implementation plan:

Short-term action: local reviews of all current inpatient stays with a view to clearly identifying the purpose of admission, anticipated length of stay and action required to achieve discharge.

Longer-term action: the establishment of systems & policies that lead to an increase in planned rather than emergency admissions, closer involvement of care co-ordinators during in-patient stays, and greater use of inpatient staff in providing advice to community staff where admission is being considered;

- a review of policies and procedures around admission, assessment care planning and discharge;
- closer work between community and inpatient teams;
- the provision of staff training in CPA and risk management for both community and in-patient staff; and
- consideration of whether inadequacies in community provision are leading to admissions that could have been prevented with earlier intervention.

Staffing Issues

3.9 Most mental health services visited by the Commission report recruitment and retention problems causing shortages of suitably trained staff who are experienced in the care of people with mental health problems. The effects of such staffing shortages are bound to have a wide-ranging effect on such hospitals' service through the increased pressure on existing staff and an overall reduction in the quality of patient care. In the worst cases, the Commission has been informed of potentially dangerous ward environments due to the numbers of staff available.

3.10 We therefore welcome the establishment by the Government of the Mental Health Workforce Action Team (WAT), set up to explore the practical solutions necessary to help deliver the workforce issues around the National Service Framework for Mental Health and the NHS Plan. In their Final Report[34], the WAT sets out the issues around recruitment and retention of staff, as well as issues around education and training, setting these elements in the context of the wider workforce issues. We are pleased to note the many references to examples of good practice as well as the recommendations made to improve recruitment and retention in particular. The Mental Health Task Force has also given clear guidance on how best to implement the WAT report and we look forward to a joint approach being taken by all the bodies mentioned to make improvements in the current position.

3.11 The WAT already report that good examples can be found of services engendering workforce plans centred around the NSF standards and Health Improvement Plans. Such workforce plans identify workforce profiles and future staffing needs, including recruitment, retention and training needs. We are particularly pleased to note examples of inter-agency working in setting up such plans to encompass both health and social services, and private and voluntary services as well as the NHS.

3.12 However, serious difficulties are faced in many areas of the service at present, all of which have very regrettable effects on patient care. We recognise that problems caused by understaffing increase the pressures on the service and can lead to:

- less time available for therapeutic interactions between staff and patients;

- strain on patients' therapeutic relationships with staff, particularly with temporary or frequently changing medical staff;

- restrictions on patients' attendance at therapeutic activities, and free access to fresh air, etc;

- poorer compliance with the Care Programme Approach requirements regarding personalised care programmes, proper risk assessments and pre-discharge planning; and

- poorer compliance with the safeguards of the Act, particularly with regard to consent to treatment, leave arrangements, etc.

3.13 Nevertheless, more imaginative approaches may help mental health services manage more effectively:

Recommendation 27

All local mental health service managers faced with staffing problems should consider the following examples of best practice identified by Commissioners:

- providing greater access to support and supervision to staff;

- wider use of psychologists and other professionals in ward-based activities, particularly at trainee level;

- bringing therapists (including art or drama therapists) onto wards on a sessional basis;

- encouraging patients and staff to contribute to ward activities through sharing their skills in activity groups; and

- providing training to staff in behaviour management, particularly de-escalation techniques.

---

34 Workforce Action Team (2001) **Mental Health National Service Framework (and the NHS Plan) Workforce Planning, Education and Training Underpinning Programme: Adult Mental Health Services: Final Report by the Workforce Action Team**. London, Stationery Office. www.doh.gov.uk/nsf/mentalhealth.htm

3.14 One area that requires particular attention is the shortage of consultant psychiatrists that is felt throughout mental health services. Many services report their reliance on locums and temporary cover for consultant vacancies. This can make the maintenance of therapeutic relationships between patients and doctors difficult. It can also threaten the establishment or continuation of good practice in operating the Act, through a lack of thorough knowledge and experience of the Mental Health Act and/or unfamilarity with the facility where it is applied.

Essential Environmental Requirements

3.15 Although issues relating to patient safety, including suicide prevention and mixed sex accommodation in mental health units, are discussed at Chapters 4 and 6 of this report (see Chapters 4.11 – 4.22, 6.33 – 6.38), it cannot be over-emphasised that acceptable standards in detained patients' surroundings are a precondition of a safe and therapeutic environment. This is recognised by various reports, including the Sainsbury Centre's *Acute Problems*[35] and the Government-sponsored *Review of Security at the High Security Hospitals*[36].

3.16 The Commission's Eighth Biennial Report contained many references to an inadequate standard of physical environment for inpatients with wards which:

- were poorly furnished and badly decorated;

- lacked privacy for patients;

- provided minimal standards of security for patients' belongings; and

- caused concern for patient safety.

3.17 In visits to all mental health units that detain patients under the Act, Commissioners encounter a wide variety of environmental standards. Some units manage to be bright, clean and cheerful, whilst others, regrettably, continue to provide bleak conditions for patients. We welcome the Government's announcement of a £30m refurbishment programme over the next two years, targeted in the first year to wards identified as being the most run-down.

3.18 There is a danger that environmental issues, such as décor, or access to fresh air and activities, rank fairly low amongst the many priorities that unit managers have to contend with. But for many detained patients, especially those housed on acute wards, being confined in unpleasant surroundings with few opportunities for respite or relief can be profoundly anti-therapeutic, contributing to management problems (see Chapter 4.32 – 4.34) and undermining attempts to provide a safe environment for vulnerable people (see Chapter 4.11 *et seq.*).

> Recommendation 28
>
> All service commissioners and providers should ensure that the general environmental quality of inpatient facilities are subject to locally agreed, systematically monitored standards.

---

35 Sainsbury Centre for Mental Health (1998) **Acute Problems: A survey of the quality of care in acute psychiatric wards**. London, Sainsbury Centre for Mental Health pp20

36 Department of Health (2000) **Report of the Review of Security at the High Security Hospitals**. London, Stationery Office p5 – 6

3.19 We have noted some imaginative and sensitive approaches to ensuring that patients feel happier with their environment:

Good Practice example

Patients being relocated from one hospital site to another in Cardiff and Vale NHS Trust were involved in choosing the décor and furnishings for their new wards. This process has been a success in so far as the new environment has had a recognisably beneficial effect on the way in which patients treat their surroundings, staff and each other. We understand that Cardiff and Vale NHS Trust are now extending this approach across its other mental health units.

Contact: Chief Executive Cardiff & Vale NHS Trust , Cardigan House, Heath Park, Cardiff CF14 4XW Tel: 02920747747

Patients' access to fresh air

3.20 In many units, particularly but not exclusively those providing medium and high secure care, patients' access to fresh air remains a problem. The former Special Health Services Authority (SHSA) specified a minimum standard for patients in the High Security Hospitals to have access to fresh air for 10 hours per week during summer months and four hours per week in winter. Sadly, even this minimal level is not always attained.

3.21 Many units do not have any substantial and secure outside area. This is particularly the case in a number of medium-secure units in urban settings. In many such cases, staff shortages or shift patterns appear to limit the availability of nursing staff to accompany those patients who cannot be allowed unescorted leave.

3.22 The patients in many medium and high secure care wards can be young and active people, for whom cramped indoor conditions exacerbate frustrations and lead to management problems. Regardless of the nature of the patients, however, access to fresh air should be regarded as a basic human need and taken very seriously by hospital managers and staff alike.

Patient activity and facilities

3.23   In a report published early in this biennial reporting period, the Department of Health's Standing Nursing and Midwifery Committee stated that *'users, carers and professionals agree that in-patient units are becoming increasingly custodial in their atmosphere. Our work suggests that users in acute care often feel that they are being deprived of therapeutic activity, have much less contact with nurses than they would wish, and at times feel unsafe.* [37] *'*

3.24   The experience of the Commission is that whilst this is a true reflection of care standards in many instances, there is no reason why services in acute and other care cannot be improved.

3.25   On visits, Commissioners pay particular attention to the levels of patient activity on and off wards. On a number of visits, some of which are unannounced, patients are observed sitting in lounges or bedroom areas with little of no discernable focus of activity and no obvious interaction with staff. Whilst it would be unrealistic for us to suggest specific standards, all too often we encounter bored patients whose only recreational activities are smoking and television. Patients often speak of their need for more recreational activities, including access to sports facilities, such as gymnasium, keep-fit or yoga sessions; a better variety of reading matter; cooking or craft activities; drama or art therapy workshops, etc.

Recommendation 31

Hospital managers should consider addressing the provision of patient activities and facilities by:

- ■ ensuring that all patients are aware of opportunities on offer, both through publicly displayed information and individual discussion with patients as a part of their care plan;

- ■ using monitoring and user-surveys to identify needs and opportunities in providing activities;

- ■ considering the use of voluntary or other agencies, or of existing contracted staff within the Trust to bolster available activities on a sessional basis; and

- ■ employing or designating an activities co-ordinator.

The provision of therapeutic interventions

3.26   The precise definition of therapeutic interventions can be a problem, specifically for hospital managers' audits and monitoring of service standards. We have noted that some services have adopted classifications for this purpose , based on the following distinctions:

Type A interventions include low-key approaches such as craftwork, current affairs discussions, etc.

Type B interventions have a defined therapeutic purpose and include social skills training, relaxation therapy and less intensive forms of group therapy.

Type C interventions have a pre-defined therapeutic methodology and specific targeted therapeutic goals such as a victim empathy group, or individual dynamic psychotherapy.

---

37 Department of Health (1999) **Addressing Acute Concerns: Report by the Standing Nursing and Midwifery Committee**. London, Stationery Office. June 1999

3.27   Patients often inform Commissioners that they feel that they are provided with inadequate therapeutic interventions, such as psychological therapy or counselling, and that their treatment appears to be limited to being administered medication. While we recognise the value of pharmacological treatment for serious mental disorder, such impressions appear to be profoundly anti-therapeutic for patients and raise concerns about the reality of multi-disciplinary working.

3.28   The Health Select Committee report on Mental Health Services recognised that there is a shortage of psychologically-based treatments in the NHS, but that it is not known whether this is primarily due to the shortage of professionals able to deliver them, lack of awareness among those responsible for purchasing mental health services as to their benefits, or cost[38]. We welcome the Government's action in relation to staffing; education and training; and clinical decision support systems, which we hope will move the NHS towards addressing this problem.

3.29   We particularly welcome the publication in February 2001 of Department of Health guidance on *Treatment Choice in Psychological Therapies and Counselling*[39]. While recognising that the guidance does not extend to the treatment of all patients who are likely to be detained under the Act (especially given the exclusion of psychotic disorders from the scope of the guidelines, despite the National Service Framework for Mental Health's recognition that there is a growing evidence of the effectiveness of psychological therapies for schizophrenia[40]), we expect that all service commissioners and providers will adopt the key implementation points and audit criteria suggested by the guidelines in assuring that the services that they pay for and provide are in accord with evidence-based practice.

> Recommendation 32
>
> Mental health service commissioners and providers should agree specific standards for the provision of recreational, educational and therapeutic activities and monitor their availability and uptake, taking account of patients' views.

3.30   The Commission has undertaken some preliminary studies of access to psychology and psychotherapy within the High Security Hospitals over the last year (see Chapter 5.19 – 5.21 below).

Survey of ECT Facilities

3.31   The way in which patients are treated while undergoing what can be the distressing experience of Electro Convulsive Treatment (ECT) is a good indicator of how seriously service providers take their responsibility of care. During 2000/2001 Commissioners made a survey of all ECT facilities in England and Wales, using a standardised form based partly on criteria published by the Royal College of Psychiatrists and partly on Commissioners' experience. The full results of this survey became available only at the end of the period covered by this report and will be described in a comprehensive analysis to be published in due course. A preliminary examination

---

38 Department of Health (2000) **The Government's Response to the Health Select Committee's Report on Mental Health Services**. London, Stationery Office, October 2000. Page 17

39 Department of Health (2001) **Treatment Choice in Psychological Therapies and Counselling : Evidence-based Clinical Practice Guideline**. www.doh.gov.uk/mentalhealth/treatmentguideline

40 Department of Health (1999) **A National Service Framework for Mental Health**. London, Stationery Office. p 46

of the results has been carried out with the help of one of the staff of the Royal College of Psychiatrists; a brief summary of this is given below.

3.32 Commissioners interviewed an informed member of staff at 230 sites and visited the ECT suite or other facility to verify certain elements of the information given. 48 standardised questions were asked, covering the main areas shown in Figure 3 (see Chapter 7.23 for a similar breakdown for Wales alone).

Fig 3

Item	Percent (n=230 sites surveyed in England and Wales)
The Arrangements for ECT Possession of a dedicated ECT suite, comprising 3 or more rooms, including a separate waiting room and recovery room	68
A Policy for ECT Clinics which were able to show the Commissioner either a copy of the Royal College of Psychiatrists Handbook or a copy of the hospital's own ECT policy	95
A Named Consultant Psychiatrist ECT clinics with a named consultant psychiatrist who visits regularly	73
Recovery and Resuscitation ECT Clinics that have, in practice, a nurse in the recovery room who is trained in Basic Life Support, Cardio-pulmonary Resuscitation and who attends refresher courses in resuscitation regularly	64

3.33 In 18 instances, the facilities visited scored very highly in each of the main criteria surveyed and in another 30 instances they appeared to comply substantially. Good practice was identified in many of these cases and will be highlighted in the forthcoming special publication.

3.34 At the other end of the scale, the survey indicated that there were substantial departures from best policy, practice or training in about 20% of cases. This does not necessarily mean that any individual patient is being adversely affected, but it does suggest unacceptable standards of service. The Commission will be writing to the relevant Chief Executives asking them to review their policies and practice in the light of the findings.

3.35 At this stage of analysis and follow-up it would not be appropriate to make any specific recommendations. During the summer and autumn of 2001, we will be reviewing the survey as a prelude to further discussions and consideration of the findings with the ECT Committee of the Royal College of Psychiatrists. The intention is to publish a fuller picture of policy and practice relating to ECT administration thereafter.

4   Safety and Security

A Safe and Therapeutic Environment

4.1   The National Service Framework for Mental Health requires local health and social care communities to provide safe hospital accommodation for those who need it (Standards Five and Seven). We welcome the Government's emphasis on patient safety in the White Paper on *Reforming the Mental Health Act* and related initiatives.

4.2   Patients are detained under the Act on the justification that this is necessary for their own health, for their safety or for the protection of others. There is very little evidence that prevailing standards of security for detained patients have caused any disproportionate risk to members of the public, but we are concerned that patients' own safety is not always adequately protected by the actions of mental health services and can be compromised by their omissions. The key issues of concern are highlighted in this chapter.

Protecting Patients from Inappropriate Placements

4.3   Among the greatest risks to the safety of detained patients are:

- fear of hospitals which prevents them from seeking early help;

- fear of other patients which prevents them from benefiting from treatment; and

- self-harm which is often increased by a poor environment, boredom, and loss of hope aggravated by being with patients who are more vulnerable than themselves.

These are matters frequently cited by patients and others in meetings with Commissioners. A major cause is the way in which people enter the acute care system and an inappropriate mix of patients in confined conditions (see Chapter 3.4 *et seq.*).

Places of Safety (Section 136)

4.4   The way in which mentally ill people who need to be taken to a place of safety by the police are treated is a cause of ongoing concern. Police stations continue to be the most common location used as places of safety, despite repeated emphasis on the undesirability of this in every Biennial Report issued by the Commission and guidance in the Code of Practice (paragraph 10.5) and the Memorandum to the Act (paragraph 315). People who are thought likely to be mentally ill should be treated as individuals whose greatest need is a sensitive response which does not itself catalyse violent reactions for which the patient is then blamed.

4.5   Section 135(6) of the Act does not restrict places of safety to police stations or hospitals but allows for them to be " a mental nursing home or residential home for mentally disordered persons or other suitable place, the occupier of which is willing temporarily to receive the patient". The Government's policy on a more holistic and primary care based approach to those with acute episodes of mental illness provides an excellent opportunity for health, social and voluntary services to work together locally to provide a much wider range of such places of safety.

4.6 One of the our key objectives over the next two years is to encourage such co-operation by monitoring the use of Section 136 on a country-wide basis and liaising with the police to see if more consistent policies and training can be provided on their response to people who appear to be mentally ill in a public place. An imaginative multi-disciplinary approach towards these particular powers must be developed so that the person held receives a responsive service that meets their needs, reduces risks, and enables the services involved to resume their other responsibilities as soon as possible.

Ensuring appropriate outcomes

4.7 While the immediate purpose of an arrest under Section 136 will be the protection of the person concerned or of other people, the Act also provides that the purpose of the subsequent holding power is to enable the detainee to be examined by a doctor and interviewed by an Approved Social Worker so that any necessary arrangements for further care or treatment can be made. (Section 136(2)). The Code of Practice's guidance on this aspect of the Act (specifically at paragraphs 10.8a and 10.14a) has been widely misunderstood by services seeking to draw up Section 136 policies, and the Commission has been frequently approached to give an interpretation.

4.8 It is our view that, if the doctor who examines a person detained under Section 136 fails to detect any form of mental disorder whatsoever, that person should be discharged from detention under Section 136 immediately, as there can be no reasonable legal grounds for the holding power to continue. If however, the doctor concludes upon examination that the person appears to be suffering from a mental disorder as defined in Section 1(2) of the Act, whether or not of a nature or degree sufficient to justify detention under Sections 2 or 3 of the Act, the detention under Section 136 should continue until an Approved Social Worker has seen the person and a decision has been reached on the arrangements needed for further care or treatment. We emphasise that this should be the case even if, on examination, the doctor feels that neither further detention under the Act nor informal admission to hospital will be required. In this way the law seeks to ensure that no mentally ill person held under Section 136 is discharged without some form of follow-up care.

4.9 We note that the above interpretation is reflected in the Police and Criminal Evidence Act Code of Practice (C, para 3.10) and is therefore a widely appreciated requirement for patients held in police stations.

Ensuring more appropriate placements

4.10   Better and more consistent police training and a wider range of places of safety should reduce the number of people who are inappropriately taken to police stations or busy hospitals where any aggressive reactions are likely to be triggered as much by fear and confusion as by any innate dangerousness. We therefore welcome the Government's proposals for:

- increases in early intervention;
- introduction of more crisis resolution teams;
- enhancement of community facilities and treatment;
- the provision of more specialised facilities for the most disruptive and dangerous patients; and
- more medium secure places.

Together these developments should all enable patients to be treated with more sensitivity and within a more appropriate patient-mix, so that the management problems which are exacerbated by poor environments, lack of activity and lack of hope may be reduced. This, in turn, should reduce the level of fear and the widely held belief that hospital settings are unsafe. Particular attention needs to be paid to the needs of specific patient groups, such as women (see chapter 6.33 – 6.39 below) .

Protecting Patients in Hospital

Environmental safety and security

4.11   All too often, references to environmental safety and security concentrate solely on removing opportunities for patients to self-harm or abscond. It is impossible to over-emphasise that these aspects must be seen as only part of a holistic approach to the care of patients. This must aim to ensure that the environment in which patients are cared for reduces the likelihood of them trying to self-harm or abscond by providing good standards of accommodation and catering, access to activities and fresh air, and – most important of all – interaction with staff who regard them as individuals with particular personal needs and wishes.

4.12   Our concerns about these broad aspects of safety and security are discussed in Chapter 3. They can all be major causative factors in management problems, generating patients' distress, aggression and self-harm. While, therefore, the following paragraphs highlight physical aspects of safety, we stress that these must be underpinned by work on making hospital wards better places to be in.

Learning from adverse events

4.13   The Commission's contribution to helping services to learn from failure was acknowledged in the report of the expert group chaired by the Chief Medical Officer, *An Organisation with a*

Memory[41], which recognised specifically that a very critical Commission visiting report was the catalyst for change in one troubled establishment. The expert group was critical, however, of the fact that what it described as 'barriers to learning' should have prevented action at the unit prior to the Commission's intervention. We wholeheartedly agree with this analysis and condemn any approach which focuses on blame rather than on learning from mistakes as well as from good practice elsewhere.

4.14 We therefore welcomed the Government's acceptance of all the recommendations in *An Organisation with a Memory*[42], which should establish a system within the NHS ensuring that lessons from adverse events in one locality are learned across the service. This philosophy has particular relevance to "untoward incidents".

4.15 In February 2000 *The Report of the Review of Security at the High Security Hospitals* (the 'Tilt Report', which is further discussed at Chapter 5) recommended that untoward incidents should be categorised according to the seriousness of outcome and in accordance with the Mental Health Act Commission's classifications. These classifications are as follows:

■ *Class A Incidents* – Incidents that result in death or cause such serious harm that they place life in jeopardy. They include, but are not limited to, homicide, attempted homicide, sudden and unexpected death and suicide.

■ *Class B Incidents* – Incidents that are not life threatening, but which acutely jeopardise the well-being of anyone involved. They include, but are not limited to, allegations of patient abuse or neglect, assaults, attempted suicide, unexplained injuries and serious errors of medication.

■ *Class C Incidents* – Incidents which seriously affect, or have the potential to seriously affect, the health or psychological well-being of individuals involved. They include, but are not limited to, errors of medication (which <u>may</u> be Class B incidents), sexual improprieties, and sexual or racial harassment. Accidental injuries, assaults and acts of deliberate self-harm may amount to either Class C or Class D incidents depending on the severity of the outcome.

■ *Class D Incidents* – Incidents which result in no injury, or only very minor injury, and do not involve any blame on the part of any member of the staff of the relevant Trust.

■ *Class E Incident*s – Any other untoward occurrence.

Recommendation 34

Service commissioners and providers should agree:

■ standard classifications for incident reporting to be adopted in relation to all incidents involving detained patients;

■ common management monitoring, audit and analysis of all untoward incidents falling within Class A, B and C to see whether any patterns emerge and what lessons can be learnt; and

■ an arrangement for joint consideration of such patterns/lessons.

---

41 Department of Health (2000) **An Organisation with a Memory: report of an expert group on learning from adverse events in the NHS chaired by the Chief Medical Officer**. London, Stationery Office . See page 33 for the example cited.

42 Department of Health (2001*)* **Building a Safer NHS for Patients: implementing An Organisation with a Memory**. London, Stationery Office (www.doh.gov.uk/buildsafenhs/)

4.16   We are glad to note that the need for separate notification of incidents involving patients detained under the Mental Health Act is recognised in the Government's plans for promoting patient safety[43]. We look forward to working with the newly established National Patient Safety Agency, which will implement and operate the overall system of data collection and analysis.

Learning from patient deaths

4.17   Standard Seven of the National Service Framework for Mental Health introduced a number of general expectations towards the reduction of suicides amongst the mentally ill. These have been further reinforced by the setting of a standard of zero suicides by inpatients from suspension from shower rails or hanging rails in wardrobes by 2002[44], as recommended in *An Organisation with a Memory*. The oversight of hanging rails within wardrobes as an opportunistic suicide risk has been a particular concern of Commissioners during the two years covered by this report and we are pleased to note that it has been highlighted so specifically.

4.18   Shower and wardrobe rails nevertheless form only a proportion of the means whereby patients attempt suicide. The Commission published its report Deaths of Detained Patients in England and Wales[45] in March 2001. This report presented the findings of our review of every patient who died whilst subject to detention under the Mental Health Act during the three year period 1997–2000. Of 1,471 such deaths, 253 were reported to the coroner as being from unnatural causes. We were able to consider 208 inquest verdicts from this group.

4.19   A summary of the main findings and recommendations from this review is at **Appendix B** to this report. The outcomes, which all underline the need for constant vigilance and awareness on the part of staff, are being followed up separately. Only two particular aspects of the findings are highlighted here because of their significant implications for safety and security. The first is that the assumption that most deaths which are categorised as hanging relate to a suspension or drop from a high point which fatally damages the central nervous system or other vital structures in the neck may be misleading. The nature of the ligatures used in our detailed study suggests that many instances of so-called hanging could be due to strangulation, where a much less robust ligature pulled tight around the neck may cause asphyxiation, reflex cardiac inhibition leading to arrest, or failure of blood supply to the brain. Strangulation of this kind requires neither a fall from a height nor the suspension of the body from a load-bearing point.

4.20   This finding implies that advice on the prevention of suicide requires continued attention to be paid, where there is a substantial risk of suicide, to the removal of a wider range of ligatures than at present, including some seemingly harmless items such as shoe-laces, dressing gown cords and belts. It also requires greater attention to the opportunities provided by some integral components of a normal ward environment such as freestanding cupboards or wardrobes, doorframes, bed frames and low level piping. Perhaps even more importantly, the finding has implications for the nature of observation, since it is much easier to see whether someone is hanging from a height than whether a supine figure is attached to a fixture which might be causing strangulation. The need to train staff in resuscitation techniques appropriate to strangulation also becomes very relevant in the light of this finding.

---

43 Department of Health (2001) **Building a Safer NHS for Patients; implementing An Organisation with a Memory**. London, Stationery Office www.doh.gov.uk/buildsafenhs/ p39

44 Department of Health (2001) **Building a Safer NHS for Patients; implementing An Organisation with a Memory**. London, Stationery Office. p54

45 Mental Health Act Commission (2001) **Deaths of Detained Patients in England and Wales: A report by the Mental Health Act Commission on information collected from 1 February 1997 to 31 January 2000**. Mental Health Act Commission. Copies of the report are available from the Commission for £7.95 + £1 p&p

> **Recommendation 35**
>
> Hospital managers should note the findings of the Mental Health Act Commission report on the deaths of detained patients (see Appendix B):
>
> ■ in assessing the physical risks in the ward environment; and
>
> ■ in considering the training to be given to staff on the management of episodes of strangulation.

4.21   The second finding to which we wish to draw particular attention relates to the location of suicides among detained patients. Of the 168 inquest verdicts of suicide considered, 38 (23%) of the patients concerned killed themselves while on authorised leave and 64 (38%) were absent without leave. This has very significant implications for the management of Section 17 leave and for the prevention and management of patients absent without leave, both of which are considered below. That the remaining 66 patients whose deaths were considered to be suicide at inquest were neither on leave or AWOL should give rise to concerns about the safety of inpatient units.

4.22   We hope to work closely with the Director for Mental Health, Professor Louis Appleby, in pursuing the issue of patient deaths in the light of the publication of the first five-year report of the National Confidential Inquiry[46] and of the work that continues to be done within Professor Appleby's Department at Manchester University on Sudden Unexplained Deaths.

Section 17 Leave

4.23   The finding that one in five suicides of detained patients occurs while the patient is on authorised leave suggests that the management of Section 17 leave could be improved. We recognise that detaining authorities must balance the need to encourage self-reliance and normalisation against the risks involved in greater freedom for patients and have noted many examples of good practice in this. Nevertheless, we continue to see far too many examples of poor practice in the granting of Section 17 leave, which could be avoided by ensuring that the following recommendation is implemented.

> **Recommendation 36**
>
> Hospital managers should ensure that sole discretion for the granting of authorised Section 17 leave is NOT left to the supervising nurse alone but is approved ONLY:
>
> ■ following consultation with involved professionals to ensure that the patient's needs for health and social care are fully assessed and addressed by the care-plan (see Code of Practice, paragraph 27.5), all of which should be recorded in the patient's clinical record;
>
> ■ following a detailed risk assessment which is similarly recorded;
>
> ■ with carefully considered contingency plans, including contact telephone numbers;
>
> ■ with clearly set down parameters, including the time of return;
>
> ■ with clearly set down supervision arrangements; and
>
> ■ with a copy of the Section 17 leave form given to the patient, and to the carer, if appropriate.

---

46 Department of Health (2001) **Safety First: Five-Year Report of the National Confidential Inquiry into Suicide and Homicide by People with Mental Illness**. London, Stationery Office.

4.24 Monitoring the use of Section 17 against these requirements will be a high priority for the Commission during the next two-year period.

4.25 We have noted a number of examples where Section 17 leave forms state that patients have been allowed leave when "escorted" by family members or friends. The implication of such a statement is that the patient would be in the legal custody of relatives while on leave (thus also implying that relatives would have specific legal powers and responsibilities to detain and convey if the patient breaks the leave conditions). In these circumstances we question whether delegating such legal responsibility to relatives or friends is appropriate or even intended. Managers are reminded that whenever a patient is to be escorted by someone other than a member of staff, that person must be given written authority by the hospital managers (Section 17(3)). In the absence of such authority it would be more appropriate to use the term "accompanied" rather than "escorted".

Section 18 and patients absent without leave (AWOL)

4.26 In our Seventh Biennial Report we emphasised the importance of clear policies to enable staff to take appropriate action when a patient goes absent without leave[47]. It is unacceptable to note that some service providers have still to develop and implement policies to deal effectively with this, as required by the Code of Practice (paragraph 21.5). This failure is even more regrettable in view of our finding that one third of the deaths by suicide mentioned above occurred when the patient was absent without leave.

Recommendation 37

Hospital managers should ensure that AWOL policies and procedures clearly indicate:

■ when the patient should be regarded as AWOL;

■ who has responsibility to return the patient;

■ which staff are authorised under Sections 137 and 138 to act to take a patient into custody, convey or detain;

■ what the expectations are of the police in terms of finding and returning patients; and

■ who should take charge of the AWOL procedure, and how they should determine:

■ who should undertake a local search and the extent of the local search;

■ when a wider search should be undertaken and by whom and what areas should be searched;

■ when to contact the police; and

■ when to contact the carers or relatives.

4.27 Patients who are absent without leave are frequently located in a different area from that served by their detaining authority. There is no nationally agreed protocol for arrangements to return such patients, although it is clearly the responsibility of the detaining authority to arrange the conveyance of a patient back to hospital. One of a number of examples which Commissioners have found of the kind of problem this causes was of a patient who had been detained at a registered mental nursing home for "out of area" treatment. The referring NHS Trust had not made clear to the registered home that the patient had a history of absconding and had not

---

47 Mental Health Act Commission (1997) **Seventh Biennial Report**. London, Stationery Office. pp51

discussed the risks that this presented with those who would be responsible for the patient's detention. Consequently, proper arrangements were not made to avoid the patient going AWOL and, when she did do so, the nursing home was ill-prepared, both in terms of having clear policies and in having experienced and available staff, to arrange for her safe return. No significant harm came to the patient in this instance, but it could easily have done so.

Good practice example.

Wirral and West Cheshire Community NHS Trust have adopted procedures that could serve as a useful model for other Trusts. The main points of this protocol are as follows:

- The responsibility for the safe return of an AWOL patient rests with the detaining authority.

- Transport should be by ambulance, with an escort of staff from the detaining authority in accordance with identified risks.

- Where a detaining authority cannot arrange immediate transport, the service provider in whose area the patient has been located should take the patient into custody pending such arrangements. The detaining authority must provide faxed authorisation for this, and should also provide copies of the patient's detention papers.

- The police should only be involved in either custodial or transportation arrangements where absolutely necessary.

Contact: Mrs Gill Edwards, Wirral and West Cheshire Community NHS Trust, St Catherine's Community hospital, Church Road, Birkenhead, Merseyside, CH42 0LG. Tel: 0151 678 7272

Recommendation 38

The Department of Health should negotiate and establish national protocols, encompassing all service providers, to ensure clarity and accountability in all instances where a patient is located out of area, whether by arrangement or because the patient has crossed boundaries without the knowledge of the detaining authority.

Safety in the Administration of Medication

4.28   In considering the administration of medicine, the greatest attention is usually paid to matters of consent, whereas what is just as important for the safety of the patient and others is that the appropriate drugs or other medicines are being prescribed and administered. This can have a significant effect not only on the safety of patients, but also on their ability to function well on leave or discharge. The role of Second Opinion Appointed Doctors (SOADs) is crucial to this aspect of treatment where consent has not been given, but in all cases the administration of medication should be subject to rigorous clinical scrutiny. The Commission encourages hospital managers to use the expertise of pharmacists as one such safeguard.

Recommendation 39

A pharmacist should check that Forms 38:

■ have been authorised by the RMO;

■ are accurately reflected in the medication chart, and:

■ comply with the RCP guidance

before releasing any prescription. Pharmacists should also check medication charts against Forms 39 where issued.

4.29 The Royal College of Psychiatrists has issued advice on dosages above the British National Formulatory (BNF) limits which should be adhered to by all psychiatrists[48]. In this connection, it is particularly important that the Responsible Medical Officer (RMO) and nursing staff are aware of aspects of the patient's past history and behaviour, or changes in current behaviour, weight or other relevant factors, which might affect his/her response to the prescribed medication. Good record-keeping is essential to such an awareness.

Recommendation 40

All service providers should obtain of the Royal College of Psychiatrists' guidelines on doses above BNF upper limit for distribution to their staff.

4.30 Generally high standards of medical record keeping are often commented upon by Commissioners during their visits, but poor practice is sometimes found in the wider aspects of the administration of medication. It is the responsibility of the RMO to keep clear, accurate, and contemporaneous patient records which report relevant clinical findings, decisions made, information given to the patient and drugs or other medication prescribed. Good clinical governance is needed to ensure that the relevant information is accurately transferred to the medication charts used by those who administer the medication and that nurses check that what they are giving accords with the RMO's original decision.

4.31 The Commission has published guidance to nurses on the administration of medication and the Act[49], which has been endorsed by the United Kingdom Central Council for Nursing, Midwifery and Health Visiting (UKCC).

Recommendation 41

Hospital managers should ensure that clear policies on the prescription and administration of medication have been agreed and that compliance is regularly audited.

---

48 Royal College of Psychiatrists **Council Report CR26: consensus statement on the use of high-dose antipsychotic medication**. A useful and readily available summary of this statement is reproduced at the beginning of Chapter 4.2 of each edition of the British National Formulary.

49 Mental Health Act Commission (2001) **Guidance Note 2/2001: Nurses, the Administration of Medicine for Mental Disorder and the Mental Health Act 1983**. Available from the Commission or at www.mhac.trent.nhs.uk.

Particular Management Problems

4.32   Patients who are compelled to enter or remain in hospital under the Mental Health Act 1983 may, perhaps more than any other patient group, behave in such a way as to disturb others around them, or to present a risk to themselves or to those charged with their care.

4.33   The very fact of compulsion, coupled with the severity and type of mental disorder being experienced by some detained patients, is likely to be a significant causative factor in this problem behaviour. However, as emphasised above and in Chapter 3, the following often very evident causes can all too easily be overlooked:

- an unsuitable mix of patients;
- boredom and lack of environmental stimulation;
- too much stimulation, noise and general disruption;
- overcrowding;
- antagonism, aggression, or provocation on the part of others;
- influence of alcohol or substance abuse; and
- the rewarding of undesirable behaviour by attention.

4.34   Many of these factors can be eliminated or reduced by effective management policies. During our visits we have witnessed a wide variety of good practice in this respect. In dealing with patients needs, however, it is important to remember that the key to successful intervention lies with the staff, whose own needs must not be overlooked. A typical example of the many adverse effects of failures in the infra-structure is of one ward where Commissioners found that 50% of the E grade nursing staff had left during the past three month period and that the Deputy Ward Manager was on sick leave after an assault by a patient. This had resulted in tremendous pressure on nursing staff, who were all doing extra shifts. The Ward Manager, as an example, was doing three extra shifts during the week of the visit, adding 17.5 hours to her normal 37.5 hour week. This is good for neither staff nor patients.

Violence Against Staff

4.35   One of the key components adding to the pressures on staffing levels (see Chapter 3.9 *et seq.*) appears to be the increasing problem of violence and aggression directed towards staff by patients. We therefore welcomed the launch of the high profile *Zero Tolerance* campaign by the Department of Health in October 1999, and are extremely pleased to note the resources now available on the NHS Zero Tolerance Zone website[50]. We commend this website to all mental health service managers, whether they work within the NHS or the independent sector. The site contains resources specific to mental health services, giving good practice examples and contacts, and the facility for case studies to be submitted by e-mail.

4.36   We are glad to note that the campaign's focus extends to a consideration of the causative factors for patient violence, and recommends risk-assessment and prevention as well as methods of dealing with aggression when it occurs.

4.37   We are also pleased to note the establishment of the National Task Force on Violence Against Social Care Staff[51] in September 1999 and the Minister's acceptance and endorsement of their interim report in March 2000. The National Action Plan, rolled out from January 2001, aims to

---

50 website address: www.nhs.uk/zerotolerance

51 website address: www.doh.gov.uk/violencetaskforce

introduce measures designed to promote the safety of all social welfare workers. We welcome and support the work of the National Task Force and hope that the Department of Health will give full consideration to its recommendations.

Seclusion

4.38   Commissioners make a practice of visiting any patient in seclusion on the day of their visit and monitoring the use of seclusion will be a high priority for the Commission during the next two years.

4.39   The Code of Practice describes seclusion as the supervised containment of a patient in a room which *may* be locked (paragraph 19.16). Seclusion may be used only for the containment of severely disturbed behaviour that is likely to cause harm to others, and should not be used for any other purpose. We deplore the practice of secluding patients under other guises, such as "cooling-off", particularly when such practices are not recorded or monitored as episodes of seclusion. The definition of 'seclusion' is not dependent on whether the door to the room is locked or even closed.

Recommendation 42

Hospital managers should audit the use of seclusion regularly to ensure that it is properly used.

Where the use of seclusion appears high, a seclusion reduction plan should be produced which includes monitoring the effects of any change in management regime on the attitude and behaviour of patients.

4.40   We frequently encounter the following particular areas of concern in relation to the proper use and recording of seclusion.

- *Poor design of seclusion rooms.* Facilities that are structurally inappropriate continue to be used. Commissioners have drawn attention to rooms with blind spots, inwardly opening doors (enabling patients in seclusion to prevent access to the room) and dangerous fittings, such as sharp corners and even ligature points.

- *Poor access to seclusion rooms.* Particularly when seclusion facilities are shared between non-connected wards or sited away from the wards that they service, getting patients into seclusion can be a dangerous and demeaning task. Commissioners have encountered facilities where, for example, patients requiring seclusion had to be taken down two floors through a busy part of a main hospital, or down dangerous staircases and through several sets of doors.

- *Poor regard for privacy and dignity.* A number of seclusion rooms fail to provide dignified facilities. Many of these are barely furnished, if at all. One particularly poor example had only a cardboard potty for toilet facilities and broken air-conditioning. Another room had one way glass that prevented the patient from seeing out but allowed the rest of the ward to see in.

- *Poor documentation of observations.* Commissioners often criticise the recording of observations. Records are often cramped and illegible, or simply fail to record that medical and nursing reviews are being carried out in accordance with the guidance in the Code of Practice (paragraph 19.20).

■ *Poor recording of reasons for seclusion.* For example, one record stated only that "behaviour has become increasingly chaotic and unpredictable, aggressive and wanting to leave the ward". Entries in the seclusion register should be clear and in accordance with the grounds for seclusion stated in paragraph 19.16 of the Code of Practice.

■ *Use of seclusion facilities for other purposes,* blurring the distinction between seclusion and other situations. One facility was used as the seclusion room, a "time-out" room post-medication and an occasional bedroom for a patient who wished to sleep away from the clamour of the ward. The limitations of the ward area should not allow for the seclusion room to be used as a bedroom, quiet room or time out area.

■ *Problems with the prompt attendance of a doctor,* if the doctor is not involved in initiating seclusion. The Code of Practice requires the immediate attendance of a doctor if seclusion is for more than five minutes (paragraph 19.19).

Where we encounter such problems on visits we will continue to expect immediate remedial action by the hospital managers.

4.41   A different kind of example of poor practice is failure to recognise relatively minor matters which may have an adverse effect on the sensory impact of seclusion. One such example is not knowing the time, which may also cause confusion for the patient. Respect for the individual should ensure that, wherever possible, seclusion rooms have a clock visible to the patient.

Recommendation 43

Hospital managers should take all the current areas of concern identified by the Commission into consideration when auditing their arrangements for seclusion

---

4.42   In our Eighth Biennial Report we provided detailed guidance on seclusion practice that was intended to be read alongside the broader guidance in the Code of Practice. This guidance, which is summarised in figure 5 below, is now endorsed by the NHS Zero Tolerance Campaign[52]. Services that use seclusion should ensure that their policies address these issues.

---

52 Department of Health (2001) **NHS Zero Tolerance Zone. Managing Violence in Mental Health. Resource Sheet Update: Seclusion,** www.nhs.uk/zerotolerance/mental/seclusion.htm

4.43   We are pleased to note that some Trusts, such as Portsmouth Healthcare NHS Trust, do not use seclusion at all. Many other services have reduced their use of seclusion significantly. Rampton Hospital is an excellent example of the way in which a range of management responses is used to avoid the use of seclusion.

Reduction in Seclusion in the Men's Intensive Care Ward, Rampton Hospital Authority

Over the last two years, the men's Intensive Care Ward at Rampton Hospital has reduced incidences of seclusion by 76%, and the average duration of seclusion episodes by 85%.

This achievement has resulted from a number of factors, some of which are highlighted below:-

Leadership – Adjustments in the balance of clinical and managerial skills have facilitated the implementation of revised seclusion policies and procedures. The Commission has noted that the ward manager's management style, clinical skills and commitment to education has been a crucial element in the personal development of each member of the nursing team.

Monitoring – New policies ensured that all confinements of patients in locked or unlocked facilities were classified as seclusion and carefully recorded and reviewed by ward staff and multi-disciplinary teams.

Use of alternative management techniques – Commissioners have observed the effective use of de-escalation techniques on the ward.

Nursing skills – The Commission has noted improved care plans, named nurses having regular one-to-one sessions with patients, and regular nursing reviews. The increase in the number of qualified staff has undoubtedly improved standards of care.

Attention to patient mix – The number of patients on the ward was reduced by one third. This has reduced overcrowding, over-stimulation of patients through noise and general disruption, and poor patient mix. As a consequence, there is now a greater turnover of patients.

Attention to environment – Efforts have been made to create a non-institutional environment. The ward has been refurbished. The daytime area has been arranged into smaller sitting areas with furniture arranged to facilitate communication. Areas affording privacy are designated for specific activities such as the occupational therapy room, interviewing room and telephone area. There is access to an open space under supervision.

Attention to patient activities – Two occupational therapists have been employed, enabling individualised and patient-focussed programmes to be developed in consultation with patients and their named nurses.

Contact: Rampton Hospital, Retford, Nottinghamshire, DN22 0PD Tel: 01777 248 321

4.44 We hope that the above achievements can be extended to women patients at Rampton Hospital. At Ashworth Hospital, the Commission and Women in Secure Hospitals (WISH) approached the hospital managers over the practice of denying access to sanitary protection products to women held in seclusion. After discussion, it was agreed that the practice is not acceptable and women who would be deemed at risk if secluded with sanitary protection are now nursed 2:1 as an alternative. We hope that the experience of this change of policy and practice will aid the hospital in its review of seclusion procedures for all women patients, and further help to reduce the use of seclusion and encourage the exploration and implementation of alternative strategies. Issues specific to women's services are discussed further at Chapter 6.33 – 6.39).

The Use of Control and Restraint

4.45   The Commission recognises that physical interventions to control and restrain patients' aggressive and dangerous behaviour are sometimes necessary in the interest of the safety of patients and staff. The Code of Practice gives clear and specific guidance on the use of control and restraint (paragraphs 19.6 – 19.14), which the Commission expects to be followed at all times.

4.46   In our Eighth Biennial Report we reported our concern over the increasing use of misleading terminology such as "care and responsibility" or "care and reassurance" that cloaks the nature of control and restraint[53]. It is likely that this increases the frustration of patients who have been subjected to control and restraint, who will often perceive the intervention as an exercise in power. It also short-circuits discussion between patients and staff over the events that led to control and restraint and the actions of staff. Such discussion is essential as a learning opportunity for both patients and staff.

> **Recommendation 44**
>
> Hospital managers should ensure that care and support is available to patients who have been subject to control and restraint interventions, in addition to the visit to the patient by a senior officer which is required at paragraph 19.13 of the Code of Practice.

4.47   Our report on *Deaths of Detained Patients* (see paragraph 4.17 *et seq.* above) noted 22 cases in which restraint had been used before death. In the 17 cases where an inquest had been completed at the time of writing, two deaths had occurred while the patient was being restrained and in four cases restraint had been used during the preceding twenty-four hours. It is clearly very important in such cases to establish immediately how far, if at all, the use of restraint may have contributed to a simultaneous or subsequent death.

4.48   In this reporting period we have noted a number of uses of the police in full riot gear in response to situations on wards where patients are detained. Such uses may have been entirely justifiable, but their incidence remains a concern. Further concerns were raised by the well-publicised incident leading to the Sines Report[54], where two teams of staff wearing riot-gear, including balaclavas under helmets with visors, were used for an internal transfer within a High Security Hospital. Such incidents, as well as our findings about deaths following or during control and restraint, reinforce the need for rigorous monitoring and evaluation of the use of these powers, which should always be a last resort.

> **Recommendation 45**
>
> Hospital managers should ensure that each use of control and restraint techniques is immediately reviewed, with regular audits to ensure that poor practice is eliminated and management and training lessons are learnt.

---

53 Mental Health Act Commission (1999) **Eighth Biennial Report** London, Stationery Office. p 225

54 Sines D (1999) **Independent Investigation into Complaints Raised by Ian Stewart Brady Relating to His Transfer to Lawrence Ward and Re-feeding at Ashworth Hospital**.

4.49 Any initial attempt to restrain aggressive behaviour should, as far as the situation will allow, be non-physical. Where physical restraint is used, it is essential that any staff involved are adequately trained. A lack of training in control and restraint techniques is a common finding on Commission visits. We are very encouraged at the work being undertaken by the British Institute of Learning Disabilities (BILD), whose practice guidelines for physical interventions in relation to adults and children with Learning Disability and/or Autism should be published later this year[55], and the Royal College of Nursing (RCN), whose working party is considering principles of good practice for control and restraint training[56]. The RCN's work, which will aim to establish generic guidance for the curricula and content of training courses, is particularly welcome given our concerns, stated in our last two Biennial Reports[57], over the proliferation of unregulated training courses which often give conflicting advice in this field. We have been involved in the UKCC's work relating to "the recognition, prevention and therapeutic management of violence in mental health care", the consultation document of which was published in January 2001. We look forward to the publication of the definitive document later in 2001.

4.50 The Code of Practice recommends that any training provider in control and restraint techniques should be suitably qualified, having completed a course designed for health care settings that has "preferably" been validated by either the English National Board or Royal College of Nursing Institute (paragraph 19.9). In our response to the Green Paper on the Reform of the Mental Health Act (**Appendix E**, paragraph 37) we urged the Government to introduce statutory regulation of the powers to exercise control and restraint. Such regulation should encompass both the initial provision of training to staff and requirements for refresher training.

> Recommendation 46
>
> New legislation should include provision for the regulation of the power to exercise control and restraint.

Locking of Wards

4.51 The Code of Practice recognises that some services require secure environments and will therefore operate locked wards. Usually such services will be in the medium or high security sector, and locked wards may be necessary in the professional judgement of the RMO or may even be a requirement of a court. Guidance on locked wards and secure areas, which stresses the importance of a proper consideration of each affected patient's individual circumstances and needs, is found at paragraphs 19.28 – 19.29 of the Code of Practice.

4.52 For most services operating at a lower security level, the Code suggests that staffing levels should be sufficient to prevent the need to lock wards, individual rooms or other areas. However, the Code also states that the nurse in charge of any shift, who is responsible for the care and protection of patients and staff and the maintenance of a safe and secure environment, has discretion to lock the ward door if the behaviour of patients makes this necessary. The Code gives precise guidance on the correct procedure to be adopted if this circumstance arises (paragraph 19.25). We have found, nevertheless, that some lower security services seem reluctant to allow staff this

---

55 See www.nhs.ukzerotolerance/mental/physical/htm

56 See www.nhs.uk/zerotolerance/mental/principles.htm

57 Mental Health Act Commission (1997) **Seventh Biennial Report** p 168, Mental Health Act Commission (1999) **Eighth Biennial Report** p 226. London, Stationery Office

discretion, which is clearly of considerable relevance to the finding mentioned above (paragraph 4.21) that one third of detained patient suicides occur whilst the patient is absent from hospital without leave.

4.53   By contrast, we continue to find wards that appear to be kept continually locked as a result of the inadequate number or management of staff, rather than because of any inherent management problems of the patients. This is a misuse of the power of compulsion, especially since some of the patients on these wards will not be detained under the Mental Health Act.

4.54   Some units, particularly those based in cities, lock wards to keep intruders out rather than to keep patients in. Where there are issues such as illicit drug dealing around the hospital (see paragraphs 4.56 – 4.61 below) or theft of items from the ward, services may have little choice but to impose some such form of security. Such measures should never impede the free movement of patients whose clinical needs do not warrant such restrictions.

4.55   The contrast between those places where wards are not locked when they should be and those where they are locked when they should not be underlines the need to balance the need for patient and staff safety against the need to ensure maximum autonomy for patients. This in turn reinforces the responsibility of management for establishing clear policies on the locking of wards.

Recommendation 47

Service providers should ensure that there are clear service-wide policies on the locking of wards and that compliance is regularly audited. The frequency of locking of doors on non-secure wards should, in particular, be scrutinised to establish whether this indicates problems with day to day practice or with inadequate staffing. In both instances, the appropriate remedial action should be taken.

Drugs and Alcohol Misuse

4.56   On numerous occasions nursing staff draw the attention of visiting Commissioners to the problem of drug and alcohol abuse on wards and the extreme difficulty of caring for patients with widely differing needs and expectations. The problems identified range from the effect of disturbed and aggressive behavior on the care and treatment of quieter patients and the difficulties in preventing street drugs entering the ward to the inappropriate use of seclusion facilities for the admission of intoxicated patients. Staff on acute wards have frequently reported that a large proportion of emergency admissions are drug related. The incidence of drug misuse appears to compound the amount of aggression experienced by staff, and in some instances by patients, and adds very significantly to the pressures ordinarily experienced in acute wards.

4.57   Many health services operate policies whereby all patients who enter their facilities are asked to sign contracts or declarations stating that they will not use drugs or alcohol whilst rresident there, and agree to the searching of their possessions or the taking of blood, urine or breath samples where there is suspicion of possession of drugs or alcohol. Such contracts can be useful as a way to reach an understanding with patients about the expectations of their behaviour whilst in the care of the service, although it is unclear what, if any, effective sanctions are available to a detaining authority if the patient is compelled to enter and remain in such care by the Mental Health Act.

4.58 In many cases an appropriate response of affected hospitals is to review their security, ensuring that the personal safety of staff and patients is as good as possible and reducing opportunities for bringing drugs and alcohol on to the premises. Some measures that should be considered on safety grounds where a patient is suspected or known to be using drugs or alcohol are: increasing observation levels; restricting leave; searching property; limiting or supervising visits; and transfer to higher security. Such measures should only be taken as a result of objective, multi-disciplinary risk-assessment on the basis of clinical need, and never as punitive sanctions[58].

4.59 In our Sixth, Seventh and Eighth Biennial Reports we raised concern over the lack of effective guidance given to service providers on the difficult issues surrounding substance misuse and its control and management amongst detained patients[59]. Although we have repeatedly highlighted the widespread lack of policy guidance on this issue, both at a national level and in the individual policies of hospitals, we must do so once again. All too often, hospital staff are not provided with effective policy guidance on what actions they can or should take when they suspect or know of substance misuse.

4.60 A number of hospitals have created their own local policies and some of these are commendable, although their preparation would have been eased by central guidance.

Good Practice Example

Tameside and Glossop Community and Priority Services NHS Trust operate a locally-produced Policy for the Management of Illicit Drug Use Incidents in Mental Health Services, which is linked with the hospital's health and safety policy. The policy sets out actions expected of staff when faced with a variety of situations involving patients or visitors, and includes guidance on what staff can and should do when taking possession of illicit substances, whether through confiscation or other means.

Contact: Mrs S McKeever, Tameside General Hospital, Fountain Street, Ashton-under Lyne, Lancashire OL6 9RW; tel 0161 331 5151

4.61 At the time of writing, elements of this policy were being reviewed on the advice of the Trust solicitor. Whilst all policies should be reviewed periodically, the need for this review indicates how useful centralised guidance from the Department of Health would be.

---

58 Williams, R and Cohen, J (2000) *Substance use and misuse in psychiatric wards; a model task for clinical governance?*; in **Psychiatric Bulletin 24**, 43–46. See also Cohen, J, Runciman, R and Williams, R (1999) *Substance Use and Misuse in Psychiatric Wards* in **Drugs: education , prevention and policy** Vol 6, No 2 1999. Carfax Publishing.

59 Mental Health Act Commission (1995) **Sixth Biennial Report**. p105 – 107; Mental Health Act Commission (1997) **Seventh Biennial Report**. p 166 – 167; Mental Health Act Commission (1999) **Eighth Biennial Report**, p231 – 4 London, Stationery Office.

> **Recommendation 48**
>
> The Department of Health should consider issuing guidance on the management of illicit-drug related incidents with a particular focus on mental health services caring for detained patients. Such guidance should clearly set out:
>
> - expected actions where there is a suspicion of illicit drug use or supply, or of alcohol consumption, whether by patients or visitors;
> - expected actions where there is knowledge of illicit drug use or supply, or of alcohol consumption, whether by patients or visitors;
> - powers of staff to search for and confiscate illicit drugs or alcohol;
> - reassurance on the powers of staff to handle and dispose of illicit drugs that come into their possession;
> - expected arrangements with police services over issues relating to illicit drugs; and
> - expectations of service agreements between mental health services and drug and alcohol teams in relation to patients presenting with dual diagnosis or co-morbidity.

> **Recommendation 49**
>
> Mental health service providers should ensure that
>
> - clear policy guidance on the management and prevention of incidents involving alcohol and illicit drugs is available to staff; and
> - that they have written service agreements with drug and alcohol teams for the joint management of patients with dual diagnosis or co-morbidity.

A Systematised Approach to Risk Management

4.62 Nearly every item to which attention is drawn in this Chapter has emphasised the importance of clear policies to protect both patients and staff and the need to introduce rigorous monitoring and audit processes to ensure that they are adhered to. A systematised approach to risk management is at the heart of all the recommendations made. This involves the proper assessment of risks and the devising of strategies to minimise them in every area of management, whether relating to the environment, the allocation of patients, their care while in hospital and their grant of leave or discharge, or to the health and safety of staff.[60]

4.63 We urge detaining authorities to adopt a stringent and pro-active risk management culture in all mental health units. Risk assessment is not simply a paper exercise but an essential tool to enable managers, staff and patients to feel more safe in a hospital environment and to have the confidence to take reasonable risks. The feeling of safety and confidence is one of the main constituents without which a truly therapeutic environment cannot be established. Commissioners find in all too many instances that risks are assessed in a haphazard and non-objective way, or not at all.

---

60 United Kingdom Central Council for Nursing, Midwifery and Health Visiting (1998) **Guidelines for Mental Health and Learning Disabilities Nursing**. London, UKCC p22.

There is therefore no chance of either managers or staff learning to incorporate risk assessment into their way of thought and behaviour so that it becomes second nature rather than an impediment to positive action.

Recommendation 50

Service providers should ensure that a full risk management strategy is introduced for all their services and that appropriate training, recording and audit are provided to ensure compliance with it. Such a strategy should include evaluation of the adequacy of existing arrangements and the need for additional measures, common systems for incident reporting, regular review systems to re-assess the risks, and a continuing programme of staff development in the assessment of risk.

Some of the main matters which must be taken into account are:

- environmental risks, including those from equipment and to staff as well as to patients;

- risks from patients of harm to self or others, including not only the nature of the illness or overt threats, but also objective assessments of family history, criminal record, substance misuse, absconding, trigger points, who is most likely to be harmed and how, and other relevant factors; and

- need to ensure that information is systematically recorded and passed on immediately when a patient moves to another location, is allowed leave or is discharged, as well as being made readily available to all relevant staff.

5 High Secure Care after the Fallon Inquiry

5.1   The issues raised in relation to inpatient care throughout this report are almost all relevant to the three High Security Hospitals serving England and Wales (Ashworth, Broadmoor and Rampton hospitals), as is shown by the use of illustrative practice vignettes from these hospitals in other chapters. The merger of Broadmoor and Rampton Hospital Authorities with their respective local NHS Trusts gives a clear sign that high security services can no longer be considered in isolation from mainstream psychiatric hospital care. We welcome this assimilation as a positive move towards an integrated service where institutions providing all types of security can learn from and teach each other. We also recognise that this process may present a challenge in terms of protecting gains in good practice prior to the mergers, and in ensuring that senior management of the new Trusts maintain a close involvement with the High Security Hospitals as institutions.

5.2   The last two years have been a period of considerable change, specific to the High Security Hospitals, stemming from the report of Sir Peter Fallon's inquiry into the Personality Disorder unit at Ashworth Hospital[61]. In response to a recommendation made in this report, the Government commissioned a review of security at the three hospitals, culminating in the report by Sir Richard Tilt[62] and the subsequent issue and implementation of new Security Directions for the hospitals[63].

5.3   These matters are of such consequence to the care of the patients in the hospitals that they are dealt with specifically in this chapter.

Inappropriate Placements in High Secure Care

5.4   The Tilt Report's recommendations on security at Ashworth, Broadmoor and Rampton hospitals (see paras. 5.23 onwards below) were acknowledged to be made on the assumption that these hospitals provide care and treatment to patients who require conditions of high security. The report itself recognised that this was not the case in relation to roughly a third of the hospitals' population, as 436 patients were in the hospitals' transfer/ discharge system at the time of the review[64]. The report stated that

---

61 Department of Health (1999) **Report of the Committee of Inquiry into the Personality Disorder Unit, Ashworth Special Hospital**. Cm 4149–11. London, Stationery Office

62 Department of Health (2000) **Report of the Review of Security at the High Security Hospitals**. London, Stationery Office

63 **The Safety and Security in Ashworth, Broadmoor and Rampton Hospitals Directions 2000** www.doh.gov.uk/hospitaldirections

64 Department of Health (2000) **Report of the Review of Security at the High Security Hospitals** London, Stationery Office p. 11

"we regard it as inappropriate, both from a civil liberties and efficient use of resources viewpoint, for a patient who can safely be accommodated in less secure conditions to remain in a high security setting for lengthy periods"[65].

5.5   The very first recommendation of the report was that the additional funding (£25 million) already identified to deal with the problem should be deployed over the period 2000 – 2003, and "used in the first instance to facilitate the movement of patients no longer needing high secure care"[66]. The report concluded that the movement of such patients would be "a crucial step towards ensuring that the hospitals are really fulfilling their true purpose of providing a service for people who require high security psychiatric care at the time when they genuinely need it"[67].

5.6   At the end of April 2001, over two years from the publication of the Tilt Report, figures available to the Commission indicated that there were 349 patients in the transfer/discharge system within the High Security Hospitals. While we accept that transfer and discharge from the hospitals is a careful process, and that some patients officially included in these lists may not be ready for immediate transfer, this is still 27% of the total patient population of the three hospitals. This does not take account of the numbers who are not yet on the list because there is no realistic hope of finding them alternative accommodation (see paragraph 5.8 below).

5.7   Under the next two subheadings we discuss obstacles to the movement of patients out of the HSHs and within the hospitals themselves, and, at recommendations 51 and 52, suggest strategies that could help to overcome them.

The Effects of Bed Pressures on the Movement of Patients from High Security Care

5.8   The intended destinations of most patients who are ready to leave the high security sector are medium secure places. All three High Security Hospitals continue to report difficulties in locating available places. It is therefore probable that, in addition to the patients who are formally counted as being within the transfer/discharge system, there is a further group of patients who are not included because there is no realistic prospect of finding a suitable alternative facility to admit them[68]. As a result it is likely that neither the Tilt Report nor the Commission has accurately reflected the true number of patients in these hospitals who could safely be transferred out.

5.9   Much more needs to be done to facilitate the freer movement of patients within psychiatric services. The problem must be approached holistically, as it is clear that the silting up of beds across the whole of mental health services is hampering the movement of patients within and across all security levels. The bed-pressures across the service (see Chapter 3.4 – 3.8) are such that patients who require a level of security other than the one in which they reside often have to wait an unacceptable length of time to be allocated a place.

5.10   There remain significant funding difficulties in effecting transfer from high secure to medium secure beds. Most NHS medium secure units are intended for shorter-stay patients and may not, for example, have the facilities or expertise to take personality disordered patients. This leaves forensic services largely dependent on the independent sector and Out of Area Treatment funding from their patients' health authorities for longer-term placements. In a number of

65 *ibid.* p. 12

66 *ibid.* p. 47

67 *ibid.* p. 12

68 *ibid.* p. 11

instances, health authorities have been reluctant to provide such funding. In this context, we are particularly concerned to learn that a number of medium secure units have explicitly stated that they will not accept patients with personality disorder from Ashworth Hospital and that this is increasing transfer delays for this group of patients. We will continue to express our concern on these issues to the relevant regional authorities and will press for action in individual cases.

5.11   For patients waiting to move to lower levels of security, transfer delays hold up their effective treatment, infringe their civil liberties and create tensions in the management of the facilities. This is particularly relevant in the case of High Security Hospital patients awaiting transfer, given the changes in culture at these hospitals in the wake of the Fallon Inquiry.

Bed Pressures within the High Security Hospitals

5.12   All three High Security Hospitals are experiencing bed pressures within their hospitals, leading to delays in admissions and in the movement of patients already admitted within the hospitals themselves.

5.13   In the case of patients residing in low and medium-secure care who require admission to higher security services, the lack of available beds has led to dangerous situations for the patients, staff and, potentially, the general public. The nursing of such patients greatly increases the burden on staff and other resources in low and medium-secure units, often to the detriment of other patients' care. On occasion, the only way in which low-secure units can manage such patients is through 1:1 or 2:1 nursing, or even the use of seclusion for long periods. Such treatment of patients is far less humane and effective, and results in a far greater curtailment of the patient's liberty, than that which would be available to the patient in an appropriately structured and secure environment (see Chapter 3.4 *et seq.* on bed pressures in general services).

5.14   Throughout the current reporting period we have remained concerned about the pressure on beds within the High Security Hospitals. As the hospitals are almost invariably full and have waiting lists, there is little flexibility in the system. We remain concerned about the inability of the hospitals to provide appropriate clinical pathways for patients admitted to their care.

■ At the beginning of their treatment, patients frequently remain on admission wards for anything up to a year after their admission case conference. As a consequence, the commencement of treatment programmes is often delayed and the patient-mix on the admission wards is such that meaningful therapeutic activity is almost impossible.

■ If a patient becomes particularly ill and requires treatment on one of the intensive care wards, their original bed is not always retained. Patients are consequently stranded on the intensive care wards much longer than their clinical need would require.

■ The patient-mix on many types of ward is too often dictated by available space rather than clinical appropriateness.

■ The limited specialist services within the hospitals that work with issues of addiction have long waiting lists. As many of the index offences of patients are in some way linked to the abuse of drugs or alcohol, we urge continued effort to address these issues in all three hospitals (see paragraphs 5.19–5.21 below).

5.15   There is clearly a vicious circle here, with some patients remaining in high security beds because beds are not available at a lower level of security and others being held in lower security than their illness warrants because all the high security beds are filled. We recognise that geographical considerations do not allow for simplistic solutions but we believe that there should be a concerted effort within each NHS Region to see how far it would be possible to make a better match between beds and individual patients. This could well reveal that the shortage of beds is less extreme than it may appear. Meanwhile there needs to be some move to increase flexibility within the high secure hospitals.

Recommendation 51

NHS Regional Offices, Regional Commissioning Bodies and Health Authorities should investigate the possibility of reviewing all patients in a particular area who are considered inappropriately placed at their current level of security to see how far patient exchanges might reduce mis-match and bed pressures.

Recommendation 52

While the Commission recognises the pressure on high security beds, maintaining a number of vacant places should be considered to create the flexibility of response necessary to benefit both patient care and throughput efficiency of the High Security Hospitals.

Staffing shortages within the High Security Hospitals

5.16   All three High Security Hospitals have problems in maintaining adequate levels of medical and nursing staff.

5.17   The struggle to maintain continuity of Responsible Medical Officer cover in the High Security Hospitals is of grave concern. The hospitals are environments where continuity of care is of the utmost importance to patients, not least because their chances of being recommended for transfer or discharge may be dependent on an effective alliance between them and their RMO. Some patients have indeed complained that the frequent changes in the consultant responsible for their care has resulted in an over-cautious approach to their rehabilitation. Whilst we have found no firm evidence to support the patients' view, the perception itself should be seen as a matter of concern to the hospitals.

5.18   Nursing shortages loom large over many of the management problems within the hospitals. It is acknowledged by the hospitals' management that staffing shortages can prevent patients' access to activities and fresh air (see also Chapter 3.20 – 3.30). Commissioners have noted staff working additional shifts to cover the basic requirements of the hospitals. Such staffing issues are of great concern, given their adverse effects on patient care and the provision of a safe and therapeutic environment (see Chapter 4).

Service Issues in High Secure Care

The Provision of Therapeutic Interventions within the High Security Hospitals

5.19   At the end of this reporting period the Commission undertook an initial review of the provision of therapeutic interventions across the three High Security Hospitals. A number of concerns have emerged at this early stage of our work, particularly in relation to:

- a lack of routinely collated information to enable audit of therapeutic interventions;

- patients waiting for long periods before psychological assessments are initiated; and

- patients waiting for long periods to access specialist treatments for specific problems, such as sex offending, alcohol and drug abuse, arson, self-harming and anger management.

5.20   We are also concerned at the increasing cessation of mixed-gender activities and therapies within the hospitals (see Chapter 6.37).

5.21   A high proportion of patients within the High Security Hospital system have particular requirements relating to psychological therapies. It is also the case that restricted patients' failure to engage in psychological therapies, for whatever reason, will be taken into account by the Home Office in considering requests for leave, transfer or discharge. For these reasons, a full range of therapeutic activities and interventions should be a part of every High Security Hospital patient's treatment options. We will be working with the hospitals over the next reporting period to address these issues.

> Recommendation 53
>
> High Security Hospital managers should instigate routine monitoring of non-pharmacological therapeutic interventions and audit for gaps in their provision.

Consent to Treatment in the High Security Hospitals

5.22   Notwithstanding the difficult circumstances described above, we are pleased to be able to report significant improvements in the quality of records and practices in relation to patients' consent to treatment in all three High Security Hospitals. In our Seventh Biennial Report we reported serious shortcomings in all three hospitals with regard to ascertaining and certifying patients' consent[69]. In our Eighth Biennial Report[70] we noted that, with some exceptions, this area still required attention and improvement. It is now the case that bad practice is the exception to an overall improvement across all three hospitals. These improvements have resulted from the auditing of consent documentation and the commitment of medical staff to instill better practices (see also Chapter 2.16 – 2.22, 2.63 – 2.67).

Effects of the Safety and Security Directions on Patient Care

An Increasingly Custodial Focus?

5.23   Revised Safety and Security Directions have been in force at all three High Security Hospitals from November 2000. We recognise the need for an increased focus on both relational and physical security in the light of the Fallon Inquiry report and the subsequent review of security by Sir Richard Tilt and his team (see paragraphs 5.2 – 5.7 above) and support the strategic goal of these interventions in the management of the hospitals.

5.24   Over the last seven months both staff and patients at the High Security Hospitals have expressed concern to the Commission at some aspects of the implementation of the Directions.

5.25   We are concerned that the implementation of the Security Directions should not impose overly time-consuming and restrictive practices in the hospitals at the expense of therapeutic interactions

---

69 Mental Health Act Commission (1997) **Seventh Biennial Report** London, Stationery Office p87

70 Mental Health Act Commission (1999) **Eighth Biennial Report** London, Stationery Office p158

between staff and patients. These concerns are heightened by the blanket application of the Directions, with a devastating result for some patients, particularly women, those undergoing rehabilitation and those who have lived in the hospitals for many years. We are particularly concerned at the depersonalising and institutionalising effect of some of the measures taken. Some of the many matters raised by patients and/or staff are highlighted in the following paragraphs.

5.26 **Searches.** While recognising the importance of searches as a tool in maintaining appropriate levels of security, both patients and staff point out the large amount of time they consume at the expense of time spent talking to patients, the effect on therapeutic relationships and the huge administrative overhead attached to recording the process.

> Recommendation 54
>
> High Security Hospital managers should review searching procedures and documentation to ensure that the Security Directions are being implemented sensitively and that staff time is used appropriately. The review should consider whether staffing levels are sufficient to provide quality care to patients given the increased demands on staff of the Security Directions.

5.27 **Property restrictions.** Commissioners have learned from many patients of the distress of losing access to many of those possessions which previously helped sustain their individuality. The diminished number of possessions that patients may keep in their room continues to cause resentment. Women patients complain of not being allowed to keep sufficient toiletries to look after their own personal hygiene. Other patients have particularly mentioned access to books, recorded music and clothes. One patient waited for five weeks in the autumn of last year for his pullovers to be released from storage; another was told, having requested his CD player from storage in November, to expect it to be returned to him in February. The mechanism for retrieving items from the property section appears to be somewhat convoluted and time-consuming. We consider that the Patients' Possessions Policies are insufficiently flexible, particularly in that the same level of restriction applies on wards on which there are patients near to discharge as on wards where there are patients of 'high dependency'.

> Recommendation 55
>
> High Security Hospital managers should monitor the time taken to approve the release of patients' personal possessions from storage, and the time taken post-approval for items to be delivered to patients. Agreed standards should be set and improvement targets initiated.

5.28 **Restrictions on patients' use of computers.** Commissioners have learned from many patients of the adverse consequences of losing access to their computers. Patients have lost old and entirely harmless machines. One patient had to abandon his Open University Course, while many lost access to an activity which gave them constructive use of their evenings and weekends. Broadmoor Hospital has made commendable efforts to compensate for this loss by the creation of a computer network in the Education Centre, but even this is limited to term-time access and dependent upon staff being available to escort patients to the facility.

> **Recommendation 56**
>
> High Security Hospital managers should consider ways to improve patients' access to computers, particularly in their leisure-time.

5.29 **Restrictions on bringing food into the hospital.** We remain concerned at the interpretation of this Security Direction, which has, in addition to stopping relatives from bringing food to patients on their visits, led to bans on patients buying-in takeaway food from previously trusted providers, patients being restricted to an authorised shopping list for therapeutic shopping, Occupational Therapists being prevented from bringing in special items for therapeutic cooking programmes, and staff being prevented from providing edible prizes for patient raffles.

> **Recommendation 57**
>
> High Security Hospital managers should review their implementation of the Security Directions relating to the importation of foodstuffs to the hospitals, to ensure that they do not result in unintended and undesirable consequences.

5.30 In an environment where matters of rules, power and control are often so overtly part of the agenda, some impositions seem counter-therapeutic and make the work of the clinical team much more difficult. We are particularly concerned to hear of instances where impositions appear to be pettily bureaucratic, such as:

- one hospital's restrictions on access to shampoo because of its minimal alcohol content, which was widely regarded as demeaning to the whole security debate; and

- a patient who had purchased a present for his mother, who visits him at weekends, was told that he would have to send the present to the stores for his mother to collect. The stores are only open during the week.

5.31 In some cases, however, staff have found ways to make the new rules less onerous for patients. Ward staff at Ashworth Hospital keep patients' recorded music items in a locked cupboard on the wards, so that patients have more ready access to them.

> **Recommendation 58**
>
> High Security Hospital managers should keep the implementation of the Security Directions under constant review, ensuring that they are imposed in appropriate ways that cause no unnecessary detriment to patient care.

5.32 In some areas the Security Directions have been approached as a positive opportunity to improve the care of patients in a better-structured environment. Commissioners visiting Cherwell Ward, Broadmoor Hospital, in May 2000 were impressed with the sense of energy, direction and purpose that seemed to have been instilled as a result of the locking-off of patient bedrooms during the day. This, and the consequent job of getting patients up in the morning, had been approached by the clinical team as a positive move towards greater activity and not simply an end in itself. Nursing staff had been deployed from the relatively unproductive task of 'monitoring the gallery' to more useful forms of patient contact.

5.33 There is a real danger that the implementation of the Security Directions could distract from a holistic approach towards safety and security in the High Security Hospitals. Action to promote a safe and therapeutic environment (see Chapter 4) needs to be continually addressed within the hospitals to make the Security Directions meaningful, particularly with regard to:

■ increasing the availability to all patients of therapeutic interventions and activities, including psychological treatments (see paragraphs 5.19 –5.21 above);

■ ensuring that women patients in the hospitals are not disadvantaged in terms of facilities and access to activities;

■ continued attention to environmental risk assessment and management, avoiding the assumption that safety and security can be assured by implementation of Security Directions alone; and

■ ensuring that the Care Programme Approach is effectively implemented for all patients across the three hospitals.

5.34 We hope that, as new systems and policies are embedded and developed in the hospitals, there can be an increased focus on the individual needs of patients based on individual risk-assessments, in line with good mental health practice, rather than blanket restrictions. This is all the more vital if decent and humane care is to be provided to the many patients who appear to have been disadvantaged by the imposition of the Safety and Security Directions, especially those who are awaiting transfer out of the hospitals, or who no longer really require very high levels of security.

Childrens' Visiting

5.35 The revised Code of Practice, published in March 1999, required all hospitals to have written policies on the arrangements for the visiting of patients by children, drawn up in conjunction with local social services authorities. Visits by children should consequently only be allowed where it is decided that such a visit is in the child's best interest, and such decisions should be regularly reviewed (paragraph 26.3).

5.36 This revision was made as it became clear that lax arrangements for such visits had put a young girl at severe risk on her visits to the Personality Disorder Unit at Ashworth Hospital. Specific directions for high security services[71] followed, in response to the report on these events by Sir Peter Fallon. General guidance on the Code's advice in relation to other psychiatric services was published later.[72] The general guidance emphasised that "in the vast majority of cases, the issue of whether or not a child should visit will be straightforward, and in these cases, policies should aim to encourage and facilitate contacts between children and adults which are considered to be in the child's interest"[73]. We recommend that this be considered as applicable across all services, including the High Security Hospitals.

5.37 We accept that security lapses such as those investigated by the Fallon Inquiry should never be allowed to happen again, and are supportive of measures that will ensure that this is the case.

---

71 HSC 1999/160, revised by HSC 2000/027.

72 Department of Health (1999) *Mental Health Act 1983 Code of Practice: Guidance on the visiting of psychiatric patients by children.* HSC 1999/222: LAC (99)32,

73 *ibid.* p 3

However, as with many aspects of the Security Directions, we are concerned that a rigid application of regulations and procedures across patient categories, rather than in response to patients' individual needs as set out in their care plans, compromises the hospitals' ability to provide patient-centred care in the context required by both the Mental Health Act Code of Practice and the National Service Framework for Mental Health.

5.38   In February and March 2001, the Commission undertook special visits to consider services provided to women patients at the three High Security Hospitals. The visits focussed on a number of issues, including arrangements for visiting by children.

5.39   Commissioners found that women patients' experience of the new visiting arrangements was the single issue that caused most distress. The new rules were described as tortuous, incomprehensible and unfair, with many women who had previously had happy and uncomplicated visits from their children or grandchildren now finding these restricted by delays and bureaucracy. A number of women patients who have been transferred from prison were surprised and disappointed to find that opportunities and facilities for their childrens' visits were greatly reduced in hospital. One woman had waited for over seven months before seeing her children, because of hold-ups in the approval process. Another patient had asked not to see her grandchildren rather than put them through what she perceived as the "ordeal" of assessment. One woman patient told a Commissioner that "the new rules make you feel like a child abuser". There was a widespread resentment that measures designed to protect against a repeat of the actions of some male patients in one hospital had produced such an effect on all patients.

5.40   The hospitals themselves are not responsible for all of the causes of delay in visiting arrangements. All three hospitals report delays in assessments by social services authorities local to the patients' families. One local authority informed Rampton Hospital that other casework precluded any such assessment in the foreseeable future. We hope that this situation will be improved by the Department's guidance that such assessments should now be fully completed within 35 days. The hospitals themselves have limited administrative time to chase up responses. We have found that uniform data on delays was not available, and have advised that it should be properly collected and monitored.

5.41   The requirement for extra vigilance during visits has, in some instances, limited the number of visits that can be arranged in each week. Although new visiting facilities are being developed at Broadmoor and Rampton hospitals, shortages of appropriately trained staff have also been cited as a limiting factor. Many patients have complained that problems in providing staff to escort or supervise visits have led to their two-hour visiting slots being significantly reduced. We hope that the hospitals will give urgent attention to these matters.

5.42   The requirement that children should be searched before and after visits has caused understandable distress to patients and to the children themselves. Rampton Hospital conducts such searches on children under the guise of a game called "hunt the sweet", so as to alleviate their embarrassment or stress. We hope that, for as long as it is considered necessary to search children, the hospitals will make every effort to do so in as appropriate and sensitive a manner as possible.

5.43   Supervision on visits can seem obtrusive to patients and their families. One patient spoke of the impossibility of having any meaningful discussion with her teenage daughter whilst a social worker, probation officer and two escort staff looked on. Patients also resent the ban on them preparing food for their visitors, or on their visitors bringing any food into the hospital (see paragraph 5.29 above).

Recommendation 59

High Security Hospital managers should review the implementation of the Security Directions with regard to the visiting of patients by children in the light of the Commission's concerns. Consideration should be given to whether certain patients are unfairly disadvantaged by the blanket imposition of all new visiting arrangements, and whether such arrangements serve any useful purpose and may be counter-therapeutic.

Recommendation 60

The Department of Health should consult with senior managers in the three High Security Hospitals to see if the adverse effects of the Security Directions can be minimised in any way.

6   Addressing Diversity

The Challenge of Diversity

"No injustice is greater than the inequalities in health which scar our nation".
(NHS Plan 2000[74])

6.1   Since its inception and First Biennial Report in 1985, the Commission has continually raised concerns with respect to the inadequate level of care and treatment afforded to particular groups of patients[75]. The requirement to meet these needs whilst respecting the individuality of every patient both in care plans and in the day to day running of inpatient units is becoming increasingly challenging as mental health services for detained patients are experiencing growing diversity in the patient population and greater awareness of the need to tackle inequalities.

6.2   The Code of Practice requires that people to whom the Act is applied should "be given respect for their qualities, abilities and diverse backgrounds as individuals and be assured that account will be taken of their age, gender, sexual orientation, social, ethnic, cultural and religious background, but that general assumptions will not be made on the basis of any one of these characteristics" (paragraph 1.1).

6.3   The National Service Framework for Mental Health contains the principle that people with mental health problems can expect services *"to be well-suited to those who use them and non-discriminatory"*. Particular expectations of services in relation to disabled patients are also raised through the Disability Discrimination Act 1995[76]. The Race Relations (Amendment) Act 2000 requires public authorities to promote good relations across all their activities and specific guidelines for the NHS are being developed by the Commission for Racial Equality.

6.4   This is further reinforced, and welcomed by the Commission, in the vision of a health service designed around the needs of the patient, as described in the NHS Plan[77]. As the then Acting Commission Chairman said in his opening remarks to the Commission's National Visit 2 Report:

"How society relates to those of its members from minority ethnic groups is a measure of its value and standards. Nowhere is this more relevant than in the provision of health and social care for those with mental health problems – especially under compulsion."[78]

---

74 Department of Health (2000) **The NHS Plan**. London, Stationery Office

75 See, for example, Mental Health Act Commission (1999) **Eighth Biennial Report** p234 – 261

76 See Department of Health (1999) **Doubly Disabled: Equality for disabled people in the new NHS**. HSC 1999/093

77 Department of Health (2000) **The NHS Plan**. London, Stationery Office

78 Warner et al (2000) **Improving Care for Detained Patients from Black and Minority Ethnic Communities Preliminary Report – National Visit 2**. Sainsbury Centre for Mental Health

6.5   This Chapter concentrates on some particular areas of service provision where additional effort must be made to allow this vision to be realised. We also suggest, at Chapter 6.16 – 19 below, one approach through which service commissioners and providers may take practical steps to address diversity in a holistic fashion.

Black and Minority Ethnic Patients

6.6   There is a widespread perception that mental health services do not have sufficient understanding of the complex and diverse religious, cultural and traditional needs of Black and minority ethnic people and that this constitutes institutional racism as defined by the Macpherson Report (1999) on the Stephen Lawrence Inquiry:

"...the collective failure of an organisation to provide an appropriate and professional service to people because of their colour, culture or ethnic origin".

6.7   From our First Biennial Report, published in 1985, we have continually drawn attention to the disproportionate numbers, and the inadequate care and treatment of patients from certain Black and minority ethnic groups who are detained. We have also raised concerns about the adequacy of the service response to Black and minority ethnic groups in general.

6.8   The Government has acknowledged that many of the issues raised in the Macpherson report have relevance for the NHS[79] and subsequently has made a number of announcements on race equality within the NHS. Perhaps understandably, these have initially concentrated on the clearly identifiable issues relating to staffing and racial harassment. Although welcome initiatives to increase the numbers of Black and minority ethnic members of NHS Boards and schemes and to teach all Board members about the need for equality and diversity in service delivery were announced in 1997, there is clearly still much to do to ensure that Black and minority ethnic mental health service users receive appropriate care from the NHS.

6.9   In February 2001, the Royal College of Psychiatrists' Council endorsed a set of recommendations that included the setting up of an Ethnic Issues Committee to work with the College in ensuring that its members receive appropriate training in cultural sensitivity and are aware of the possibility of discrimination when applying the Mental Health Act. As this report goes to press, the pages of the *Psychiatric Bulletin* have been opened to a debate over the extent and effects of institutional racism in British Psychiatry[80]. Indeed, our own collection of data on the ethnicity of patients admitted under the Act for the past four years, though not scientifically rigorous, (particularly in the use of the now out-dated 1991 census – see Appendix B paragraph 31) supports the notion that certain Black and minority ethnic groups are disproportionately detained within psychiatric settings (see Figure 6 below).

79 HSC 1999/060 (12 March 1999): **Tackling Racial Harassment in the NHS – a Plan for Action**.

80 Shashidaran S P *Institutional Racism in British Psychiatry* & Cox J L *Commentary: Institutional Racism in British Psychiatry*. **Psychiatric Bulletin** 25:7 July 2001 p244–249

Figure 6 : Mental Health Act by Ethnicity in England and Wales[81]

Ethnic Group	Mental Health Act Data				Census Data (1991)
	1996/7 (n=29,426)[1]	1997/8 (n=33,552)[2]	1998/9 (n= 35,097)[3]	1999/2000 (n=40,024)[4]	
	%	%	%	%	%
White	84.0	83.3	85.0	88.2	94.5
Black Caribbean	5.4	6.2	5.2	3.6	0.9
Black African	2.7	2.5	2.4	1.7	0.4
Black other	1.8	2.0	1.5	1.1	0.3
Indian	1.7	1.6	1.4	1.5	1.5
Pakistani	1.3	1.0	1.4	1.2	0.9
Bangladeshi	0.4	0.6	0.4	0.4	0.3
Chinese	0.3	0.3	0.3	0.2	0.3
Other groups	2.4	2.5	2.4	2.1	0.9

1 ethnicity not known (1996/7) = 2,102 – not included in table
2 ethnicity not known (1997/8) = 1,505 – not included in table
3 ethnicity not known (1998/9) = 1,204 – not included in table
4 ethnicity not known (1999/2000) = 5,029 – not included in table

(n.b. the growth in "ethnicity unknowns" has possibly distorted the residual analysis shown)

6.10 Figure 7 suggests that not only is there a disproportionate detention rate of Black and minority ethnic people under the Act but also that, having been detained, the rate at which they are referred to the SOAD service and the number requesting the support of a Commissioner are incrementally higher still.

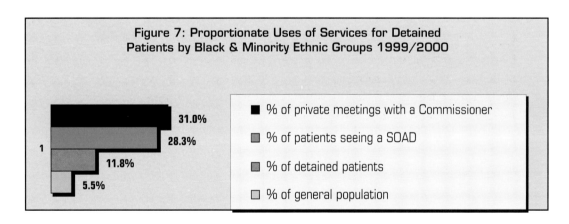

Figure 7: Proportionate Uses of Services for Detained Patients by Black & Minority Ethnic Groups 1999/2000

- 31.0% ■ % of private meetings with a Commissioner
- 28.3% ■ % of patients seeing a SOAD
- 11.8% ■ % of detained patients
- 5.5% □ % of general population

6.11 This analysis adds a new dimension to data previously reported separately and heightens the need for research into the possibility of institutional racism both pre and post detention.

81 based on information supplied to the Commission by 269 establishments out of a possible 281 respondents.

6.12 In respect of our collection of in-patient data, we make no claim to be adding significantly to research studies already undertaken on the use of the Act on ethnic minorities. In fact, we support the view published in the Department of Health-sponsored publication *Assessing Health Needs of People from Minority Ethnic Groups*[82] that hospital in-patient statistics alone are inadequate as epidemiological data, and that research into the wider aspects of ethnicity and health provision, including the take-up of services in the community, must take place if real planning and health targeting can occur.

6.13 It is not merely enough to provide training programmes, or to employ one or two token Black staff, or to produce an equality of opportunity policy, or to provide a 'special pot' of money to tackle what are – in the final analysis – fundamental components of an effective mental health service. None of these areas are mutually exclusive. It is crucial to have a holistic, multi-dimensional approach and not instigate activities in isolation. Services need to have clear strategic programmes coupled with long-term mainstream funding.

The Commission's strategic approach: the Equal Opportunities Programme

6.14 As early as 1996 (two years prior to the Macpherson report), the Commission recognised that institutional racism was an issue that needed addressing within its own structures, policies, practices and day-to-day operations. In recognition of this and the need to develop and implement a more proactive response to the fundamental issues of inequality, and to demonstrate to external agencies the implementation of sound principles of equality into our own internal policies and practices, we developed a long-term strategic Equal Opportunities Programme (EOP). In our Seventh Biennial Report (1997) we published an EOP statement (see Figure 8 below) and a set of clear goals identifying specific areas of implementation.

Figure 8: The Commission's Equal Opportunities Programme

Five Key Goals Set:

❑ To be committed to the identification of unequal and discriminatory services in the mental health field;

❑ To establish an effective monitoring & quality assurance system;

❑ To set specific foci for commission activities – e.g.: women's issues and race and culture;

❑ To build Equal Opportunities awareness into the development of members and staff;

❑ To increase the number of under-represented groups amongst staff, Commission members and appointees.

These measures aim to enhance public understanding of the Mental Health Act Commission's commitment to Equal Opportunities.

6.15 In our Eighth Biennial Report we highlighted the key activities that took place under Phase 1 of the EOP strategy[83]. Two central achievements included the training of 98% of all Commissioners in issues of race and culture, and the undertaking of National Visit 2, which looked at nationwide provision of ethnic monitoring, interpreting services and strategies to deal with racial harassment.

---

82 Shashidaran & Commander (1998) *Mental Health* in Rawaf & Bahl (eds) **Assessing Health Needs of People from Minority Ethnic Groups**. London, Royal College of Physicians.

83 Mental Health Act Commission (1999) **Eighth Biennial Report**. London, Stationery Office p 20 – 22

Phase 2 of the Commission's strategy was to establish consultation exercises within Black and minority ethnic communities, both as a way of addressing the recruitment issues within the Commission and to hear such communities' perceptions of service provision for detained patients. A summary of the findings from the National Visit 2 and details of the Regional Consultation Exercises is given in **Appendices C and D**: in this chapter we concentrate on the lessons for services that have emerged from these exercises and from the Commission's general experience of visiting hospitals.

The Commission's Regional Consultation Exercises

6.16   The Commission's Regional Consultation Exercises took place over this biennial reporting period around three geographical areas: Greater Manchester, the West Midlands and the North East of England. The exercises were structured through interviews and focus-groups involving approximately 50 organisations (including Black and minority ethnic community members, mental health service providers, police and probation officers and voluntary organisations) in each region, followed by a local seminar in which the Commission discussed its role and remit and attendees could explore mental health service issues through workshops facilitated by local Black and minority ethnic groups.

6.17   The exercises highlighted five key areas:

- mental health services for Black and minority ethnic communities;
- detention under the Mental Health Act 1983;
- race equality initiatives;
- ethnic monitoring; and
- services for women.

Details of the way in which the consultations and seminars were organised and particular findings from them are given in **Appendix D** to this Report.

6.18   Building services to meet the needs of and to support diversity amongst patient populations requires consultation and working with the voluntary sector and other stakeholders in such services, such as Black and minority ethnic communities. We were particularly pleased to note that our consultation exercises were used by service providers as a platform for further local development in building contacts with such organisations and groups. For example, in Manchester, the local authority and mental health service commissioners organised a follow-up seminar which was attended by eighty local people and led to a number of specific goals for improved partnership working in that area.

6.19   We view our national consultation exercises as a model for the engagement of Black and minority ethnic communities, mental health service users, service providers and commissioners. The findings from this project will contribute to forging true partnerships between people from Black and minority ethnic communities and the providers of mental health services and other relevant organisations, on both local and national levels. In this way, the challenge of delivering mental health services that consistently and effectively meet the needs of diverse communities can be addressed. Developing these partnerships will require strategic thinking; commitment from all parties especially statutory authorities and other providers; and the development and cherishing of local networks.

Services for Black and minority ethnic groups – what is to be done?

6.21 Over the years, we have suggested many policy and practice measures to address the diverse needs of Black and minority ethnic groups, including the provision of translated leaflets and appropriately sensitive environments taking into account patients' dietary, religious and cultural backgrounds. The issues of ethnic monitoring, racial harassment and the provision of and access to interpreters have been consistently raised as matters requiring urgent attention. Although some of these measures have met with positive change, service development in these areas has remained ad hoc, patchy and piecemeal.

6.22 We believe that the key to improvement in this whole area is Board leadership in producing a long-term, proactive, strategic equality programme that addresses all aspects of inequality. This programme should be endorsed and driven by the Board and senior management of the organisation and be developed with clear action points, providing realistic timescales and led by identified senior staff. The Race Relations (Amendment) Act provides a useful list of the key areas of focus[84].

6.23 The strategic programme should produce clear policies, procedures and guidelines in all aspects of service delivery together with robust monitoring, implementation and review procedures. The programme should include the following:

- the development of innovative methods of effective and meaningful consultation and active involvement of community and user groups in developing and delivering policy and practice;
- the recruitment, retention and training of staff;
- the establishment of partnerships with a wide variety of groups;
- the regular dissemination of information;
- increased initiatives in respect of prevention, education and early access, particularly within primary care services;
- the raising of awareness of the stigma and discrimination faced by users;
- access to trained and qualified interpreters; and
- clear unambiguous polices with respect to racial harassment.

Above all there should be clear procedures for actively identifying and responding to individual patients' needs.

6.24 Central to the success of any such programme is the need to acknowledge the diversity of individuals and communities. It is necessary to recognise the differences between well-established communities (who have up to four generations living in the UK), and those who are newly

---

84 Home Office (2001) **Race Relations (Amendment) Act 2000 New laws for a successful multi-racial Britain: proposals for implementation.** London Home Office. Chapter 6.

arrived with a variety of additional health and social care issues. There is also a fundamental need to collect and analyse ethnic monitoring data so that this information can feed directly back into the monitoring and evaluation process.

Recommendation 62

Service commissioners and providers should engender clear strategic equality programmes, endorsed and driven by their Board and senior management, and allocated mainstream funding, taking account of the suggestions presented at paragraphs 6.22 – 24 above.

6.25   While we are firmly of the view that services cannot successfully address the needs of Black and minority ethnic groups, or indeed any minority group of patients, without a strategical holistic, multi-dimenional approach with long-term mainstream funding, certain issues must be addressed within such an approach and, where such an approach is slow in starting, should be addressed immediately. These are highlighted in the following paragraphs.

6.26   **Racial harassment** is a serious problem and occurs in all sectors. Racial harassment not only includes physical attacks on people but also verbal abuse and any other form of behaviour that deters people from using or participating in a particular service. It is important that all service providers should have clear policies and procedures to deal with inter-patient racial harassment and of racial harassment of patients by staff. These should require staff to intervene when harassment is apparent, and to ensure that the victim of racial harassment is not further disadvantaged by any such intervention. Following the National Visit 2 we found that three quarters of the units visited in England had no such policies. All too often we learn of patients who have been subject to racial harassment being isolated from the environment where harassment is taking place, whilst the perpetrators go unchallenged and unaffected by their actions. As well as the obvious injustice of such an approach, this can cause or exacerbate problem behaviour from the patient who has been subject to the harassment, leading to an escalation of the problem and further alienating that patient.

6.27   In one well-publicised case that we have followed closely during this reporting period, this approach had tragic consequences. David Bennett was a young black man who, when acting out in response to racist taunting from fellow patients, was isolated from those patients and subsequently died whilst struggling under restraint. The lack of a clear racial harassment policy was recognised by the coroner as being one factor in the events that led to his death.

6.28   **Ethnic Monitoring** remains patchily implemented, although it is has been a mandatory requirement since April 1995. The need for and advantages of ethnic monitoring may be a training issue amongst staff where ethnicity is neither routinely nor accurately determined. Some services have developed innovative practices, whereby patients are given a list of statements of ethnicity in various languages and asked to indicate which statement applies to them.

6.29   With some exceptions, data from ethnic monitoring is not being put to good use. One of the main reasons for requiring such information is to enable ward staff to identify patients' ethnicity so that appropriate action is taken to provide care in a culturally appropriate framework, taking account of **linguistic, cultural and religious needs**. This information, and the views of the patients as to their specific needs, should be an integral part of their care plans.

6.30   **Interpreting services** are widely used, but two-thirds of wards visited on the National Visit 2 and many service providers engaged in the national consultation exercises had used patients' relatives or friends for this purpose in the recent past. Nearly a half of wards visited in this reporting period only had patient information leaflets in English, despite their availability in a number of other languages (see Chapter 2.8 – 2.10).

6.31   Links with Black and minority ethnic groups should extend, wherever possible, to contacts with **culturally appropriate advocacy groups** and voluntary organisations.

6.32   We reiterate the need for over-arching strategies to cover all these points. We welcome the on-going development of guidance in codes of practice in relation to the NHS and the Race Relations (Amendment) Act 2000, and hope that the duties imposed by that Act on public authorities will serve as a useful lever to ensure race equality in access to services and treatment. Through our focus on this area of work and our programme of activities over the past four years, we have laid solid foundations for addressing the requirements of the Race Relations (Amendment) Act 2000. We will continue to build on our established equality programme over the next two years to ensure that we meet the new duties, and will be actively looking for similar compliance and a general sensitivity to the special needs of patients from Black and minority ethnic backgrounds in services that we visit.

Women Patients

Safety, privacy and dignity in mixed environments

6.33   Women patients are normally in a minority on any mixed ward at any given time[85]. This is particularly the case in acute care and in some medium secure units. It is of paramount importance that women patients are able to feel safe and retain their privacy and dignity on such units, and the Commission welcomes the Government's action to ensure this.

6.34   The NHS Executive issued EL(97)3 on the 24 January 1997, requiring health authorities to set local performance targets with Trusts within their boundary, to deliver the following objectives:

■ ensure that appropriate organisational arrangements are in place to secure good standards of privacy and dignity for hospital patients;

■ achieve fully the standard for segregated washing and toilet facilities across the NHS; and

■ provide safe facilities for patients in hospital who are mentally ill which safeguard their privacy and dignity.

---

85 Mental Health Act Commission (1999) **Eighth Biennial Report**, London, Stationery Office para 10.57

Central monitoring arrangements within the NHS Executive have been tracking the progress in achieving these objectives from an original target of 95% implementation by 2002. The first annual report on this monitoring (1999) showed a 93% expectation and urged greater effort.

6.35 As well as finding some units that have yet to comply with the Directive at all, Commissioners also find some that have complied with the basic requirements to provide gender-differentiated toilet and washing facilities, yet do so in a way that still does not afford women patients the safety and security that they should be able to expect. In particular, women-only washing and toilet facilities may be provided, but these are placed within wards in such a way that women have to pass male sleeping areas at night to reach them. Other services have not yet managed to protect women patients adequately from harassment or even serious danger. For example, in some services women are provided with individual rooms that are not furnished with patient-operated locks that can be overridden by staff, even though they share corridor access with mens' rooms.

6.36 The National Service Framework for Mental Health states that "while accommodation for social and therapeutic activities will usually be mixed, Government wants to ensure that single sex day space is always provided" (page 50). It is now a requirement that newly built units must provide secure day rooms for women patients only. Older hospitals may have to adopt more imaginative solutions, but it is not acceptable that the only women-only spaces in mental health units can be patients' bedrooms and bathrooms.

Good Practice Example

West Hampshire NHS Trust facilitated a working party comprised of staff and patients to address the concerns raised over women's safety and access to facilities on a particular unit. The working party was charged with:

- evaluating the delivery of care to women patients at the unit and identifying shortfalls and examples of good practice, taking account of the differing needs of women on each of the wards and using questionnaires or other means to ascertain the views of all patients and staff;

- formulating an audit tool to establish and monitor base-line standards; and

- making policy recommendations on all of these issues, including recommendations for evidence based practice in the care of women.

The group was also linked to another in-house group setting standards and looking at quality assurance for all of the patients within the unit.

The Commission commends this as an imaginative approach to addressing issues of women's care.

Contact Jayne Dollery, CBT Nurse Specialist, Ravenswood House MSU, Fareham, Hampshire SO51 7ZA Tel 01329 836000

6.37 We would not wish to see these guarantees for women's safety and security resulting in the creation of entirely segregated hospitals. We have found that some services, whether by design or inadvertently, appear to be losing sight of the continued need for women and men patients to engage in social and therapeutic activities in a mixed environment. This could lead not only to a lack of normalcy in hospital environments, but also to a serious diminution of activities and therapies available to the often small group of women living in such environments. We have particular concerns over this issue at the three High Security Hospitals, following strong representation from both patients and staff at the hospitals (see Chapter 5.20). Services must ensure that women are safe when undertaking mixed activities, but such activities must continue to be provided.

6.38   In the coming period we will continue our involvement with the UKCC in developing standards of care for women in secure environments. The Commission looks forward to the outcome of this project, which will involve a wide range of interested parties.

Recommendation 63

Service commissioning bodies and service providers should agree and monitor services for women patients to ensure that such patients can:

- lock bedroom doors, using a system capable of being overridden by staff in emergency;

- have a choice of a female key-worker;

- be in contact with other women;

- have the opportunity to take part in women-only therapy groups and social activities, but have the choice of taking part in mixed groups where appropriate;

- engage safely in a full range of such activities, even where their number is small compared to the hospital population;

- have physical health-checks on admission;

- have access to a female doctor for medical care;

- have access to a female member of staff at all times; and

- be assured of adequate supervision at night.

6.39   Issues relating to women and seclusion are discussed at Chapter 4.44 above.

Children and Adolescents

6.40   In our last two Biennial Reports we have expressed our concern over the uneven provision of services for children and adolescents who are detained under the Mental Health Act[86]. We welcomed the inclusion in the 1998 National Priorities Guidance[87] of an objective to improve the provision of appropriate, high-quality care and treatment for children and adolescents through building up locally based child and adolescent mental health services (CAMHS). The Government has reported significant investment in the period covered by this report towards meeting all the objectives set by the National Priorities Guidance, also taking account of the recommendations of the Audit Commission's *Children in Mind* report[88]. Work also continues at a national policy level, and the Government has announced its intention to publish a Children's National Service Framework, encompassing CAMHS, in 2003/4[89]. An All-Wales Strategy for CAMHS was also in preparation at the end of this reporting period.

---

86 Mental Health Act Commission (1997) **Seventh Biennial Report** p187–8, Mental Health Act Commission (1999) **Eighth Biennial Report** p 247 – 250 London, Stationery Office

87 Department of Health (1998) **Modernising Mental Health Services: National Priorities Guidance 1999/ 00 – 2001/02.** LAC(98)22

88 Audit Commission (1999) **Children in Mind.** Oxford, Audit Commission Publications.

89 See www.doh.gov.uk/nsf/children.htm

6.41 However, the difficulties faced by mental health services in responding adequately to the needs of detained children mean that a great deal of work remains to be done. Inpatient service provision for distressed children and adolescent patients remains problematic across England and Wales. We are particularly concerned about those cases where adolescents are admitted through necessity to adult units, or where, through a lack of facilities, they are not admitted when at their most vulnerable.

6.42 Even in the best circumstances, children admitted to adult wards are likely to be isolated and unhappy, and their social, educational and emotional needs are unlikely to be met. In some cases, the facilities in which children are detained are so poorly suited to accommodate them that service providers are reluctantly forced to take extreme measures. In this reporting period Commissioners met with one 14 year old girl who was being nursed one-to-one in her own room and in the corridors of a central London hospital, because she was seen as vulnerable if housed on the overcrowded wards. The hospital had reluctantly agreed to admit her for a few days whilst suitable accommodation was located, but, eight weeks from admission, no such place had been found. Whilst staff were doing their best in such a situation, the girl's detention amounted to little more than containment of dubious therapeutic value and was potentially extremely damaging to her own morale and to that of staff and other patients. Many less dramatic but no less concerning examples could be given.

6.43 One problem faced by services is the relative infrequency of admission of children and adolescents under the Act. In visits to CAMHS and general services in this reporting period Commissioners met with slightly more than 200 detained children and adolescents, which it estimates to be roughly one fifth of all the children and adolescents detained in this period. The Commission surveyed all hospitals and Registered Mental Nursing Homes that detain patients on the numbers of admissions of children and adolescents under the Act in this reporting period. The results (based upon 230 responses out of 281 establishments) are presented in Figure 9 below. These figures suggest that:

■ 25% of all children (i.e. under 16 years old) admitted under the Act are placed in adult facilities;

■ 82% of all adolescents (i.e. aged 16–18) admitted under the Act are placed in adult facilities; and

■ within both groups, males are most disadvantaged by current arrangements, with 32% of detained male children and 84% of detained male adolescents admitted to adult facilities.

Fig. 9 Children and Adolescents admitted under the Mental Health Act, 1/4/99 – 31/3/01

Type of ward admitted to	Adult male	Adult female	CAMHS male	CAMHS female	TOTAL
Children (under 16 years)	71	46	150	193	460
Adolescents (16–18 years)	307	200	58	57	622
TOTAL	378	246	208	250	1082

6.44 When it is unavoidable to admit children or adolescents to adult wards, strategies such as that reported in the Eighth Biennial Report[90] in relation to Gwent Healthcare NHS Trust can ensure that the best possible arrangements are made. In essence the arrangements, which are agreed in protocol form and can be brought into action on the admission of any child or adolescent patient, are as follows:

■ one unit is identified as the most appropriate placement for children and adolescents in emergencies;

■ that unit has access to a pool of bank nurses trained to care for children and adolescents;

■ daily assessment by a child psychiatrist or a designated junior is arranged;

■ an on-call child psychiatrist is available for queries and advice out of hours; at other times an identified clinical services manager provides this service; and

■ staff caring for the patient are treated as a part of the ward tem and rotated, to avoid isolation of either staff members or the patient.

At Chapter 7.26 we note that all Welsh facilities that provide inpatient psychiatric care for children and adolescents are required to meet standards set by the Health Advisory Service 2000, including having explicit protocols relating to the admission of young people to adult mental illness units. We hope that the all services will consider whether such strategic arrangements should be agreed within their localities, and that the Department of Health will consider making this a requirement for all English services.

Recommendation 64

All mental health services providing care to children and adolescents detained under the Act should have agreed working and referral arrangements with appropriate medical and psychiatric expertise in CAMHS.

---

90 Mental Health Act Commission (1999) **Eighth Biennial Report**. London, Stationery Office p 249

> **Recommendation 65**
>
> All NSF local implementation strategies should identify the mental healthcare needs of children and adolescents and plan appropriate provision to meet those needs.

> **Recommendation 66**
>
> The Department of Health should consider the need for England to have standards and protocols for the care of mentally ill minors detained in adult units, as already exists in Wales

6.45 We look forward to working with the Department of Health in discussions over the formulation of the Children's National Service Framework. Our review of our own information leaflets (see Chapter 2.12) will consider formats that will be accessible to children.

> **Recommendation 67**
>
> The Department of Health should consider formats for its information leaflets on the Mental Health Act that will be accessible to children.
>
> (see recommendation 5, Chapter 2.11)

Commissioner and SOADs' visits to detained children

6.46 At the end of this reporting period, the Commission Board agreed that, as all Mental Health Act Commissioners have significant contact with child and adolescent patients, and have legal authority to meet with them in private as well as access to their records, two Commissioners would be present at any private meeting with such patients unless one of those Commissioners had been police-checked.

6.47 We have also initiated the establishment of a small panel of SOADs with expertise in child psychiatry, so as to ensure that suitable safeguards under Part IV of the Act are provided to child and adolescent patients. Such SOADs will also be police-checked.

Deaf Patients

6.48 Approximately one in every 1000 of the population is deaf, using "sign" as their preferred language[91]. Despite normal intelligence, the ability of people with early profound deafness to understand spoken or written English, and therefore lip-reading or the written word, is limited. Given the centrality of communication to every aspect of psychiatric practice, such people can be seriously disadvantaged by the general lack of appreciation of these considerable difficulties.

6.49 Deaf patients have been reported to be grossly over-represented in mental hospitals as a result of poor diagnosis, miscommunication and misguided treatment programmes[92]. The three national specialist mental health services for deaf people are neither commissioned nor resourced to

---

91 Pathfinder Mental Health Services NHS Trust [n.d.] **National Deaf Services: Mental Health Services in Sign Language for Deaf Adults, Children and Families.** London, Pathfinder Mental Health Services NHS Trust. p 1

92 *ibid.* p 2

provide intensive care. In a few cases, deaf patients requiring detention under the Act may be treated in a neighbouring facility to one of the national centres, so allowing for some input from the national centre to their care, but, if no bed is available locally, they may be deprived of any significant input from the national centres.

6.50　Problems in services for deaf mentally ill patients, particularly in crisis situations, were brought into sharp focus by the publication of the report from the Inquiry into the care and treatment of Daniel Joseph in September 2000[93]. We were pleased to note the Government's acceptance of the recommendations of this Inquiry, which included the development of a nationally co-ordinated strategy for deaf people with mental health problems, a review of the commissioning of sign-language interpreters in health and social services and increased priority for the specialist services for deaf people on the NHS Executive agenda.

6.51　We welcome the expected publication of the Consultation Paper *Modernising Mental Health Services for People who are Deaf*[94] and look forward to working with the Department of Health in the development of a national strategy for deaf people.

6.52　Article 5(2) of the European Convention of Human Rights provides a right to anyone deprived of their liberty to be informed promptly of the reasons for this deprivation "in a language which he understands." We believe that deaf patients are especially vulnerable to failures to secure this right, which may be symptomatic of the many disadvantages faced by such patients who do not come into early and appropriate contact with the three national specialist mental health services for deaf people.

6.53　The importance of acknowledging and dealing with problems in communication, including deafness, is specifically referred to in the Code of Practice (see guiding principles, paras 1.3 – 1.7). In circumstances where there is doubt as to whether oral/aural and written methods of communication are adequate, the assistance of either a local authority Social Worker with Deaf People or a voluntary agency worker with the deaf must be sought.

6.54　In our review of the appropriateness of our own information leaflets for particular groups of patients (see Chapter 2.12), we will consider the unique communication needs of the Deaf community (see paragraph 6.48 above). We urge the Department of Health to similarly review its information leaflets on the Mental Health Act.

Recommendation 68

The Department of Health should consider formats for its information leaflets on the Mental Health Act that will be accessible to deaf patients whose first language is BSL. (see recommendation 5, Chapter 2.11)

---

93 **Report of the Independent Inquiry Team into the Care and Treatment of Daniel Joseph** (2000) Commissioned by Merton Sutton & Wandsworth and Lambeth, Southwark & Lewisham Health Authorities. April 2000.

94 In preparation at the time of writing.

Elderly Patients

6.55 At the end of this reporting period the Government published the National Service Framework for Older People[95]. We welcome the setting of these standards, particularly Standard Seven, promoting access to integrated mental health services to ensure effective diagnosis, treatment and support; Standards One and Two promoting anti-discrimination and person-centred care; and Standard Four ensuring that care in hospital will be provided appropriately by properly trained staff.

6.56 We also welcome the publication of guidelines for implementing the medicine-related aspects of the NSF for Older People[96]. We hope that this can set the groundwork for further and more comprehensive guidelines on the use of medication for mental disorder with older people.

6.57 Two particular cases of deaths of elderly detained patients have caused us concern in this period:

- A frail 79 year old man with a confusional state was admitted to a psychiatric ward under Section 2 for assessment of his condition. His haemoglobin was noted to be 25% and he was transferred to the general care of an elderly ward. His psychiatric records were not transferred with him. After he had become agitated and assaultative towards staff, he was given a prescribed rapid tranquillisation combination of drugs in a dosage more suitable to an active fit young man. When he woke up, he was unsteady on his feet and fell on several occasions sustaining injuries to his head. He later died from a large skull fracture.

- A 76 year old woman was admitted to a psychiatric ward for assessment under Section 2. She was noted to be eating and drinking little over the ten-day period before she died of dehydration, but little or no specific action seems to have been taken to address the problem.

6.58 In both cases Commissioners attended the inquests with Properly Interested Person status and pursued matters with the Trusts concerned. In the second case, although an internal inquiry concluded that the standard of care was poor and changes were implemented to prevent a recurrence, an unannounced visit by a specialist nurse Commissioner two months later showed that little had changed and that two patients were in imminent danger. These cases were brought to the attention of the Medical Director.

6.59 The dangers of services failing to take account of the particular needs of elderly patients are evident from these examples. In the first example, a general hospital ward mishandled psychiatric treatment with tragic consequences; in the second, a ward providing psychiatric treatment was failing to provide the most basic care needed to maintain patients' lives.

6.60 The service model outlined for mental health services in the NSF for Older People[97] could help to ensure that these failures do not happen. Specialist mental services should be multi-disciplinary and have agreed working and referral arrangements with, amongst others, dieticians and pharmacists. Specialist services are expected to provide outreach and advice services to other parts of the service.

95 Department of Health (2001) **National Service Framework for Older People**. London, March 2001. www.doh.gov.uk/nsf/olderpeople.htm

96 Department of Health (2001) **Medicines and Older People: Implementing the medicines-related aspects of the NSF for Older People**. London, March 2001. www.doh.gov.uk/nsf/olderpeople.htm

97 Department of Health (2001) **National Service Framework for Older People**. London, March 2001. p103–6

6.61 Commissioners all too frequently note particular problems in the care environments of elderly patients. A common problem is the management of urinary incontinence, as evidenced by strong urine smells in certain wards. Affected wards should review their management of this issue and check that floor-coverings are appropriate.

6.62 Many older patients without mental capacity to give consent to their care and treatment, particularly those with dementia-related disorders, are not necessarily detained under the Mental Health Act. Being essentially compliant with their care and treatment, they are provided with this under common-law powers. It is widely acknowledged that such patients may be inappropriately prescribed neuroleptic drugs to treat behavioural complications of their disorder, sometimes with adverse effects on their cognitive state[98]. We welcome the Department's guidance on this, which applies to detained patients as well as informal ones[99]. However, there is, as yet, little overview of these and more general standards of care and treatment for patients who lack mental capacity but who are not detained under the Act. We discuss our concerns over such patients at paragraphs 6.68 – 6.69 below.

Needs of Patients with Learning Disabilities

6.63 The National Service Framework for Mental Health aims to enable people with Learning Disability to access mainstream psychiatric services in the same way as anyone else wherever possible. It recognises that this will require mainstream services to be more responsive to the needs of such patients. The NSF for Mental Health also recognises the need for specialist learning disability services, both to provide specialist treatment to learning disabled patients and to provide facilitation and support to mainstream services.

6.64 One of the challenges faced by all services that detain learning disabled patients is to provide information to such patients. This applies to fulfilling the statutory duty to provide detained patients with information on their legal situation and rights (Section 132) just as it does to providing suitable information to enable them to participate in their treatment to the fullest extent possible. We welcome the Government's assurance that it will take steps to ensure that

---

98 Department of Health (2001) **Medicines and Older People: Implementing the medicines-related aspects of the NSF for Older People**. London, March 2001 p 15; Department of Health (2001) **National Service Framework for Older People**. London, March 2001. P99

99 10 Department of Health (2001) **National Service Framework for Older People**. London, March 2001. www.doh.gov.uk/nsf/olderpeople.htm p 99

mental health promotion materials and information are available in formats accessible to people with learning disabilities, including those from minority ethnic groups[100], and trust that this will extend to patient leaflets on the Mental Health Act 1983. We will be similarly reviewing our own patient information leaflets (see Chapter 2.12).

Good practice example

Dr Anna Thomas, now working for Independent Community Living Ltd, has aided the Commission in producing a "Symbol" Mental Health Act Commission poster, aimed at people with mental impairment or reading difficulties, which has been a success in Learning Disabilities Units. Dr Thomas has also produced a pictorial information leaflet explaining Section 37 for patients in her own care, which other services may wish to adapt for their own use.

(Contact: Dr A Thomas, ICL ltd, Lys Ifor, Crescent Road, Caerphilly, South Wales CF83 1XY tel 029 2088 1994 fax 029 2085 3111)

Recommendation 71

The Department of Health should consider formats for its information leaflets on the Mental Health Act that will be accessible to patients with learning disabilities. Such formats could include pictoral or "symbol" text, or video.

(see recommendation 5, Chapter 2.11)

6.65 Relatively few patients in specialist learning disability units are detained under the Mental Health Act. Planned Commission visits to such units may be postponed due to the fact that there are no detained patients for Commissioners to see. Although Commissioners have encountered some excellent facilities and services for this group of patients, they have also encountered some alarmingly poor services. The limit to the Commission's oversight of the many small units providing services for the learning disabled is of considerable concern.

6.66 In one particularly worrying example, a Commissioner visited a learning disability unit on world mental health day (10 October 2000). Patients resident on the men's villa (none of whom were detained under the Act) were housed on a locked ward in appalling conditions. A strong smell of urine pervaded the ward, and patients had little or no available activities or access to fresh air. The Commissioner recorded that she was shocked at the conditions and the aura of low expectation on the unit. It was even more disturbing that, as there were no detained patients on the ward, these conditions had come to the Commission's attention by chance.

6.67 We believe that there are important lessons to be learned from such examples about the need for regular visits to services where vulnerable patients are detained. These are discussed briefly below.

---

100 Department of Health (2001) **Valuing People: A New Strategy for Learning Disability for the 21st Century.** London, Stationery Office. p 66.

The Vulnerable Position of Long-Term Mentally Incapacitated Patients

6.68   Every Commission Biennial Report (starting in 1985) has expressed concern at the de facto detention of mentally incapacitated patients[101], whether they are patients with learning disability, dementia or head-injuries. The judgement in R v Bournewood Community & Mental Health NHS ex parte L [1998] 3 AER[102] confirmed that, under the present law, it is acceptable for such patients to be kept informally in hospital where they are compliant with such action, even though this was described in the judgment of Lord Steyn as "an indefensible gap in mental health law". We remain extremely concerned at the lack of legal protection offered to such patients, not only with regard to the possibility that they may be held in hospital where such action is unwarranted or unlawful, but also because such patients are denied the protections offered to patients detained under the Mental Health Act regarding consent to treatment, aftercare and visitorial oversight by the Commission.

6.69   We acknowledge and welcome the Government's intention to provide safeguards in relation to the long-term mentally incapacitated[103], including bringing such patients within the remit of the successor body to the Commission. The experience of Commissioners (see paragraph 6.66 above) suggests that an important aspect of this protection must be a visitorial role, whether this is given to the successor body or to any other organisation with appropriate experience and expertise.

Recommendation 72

The Commission urges the Government to consider ways in which long-term incapacitated patients can be protected while new legislation is awaited.

---

101 Mental Health Act Commission (1985) **First Biennial Report** p 11; (1987) **Second Biennial Report** p50; (1989) **Third Biennial Report** p 35; (1991) **Fourth Biennial Report** p43; (1993) **Fifth Biennial Report** p.47; (1995) **Sixth Biennial Report** p 66; (1997) **Seventh Biennial Report** p 180–181 (1999); **Eighth Biennial Report** p 35, 254 –255. London, Stationery Office.

102 see Mental Health Act Commission (1999) **Eighth Biennial Report**. London, Stationery Office p 33–35

103 Department of Health (2000) **Reforming the Mental Health Act: Part I The New Legal Frarmework**. London, Stationery Office. Chapter 6

7   The Commission in Wales

The National Assembly for Wales

7.1   The Mental Health Act Commission serves both England and Wales. Since we started work in 1983, there have often been differences in service provision and practice between England and Wales. This situation has been accentuated since 1999 by the creation of the National Assembly for Wales, the election of its members and its appointment of a Minister of Health and Social Services. These changes have significantly increased the importance of the Commission paying attention to differences in policy and practice while continuing to fulfil our main function of visiting patients to ensure satisfactory compliance with the provisions of the Mental Health Act 1983.

7.2   In recognition of this new situation, the Vice-Chairman of the Commission's Board, Professor Richard Williams, has taken the lead on Welsh matters which are of concern to the Commission and has established positive links between the Commission's Board and Members and staff of the National Assembly. Although Professor Williams will unfortunately be leaving the Commission at the end of September 2001, we intend to continue the practice of having a Board Member with this special focus.

7.3   In March 2001, the Commission held a Board Meeting at the Assembly building in Cardiff Bay. Board Members were able to discuss matters of mutual interest with the Minister, Jane Hutt AM, and the Chair of the Health and Social Services Committee, Kirsty Williams AM. The Commission's Board greatly welcomed this opportunity and were encouraged by the keen interest shown in the work of Commissioners. The Board intends to continue to hold at least one meeting a year in Wales to demonstrate its recognition of the differences between England and Wales.

Welsh Language Policy

7.4   The Commission has been active in developing its Welsh Language Policy in accordance with the requirements of the Welsh Language Act 1993. This policy, which has been endorsed by the Welsh Language Board and cited as a model of good practice, ensures that anyone who wishes to use the Welsh language in correspondence with or talking to Members or staff of the Commission may do so. Wherever possible, a Welsh-speaking Commissioner attends Commission visits in Wales and arrangements are made for any detained patient who wishes to speak to a Commissioner in Welsh to do so.

Mental Health Strategy and Policy in Wales

7.5   In reading Chapters 1 – 6 of this Biennial Report, it is important to recognise that many of the strategies and policies mentioned there do not apply to Wales. One example of this is "Modernising Mental Health". It is therefore necessary to distinguish between the NHS Framework for England and that for Wales. Wales has not adopted anything similar to the NHS Zero Tolerance policy which is welcomed in Chapter 4.35, but we would strongly recommend that the National Assembly looks seriously at the possibility of doing so. The Commission for Health Improvement and the National Institute for Clinical Excellence both have responsibilities for aspects of mental health in Wales, but there is a separate Welsh Care Standards Commission.

7.6 We welcome the decision of the National Assembly to place mental health as one of its three top health priorities, as in England. In June 2000, two Welsh mental health strategy documents were issued for consultation. *"Everybody's Business"*[104], is groundbreaking as the first plan of its kind in the UK to cover the whole field of mental health services for children and adolescents. In Chapter 6.44, we commend such a strategy to England. We look forward to seeing the plan fully implemented and developed into practices which may serve as an example to mental health services in England as well as Wales.

7.7 The Commission was pleased to see detained patients specifically mentioned in the section on empowerment in *"Equity, Empowerment, Effectiveness, Efficiency"*[105], the draft strategy for adult services. This states that such patients should be encouraged to participate actively and willingly in their own care. Commissioners comment frequently on the beneficial effect which such involvement has on the health of the patients concerned. We understand that the National Assembly intends to develop a National Service Framework for Wales from the strategy.

7.8 Although the strategy plans which have emerged from these two consultation exercises have not yet been published, the Commission understands that the Minister, Jane Hutt, has confirmed them and that they will be launched in September this year. We look forward, in particular, to seeing how individual detained patients will be affected by those objectives which will address some of the issues covered in this report, such as:

■ the development of advocacy services for all patients;

■ the adoption of the Care Programme Approach for the first time in Wales; and

■ the improvement of discharge plans to include suitable support and follow-up.

All of these go towards the over-riding objective of providing mental health services in settings which are fit for purpose and which provide dignity and privacy. The importance which the Commission attaches to this objective is emphasised in Chapters 3 and 4 of this Report.

Structural Change

7.9 Prior to devolution, the Welsh Office reconfigured the NHS Trusts and, in April 1999, reduced them by almost one half. Wales now has no mental health or community Trusts – a significant difference compared to the development of some very large combined mental health and community Trusts in England. Similarly, in 1998, when Primary Care Groups were created in England with a view to the development of Primary Care Trusts independent of Health Authorities, in Wales 22 Local Health Groups were created as sub-committees of the five Health Authorities, each one co-terminous with one of the County Borough Councils and having local authority representation on its Board.

7.10 Commissioners have not observed that these differences in structure have had any direct effect on the experiences of individual mentally ill patients in Wales, perhaps because the commissioning of mental health services has not yet been devolved to the Local Health Boards.

---

104 **Child and Adolescent Mental Health Services.** *Everybody's Business.* Consultation Strategy Document June 2000

105 **Adult Mental Health Services for Wales:** *Equity, Empowerment, Effectiveness, Efficiency.* Draft Strategy document June 2000

7.11 The consultation document *Improving Health in Wales– Structural Change in the NHS in Wales* (published in July 2001– after the period covered by this Report) proposes to replace all five health authorities by twenty-two Local Health Boards. These will be statutory bodies grouped under three Health Economy Teams (for North Wales, South and East Wales and Mid and West Wales). Although the Commission understands that the new system will pay particular attention to the commissioning arrangements for mental health services, we are concerned that already over-pressed managers and staff, heavily engaged in adapting to changes in management arrangements, may lose sight of the priority which should be accorded to mentally ill patients, especially those detained against their will.

The Commission's Activities in Wales

7.12 All visits to mental health facilities in Wales are carried out by one of the Commission's seven Commission Visiting Teams (CVT6). The Commissioners who are regular members of this team are highlighted in Appendix A. This Team covers the West Midlands as well as Wales and so its members have to be familiar with the structures of two health services and with two different approaches to mental health policy. Welsh Trusts that have borders with England and English Trusts which border on Wales similarly find themselves working with patients from both countries and with two structures and policies. The Commissioners are therefore able to appreciate the demanding challenges this duality poses for professionals and managers in those services and the need for greater recognition and better training to take account of the position.

> Recommendation 73
>
> Welsh Trusts with boundaries with England and English Trusts with Welsh boundaries should ensure that there is at least a nucleus of staff who know both systems well enough to offer advice as necessary to those who deal with cross-boundary patients.

7.13 During the two years under review, Commissioners visited every mental health facility in Wales which held detained patients on a rolling programme. Most units will have received at least three visits in the period. A total of 51 visits were made overall.

7.14 As explained in the Introduction to this report (Chapter 1), we do not wish to name and blame but to provide an overview of how the implementation of the Act is affecting the people it aims to protect, to help the facilities visited to improve their own practice, and to draw attention to general areas of poor practice and advise on possible remedies. Commissioners are greatly impressed by the general level of commitment and care shown by staff and managers on their visits. With very few exceptions, the general areas of poor practice which have been identified in Wales reflect those in England. The recommendations made in earlier chapters and the Commentary and Schedule of Recommendations in Chapter 9 therefore apply as much to Wales as to England. The following paragraphs accordingly highlight only those issues which we believe are of particular significance in Wales.

Rights and Respect

Doctors appointed under Section 12 of the Mental Health Act

7.15 Chapter 2.57 *et seq.* stresses the importance of Section 12 doctors and recommends a number of actions by Health Authorities to try to increase the number and availability of such doctors so that patients are not subjected to long delays in assessment. Commissioners in Wales have also identified problems over the availability and location of suitably approved doctors, but our particular concern relates to the mechanisms for considering applications for Section 12 approval in Wales, the standards applied to applicants and the training required of them. We note that these all vary considerably amongst the Health Authorities in Wales. In particular, some Health Authorities require specific training but some require none.

7.16   The Commission takes the view that all patients are entitled to receive a common standard of assessment for detention and believes that there should be at least minimum national requirements for training. There may be concerns that raising the threshold for approval would reduce the number of doctors applying to be approved but experience in England suggests that many potential applicants feel re-assured by the offer of training. In this respect, we are glad to note that both the National Assembly for Wales and the Department of Health have made funding available to the Royal College of Psychiatrists towards the training of child and adolescent psychiatrists as Section 12 doctors.

Recommendation 74

In considering how responsibilities for approving Section 12 doctors should be exercised under the proposed restructuring, the National Assembly for Wales should review the current system for approving Section 12 doctors with a view to ensuring greater consistency and a minimum level of initial and ongoing training.

Approved Social Worker (ASW) Issues

7.17   Chapter 2 also highlights the important role of ASWs and the need for them to complete standardised forms to ensure that all the relevant information about a detained patient is left with the receiving hospital. Commissioners regularly scrutinise forms completed by ASWs in relation to individual patients and have been glad to note that, although the quality and comprehensiveness of such forms varies widely across Wales, there are several examples of good practice.

Quality and Standards of Care

Bed pressures

7.18   Commissioners frequently express concerns about the adequacy of facilities for acutely ill and disruptive patients, especially those who require medium secure beds. We nevertheless believe that it is difficult to establish whether there is a true shortage of secure beds in Wales without a detailed analysis of the extent to which patients are being kept unnecessarily in such accommodation because of the shortage of low secure beds.

Recommendation 75

The Specialist Health Services Commission for Wales should encourage a holistic assessment of bed needs across all security levels so that patients are not kept at a higher level of security than their condition justifies.

Staffing issues: shortage of psychiatrists

7.19 As in England, workforce issues are likely to be the key to the development of mental health services for patients of all ages. Commissioners report that there is a significant shortage of psychiatrists in Wales, although closer analysis suggests that the proportion of vacant posts is actually lower than in England. The position varies considerably across the country, with worrying numbers of vacancies in particular parts of Wales, and especially a shortage of forensic psychiatrists. We understand that although there are sufficient training posts in Wales to fill present and predicted consultant vacancies, the out-turn of trainees is not sufficient to fill those vacancies. We welcome the National Assembly's recognition of the problem and the initiative it has taken to review the situation.

Essential Environmental Requirements

7.20 Staffing issues naturally impact on delivery of the standard of care which should be provided. A number of in-patient facilities in Wales remain housed in old unsuitable buildings. Some progress has been made during the period under review in that a number of wards have been up-graded and refurbished while others, such as the Mid-Wales Hospital in Talgarth, have been relocated in completely new units. Particular concerns continue to be:

■ the provision of single sex facilities for men and women;

■ access to fresh air;

■ lack of activity; and

■ an inappropriate mix of patients on wards.

As an example of the latter, Commissioners visited one ward on which staff were caring for patients with conditions ranging from chronic psychosis and personality disorders to substance misuse and learning disabilities.

7.21 In spite of continuing concerns, we have been greatly encouraged by the positive response of Trusts which have sought to implement coherent ward management policies and by the many examples of good practice which have been encountered in Welsh facilities. One such example, involving Cardiff and Vale NHS Trust, is highlighted at Chapter 3.19.

ECT in Wales

7.22 The Commission's study of ECT facilities is described at Chapter 3.31 *et seq.*, where we report the figures from our initial analyses of the ECT survey combined for England and Wales. Fourteen of the 230 clinics reviewed were in Wales. A summary of the findings relating to these clinics is provided in Figure 10 below.

7.23 Three of the 18 clinics which were rated highly in the total survey were in Wales and another three Welsh facilities were in the group of 30 which complied to all requirements to a substantial extent. At the other end of the scale, one clinic had less than three rooms and at least one other departure from the standards expected. Although the proportion of ECT facilities scoring well in Wales was much higher than in England (40% compared with 18%), the relatively small number of suites involved is obviously a relevant factor.

Figure 10

Item	Percent (n=14 sites surveyed in Wales)	No. of units
The Arrangements for ECT Possession of a dedicated ECT suite, comprising 3 or more rooms, including a separate waiting room and recovery room	79	11
A Policy for ECT Clinics which were able to show the Commissioner either a copy of the Royal College of Psychiatrists Handbook or a copy of the hospital's own ECT policy	100	14
A Named Consultant Psychiatrist ECT clinics with a named consultant psychiatrist who visits regularly	93	13
Recovery and Resuscitation ECT Clinics that have, in practice, a nurse in the recovery room who is trained in Basic Life Support, Cardio-pulmonary Resuscitation and who attends refresher courses in resuscitation regularly	86	12

7.24 As recorded in Chapter 3.35, a full analysis of the findings from this survey in both England and Wales will be published later in 2001.

Addressing Diversity

7.25 The difficulties highlighted in Chapter 6 in relation to small groups of diverse patients are in general similar in Wales to England. The problems of Black and minority ethnic groups are, however, more easily overlooked because only Cardiff reaches the national average for people from such minorities. Because the population is so much more dispersed in Wales, it is difficult to address the needs of relatively isolated individuals. This is one of the reasons why the Commission, in consultation with the National Assembly for Wales, has decided to carry out a National Visit in Wales which will focus on the needs of Black and minority ethnic groups, following up some of the issues raised in our second National Visit to the whole of England and Wales.[106]

Children and adolescents

7.26 One major difference between Wales and England is the creation of standards by the Health Advisory Service 2000 for the inpatient psychiatric care of adolescents in the NHS in Wales. All psychiatric facilities that admit young people are required to meet these standards. In particular, all mental health services must have in place explicit protocols covering the arrangements for and management of young people admitted to adult mental illness units. This includes specific items relating to child protection and the availability of staff who have been trained to work with

106 Warner et al (2000) **Improving Care for Detained Patients from Black and Minority Ethnic Communities Preliminary Report – National Visit 2.** Sainsbury Centre for Mental Health.

children and are police checked. In Chapter 6.44 we recommend that the Department of Health considers the adoption of similar standards and protocols.

7.27   Commissioners have found that, in practice, problems in finding appropriate places for adolescents in Wales and in applying the protocols to adolescents in adult facilities are increasing because of the pressure on adult psychiatric units from the rise in numbers of adults who need urgent or emergency admission. The number of young people who need such help has also risen and yet we understand that the number of dedicated places for adolescents is proportionately less in Wales than in any NHS region in England. We therefore welcome the commitment in *"Everybody's Business"* to review this problem.

7.28   In Wales as in England, the Commission has recently required Commissioners who have not been police-checked not to hold any private meeting with a child or adolescent patient unless another Commissioner is present. A small panel of Second Opinion Appointed Doctors with expertise in child expertise is also being identified. The Commission will ensure that they are police-checked for attendance on such patients.

7.29   These observations underline the key importance, as stressed in Chapter 6, of ensuring that general strategies and policies for the protection of children are applied to this especially vulnerable group of children and adolescents.

Conclusion

7.30   In carrying out their functions during the past two years, Commissioners have noted very few significant differences in the implementation of the Mental Health Act 1983 between Wales and England. The development of different policies and strategies and perhaps of different legislation and priorities may alter this position over the years to come. This chapter has highlighted some of the current differences. We will continue to note significant differences in the hope that this may encourage the better sharing of good practice throughout Wales and England.

7 Y Comisiwn yng Nghymru

Cynulliad Cenedlaethol Cymru

7.1 Mae'r Comisiwn Deddf Iechyd Meddwl yn gwasanaethu Cymru a Lloegr. Ers i'r Comisiwn ddechrau ar ei waith ym 1983, yn aml fe fu gwahaniaethau yn narpariaeth y gwasanaeth a'r arfer rhwng Cymru a Lloegr. Fe gafodd y sefyllfa hon ei amlygu ers 1999 oherwydd creu Cynulliad Cenedlaethol Cymru, ethol ei aelodau a phenodi Gweinidog Iechyd a Gwasanaethau Cymdeithasol. Mae'r newidiadau hyn wedi cynyddu'n arwyddocaol ar y pwysigrwydd i'r Comisiwn dalu sylw i'r gwahaniaethau mewn polisi ac arfer tra'n parhau i gyflawni ei swyddogaeth o ymweld â chleifion er mwyn sicrhau cydymffurfio boddhaol gyda darpariaethau Deddf Iechyd Meddwl 1983.

7.2 I gydnabod y sefyllfa newydd hon, mae Is-Gadeirydd Bwrdd y Comisiwn, Yr Athro Richard Williams, wedi rhoi arweiniad ar y materion Cymreig sydd o bryder i'r Comisiwn ac mae wedi sefydlu dolenni cyswllt cadarnhaol rhwng Bwrdd y Comisiwn ac Aelodau a Staff y Cynulliad Cenedlaethol. Er y bydd Yr Athro Williams yn anffortunus yn gadael y Comisiwn ddiwedd Medi 2001, mae'r Comisiwn yn bwriadu parhau gyda'r arfer o gael Aelod o'r Bwrdd sy'n meddu'r canolbwynt arbennig hwn.

7.3 Ym Mawrth 2001, fe gynhaliodd y Comisiwn Gyfarfod o'r Bwrdd yn adeilad y Comisiwn ym Mae Caerdydd. Roedd Aelodau'r Bwrdd yn gallu trafod materion a oedd o gyd-ddiddordeb iddynt gyda'r Gweinidog, Jane Hutt AC, a Chadeirydd y Pwyllgor Iechyd a Gwasanaethau Cymdeithasol Kirsty Williams AC. Fe groesawodd Bwrdd y Comisiwn y cyfle hwn yn fawr iawn ac fe'u calonogwyd gan y diddordeb byw a ddangoswyd yng ngwaith y Comisiynwyr. Mae'r Bwrdd yn bwriadu parhau i gynnal o leiaf un cyfarfod y flwyddyn yng Nghymru i arddangos ei gydnabyddiaeth o'r gwahaniaethau sydd rhwng Cymru a Lloegr.

Polisi'r Iaith Gymraeg

7.4 Mae'r Comisiwn wedi bod yn weithredol mewn datblygu ei Bolisi Iaith Gymraeg yn unol â gofynion Deddf yr Iaith Gymraeg 1993. Mae'r polisi hwn, sydd wedi cael ei gymeradwyo gan Fwrdd yr Iaith Gymraeg a'i enwi fel model o ymarfer dda, yn sicrhau bod unrhyw un sy'n dymuno defnyddio'r iaith Gymraeg mewn gohebiaeth â, neu mewn siarad ag Aelodau neu staff y Comisiwn, yn gallu gwneud hynny. Pryd bynnag mae hynny'n bosibl, mae Comisiynydd Cymraeg ei iaith yn mynychu ymweliadau'r Comisiwn yng Nghymru ac fe wneir trefniadau i unrhyw glaf dan orchymyn sy'n dymuno siarad â Chomisiynydd yn Gymraeg wneud hynny.

Strategaeth a Pholisi Iechyd Meddwl yng Nghymru

7.5 Wrth ddarllen Penodau 1 – 6 o'r Adroddiad Dwyflynyddol, mae hi'n bwysig cydnabod nad yw llawer o'r strategaethau a'r polisïau a grybwyllir yno yn cymhwyso at Gymru. Un enghraifft o hyn yw "*Modernising Mental Health*." Mae'n angenrheidiol gan hynny i wahaniaethu rhwng Fframwaith GIG ar gyfer Loegr a'r un ar gyfer Cymru. Nid yw Cymru wedi mabwysiadu unrhyw beth sy'n debyg i bolisi Goddefgarwch Sero'r GIG sy'n cael ei groesawu ym Mhennod 4.35, ond fe fyddem yn argymell yn gryf bod y Cynulliad Cenedlaethol yn edrych yn ddifrifol ar y posibilrwydd o wneud hynny. Mae gan y Comisiwn ar gyfer Gwelliant Iechyd a'r Sefydliad Cenedlaethol ar gyfer Ardderchowgrwydd Clinigol gyfrifoldebau am agweddau ar iechyd meddwl yng Nghymru, ond y mae Comisiwn Safonau Gofal Cymru ar wahân.

7.6 Yr ydym yn croesawu penderfyniad y Cynulliad Cenedlaethol i osod iechyd meddwl fel un o'i dri prif flaenoriaeth iechyd, fel y digwydd yn Lloegr. Ym Mehefin 2000, fe gyflwynwyd dwy ddogfen strategaeth iechyd meddwl Gymreig ymgynghorol. Mae *Busnes Pawb*[107], yn torri tir newydd fel y cynllun cyntaf o'i fath yn y DG, i gwmpasu maes cyfan gwasanaethau iechyd meddwl ar gyfer plant a phobl ifanc. Ym Mhennod 6.34, yr ydym yn cymeradwyo strategaeth o'r fath ar gyfer Lloegr. Yr ydym yn edrych ymlaen at weld y cynllun yn cael ei weithredu a'i ddatblygu'n llawn mewn arferion a all weithredu fel enghraifft i wasanaethau iechyd meddwl yn Lloegr yn ogystal â Chymru.

7.7 Roedd y Comisiwn yn falch o weld cleifion dan orchymyn yn cael eu crybwyll yn benodol yn yr adran ar awdurdodi yn *Cyfiawnder, Nerthu, Effeithilrwydd, Effeithlonrwydd*[108], y strategaeth ddrafft ar gyfer gwasanaethau oedolion. Mae hon yn datgan y dylai'r cyfryw gleifion gael eu hannog i gymryd rhan weithredol ac un sydd o'u gwirfodd yn eu gofal hwy eu hunain. Mae'r Comisiynwyr yn gwneud sylwadau'n aml ar yr effaith llesol a gaiff ymwneud o'r fath ar iechyd y cleifion dan sylw, Yr ydym ar ddeall bod y Cynulliad Cenedlaethol yn bwriadu datblygu Fframwaith Gwasanaeth cenedlaethol ar gyfer Cymru o'r strategaeth.

7.8 Er nad yw'r cynlluniau strategaeth sydd wedi ymddangos o'r ddau ymarfer ymgynghori hyn wedi cael eu cyhoeddi hyd yma, mae'r Comisiwn ar ddeall bod y Gweinidog, Jane Hutt, wedi eu cadarnhau ac y byddant yn cael eu lansio ym Mis Medi eleni. Edrychwn ymlaen, yn neilltuol, at weld sut yr effeithir ar gleifion unigol dan orchymyn gan yr amcanion hynny a fydd yn ymdrin â rhai o'r materion a gynhwyswyd yn Rhan 1 yr Adroddiad hwn, megis:

■ datblygiad gwasanaethau eiriolaeth ar gyfer yr holl gleifion;

■ mabwysiadu'r Dull Gweithredu Rhaglen Ofal am y tro cyntaf yng Nghymru;

■ pwysigrwydd y cynlluniau rhyddhau i gynnwys cefnogaeth addas a dilyniant.

Mae'r rhain i gyd yn cyfrannu at yr amcan pwysicaf o ddarparu gwasanaeth iechyd meddwl mewn lleoliadau sy'n addas i'r perwyl ac sy'n darparu urddas a phreifatrwydd. Mae'r pwysigrwydd y mae'r Comisiwn yn ei osod ar yr amcan hwn yn cael ei bwysleisio ym Mhenodau 3 a 4 yr Adroddiad hwn.

Newid Strwythurol

7.9 Cyn datganoli, fe ailgyflunwyd Ymddiriedolaethau GIG gan y Swyddfa Gymreig ac, yn Ebrill 1999, fe'u cwtogwyd gan ymron i'r hanner. Nid oes gan Gymru erbyn hyn unrhyw Ymddiriedolaeth iechyd na chymuned. – gwahaniaeth arwyddocaol o'i gymharu â'r datblygiad mewn rhai Ymddiriedolaethau iechyd meddwl a chymunedol cyfunedig mawr iawn yn Lloegr. Yn yr un modd, ym 1998, pan grëwyd Grwpiau Gofal Cynradd yn Lloegr gyda'r bwriad o ddatblygu Ymddiriedolaethau Gofal Cynradd fyddai'n annibynnol o'r Awdurdodau Iechyd, yng Nghymru, fe grëwyd 22 Grp Iechyd fel is-bwyllgorau o'r pump Awdurdod Iechyd, pob un

107 **Gwasanaethau Iechyd Meddwl Plant a Phobl Infanc:** *Busnes Pawb*: Dogfen Ymgynghori Strategol. Mehefin 2000

108 **Cymru Gwasanaethau Iechyd Meddwl Oedolion ar gyfer Cymru** *Cyfiawnder, Nerthu, Effeithilrwydd, Effeithlonrwydd* Dogfen Strategaeth Ddrafft Mehefin 2000

ohonynt yn ffinio ag un o'r Cynghorau Bwrdeistrefol Sirol ac â chynrychiolaeth awdurdod lleol ar ei fwrdd.

7.10   Nid yw'r Comisiynwyr wedi sylwi bod y gwahaniaethau hyn mewn strwythur wedi cael unrhyw effaith uniongyrchol ar brofiadau cleifion unigol ag afiechyd meddwl yng Nghymru, efallai oherwydd nad yw'r comisiynu gwasanaethau iechyd meddwl hyd yma wedi ei ddatganoli i'r Byrddau Iechyd Lleol.

7.11   Mae'r ddogfen ymgynghorol *Gwella Iechyd yng Nghymru: Newidiadau Strwythurol yn yr NHS yng Nghymru* (a gyhoeddwyd yng Ngorffennaf 2001– ar ôl y cyfnod a gwmpesir yn yr Adroddiad hwn) yn cynnig disodli pob un o'r pump awdurdod iechyd gan ddau ar hugain o Fyrddau Iechyd Lleol. Fe fydd y rhain yn gyrff statudol wedi eu grwpio o dan Dimau Economi Iechyd (ar gyfer Gogledd Cymru, De a Dwyrain Cymru, a Chanol a Gorllewin Cymru). Er bod y Comisiwn ar ddeall y bydd y system newydd yn talu sylw neilltuol i'r trefniadau comisiynu ar gyfer gwasanaethau iechyd meddwl, yr ydym yn bryderus y gall rheolwyr a staff sydd eisoes wedi eu gorlwytho, ac â rhan drom mewn addasu i newidiadau mewn trefniadau rheolaethol, golli golwg ar y flaenoriaeth y dylid ei rhoi i gleifion ag afiechyd meddwl, yn enwedig y rhai hynny sydd dan orchymyn yn erbyn eu hewyllys.

Gweithgareddau'r Comisiwn yng Nghymru

7.12   Mae'r holl ymweliadau â chyfleusterau iechyd meddwl yng Nghymru yn cael eu cynnal gan un o saith Tîm Ymweld Comisiynol y Comisiwn (CVT6). Mae'r Comisiynwyr sy'n aelodau rheolaidd o'r tîm hwn yn cael eu hamlygu yn Atodiad A. Mae'r tîm hwn yn cwmpasu Gorllewin Canolbarth Lloegr yn ogystal â Chymru ac felly mae'n rhaid i'w aelodau fod yn gyfarwydd â strwythurau dau wasanaeth iechyd ac â dau wahanol ddull gweithredu tuag at bolisi iechyd meddwl. Mae Ymddiriedolaethau Cymreig sydd â ffiniau â Lloegr ac Ymddiriedolaethau Saesnig sy'n ffinio ar Gymru yn yr un modd yn eu canfod eu hunain yn gweithio gyda chleifion o'r ddwy wlad a chyda dau strwythur a pholisi. Mac'r Comisiynwyr gan hynny yn gallu gwerthfawrogi'r sialens anodd y mae'r ddeuoliaeth hon yn ei osod ar bobl broffesiynol a rheolwyr yn y gwasanaethau hynny a'r angen am fwy o gydnabyddiaeth a gwell hyfforddiant i ymdopi â'r sefyllfa.

> Argymhelliad
>
> Fe ddylai Ymddiriedolaethau Cymreig sydd â ffiniau â Lloegr ac Ymddiriedolaethau Saesnig sydd â ffiniau â Chymru sicrhau bod o leiaf gnewyllyn o staff sy'n gwybod am y ddwy system yn ddigon da i roi cyngor fel y bo angen i'r rhai sy'n delio â chleifion traws-ffiniol.

7.13   Yn ystod y ddwy flynedd a oedd dan adolygiad, fe ymwelodd y Comisiynwyr yn ôl rhaglen dreiglol a phob un cyfleuster iechyd meddwl yng Nghymru a oedd yn cadw cleifion dan orchymyn. Fe fydd y rhan fwyaf o'r unedau wedi derbyn o leiaf dri ymweliad yn ystod y cyfnod hwn. Fe wnaed cyfanswm o 51 o ymweliadau yn gyfangwbl.

7.14   Fel yr eglurwyd yn y Cyflwyniad i'r Adroddiad hwn (Pennod 1), nid ydym yn dymuno enwi a beio ond yn hytrach darparu arolwg o sut y mae gweithredu'r Ddeddf yn effeithio ar y bobl y mae'n fwriad ganddi eu hamddiffyn, i wella'r cyfleusterau yr ymwelwyd â hwy er mwyn gwella eu harfer hwy eu hunain, ac i dynnu sylw at ardaloedd cyffredinol o ymarfer sâl a chynghori ar ddulliau posibl i wella arnynt. Fe wnaethpwyd argraff dda ar y Comisiynwyr gan lefel gyffredinol yr ymrwymiad a'r gofal a ddangoswyd gan y staff a'r rheolwyr ar eu hymweliadau. Gydag ond ychydig iawn o eithriadau, mae'r meysydd cyffredinol o arfer sâl a ganfyddwyd yng Nghymru yn adlewyrchu'r rhai sy'n Lloegr. Mae'r argymhellion a wnaethpwyd mewn penodau cynharach a'r Sylwebaeth a'r Crynodeb o Argymhellion ym Mhennod 8 yn cymhwyso gan hynny yn gymaint at Gymru ag y mae at Loegr. Nid yw'r Penodau canlynol felly ond yn amlygu'r materion hynny y credwn eu bod o arwyddocâd neilltuol yng Nghymru.

Hawliau a Pharch

Doctoriaid a benodwyd o dan Adran 12 y Ddeddf Iechyd Meddwl

7.15 Mae Pennod 2 yn pwysleisio pwysigrwydd doctoriaid Adran 12 ac mae'n argymell nifer o ffyrdd y gall yr Awdurdodau Iechyd weithredu i geisio cynyddu nifer ac argaeledd Meddygon o'r fath fel na bo'r cleifion yn wrthrych oedi maith mewn asesiadau. Mae'r Comisiynwyr yng Nghymru wedi canfod anawsterau yng Nghymru yn ogystal gydag argaeledd a lleoliad meddygon a gymeradwywyd ond y mae ein pryderon neilltuol yn berthynol i'r peirianwaith ystyried ceisiadau ar gyfer cymeradwyaeth Adran 12 yng Nghymru, y safonau a gymhwysir at ymgeiswyr a'r hyfforddiant sy'n ofynnol. Yr ydym yn nodi bod y rhain i gyd yn amrywio'n helaeth ymysg awdurdodau iechyd yng Nghymru. Yn neilltuol, mae rhai awdurdodau iechyd yn gofyn am hyfforddiant penodol a rhai nad ydynt yn gofyn am ddim.

7.16 Mae'r Comisiwn o'r farn bod yr holl gleifion â'r hawl i dderbyn safon asesu gyffredinol ar gyfer gorchymyn ac yn credu y dylasai bod gofynion lleiaf yn bod yn genedlaethol ar gyfer hyfforddiant. Fe all bod pryderon y byddai codi'r trothwy ar gyfer cymeradwyaeth yn lleihau nifer y meddygon fyddai'n ceisio cymeradwyaeth ond mae'r profiad yn Lloegr yn awgrymu y byddai llawer o ymgeiswyr posibl yn teimlo'n fwy bodlon o gael cynnig hyfforddiant. Parthed hyn yr ydym yn falch o nodi bod Cynulliad Cenedlaethol Cymru a'r Adran Iechyd fel ei gilydd wedi gwneud cyllid ar gael i Goleg Brenhinol y Seiciatryddion tuag at hyfforddi seicolegwyr plant a phobl ifanc fel meddygon Adran 12 (gweler Pennod 6.34).

Argymhelliad

Wrth ystyried sut y dylasid gweithredu'r cyfrifoldebau ar gyfer cymeradwyo meddygon Adran 12 yn ôl yr ail strwythuro arfaethedig, fe ddylai Cynulliad Cenedlaethol Cymru adolygu'r system bresennol ar gyfer cymeradwyo meddygon Adran 12 gyda'r bwriad o sicrhau mwy o gysondeb a lleiafswm o lefel hyfforddiant dechreuol a chyfredol.

Materion Gweithiwr/wraig Cymdeithasol Cymeradwyedig (GCC)

7.17 Mae Pennod 2 yn amlygu yn ogystal swyddogaeth bwysig GCCau a'r angen am iddynt gwblhau ffurflenni safonedig er mwyn sicrhau bod yr holl wybodaeth berthnasol ynglŷn â chlaf dan orchymyn yn cael ei adael gyda'r ysbyty derbyn. Mae'r Comisiynwyr yn archwilio'r ffurflenni a gwblhawyd gan GCCau yn rheolaidd yn berthynol â chleifion unigol ac maent wedi bod yn falch o nodi, er bod ansawdd a hollgynhwysedd ffurflenni o'r fath yn amrywio'n eang lledled Cymru, bod llawer o enghreifftiau o arfer dda.

Ansawdd a Safonau Gofal

Y pwysau am welyau

7.18 Mae'r Comisiynwyr yn aml yn mynegi pryderon ynglŷn â pha mor addas yw'r cyfleusterau ar gyfer y difrifol wael a chleifion trafferthus, yn enwedig y rhai sydd ag angen gwelyau diogelwch canolig. Yr ydym yn credu fodd bynnag ei bod hi'n anodd sefydlu pa un a oes prinder gwirioneddol o welyau diogel yng Nghymru heb ddadansoddiad manwl o'r graddau y cedwir cleifion yn ddiangen mewn llety o'r fath oherwydd prinder gwelyau diogelwch isel.

Argymhellion

Fe ddylai'r Comisiwn Gwasanaethau Iechyd Arbenigol dros Gymru annog asesiad holistaidd o anghenion gwelyau ar draws yr holl lefelau diogelwch fel nad yw'r cleifion yn cael eu cadw ar lefel diogelwch uwch nag y mae eu cyflwr yn cyfiawnhau.

Materion staffio; prinder seiciatryddion

7.19 Fel yn Lloegr, mae materion gweithlu yn debygol o fod yn allweddol i ddatblygiad iechyd meddwl ar gyfer cleifion o bob oed. Mae'r Comisiynwyr yn adrodd yn ôl bod prinder arwyddocaol o seiciatryddion yng Nghymru, er bod dadansoddiad mwy manwl yn awgrymu bod y gydran o swyddi gweigion mewn gwirionedd yn llai nag ydynt yn Lloegr. Mae'r sefyllfa'n amrywio'n sylweddol ar draws y wlad, gyda niferoedd sy'n achosi pryder mewn rhannau neilltuol o Gymru, ac yn arbennig prinder seiciatryddion fforensig. Yr ydym ar ddeall er bod digon o swyddi hyfforddi yng Nghymru i lenwi swyddi gwag ar gyfer ymgynghorwyr ar hyn o bryd ynghyd â'r rhai a arfaethir, nid yw'r nifer sy'n derbyn hyfforddiant yn ddigonol i lenwi'r swyddi gwag hynny. Yr ydym yn croesawu bod y Cynulliad Cenedlaethol wedi cydnabod y broblem a'r fenter a gymerodd i adolygu'r sefyllfa.

Gofynion amgylcheddol hanfodol

7.20 Mae materion staffio yn naturiol yn effeithio ar gyflenwi'r safon gofal y dylid ei ddarparu. Mae nifer o gyfleusterau cleifion mewnol yng Nghymru yn parhau i fod mewn hen adeiladau anaddas. Fe wnaethpwyd peth cynnydd yn ystod cyfnod yr arolwg oherwydd fe gafodd nifer o wardiau eu huwchraddio a'u hadnewyddu tra bod rhai eraill, fel Ysbyty Canolbarth Cymru yn Nhalgarth, wedi cael eu hadleoli i unedau cyfan gwbl newydd. Mae pryderon neilltuol yn parhau yngln â

- darpariaeth cyfleusterau un rhyw ar gyfer dynion a merched;
- mynediad at awyr iach;
- diffyg gweithgareddau;
- a chymysgedd amhriodol o gleifion ar wardiau.

Fel enghraifft o'r pwynt olaf, fe ymwelodd y Comisiynwyr ag un ward ble roedd y staff yn gofalu am gleifion gyda chyflyrau a oedd yn amredeg o seicosis cronig ac anhwylderau personoliaeth hyd at gamddefnyddio sylweddau ac anableddau dysgu.

7.21 Er gwaetha'r pryderon sy'n parhau, fe gawsom ein calonogi'n fawr gan ymateb cadarnhaol yr Ymddiriedolaethau sydd wedi ceisio rhoi polisïau cydlynus rheolaeth wardiau mewn grym a chan y llu o enghreifftiau o arfer dda y daethpwyd ar eu traws mewn cyfleusterau Cymreig. Fe gaiff un enghraifft o'r fath, a oedd yn ymwneud ag Ymddiriedolaeth GIG Caerdydd a Bro Morgannwg, ei hamlygu ym Mhennod 3.19.

Therapi Electrogynhyrfol (ECT) yng Nghymru

7.22 Fe ddisgrifir astudiaeth y Comisiwn o ECT ym Mhennod 3.31 uchod, ble yr ydym yn rhoi adroddiad ar y ffigyrau o'n dadansoddiadau dechreuol o'r arolwg ECT a gyfunwyd ar gyfer

Cymru a Lloegr. Roedd pedwar ar ddeg o'r 230 clinig a adolygwyd yng Nghymru. Fe ddarperir crynodeb o'r canlyniadau sy'n berthynol i'r clinigau hyn yn Nhabl Y isod.

7.23   Roedd tri o'r 18 clinig y rhoddwyd dyfarniad uchel iddynt yn yr arolwg cyfan yng Nghymru ac yr oedd tri chyfleuster Cymreig arall yn y grp o 30 a oedd yn cydymffurfio â'r holl ofynion i raddau sylweddol. Yn y pegwn arall, roedd llai na thair ystafell mewn un clinig ac yr oedd o leiaf un arall a oedd heb gyrraedd y safonau a ddisgwylid. Er bod y gydran o gyfleusterau ECT a oedd yn cyrraedd sgôr dda yng Nghymru yn llawer uwch nag yn Lloegr (40% o'i gymharu â 18%). mae'r nifer gymharol fechan o'r cyfleusterau dan sylw yn amlwg yn ffactor perthnasol.

Tabl Y

Eitem	Canran (n=14 safleoedd a arolygwyd yng Nghymru)	Clinig
Y trefniadau ar gyfer ECT Yn meddu ystafelloedd ECT penodedig, sy'n cynnwys 3 neu fwy o ystafelloedd, gan gynnwys ystafell aros ar wahân, ac ystafell ddadebru	79	11
Polisi ar gyfer ECT Clinigau a oedd yn gallu dangos i'r archwilydd naill ai gopi o Lawlyfr Coleg Brenhinol y Seiciatryddion neu i bolisi ECT yr ysbyty ei hun	100	14
Seiciatrydd Ymgynghorol a Enwyd Clinigau ECT gydag arbenigwr seiciatryddol a enwir sy'n ymweld yn rheolaidd	93	13
Adferiad a Dadebriad Clinigau ECT sydd, yn ymarferol, â nyrs yn yr ystafell ddadebru sydd wedi'i hyfforddi mewn Cynnal Bywyd Sylfaenol, Adferiad Cardio-ysgfeiniol, ac sy'n mynychu cyrsiau gloywi mewn dadebru'n rheolaidd.	86	12

7.24   Fel y cofnodwyd ym Mhennod 3.35, fe fydd dadansoddiad llawn o ganfyddiadau'r arolwg hwn yng Nghymru a Lloegr fel ei gilydd yn cael eu cyhoeddi'n ddiweddarach yn 2001.

Amrywiaeth: ymdrin ag anghenion grwpiau amrywiol o gleifion

7.25   Mae'r anawsterau a amlygir ym Mhennod 6 parthed grwpiau bychain o gleifion amrywiol yn gyffredinol yn gyffelyb yng Nghymru ac yn Lloegr. Mae problemau lleiafrifoedd Duon ac ethnig fodd bynnag, yn haws eu hanwybyddu oherwydd mai dim ond Caerdydd sy'n cyrraedd y cyfartaledd cenedlaethol ar gyfer y cyfryw leiafrifoedd. Oherwydd bod y boblogaeth yn llawer mwy gwasgaredig yng Nghymru, mae'n anodd ymdrin ag anghenion unigolion sy'n weddol ynysig. Dyma un o'r rhesymau pam y mae'r Comisiwn, mewn ymgynghoriad â Chynulliad Cenedlaethol Cymru, wedi penderfynu cynnal Ymweliad Cenedlaethol yng Nghymru a fydd yn canolbwyntio ar anghenion lleiafrifoedd Duon ac ethnig, gan fynd ar ôl rhai o'r materion a godwyd yn ein hail Ymweliad Cenedlaethol â Chymru a Lloegr gyfan.[1]

Plant a phobl ifanc

7.26 Un gwahaniaeth mawr rhwng Cymru a Lloegr ydyw'r creu ar safonau gan y Gwasanaeth Iechyd Ymgynghorol 2000 ar gyfer gofal seiciatrig mewnol pobl ifanc yn y GIG yng Nghymru. Mae'n ofynnol ar i'r holl gyfleusterau seiciatrig sy'n derbyn pobl ifanc ddiwallu'r safonau hyn. Yn neilltuol, mae'n rhaid i'r holl wasanaethau iechyd meddwl fod â phrotocol pendant yn cwmpasu'r drefniadaeth ar gyfer, a'r rheolaeth ar, bobl ifanc sy'n cael eu derbyn i unedau iechyd meddwl i oedolion. Mae hyn yn cynnwys eitemau penodol parthed amddiffyn plant ac argaeledd staff sydd wedi cael eu hyfforddi i weithio gyda phlant ac wedi eu gwirio gan yr heddlu. Ym Mhennod 6.44 yr ydym yn argymell bod yr Adran Iechyd yn ystyried mabwysiadu safonau a phrotocolau cyffelyb.

7.27 Mae'r Comisiynwyr wedi darganfod, yn ymarferol, bod problemau mewn canfod lleoedd priodol ar gyfer pobl ifanc yng Nghymru ac mewn cymhwyso'r protocolau at y bobl ifanc mewn cyfleusterau i oedolion yn cynyddu oherwydd y pwysau sydd ar yr unedau seiciatrig gan y cynnydd yn y nifer o oedolion sydd angen derbyniad brys neu argyfwng. Mae nifer y bobl ifanc sydd angen cymorth o'r fath wedi codi'n ogystal, ac eto, yr ydym ni ar ddeall bod nifer y lleoedd penodol ar gyfer y bobl ifanc ar gyfartaledd yn llai yng Nghymru nag mewn unrhyw ranbarth GIG yn Lloegr. Yr ydym gan hynny'n croesawu'r ymrwymiad yn *Busnes Pawb* i adolygu'r broblem hon.

7.28 Yng Nghymru fel yn Lloegr, mae'r Comisiwn wedi ei gwneud hi'n ofynnol i'r Comisiynwyr na chawsant eu gwirio gan yr heddlu i beidio â chynnal cyfarfod preifat gyda phlentyn neu berson ifanc sy'n glaf os nad oes Comisiynydd arall yn bresennol. Mae panel bychan o Ddoctoriaid Ail Farn a Benodwyd gydag arbenigedd plant hefyd yn cael eu nodi. Fe fydd y Comisiwn yn sicrhau eu bod wedi cael eu gwirio gan yr heddlu ar gyfer ymweld â chyfryw gleifion.

7.29 Mae'r sylwadau hyn yn tanlinellu pwysigrwydd allweddol, fel y'i pwysleisir ym Mhennod 6, o sicrhau bod y strategaethau a'r polisïau cyffredinol ar gyfer amddiffyn plant yn cael eu cymhwyso at y grp o blant a phobl ifanc sy'n neilltuol o hawdd eu niweidio.

Casgliad

7.30 Wrth iddynt gynnal eu swyddogaethau yn ystod y ddwy flynedd ddiwethaf, ychydig iawn o wahaniaethau arwyddocaol y mae'r comisiynwyr wedi eu nodi yng ngweithrediad Deddf Iechyd Meddwl 1983 rhwng Cymru a Lloegr. Fe all datblygiad ar wahanol bolisïau a strategaethau ac efallai ar wahanol ddeddfwriaeth a blaenoriaethau newid y sefyllfa dros y blynyddoedd sydd i ddod. Mae'r bennod hon wedi amlygu rhai o'r gwahaniaethau presennol. Fe fyddwn yn parhau i nodi gwahaniaethau arwyddocaol yn y gobaith y gall hyn annog gwell rhannu ar arfer dda ledled Cymru a Lloegr.

8 The Organisation and Work of the Commission

8.1 Earlier chapters of this report have stressed that the findings and recommendations are all founded on our work during this reporting period. In support of that assertion, this chapter gives a brief summary of how the Commission is organised and the main areas of work which have not only contributed to the contents of the report but have ensured that the interests of detained patients are not overlooked in a wide range of circumstances. Some details relating to the Commission's work, and in particular its governance and financial management, are briefly discussed below. Full financial details can be found in the **Appendix G** to this report.

8.2 This chapter is followed by a commentary and schedule of the recommendations discussed in previous chapters and evidenced by the work and activities described below.

The Function of the Commission

8.3 The Mental Health Act Commission is a Special Health Authority whose functions are set out in Section 121 of the Mental Health Act 1983 and subsidiary legislation. The Commission's primary responsibility is monitoring the application of the Mental Health Act as it relates to the care and treatment of detained patients in England and Wales. We discharge this function mainly by visiting such patients and checking that the legal requirements for their detention appear to have been met. On such visits we also look at the arrangements and procedures which ensure that detained patients' care and treatment is provided in accordance with the Act and the Code of Practice. All reviews of arrangements and procedures are validated by testing them in operation and checking that staff are aware of and comply with their obligations under the Act. Broader responsibilities relate to the appointment of Second Opinion Appointed Doctors and neurosurgery panels, reviewing deaths in detention and dealing with complaints about the implementation of the Act.

8.4 The Commission's functions are fulfilled in the following ways:

■ a programme of visits by teams of Commissioners to all hospitals or nursing homes caring for detained patients;

■ the appointment by the Commission of a panel of Second Opinion Appointed Doctors (SOADs) who visit and give a second opinion on certain treatments for patients who are unable or unwilling to give consent (Section 58);

■ appointing multi-disciplinary panels to consider the authorisation of neurosurgery for mental disorder for consenting patients, whether or not they are detained (Section 57);

■ advice on, monitoring and sometimes investigation of complaints by detained patients;

■ monitoring of deaths of detained patients, including review of any enquiry reports and attendance at some inquests;

■ considering appeals against the withholding of postal packets (and, since the introduction of new Security Directions, internal mail and telephone calls) in relation to patients in the High Security Hospitals;

- giving advice on policy and practice, based on established views or where necessary following discussion amongst groups of Commissioners with relevant professional expertise; and

- offering training on aspects of the Mental Health Act and Code of Practice for service providers and others concerned with the implementation of the Act.

Commission Membership

8.5   The Commission consists of a Chairman, Vice-Chairman and up to 180 Commissioners, all of whom are appointed by the Secretary of State after open competition and formal interview. A list of all those who have been Commissioners in the period under review is given in **Appendix H**. Those who have served on the Commission's Board during the period of this report are indicated on this list. Additionally, the Commission's Chief Executive and Chief Financial Officer are executive members of the Board.

8.6   Figure 11 below analyses Commission membership by gender and shows the representation of members from Black and minority ethnic groups. Figures are shown as at March 2000 and March 2001 to illustrate current trends in membership.

Figure 11: Commission Membership Profile & Changes 2000/01

Analysis By Source	Numbers @ March 2000				Numbers @ March 2001			
	Male	Female	Total		Male	Female	Total	
White	73	68	141	82.9%	75	59	134	77.9%
Black & Minority Ethnic Groups	18	11	29	17.1%	22	16	38	22.1%
	91	79	170		97	75	172	
Total	53.5%	46.5%		100.0%	56.4%	43.6%		100.0%

8.7   One success of the efforts to improve our profile with Black and minority ethnic groups (see Chapter 6.14 and Appendix D) is reflected in the fact that membership from these groups has risen from 17% at 1 April 1999 to 22% by 31 March 2001. During the same period, the proportion of members who are female decreased slightly, but with a much higher number now drawn from Black and minority ethnic populations. Overall, therefore, the male/female membership balance of members drawn from Black and minority ethnic communities is now more reflective of the overall gender balance. We believe that this analysis demonstrates our commitment to the diversity that has been emphasised in Chapter 6.

8.8   Similarly, the diverse professional backgrounds of our Commissioners mirrors our belief in a multi-disciplinary approach, both to our own services and to mental health services in general. Nearly half our Commissioners have a nursing or social work background; 15% are lawyers, 11% are consultants or GPs and 26% come from other disciplines, such as psychology, pharmacy or mental health administration, or from non-professional backgrounds. Many of our Commissioners from all backgrounds are or have been service users or carers.

Members of the Second Opinion Appointed Doctor (SOADs) Panel

8.9   Doctors who have been acting as SOADs between 1999 and 2001 are listed in **Appendix I**. Figure 12 below provides a breakdown of gender and ethnicity for SOADs appointed by the Commission.

Figure 12: SOAD Panel Profile Of Active SOADs and Changes 2000/01

Source	Numbers @ March 2000				Numbers @ March 2001			
	Male	Female	Total		Male	Female	Total	
Black & Minority Ethnic Groups	34	2	36	23.1%	57	5	62	33.9%
White	94	26	120	76.9%	96	25	121	66.1%
Total	128	28	156			153	30	183
	82.1%	17.9%		100.0%	83.6%	16.4%		100.0%

8.10 The escalation of SOAD demand since 1997/98 (see paragraph 8.18 *et seq.* below) has made SOAD recruitment a priority issue for the Commission during this period. The SOAD panel has increased significantly throughout the period, with SOADs from Black and minority ethnic groups now providing one third of the panel membership. Although the total number of female SOADs has increased, the proportion of SOADs who are female has fallen slightly to one in six.

8.11 The recruitment drive also took account of the fact that a large proportion of the SOAD panel is made up of older doctors, with a significant reliance on SOADs who are past retirement age. This potentially signals future difficulties and efforts have been made to encourage applications from younger age groups. However, whilst the majority of new appointments are now under 55 years of age, it remains difficult to recruit working consultant psychiatrists to the SOAD panel and one in five SOADs are currently over retirement age.

The Commission's Visiting Activities

8.12 Commissioners are divided into seven Commission Visiting Teams (CVTs), covering different geographic areas. Each of the High Security Hospitals also has a dedicated team. The CVTs work to a two-year programme, during which time every Trust or Registered Mental Nursing Home in their area which holds detained patients is visited at least three times. The Commission will visit establishments where there are particular difficulties or large numbers of patients more often. The primary purpose of the visits is to meet patients currently detained, to check their documentation and to validate in practice that arrangements ensure that they are being treated in accordance with the provisions of the Act and the Code of Practice. This inevitably raises many of the general issues highlighted in Chapters 2 – 7 above.

8.13 Figure 13 summarises key visiting activity during the reporting period and compares this to the previous period. The number of visits made each year cannot easily be compared because we record them by number of Trusts rather than by number of facilities visited. The major reconfiguration of Trusts which has occurred recently therefore means that where there may previously have been one visit to a Trust managing two facilities, one visit to a large amalgamated Trust may now cover, say, eight or nine facilities.

8.14 In comparison to the previous period, in this reporting period there has been a substantial increase in all patient related activity. Whilst private meetings are driven by patient requests and can, in some years, show a reduction, all other areas are managed by Commissioners and show by far the largest gains. Translated into more personal measures, and after allowing for patients seen more than once, the following patient contact frequencies are estimated:

- At the High Security Hospitals, all patients meet a Commissioner and have their rights protected by document checks at least once in any year; and

- At other providers, on average Commissioners meet with about 1 in 15 of all detained patients in private and check the documentation of or meet informally with a further 1 in 6 of all such patients.

It is this high level of contact that gives us confidence regarding the depth of knowledge that Commissioners have about services to detained patients and the strength of evidence that underlies the conclusions and generalisations made in the preceding chapters of this report.

Figure 13 – Visiting Activity

Details of Patient Contacts and Documentation Checks	1997/98 to 1998/99	1999/2000 to 2000/01	Increase
Direct Patient Contacts			
– Private Meetings with Document Checks[†]	12394	13042	5.2%
– Individual Patients Met Informally	6580	8656	31.6%
– Individual Patients Met in Group Situations	742*	895	20.6%
– Total Direct Patient Contacts	19716	22593	14.6%
Documentation Checks[†]			
– Documents Checked but Patient Not Seen	7910*	11285	42.7%

* Data not collected in 1997/98, therefore estimated at 1998/99 activity levels

† Total document checks = 20304 (1997-99), 24327 (1999-2001). Increase = 19.8%

8.15   Because of the wide range of services involved in the provision of care to detained patients, at least one of the visits to each Trust is used by Commissioners to seek the views of others who are involved with those patients. The most significant of these is Social Services, which are visited separately at least once in every two-year period to ensure that they too are properly fulfilling their functions under the Act. Additionally, when Commissioners undertake a full visit to a Trust, they invite representatives of users and carers, Patient Councils or similar bodies, relevant voluntary organisations, including advocacy services, and other statutory services such as the police and ambulance service to attend a general discussion so that concerns relating to the treatment of the patients can be fully discussed.

8.16   During the course of each visit, Commissioners raise issues about particular patients with the staff who are directly responsible for them and in so doing are able immediately to resolve many difficulties. At the end of each visit, there is a meeting with senior managers from the Trust or nursing home at which Commissioners discuss their findings. This is followed by a formal written report to the Chief Executive which comments on what Commissioners have found and, where necessary, suggests remedial action. Commissioners see their visits as not only providing safeguards for the patients but also offering support to staff and managers who often find the observations and guidance of an outside expert body of considerable assistance.

8.17 The visits and meetings described in the preceding paragraphs have been the primary source of evidence for the general and specific points made throughout this report. The need to synthesise what is learned from the experience of individual patients and validation work based on more focussed and better documented surveys of how the Act and Code of Practice are being implemented has led to the changes in our administrative and visiting arrangements which are described in paragraphs 8.34 – 8.37 below.

Matters requiring particular attention

8.18 In addition to patient visits and document checks (see paragraph 8.12 above), we selected four aspects of implementation for structured scrutiny during the period under review. Three of these were monitored by detailed questionnaires and interviews with staff completed in every ward visited. These related to:

- the provision of information on patients' rights;

- contact with Responsible Medical Officer; and

- knowledge of and contact with named nurse.

8.19 The information gained from these surveys is still being collated and analysed, but an initial analysis of information provided to patients on their rights under the Act is discussed at Chapter 2.8 – 2.10.

8.20 The fourth area of special investigation was ECT, which was based on facilities rather than wards. The initial findings from this exercise are discussed in Chapters 3.31 – 3.35 and 7.22 – 7.24.

SOAD ACTIVITY

8.21 SOAD activity is demand-led. Although the Commission can and does initiate a small number of visits by using our powers to withdraw previous certificates (for which purpose we review the treatment of all patients subject to treatment under Section 58 for a certain period of time[111]) the large majority of SOAD visits are initiated by requests from individual patients' RMOs. Fluctuations in the number of SOAD visits is therefore wholly outside the control of the Commission. The Commission responds to these requests by allocating SOADs on a rotational basis linked to proximity to the hospital or nursing home in which the patient is receiving treatment.

8.22 Figure 14 shows that, following the significant increase in demand in 1998, the number of requests for Second Opinions has remained relatively stable.

Figure 14: SOAD Activity 1997/98 to 2000/01

	1997/98	%Change	1998/99	%Change	1999/00	%Change	2000/01
Medication Only	4,732	29.2%	6,116	–5.8%	5,761	4.7%	6,033
ECT Only	2,197	1.5%	2,229	–2.7%	2,169	–3.0%	2,105
ECT and Medication	74	6.8%	79	27.8%	101	–12.9%	88
TOTAL	7,003	20.3%	8,424	–4.7%	8,031	2.4%	8,226

---

111 See Section 61, Mental Health Act 1983.

Section 57 Activity: Neurosurgery for Mental Disorder

8.23 During this reporting period we arranged visits to consider the authorisation of neurosurgical procedures for the treatment of mental disorder in relation to nine patients (seven in 1999/2000, two in 2000/01). The Commission's role in this matter is to appoint a multi-disciplinary panel to consider whether the patient is giving fully informed, valid consent and whether the treatment can be given[112]. In one case, the appointed panel deferred their decision, requesting that the patient's records and aftercare plan be fully completed, before certifying that the operation could go ahead. All nine operations were eventually certified to go ahead.

Complaints

8.24 The Complaints Co-ordinator is a Commissioner who oversees the administrative arrangements for dealing with complaints made directly to the Commission. During the two years under review, 747 new written complaints were received and followed up by the Commission and 244 formal complaints were raised or reviewed during visits. None of these led to a full investigation by the Commission (see Chapter 2.25 *et seq.*).

Deaths of Detained Patients

8.25 All hospitals and Registered Mental Nursing Homes are required by the Commission to notify us of the death of a detained patient within 72 hours of the event. A panel of experienced and specially trained Commissioners is available to attend inquests, with Properly Interested Person Status where appropriate, and/or to follow up any subsequent Commission concern with service providers. In the two years under review, we were notified of 881 deaths and attended 127 inquests. In February 2001 we published a report, *Deaths of Detained Patients in England and Wales[113]*, analysing information collated as a result of these activities (see Chapter 4.17 *et seq.* and **Appendix B**).

Section 134 – Reviewing Withheld Mail / Telephone calls

8.26 The Commission is empowered to consider appeals over the withholding of patients' mail in the High Security Hospitals[114]. We undertook fifteen such reviews in this period and, after consideration of all the circumstances, directed in five cases that the withheld item should be released to the mail's intended recipient. In one further case, we directed that part of the withheld item should be released.

8.27 Although the High Security Hospital Safety and Security Directions (see Chapter 5) provided the Commission with a power to review the withholding of internal mail and telephone calls from the 30 November 2000, no requests for such a review were made of the Commission from that time to the end of the reporting period.

Advice on Policy and Practice

8.28 The Commission's Secretariat provides help and informal advice to services and patients, utilising the expertise of Commissioners where appropriate. We estimate that, annually, we deal with

---

112 See Section 57, Mental Health Act 1983.

113 Mental Health Act Commission (2001) **Deaths of Detained Patients In England and Wales: A report by the Mental Health Act Commission on information collected from 1 February 1997 to 31 January 2000.** Mental Health Act Commission. Copies available from the MHAC office for £7.95 & £1 p&p.

114 See Section 134, Mental Health Act 1983

some 2000 such queries by telephone and 400 by letter. The Commission also publishes advice and guidance on aspects of the implementation of the Act. A list of published guidance is given in **Appendix K**.

Public Consultations

8.29   The period from 1999–2001 was a particularly busy one in terms of the formulation of national policy. We played a significant role in offering policy advice on matters relating to detained patients. Our main inputs were as follows:

■ **Expert Committee on the Review of the Mental Health Act 1983**

We provided a detailed response to the Expert Committee's consultation in 1999.

■ **Response to the consultation paper on "Managing Dangerous People with a Severe Personality Disorder"**

■ **Response to the consultation paper on "Reforming the Mental Health Act"**

The responses to these two documents set out clearly the Commission's position on the main consultation issues. Since these documents were not published, the Summary of the Commission's Views from each of them is reproduced in full in **Appendices E and F**. We were pleased to note that the proposals in both Parts of the subsequent White Paper accorded very closely to the views we had expressed.

■ **Submission of a separate document to the Department of Health giving the Commission's detailed views on a successor body.**

The proposals for a Commission for Mental Health closely follow the Commission's suggestions, with particular regard to greater monitoring capability and increased ability to analyse findings and offer support and advice. We shall maintain an ongoing dialogue with the Department about the need to ensure that the omission of a visiting function from the remit of our successor body will be adequately covered by the arrangements proposed in the White Paper.

■ **Submission of evidence to the Health Committee on the Regulation of Private and Other Independent Healthcare and a response to the subsequent consultation paper.**

We were glad to see that the establishment of the Care Standards Commission drew particular attention to the need to focus on mentally people in private care facilities.

Equal Opportunities

8.30   The Commission's Equal Opportunities Strategy, launched in 1997, is discussed at Chapter 6.14. *et seq.* This reporting period saw the launch of Phase 2 of the strategy: the Commission's Regional Consultation Exercises. Three multi-disciplinary events were organised by the Commission in collaboration with the University of Central Lancashire during the period, each preceded by consultation interviews and seminars in which Commissioners met with representatives of the Black and minority ethnic communities, voluntary organisations, service providers and other relevant groups. The lessons for services that emerged from these exercises are discussed at Chapter 6.21 *et seq.*, while a synopsis of the reports now published on these three events is provided in **Appendix D**.

8.31   During the period under review, we have established an Equal Opportunities Advisory Group consisting of experienced Commissioners from each of the visiting teams, whose remit is to provide ongoing advice to the Board on wider equal opportunities issues, disseminate relevant information to their teams, assist in monitoring the impact of our Equal Opportunities Programme, both internally and externally, and help to develop relevant monitoring tools. These Commissioners will be closely involved in carrying forward the next stage of our work in this area.

External Training

8.32 Following the issue of the revised Code of Practice in 1999, the Commission developed training on the application of the Code which was offered to all service providers. 157 days of such training were delivered by a panel of specially selected and trained Commissioners to 126 service providers.

8.33 The demand for and appreciation of this training were so high that a further set of training modules were developed concentrating on particular aspects of good practice and the Mental Health Act. From May 2000 to the end of the reporting period 83 further days of training were provided by Commissioners to 65 services. The level of satisfaction expressed by service providers for this training is high and there is an ongoing demand for it.

Administration and Corporate Governance

Administrative support

8.34 Commissioners, SOADs and the Board are supported by a Secretariat consisting of an average of 31 staff, led by a Chief Executive who is accountable to the Chairman and the Commission Board. The Commission is grateful for the commitment and goodwill of the staff, who have coped with an exceptionally difficult period despite significant vacancies and changes at senior level. The period under review has been difficult not only because there have been many changes in national policies and structures but also because the Commission itself has been undergoing considerable administrative changes.

Corporate strategy and business plan

8.35 At the end of the last biennial reporting period, the Commission undertook a review of its central organisational structure and associated costs.[115] The changes suggested by that review could not be implemented immediately because of significant vacancies and changes in staffing, but the work has been carried forward steadily since then. In 2000/2001, the Commission put forward to the Department of Health a Corporate Strategy and Business Plan which showed that, even after re-investing the savings identified to be available, its functions in relation to detained patients could not properly be fulfilled without substantial new investment. Both the Department of Health and the National Assembly of Wales have now allocated additional resources for 2001/2002. These new funds will enable the employment of a more professional administrative and support staff structure and allow for the development of our Information Technology strategy (see paragraph 8.37 below).

Review of visiting practice

8.36 A major part of the Corporate Strategy was the development of current visiting activities to ensure that, while the commitment to visiting patients was wholly maintained, better arrangements could be made regarding validation checks and the follow-up of action by Trusts

---

115 Mental Health Act Commission (1999) **Eight Biennial Report** London, Stationery Office p19–20

and Nursing Homes on issues of concern raised during visits. At Commission Conferences late in 2000 and Workshops early in 2001, all Commissioners were involved in developing detailed plans for organising visits and feed-back to service providers in ways which would help everyone concerned to improve the services to detained patients. This work is ongoing, with a further Commission Conference in September 2001, leading to discussions with stakeholders at strategic, management and operational level early in 2002. Service users and carers will be involved in these discussions and the publication of this Biennial Report will be a significant contribution to them.

Increased support for Commissioner activities

8.37   Both the Central Cost Review and the Review of Visiting Practice showed that better use could be made of the professional skills of Commissioners if the staff at the Commission's Secretariat could be strengthened, particularly at senior level, and if better technological tools were available to enable more sophisticated data input and analysis. As a result of the additional resources mentioned in paragraph 8.35 above, we are, at the time of writing this report, in the process of recruiting staff to provide the additional support needed to ensure that the evidential base and follow up to all our visits can be more systematised and consistent while simultaneously reducing the time which Commissioners need to spend on administration. Additional skilled staff are also being recruited to develop a technological infra-structure which will enable the Commission to record and analyse its data more efficiently and to communicate more effectively with all the relevant stakeholders in mental health services.

Corporate governance

8.38   The Commission is almost wholly funded by the Department of Health and the National Assembly for Wales and is therefore accountable for its use of public monies. We are also required to conform to the corporate governance requirements applicable to all public bodies. During the period under review, we have undertaken a full review of all our corporate governance policies and documentation and have improved arrangements for planning, managing and accounting for expenditure.

Financial management

8.39   During the reporting period, the Commission's financial management was subject to the scrutiny of a Finance and Audit Committee and external audit. Our gross expenditure in 1999/2000 was £3.23m and in 2000/2001 it was £3.4m. Efficiency savings were achieved in each year without any detriment to the visiting programme and budget underspends on other Commission activities helped offset an unfunded deficit on SOAD fees and expenses. The Commission has no control over expenditure on SOAD fees since this is dependent wholly on the demand for second opinions. We wish to make clear that, without unfunded overspends in this area, a balanced outturn would have been reported in both years. **Appendix G** summarises expenditure, relevant notes and the balance sheet of the Commission extracted from the accounts as certified for presentation in this report by the statutory auditor. A full set of the accounts is available on application to the Commission.

Conclusion

8.40   We hope that this relatively brief description of the way in which the Commission has been developing demonstrates our commitment to the self-assessment and self-regulation processes which we are commending to others throughout this report. During the next biennial reporting period we shall not only have to maintain this positive development of the Mental Health Act Commission, but also consider and advise on the arrangements which will be necessary to make a smooth transition to the proposed Commission for Mental Health. We believe that the action which is currently being taken to strengthen our infrastructure and enhance our current visiting capacity will help us to do this without any adverse effect on our ongoing capacity to monitor the implementation of the existing legislation. We hope that the Commentary and Schedule of Recommendations in the following chapter will provide a useful tool for us to do so in full co-operation with policy makers, service commissioners and service providers.

9 Commentary and Schedule of Recommendations

9.1 This chapter puts the comments and findings in the preceding chapters in the context of the wider mental health environment and comments on the implications of this environment for them. It also groups the recommendations in a way which we hope will be useful to those who are responsible for implementing the Act in general and, in particular, to the mental health facilities which we shall be visiting during the next two years.

Mental Health Strategy

9.2 National policy on mental health has developed more quickly and more dynamically since the period covered by the Eighth Biennial Report than at any time in the history of state intervention in mental illness. The recognition of mental illness as one of the three top healthcare priorities of the present Government – on a par with cancer and cardiac illnesses – is a step whose importance is difficult to over-estimate. This major Governmental thrust is reinforced and emphasised by the bringing into effect of the Human Rights Act 1998, which puts a new and different stress on the recognition of individual rights.

9.3 The Commission's comments and recommendations are intended to be read in the context of the following major Government documents and the emerging strategies of the National Assembly for Wales:

- Modernising Mental Health Services
- The National Health Service Plan
- The NHS Framework and Standards

(see **Appendix J** for a fuller list of background documents to this report)

9.4 These documents set a clear strategy for the future development of mental health services and provide leadership and a sense of direction which the Commission greatly welcomes. In particular, we welcome the recognition that acutely ill patients do not necessarily have to be in residential care but can be treated within the community if the health and social services infra-structure can be made sufficiently robust. Any changes which reduce the number of patients initially admitted to hospital under the Act or re-admitted constantly because of their alleged "failure" to cope outside must be in the overall interests of the patient.

9.5 In our view, full implementation of this strategy, together with a continued commitment to the removal of stigma, will be key factors in reducing the number of detained patients so that the quality and standard of their care can begin to match the requirement of reciprocity in relation to such detention.

Structural changes

9.6 The structural changes which directly affect mental health are far-reaching. In England, they include:

- establishment of Primary Care Trusts;

- amalgamation of many Acute and Community Mental Health Trusts;

- development of joint Health and Social Care Trusts; and

- integration of High Secure Hospitals with broader-based Trusts.

Of less direct impact but nevertheless of relevance is the forthcoming major reduction in the number of Health Authorities and changes in the configuration and role of the National Health Service Executive Regional Offices. Similar structural changes are underway or proposed in Wales.

9.7 These are valuable foundation stones for the positive development of mental health care services in the 21ˢᵗ century and should clearly contribute to the development of the integrated infra-structures necessary to give effect to our recommendations on the care of detained patients. The Commission nevertheless wishes to emphasise that structural change needs to be phased and managed so that:

- mental health priorities are maintained throughout the period of change;

- the changes do not adversely affect individual patients;

- there is ongoing and effective implementation of the Mental Health Act;

- significant recommendations relating to improvements in practice can still be achieved; and

- there is a properly planned and integrated approach to how the structural changes interact with each other and the patients whom they affect.

Regulatory changes

9.8 In parallel with these structural changes, the Government has set up or announced a number of new bodies with responsibilities for ensuring the delivery of services in different contexts or from different perspectives:

- Commission for Health Improvement;

- National Institute for Clinical Excellence;

- Care Standards Commission; and

- National Patient Safety Agency.

9.9 This increase in regulatory bodies should similarly improve the likelihood of patients in general receiving the standard of service they are entitled to expect. None of them is, however, specifically concerned with detained patients, who are unlikely to be high in their priorities because of stronger demands from elsewhere in the National Health Service. Our particular concerns in relation to detained patients are that:

- boundaries may not be sufficiently clearly defined to prevent duplication of demands on those who are managing facilities with detained patients;

- responding to such demands may distract service managers from their core functions; and

- managers may assume that greater regulation diminishes their own responsibility for performance management.

We are sure that the Director for Mental Health will be well aware of the first two risks in carrying out his co-ordinating role in relation to the delivery of the Mental Health Plan. One of our aims in making the recommendations in this report is to help managers address both the second and the third risks by signalling ways in which self-regulation may be made so effective that external regulatory action becomes a quality re-assurance process rather than a primary safeguard.

Managing in a period of uncertainty

9.10   The Commission recognises the strains which strategic, structural and regulatory changes are placing and will continue to place on the managers and staff of facilities which provide services to detained patients. We regularly observe their commitment and see the efforts they make to meet the needs of their patients in the face of practical difficulties caused by shortages of staff, money and/or alternative placements. We understand and empathise with these difficulties and hope that the points made above will help to reduce any adverse effects of change. None of this can, however, allow us to overlook the extent to which detained patients are disadvantaged by failure to implement the various provisions of the Act and the guidance in the Code of Practice.

9.11   The recommendations made throughout this report are all based on good practice which Commissioners have seen on visits to facilities where detained patients are held. Good practice in one area of implementation of the Act does not, of course, mean that it exists across all areas in any particular facility. We nevertheless believe that the good practice established by many managers and staff has general relevance and can be applied elsewhere to maintain and improve existing services in a constantly changing environment.

9.12   Where good systems are in place and well understood, managers and staff are better able to work together in the interests of the patients. Those who can demonstrate by regular monitoring of such systems that they are implementing the provisions of the existing legislation are far less likely to come into conflict either with regulatory bodies or with the provisions of the Human Rights Act. The less time that managers spend in responding to criticisms of their service, the more they have to spend in ensuring that the services for which they are responsible are properly delivered. Good management enhances the confidence of staff and frees them to spend more time with patients.

9.13   We do not therefore share the view that good management systems are a bureaucratic end in themselves. We believe that good systems are major cogs to connect the engine of policy to the wheels of practice so that detained patients actually receive the service intended by the legislation and related guidance. In the following paragraphs, we comment on how the way in which our recommendations are presented is intended to help managers at different levels to create and oil such cogs.

Grouping of Recommendations

9.14   The summary of recommendations that follows has been divided into four sections:

- ■ Strategic recommendations for action at national or regional/Health Authority level.

- ■ Recommendations for agreed action between service commissioners and service providers.

- ■ Recommendations for action by those with direct responsibilty for service delivery (i.e. local hospital managers, whether NHS or independent sector; High Security Hospital managers; and social service managers).

- ■ Recommendations for action at an operational level.

9.15   The terms used in these divisions are deliberately generic because of the structural changes mentioned above. During the next few years, for instance, "service commissioners" may be Health Authorities, Primary Care Trusts, or possibly other new specialised agencies with a strategic responsibility. Similarly, "service providers" may be Primary Care Trusts, Mental Health NHS Trusts, Health and Social Care Trusts or various private agencies, any of whom may be "hospital managers" within the definition of the Mental Health Act 1983 (i.e. anyone with direct responsibility for managing a facility which has the authority to hold detained patients[116]). All these terms may differ between England and Wales. The recommendations listed and the comments made will apply regardless of the nomenclature.

Strategic action

9.16　The number of recommendations for strategic action is small because they are intended only to highlight particular concerns of the Commission which are not already specifically addressed in the current range of strategic proposals.

9.17　We hope that focussing on a few key areas may not only highlight the issues of particular relevance to detained patients but also help to identify areas which would serve as a useful basis for discussion between the various new regulatory bodies. Discussions on the need for national protocols on out of area placements (recommendation 39) or for the care of children in adult units (recommendation 64) could, for instance, help to establish boundaries and areas of co-operation between regulatory bodies which will ensure positive corporate working. We should be glad to facilitate or be involved in any such discussions.

Action between service commissioners and providers

9.18　The recommendations under this heading are similarly limited because the main intention is to emphasise the need for those who commission services to work closely with service providers to establish policies and systems which apply as widely as possible to a range of providers. This will help to establish more consistent levels of care for patients as well as enabling commissioning bodies to establish monitoring and audit systems which will help to reveal best practice. The areas selected are those of particular concern to the Commission which we shall be closely monitoring during the next biennial period.

Action by those with direct responsibility for service delivery

9.19　By far the largest number of recommendations is intended for action by those with direct responsibility for the delivery of services. These are the managers with whom Commissioners have the most contact when visiting detained patients and establishing how far they are being treated within the terms of the Act and the Code of Practice.

9.20　The recommendations here are a clear indication of the issues which we shall be following through on our visits during the next two years. As implied in paragraph 9.10 above, we are well aware that many of the recommendations will be regarded as adding to administrative burdens rather than improving the service to patients. The key point which we wish to underline is that good systems and effective monitoring and feed-back can provide valuable support to those who are at the interface with patients and allow them to concentrate better on the staff/patient relationship. We believe that it is the nature of this relationship which ultimately determines the therapeutic value of detention.

Action at an operational level

9.21　Finally, there are a few recommendations intended specifically for those at the interface with patients. We have been especially selective here because we believe that it is for managers to determine operational requirements and that the recommendations for managers will translate readily into such requirements. The three issues which we have highlighted are ones which observation leads us to conclude are particularly likely to be overlooked unless staff at operational level take a personal interest in them.

116　See Mental Health Act 1983, Section 145. (The definition given at paragraph 9.15 above is a précis of the statutory definition).

Performance Management

9.22 Our recommendations have deliberately not been prioritised. We wish to emphasis that there is good and bad practice in all the facilities we visit and that we are constantly impressed by the quality and commitment of the managers and staff we meet. In our view, it is for them to examine the recommendations so that they may decide which are already being satisfactorily fulfilled and which areas need to take priority in improving their own service delivery. Self-assessment and Commission Visit Reports should both contribute to this process. High priority areas will depend on weaknesses identified, and may differ even within individual providers.

9.23 Similarly, we have not included any specific recommendation relating to performance management in the provision of mental health services. We assume that service providers wish to achieve good services in the first instance rather than having shortcomings identified by others. That is certainly the impression we have gained from the positive response which most providers make to the various matters raised by Commissioners at the end of each visit. "Getting it right first time" requires a rigorous process of self-assessment and improvement at local level, with commissioning and regulatory bodies undertaking regular monitoring and auditing functions. Our recommendations are intended to make a positive contribution to this process and it is with that in mind that we shall be looking to see how far they have been implemented during our visits over the next biennial period.

9.24 Finally, although most of our recommendations are resource neutral, and others could lead to overall savings, we recognise that many will have staffing or financial implications. At commissioning and local management levels, it is therefore essential that action plans are supported by a realistic assessment of resource needs and of how such resources will be provided. At a strategic level, the total resource requirement needs to be clearly identified and given high priority in the light of the Government's commitment to mental health as one of its top three priorities for both England and Wales.

Conclusion

9.25 The Commission itself is in the same position as other bodies concerned with mental health services in facing the challenges and opportunities which the current far-seeing agenda for mental health reform poses. We have the great advantage of a single focus on patients who are detained or liable to be detained under the Mental Health Act but this in itself touches on the most difficult issues which face us all. We therefore intend to do all we can to help facilitate the many changes mentioned at the beginning of this chapter. At the same time we shall continue to ensure that the implementation of the 1983 Act and the Code of Practice are given the priority they deserve by drawing attention to those aspects which fall far short of what is expected. The right of detained mentally disordered patients to be treated with the same respect and humanity as every other free member of society must be safeguarded.

Schedule of Recommendations

Strategic Recommendations for Action at National and Regional / Health Authority level.

References to the Department of Health should be taken as relating also to the National Assembly of Wales where appropriate.

Recommendation 1 (Chapter 2.3)

The Department of Health and National Assembly for Wales should take every opportunity to challenge inaccurate representation of mentally ill people, in the media and elsewhere, based upon stigmatising attitudes and stereotypes.

Recommendation 5 (Chapter 2.11)

The Department of Health should ensure that patient information leaflets on the Mental Health Act 1983 are available in formats appropriate to the following groups of patients:

- children and adolescents;
- deaf patients;
- blind patients;
- deaf/blind patients; and
- patients with Learning Disabilities

(see also Recommendations 67 (para 6.45), 68 (6.54) & 71 (6.64))

Recommendation 8 (Chapter 2.24)

The Department of Health should issue guidelines on good practice in the provision of advocacy services as soon as possible, in advance of whatever is decided on the special advocacy service proposed in the new legislation.

Recommendation 11 (Chapter 2.29)

The Government should ensure that the new mental health legislation provides the Commission's successor body with an exceptional, discretionary power to investigate complaints or whistle-blowing allegations where appropriate.

Recommendation 13   (Chapter 2.38)

The Department of Health should commission research to examine the possible reasons for the nationally high use of Section 5(2), particularly with a view to investigating whether the physical and / or therapeutic environment is an influencing factor.

Recommendation 21   (Chapter 2.61)

The lead Health Authority responsible for the approval of doctors under Section 12(2) in each region, in partnership with the other relevant services, should ensure that :

- there is systematic high level collation of data from ASWs on the numbers of telephone calls made, the time taken to locate a Section 12 Approved doctor and the sharing of workload between doctors so that baselines and targets for improvement can be established;
- regular monitoring meetings between Health Authorities, Trusts, Social Services and Police are held to ensure that targets are met;
- intensive, possibly modular, training courses are established to enable a wider range of GPs to carry out the assessment function with confidence; and
- approved training courses are monitored to ensure both quality and consistency.

Recommendation 25   (Chapter 3.6)

The Department of Health should ensure that national statistics on bed occupancy take account of detained patients who are on leave from inpatient beds, so that available beds and bed occupancy can be monitored more meaningfully.

Recommendation 38   (Chapter 4.27)

The Department of Health should negotiate and establish national protocols, encompassing all service providers, to ensure clarity and accountability in all instances where a patient is located out of area, whether by arrangement or because the patient has crossed boundaries without the knowledge of the detaining authority.

Recommendation 46   (Chapter 4.50)

New legislation should include provision for the regulation of the power to exercise control and restraint.

Recommendation 48   (Chapter 4.61)

The Department of Health should consider issuing guidance on the management of illicit-drug related incidents with a particular focus on mental health services caring for detained patients. Such guidance should clearly set out:

- expected actions where there is a suspicion of illicit drug use or supply, or of alcohol consumption, whether by patients or visitors;
- expected actions where there is knowledge of illicit drug use or supply, or of alcohol consumption, whether by patients or visitors;
- powers of staff to search for and confiscate illicit drugs or alcohol;

- reassurance on the powers of staff to handle and dispose of illicit drugs that come into their possession;

- expected arrangements with police services over issues relating to illicit drugs; and

- expectations of service agreements between mental health services and drug and alcohol teams in relation to patients presenting with dual diagnosis or co-morbidity.

Recommendation 51   (Chapter 5.15)

NHS Regional Offices, Regional Commissioning Bodies and Health Authorities should investigate the possibility of reviewing all patients in a particular area who are considered inappropriately placed at their current level of security to see how far patient exchanges might reduce mis-match and bed pressures.

Recommendation 52   (Chapter 5.15)

While the Commission recognises the pressure on high security beds, maintaining a number of vacant places should be considered to create the flexibility of response necessary to benefit both patient care and throughput efficiency of the High Security Hospitals.

Recommendation 60   (Chapter 5.43)

The Department of Health should consult with senior managers in the three High Security Hospitals to see if the adverse effects of the Security Directions can be minimised in any way.

Recommendation 66   (Chapter 6.44)

The Department of Health should consider the need for England to have standards and protocols for the care of mentally ill minors detained in adult units, as already exist in Wales.

Recommendation 72   (Chapter 6.69)

The Commission urges the Government to consider ways in which long-term incapacitated patients can be protected while new legislation is awaited.

Recommendation 74   (Chapter 7.16)

In considering how responsibilities for approving Section 12 doctors should be exercised under the proposed restructuring, the National Assembly for Wales should review the current system for approving Section 12 doctors with a view to ensuring greater consistency and a minimum level of initial and ongoing training.

Recommendation 75   (Chapter 7.18)

The Specialist Health Services Commission for Wales should encourage a holistic assessment of bed needs across all security levels so that patients are not kept at a higher level of security than their condition justifies.

Recommendations for Agreed Action between Service Commissioners and Service Providers

Recommendation 26 (Chapter 3.8)

Where shortage of beds appears to be adversely affecting services, service commissioners and providers should jointly consider and identify within the NSF local implementation plan:

Short-term action: local reviews of all current inpatient stays with a view to clearly identifying the purpose of admission, anticipated length of stay and action required to achieve discharge.

Longer-term action: the establishment of systems & policies that lead to an increase in planned rather than emergency admissions, closer involvement of care co-ordinators during in-patient stays, and greater use of inpatient staff in providing advice to community staff where admission is being considered;

- a review of policies and procedures around admission, assessment care planning and discharge;
- closer work between community and inpatient teams;
- the provision of staff training in CPA & risk management for both community and in-patient staff; and
- consideration of whether inadequacies in community provision are leading to admissions that could have been prevented with earlier intervention.

Recommendation 28 (Chapter 3.18)

All service commissioners and providers should ensure that the general environmental quality of inpatient facilities are subject to locally agreed, systematically monitored standards.

Recommendation 29 (Chapter 3.18)

Where remedial action is required in relation to general environmental quality, at whatever level, this should be the subject of an agreed action plan with resources needed for implementation clearly identified within the NSF local implementation plan.

Recommendation 30 (Chapter 3.22)

Service commissioners and providers should agree and monitor specific standards for access to fresh air for all detained patients.

Recommendation 32 (Chapter 3.29)

Service commissioners and providers should agree specific standards for the provision of recreational, educational and therapeutic activities and monitor their availability and uptake, taking account of patients' views.

Recommendation 34 (Chapter 4.15)

Service commissioners and providers should agree:

- standard classifications for incident reporting to be adopted in relation to all incidents involving detained patients;
- common management monitoring, audit and analysis of all untoward incidents falling within Class A, B and C to see whether any patterns emerge and what lessons can be learnt; and
- an arrangement for joint consideration of such patterns/lessons.

Recommendation 61 (Chapter 6.20)

Service commissioners and providers should consider the consultation model used by the Commission when planning their own strategies to address diversity amongst their own patient populations. This model could be adapted and applied to the planning services for any identifiable groups of patients, including each of those that are presented in Chapter 6 of this report, and not only to Black and minority ethnic groups.

Recommendation 62 (Chapter 6.24)

Service commissioners and providers should engender clear strategic equality programmes, endorsed and driven by their Board and senior management, and allocated mainstream funding, taking account of the suggestions presented at 6.12 – 29 above.

Recommendation 63 (Chapter 6.38)

Service commissioning bodies and service providers should agree and monitor services for women patients to ensure that such patients can:

- lock bedroom doors, using a system capable of being overridden by staff in emergency;
- have a choice of a female key-worker;
- be in contact with other women;
- have the opportunity to take part in women-only therapy groups ands social activities, but have the choice of taking part in mixed groups where appropriate;
- engage safely in a full range of such activities, even where their number is small compared to the hospital population;
- have physical health-checks on admission;
- have access to a female doctor for medical care;
- have access to a female member of staff at all times; and
- be assured of adequate supervision at night.

Recommendation 64 (Chapter 6.44)

All mental health services providing care to children and adolescents detained under the Act should have agreed working and referral arrangements with appropriate medical and psychiatric expertise in CAMHS.

Recommendation 65   (Chapter 6.44)

All NSF local implementation strategies should identify the mental healthcare needs of children and adolescents and plan appropriate provision to meet those needs.

Recommendation 69   (Chapter 6.60)

Non-specialist services who care for elderly detained patients should look to the expectations placed on specialist services by the National Service Framework for Older People (p103 – 6) and try to meet those expectations as far as they are able.

Recommendation 70   (Chapter 6.60)

All mental health services providing care to elderly detained patients should have agreed working and referral arrangements with appropriate medical and psychiatric expertise in the care of older people.

Recommendations for Action at Local Hospital Management Level (including private providers).

Recommendation 2   (Chapter 2.6)

Service providers should ensure that a system of verification using a standardised form is used to record that information has been given to patients about their legal position and rights under the Act. The form should have space for recording:

- the name of the person giving the information;
- the date that the information was given;
- whether the patient understood the information;
- subsequent attempts to give the information; and
- the planned date for the next attempt.

Recommendation 3   (Chapter 2.7)

Hospital managers should ensure that patients' wishes in relation to Sections 132(4) and 133 are ascertained and recorded, and that information is provided to the Nearest Relative if the patient has not objected.

Recommendation 4   (Chapter 2.10)

Hospital managers should ensure that the Department of Health's patient information leaflets on the Mental Health Act are available on all units in an appropriate range of languages and formats.

Recommendation 6   (Chapter 2.13)

Hospital managers should ensure that each ward is issued with a copy of the Legal Services Commission list of franchised solicitors to assist in the process of securing representation at Mental Health Review Tribunals.

Recommendation 7 (Chapter 2.20)

Hospital managers should arrange for effective audit, monitoring and flagging systems to be in place to ensure that the capacity of each detained patient to consent to treatment is assessed and reviewed regularly from the time of admission, that treatment is regularly discussed with patients, that they should be given the opportunity to discuss such treatments on a one-to-one basis and that such discussions are recorded, as required by Chapters 15 and 16 of the Code of Practice.

(see also recommendation 22, Chapter 2.67)

Recommendation 9 (Chapter 2.27)

Hospital managers should closely monitor the handling and outcome of all complaints, both to ensure minimum delay and to note any quality implications arising from the complaint.

Recommendation 10 (Chapter 2.27)

Complaints managers should ensure that complaints made by detained patients are not regarded less seriously than those from other patients, and should be sensitive to the potentially adverse effects on the progress of such patients of delays in handling complaints.

Recommendation 12 (Chapter 2.33)

All those involved with the care and treatment of detained patients should encourage multi-disciplinary liaison to develop protocols which balance the need for confidentiality against the need to share essential information.

Recommendation 14 (Chapter 2.39)

Hospital managers should arrange for the routine collation of detailed statistics on the use of Section 5(2), including the time taken to complete assessments, for audit purposes.

Recommendation 15 (Chapter 2.40)

All providers should ensure that risk assessments of informal patients take account of the likelihood of and risks involved in their leaving the ward, and if both are high, an assessment for detention under the Act should be considered.

Recommendation 17 (Chapter 2.44)

Hospital and social services managers should ensure, through audit and review, that if a patient who is detained under Section 2 appears to require further detention, a Section 3 assessment is arranged at the earliest opportunity and undertaken according to the requirements of the Code of Practice.

Recommendation 18 (Chapter 2.45)

Hospital managers, through audit and review, should ensure that:

- the detention of each patient is kept under constant review by the clinical team;

- decisions on the continuation of detention are based upon clinical need and not administrative convenience;

- detentions are not allowed to lapse, but are actively rescinded unless a decision is made to renew detention; and

- RMOs have access to a suitable form to rescind detentions, a copy of which is given to the patient upon discharge.

Recommendation 22 (Chapter 2.67)

All service providers should have adequate audit tools and flagging systems to record and trigger specific actions to ensure compliance with the consent to treatment provisions of the Act.

(see also recommendation 7, para 2.20)

Recommendation 24 (Chapter 2.70)

All relevant agencies should take particular note of discharge planning requirements for patients subject to Section 117 of the Act.

Recommendation 27 (Chapter 3.13)

All local mental health service managers faced with staffing problems should consider the following examples of best practice identified by Commissioners:

- providing greater access to support and supervision to staff;

- wider use of psychologists and other professionals in ward-based activities, particularly at trainee level;

- bringing therapists (including art or drama therapists) onto wards on a sessional basis;

- encouraging patients and staff to contribute to ward activities through sharing their skills in activity groups; and

- providing training to staff in behaviour management, particularly de-escalation techniques.

Recommendation 31 (Chapter 3.25)

Hospital managers should consider addressing the provision of patient activities and facilities by:

- ensuring that all patients are aware of opportunities on offer, both through publicly displayed information and individual discussion with patients as a part of their care plan;

- using monitoring and user-surveys to identify needs and opportunities in providing activities;

- considering the use of voluntary or other agencies, or of existing contracted staff within the Trust to bolster available activities on a sessional basis; and

- employing or designating an activities co-ordinator.

Recommendation 33 (Chapter 4.9)

Service providers, including the police, should ensure that their policies on Section 136 reinforce the need to wait for an Approved Social Worker to attend a person who is believed to have any kind of mental disorder as defined in the Act before releasing such a person and that the implementation of the policy is monitored.

Recommendation 35 (Chapter 4.20)

Hospital managers should note the findings of the Mental Health Act Commission report on the deaths of detained patients (see appendix B):

- in assessing the physical risks in the ward environment; and
- in considering the training to be given to staff on the management of episodes of strangulation.

Recommendation 36 (Chapter 4.23)

Hospital managers should ensure that sole discretion for the granting of authorised Section 17 leave is NOT left to the supervising nurse alone but is approved ONLY:-

- following consultation with involved professionals to ensure that the patient's needs for health and social care are fully assessed and addressed by the care-plan (see Code of Practice, paragraph 27.5), all of which should be recorded in the patient's clinical record;
- following a detailed risk assessment which is similarly recorded;
- with carefully considered contingency plans, including contact telephone numbers;
- with clearly set down parameters, including the time of return;
- with clearly set down supervision arrangements; and
- with a copy of the Section 17 leave form given to the patient, and to the carer, if appropriate.

Recommendation 37 (Chapter 4.26)

Hospital managers should ensure that AWOL policies and procedures clearly indicate:

- when the patient should be regarded as AWOL;
- who has responsibility to return the patient;
- which staff are authorised under Sections 137 and 138 to act to take a patient into custody, convey or detain;
- what the expectations are of the police in terms of finding and returning patients; and
- who should take charge of the AWOL procedure, and how they should determine:
  - who should undertake a local search and the extent of the local search;
  - when a wider search should be undertaken and by whom and what areas should be searched;
  - when to contact the police; and
  - when to contact the carers or relatives.

Recommendation 40 (Chapter 4.29)

All service providers should obtain the Royal College of Psychiatrists' guidelines on doses above BNF upper limit for distribution to their staff.

Recommendation 41 (Chapter 4.31)

Hospital managers should ensure that clear policies on the prescription and administration of medication have been agreed and that compliance is regularly audited.

Recommendation 42 (Chapter 4.39)

Hospital managers should audit the use of seclusion regularly to ensure that it is properly used. Where the use of seclusion appears high, a seclusion reduction plan should be produced which includes monitoring the effects of any change in management regime on the attitude and behaviour of patients.

Recommendation 43 (Chapter 4.41)

Hospital managers should take all the current areas of concern identified by the Commission into consideration when auditing their arrangements for seclusion

Recommendation 44 (Chapter 4.46)

Hospital managers should ensure that care and support is available to patients who have been subject to control and restraint interventions, in addition to the visit to the patient by a senior officer which is required at paragraph 19.13 of the Code of Practice.

Recommendation 45 (Chapter 4.47)

Hospital managers should ensure that each use of control and restraint techniques is immediately reviewed, with regular audits to ensure that poor practice is eliminated and management and training lessons are learnt.

Recommendation 47 (Chapter 4.55)

Service providers should ensure that there are clear service-wide policies on the locking of wards and that compliance is regularly audited. The frequency of locking of doors on non-secure wards should, in particular, be scrutinised to establish whether this indicates problems with day to day practice or with inadequate staffing. In both instances, the appropriate remedial action should be taken.

Recommendation 49 (Chapter 4.61)

Mental health service providers should ensure that:

- clear policy guidance on the management and prevention of incidents involving alcohol and illicit drugs is available to staff; and
- that they have written service agreements with drug and alcohol teams for the joint management of patients with dual diagnosis or co-morbidity.

Recommendation 50 (Chapter 4.63)

Service providers should ensure that a full risk management strategy is introduced for all their services and that appropriate training, recording and audit are provided to ensure compliance with it. Such a strategy should include evaluation of the adequacy of existing arrangements and the need for additional measures, common systems for incident reporting, regular review systems to re-assess the risks, and a continuing programme of staff development in the assessment of risk.

Some of the main matters which must be taken into account are:

- environmental risks, including those from equipment and to staff as well as to patients;
- risks from patients of harm to self or others, including not only the nature of the illness or overt threats, but also objective assessments of family history, criminal record, substance misuse, absconding, trigger points, who is most likely to be harmed and how, and other relevant factors; and
- the need to ensure that information is systematically recorded and passed on immediately when a patient moves to another location, is allowed leave or is discharged, as well as being made readily available to all relevant staff.

Recommendation 73 (Chapter 7.12)

Welsh Trusts with boundaries with England and English Trusts with Welsh boundaries should ensure that there is at least a nucleus of staff who know both systems well enough to offer advice as necessary to those who deal with cross-boundary patients.

Recommendations specific to High Security Hospital Managers

Recommendation 53 (Chapter 5.21)

HSH managers should instigate routine monitoring of non-pharmacological therapeutic interventions and audit gaps in their provision.

Recommendation 54 (Chapter 5.26)

HSH managers should review searching procedures and documentation to ensure that the Security Directions are being implemented sensitively and that staff time is used appropriately. The review should consider whether staffing levels are sufficient to provide quality care to patients given the increased demands on staff of the Security Directions.

123

Recommendation 55 (Chapter 5.27)

HSH managers should monitor the time taken to approve the release of patients' personal possessions from storage, and the time taken post-approval for items to be delivered to patients. Agreed standards should be set and improvement targets initiated.

Recommendation 56 (Chapter 5.28)

HSH managers should consider ways to improve patients' access to computers, particularly in their leisure-time.

Recommendation 57 (Chapter 5.29)

HSH managers should review their implementation of the Security Directions relating to the importation of foodstuffs to the hospitals, to ensure that they do not result in unintended and undesirable consequences.

Recommendation 58 (Chapter 5.31)

HSH managers should keep the implementation of the Security Directions under constant review, ensuring that they are imposed in appropriate ways that cause no unnecessary detriment to patient care.

Recommendation 59 (Chapter 5.43)

HSH managers should review the implementation of the Security Directions with regard to the visiting of patients by children in the light of the Commission's concerns. Consideration should be given to whether certain patients are unfairly disadvantaged by the blanket imposition of all new visiting arrangements, and whether such arrangements serve any useful purpose and may be counter-therapeutic.

Recommendations specific to Social Service Managers

Recommendation 19 (Chapter 2.52)

Social service authorities should develop standard forms for ASWs to complete on the admission of a patient to hospital under the Act, to ensure that all the relevant information is left with the receiving hospital.

Recommendation 20 (Chapter 2.56)

Standard formats should be developed for ASWs' reports which ensure that details of how the Nearest Relative was identified and consulted are included. This will enable hospital administrators to include these issues in their scrutiny of admission documents and ensure that the papers are legally valid.

> **Recommendation 24** (Chapter 2.70)
>
> All relevant agencies should take particular note of discharge planning requirements for patients subject to Section 117 of the Act.

Recommendations for Action at Operational Level

> **Recommendation 16** (Chapter 2.40)
>
> Nursing and Medical staff must ensure that all patients who are not detained under the Act have a clear understanding of their legal status.

> **Recommendation 23** (Chapter 2.76)
>
> A copy of the relevant statutory Form 38 or 39 (Consent to Treatment) should be kept attached to patients' medicine charts, and pharmacists ahould be asked to check against this for authorisation before dispensing medication for patients.

> **Recommendation 39** (Chapter 4.28)
>
> A pharmacist should check that Forms 38:
>
> - have been authorised by the RMO;
> - are accurately reflected in the medication chart, and:
> - comply with the RCP guidance
>
> before releasing any prescription. Pharmacists should also check medication charts against Forms 39 where issued.

The Commission is a signatory to the following declaration of intent of the Royal College of Psychiatrists' *Changing Minds* campaign.

Declaration of Intent

1   We, the Council, Fellows and Members of the Royal College of Psychiatrists, are seriously concerned at the stigma encountered by people suffering from mental disorders, their relatives and those who care for them.

2   The experience of our patients is that discriminatory attitudes are widespread within the general public of all ages, the media, the medical profession, employers, banks, insurance companies, building societies, educational bodies, housing authorities, and many other organisations.

3   The Royal College has launched a new Campaign - Changing Minds: Every Family in the Land which will:

- increase public and professional understanding of
    - anxiety
    - depression
    - schizophrenia
    - alcohol and drug misuse
    - dementia
    - eating disorders;
- emphasise how all of us may be affected directly or through those close to us;
- reduce the stigma attached to those disorders and discrimination arising from it;
- narrow the gap between the beliefs of health care professionals and the public about the nature and effectiveness of treatment.

4   The Campaign will challenge inaccurate representation, in the media and elsewhere, based on stigmatising attitudes and stereotypes ("nutter", "psycho", "schizo"), myths ("all people with schizophrenia are violent"), misunderstandings ("mental illness cannot be cured") and discriminatory attitudes ("I don't want nutters living in my backyard").

5   The Campaign will stress the importance of mental health promotion as an issue for all of us. It will re-affirm the role of diagnosis and treatment - psychological, social and physical - in the effective management of mental disorders.

6   Within the Campaign, the College will work collaboratively with other organisations to seek changes, not only in attitudes and behaviour, but also in legislation. We aim for the same success as that achieved against discrimination based on race, gender and sexuality. There should be no room for stigma in the third millennium.

Deaths of Detained Patients in England and Wales

A Report by the Mental Health Act Commission on information collected from 1 February 1997 to 31 January 2001

Executive Summary

Introduction

1   Since 1996, it has been the policy of the Mental Health Act Commission (MHAC) to maintain a record of every patient who has died while subject to detention under the Mental Health Act 1983 and to enquire into any such death when this has been considered to fall within the terms of the Commission's remit. The purpose of the MHAC report on their findings from 1 February 1997 to 31 January 2000 is to contribute both to the ongoing debate about the care of patients subject to the 1983 Act and to the NHS priority of making a substantial reduction in the number of suicides among patients and in the population as a whole.

2   The work recorded in the main report was done by the Commission's Vice-Chairman, Professor Richard Williams, with the assistance of Professor Gethin Morgan. They have taken great care to stress the methodological limitations of the study. These concern:

■ uncertainty about the comprehensiveness of the basic information, which is provided on request and not as a statutory requirement;

■ incomplete data insofar as the number of deaths reported during the period is still awaiting the outcome of inquests;

■ the inability of the Commission to compare the data in detail with relevant figures relating either to the general population or the population of those who may be mentally disordered but not subject to the 1983 Act; and

■ the absence of any directly comparable earlier or contemporary data. (But broad comparisons are made with the outcome of an earlier MHAC Review in 1995[117] and with the National Confidential Inquiry[118]).

3   In spite of these reservations, it is considered that the conclusions drawn are robust enough to confirm conclusions drawn in the earlier reviews of similar material and to suggest that more still needs to be done to ensure that the messages drawn from analytical material are effectively

117   Banerjee, S. Bingley, W, Murphy E (1995) **Deaths of Detained Patients: a review of reports to the Mental Health Act Commission**. London, Mental Health Foundation.

118   National Confidential Inquiry into Suicide and Homicide by People with Mental Illness (1999) **Safer Services**. London, Department of Health.

translated into practice. The full report contains a wealth of detail which should be of interest to all practitioners and includes a summary of main findings and recommendations. The purpose of this extended summary is to provide ready access to some of the key information.

4   The report considers the deaths of 1,4471 people subject to detention under the Mental Health Act during the chosen three year period. Hospital staff reported 1,218 of them to the MHAC as having died from natural causes.

Deaths from Natural Causes

5   Not unexpectedly, there is a preponderance of elderly patients in this group - 76% over 65 years of age and 56% over 75 years of age. 53% were men and 94% were white. The estimated rate of death from natural causes is 822/100,000 sections per annum for 1997-2000.

6   The most significant finding in relation to these patients is that 47% of them died within one month of admission and 18% between one month and ten weeks. This reflects findings in the earlier review. It suggests that close monitoring and analysis of deaths within a short period of admission might throw light on the types of illness or experience which led to them and could have significant implications for the treatment of mentally disordered patients before they reach the stage at which compulsion becomes necessary.

Unnatural Deaths

All Unnatural Deaths

7   Two hundred and fifty-three (17%) of the 1,471 cases under review resulted in an inquest. 168 verdicts were recorded as suicide or open, 31 as accident or misadventure, 4 as due to drug abuse and 5 as natural causes. The outcome of 45 of these inquests was not known at the time of the report.

8   Only 2% of the unnatural deaths were over the age of 75 and 78% were less than 45 years. 72% were men and 83% were white. The most common causes of death were:-

   ■ Hanging   34%
   ■ Jumping from a height   14.2%
   ■ Being hit by a train   11.5%
   ■ Drowning   8.3%
   ■ Overdose   5.1%

9   Forty-nine per cent of those who died unnaturally were diagnosed as suffering from schizophrenia and 20% from depression. The diagnostic categories of all psychoses and depression, with associated disorders, accounted for 78% of all unnatural deaths. Personality disorders were included in 11% of cases.

10   Only 32% (82) of unnatural deaths occurred within a psychiatric unit. Nineteen per cent (48) were patients on agreed leave and 33% (83) were absent without leave. This reflects the findings of the previous reviews and emphasises the importance of risk assessment, security, and the need for clear policies on leave under Section 17 of the 1983 Act, particularly when a patient fails to return at the expected time. Absence without leave implies that the patient has deliberately

broken the rules and that staff have been caught unawares. Suicide while the patient is on agreed leave suggests that the suicide risk was not anticipated. Post death audit may help to clarify problems of assessment and management.

Deaths by Accident or Misadventure

11   Thirty-one (12.5%) of the unnatural deaths were categorised as by accident or misadventure. 58% (18) were men and 42% (13) women. 68% (21) were less than 45 years of age. 12 deaths were in a psychiatric ward, 8 in general hospital units, 5 in a public place, 4 in hospital grounds and 2 at home. 4 were on leave and 7 absent without leave.

12   Because of the small number of deaths by accident or misadventure, they were not compared in detail with the deaths that were found at inquest to be due to suicide. There is imprecision in the categorisation of deaths at inquest that makes valid analysis difficult without detailed case-by-case examination. Nevertheless, the information provided suggests that the inquest verdicts of accidental death encompassed many deaths which might, on clinical grounds, have been regarded as suicides (14 of them had been regarded as at risk of self-harm and were under special observation for that reason).

Suicide

13   For the purpose of the MHAC report, open verdicts at inquest have been included as suicides to avoid under-estimation of death by suicide on clinical grounds. This is similar to the practice of the Confidential Inquiry. This approach gives 168 cases of suicide, excluding the 45 where the inquest verdict has not yet been returned.

14   Seventy-six per cent (128) of the detained patients identified as suicides were men and 24% (4) women. 80% of all the suicides in the present study were aged 45 years or less at the time of death; the median age was 34, with a range from 18-73. This suggests that younger people who are detained because of a mental disorder are certainly more at risk of suicide than older people. (Middleton and Gunnell have presented recent data supporting their view that there has been a continuing increase in the rate of suicide among males aged 25-34 years.)

15   The most common methods of suicide were:-
- Hanging   40%
- Jumping from a height   17%
- Jumping before a train etc   15%
- Drowning   10%
- Drug overdose   4%

16   The most common categories of mental disorder among the suicides were schizophrenia and related disorders (49%), affective disorders (24%) and psychotic episodes (10%) – a total of 83% (cf 89% in the 1995 review).

17   Only 29% (48) of the suicides occurred in a psychiatric ward and 4% (6) in hospital grounds. The majority, 41% (69) took place in a public place while the patient was on approved leave or absent without leave. This underlines the importance of risk assessment and careful Section 17 procedures, as mentioned in paragraph 10 above.

18   Twenty-five per cent (41) of suicides occurred while the patient was being observed every 15 minutes or less. This finding emphasises the need to review observation procedures. Post-death audit should focus on this.

Hanging

19   The work by Middleton and Gunnell suggests that hanging as a general method of suicide has increased threefold in 15-24 year old men and twofold in young women since 1979. Hanging was reported to the MHAC as the cause of death in 34% (86 – 66 men and 20 women) of the 253 cases reported to the coroner as unnatural. 40% of suicides and 16% of deaths by accident or misadventure were due to hanging. Hanging is therefore a key factor in the prevention of suicide.

20   Death by hanging implies a fracture of the second cervical vertebra. The current review's closer analysis of ligatures and load-bearing supports used in cases reported as hanging suggests that many of these hangings could be due to strangulation. For example, a ligature less robust than one likely to cause a fracture may cause:

■ Compression and/or trauma to the larynx or trachea in the neck causing asphyxiation;

■ Reflex cardiac inhibition leading to cardiac arrest; or

■ Failure of blood supply to the brain.

21   If this hypothesis is correct, it is highly relevant to the care of suicidal patients, whether detained or not. Since 58% of the hangings occurred in a psychiatric unit, the possibility of strangulation suggests that attention needs to be paid to the removal of a wider range of ligatures than may be necessary to avoid cervical fracture, greater attention given to the load-bearing capacity of some integral components of a normal ward environment and fundamental changes in design considered to achieve long-term improvement. It also has implications for the immediate management of episodes of hanging and for the application of appropriate resuscitation techniques.

Observation Procedures

22   Perhaps more importantly, the hypothesis has implications for the nature of observation, since it is much easier to see whether someone is hanging from a height than whether a supine figure is attached to a fixture at the same height that may be causing strangulation. This is particularly relevant because 25% of all hangings occurred despite observation every 15 minutes or more frequently.

23   The 1999 Report of the Confidential Inquiry comments on the variations in how observation procedures concerning suicide risk are implemented. It questions the rationale and value of intermediate levels of supervision. Without knowing the number of patients who undergo special observation at all levels and the rate of suicide exhibited by them, the MHAC review suggests that it is premature to dismiss the value of these long-established procedures. The figures on suicide by hanging, in particular, suggest that there needs to be a judicious balance between the level of ward security, one-to-one contact between patients and staff, and a gradual reduction in the intensity of supervision during the period of recovery so that each patient may eventually acquire the freedom and responsibilities inherent in a normal ward routine.

Restraint

24   Among the deaths reported to a coroner, the MHAC information showed 22 instances in which restraint had been used in the week before death. Three of the 22 people who died after or during an instance of restraint were from African or Caribbean ethnic cultural groups. Such small numbers render any kind of statistical analysis hazardous. At the time of writing (July 2001), inquests had been completed in only 17 of these cases, in two of which death had occurred while the person concerned was being restrained and in four restraint had been used during the

preceding four hours. It is clearly very important to be able to establish how far, in any individual case, the use of restraint may have contributed to a simultaneous or subsequent death. Knowledge of whether and how it did so should contribute to the development of safer methods of restraint.

Incidence and Trends

25   The data available are not at present sufficiently consistent or reliable to enable any assumptions to be made with confidence about either incidence or trends in any of the factors examined. It is likely that the 1995 review under-estimated the number of suicides whereas this review may have slightly over-estimated, partly because of the combination of open verdicts with suicides and partly because of assumptions made in those cases where the inquest verdict is not yet known. There are also several different ways in which the number of detentions under the 1983 Act can be calculated.

26   The deaths reported to the MHAC during the 1990s occurred over periods of time in which the detention rate was rising. There were also fluctuations over short periods in the numbers of informal in-patients who became subject to detention after admission. (This was particularly true in 1998-1999, probably as a result of the Bournewood case). In order to provide a basis for comparison, the authors of the report considered the number of uses of the Act for one year in each period of the two MHAC reviews, i.e. 1993-94 and 1998-1999. In each selected year, the number of initial admissions under the Act was added to the number of informal in-patients subsequently made subject to detention. The resulting figures for comparison were 39,582 in 1993-94 and 49,648 in 1998-1999, an increase of 25.4%.

27   Bearing in mind all these uncertainties, the report estimates that the <u>number</u> of deaths by natural causes is approximately 408 a year, giving an estimated <u>rate</u> of 822 per 100,000 detentions. A comparable rate for 1993-94 cannot be calculated because of the different reporting system then in place.

28   On the same tentative basis, the *number* of suicides among detained patients may have increased by 42% - from a total of 95 "probable suicides" in the two years from 1992-1994 to an estimated projected total of 204 in the three years from 1997-2000 and the *rate* of suicide among detained patients during the same period may have increased by 14%. The rate of suicide among detained patients now is estimated at about 137 per 100,000 sections, compared with an estimated 120 per 100,000 at the time of the 1995 review. This compares with a rate of 11 per 100,000 in the general population in 1992. This is hardly unexpected, given that suicidal tendency or an expression of intent are often the cause for an application for detention under the 1983 Act, but underlines the importance of reducing suicides among detained patients.

29   However tentative these figures may be, it seems probable that there has been a true increase in the number of suicides and a possible increase in the rate of suicide among detained patients in the period under review. This attempt to provide comparative data, however cautious, highlights the need to create a credible and consistent database against which to measure progress and to identify the factors most likely to lead to prevention.

Gender, Age and Ethnicity

30   There is no clear indication of any changes in incidence or trends in age, gender or ethnicity as compared with the 1995 review. Partly because of the very small numbers involved, it is virtually impossible to assess whether ethnicity has any bearing on the likelihood of unnatural death.

31   The major ethnic groupings in this study, with the 1995 figures in brackets, were 83% white (76%) and 5% Black Caribbean (7%). This proportionality cannot be compared with national figures because the information in the last census of population in England and Wales is almost certainly inaccurate now. It appears likely that the number of young people from black and ethnic communities has risen rapidly – the CRE factsheet for 1995 shows that ethnic minority populations now have proportionately more young people than the white population. This situation poses challenges in analysis of any data on ethnicity.

32   Whatever the position may be, the need to recognise diversity and concern about the disproportionate number of people from Black and minority ethnic groups who are detained under the 1983 Act make it essential to improve the ability to analyse and compare relevant data in order to assess whether ethnicity has any bearing on deaths among detained patients. It also underlines the need for comprehensive post-death audits.

Monitoring and Data Collection

33   The authors of the report stress the need for clinical skills to be informed by attention to the evidence from systematic research as well as by awareness of the individuality of each patient. Qualitative as well as quantitative information is necessary to produce good clinical practice. The interpretation of quantitative data often requires return to the narrative gained from good reflective clinical practice. In this way, the two broad approaches to inquiry can reverberate and mutually interact.

34   This approach is illustrated by the methodology adopted by the MHAC to inquire into the deaths of detained patients. Although the data presented in the report provides a good basis for ongoing monitoring and comparative work, attempts at analysis have revealed gaps and suggested ways in which the data could be improved and refined to enable the material it produces to be even more informative. The MHAC is amending its database and adjusting its methodology to close the gaps identified, thus increasing the value of future analysis.

Summary of Recommendations

35   The MHAC report makes the following recommendations. Those which reflect this Extended Summary are as follows (paragraph numbers refer to this Summary):

   ■ Closer monitoring and analysis of the deaths of patients who die within a short period after being detained should be undertaken, possibly as part of a wider research project (paragraph 6);

- In revising guidance on and training in risk assessment, particular attention should be paid to the findings on unnatural death while patients are on approved leave or absent without leave (paragraphs 10 and 17);

- Ways of improving the categorisation of inquest data for research purposes should be explored further, possibly in conjunction with the Confidential Inquiry (paragraph 12);

- Deaths by hanging should be more closely analysed to establish how far they include strangulation and the implications of such an analysis for preventative measures (paragraphs 19-21);

- The use of restraint should continue to be recorded and carefully monitored in all cases and where there is an unnatural death the post-death audit should pay careful attention to the use of restraint during and prior to the death (paragraph 24);

- The figures on incidence and trends should be treated with extreme caution. There are difficulties inherent in comparing the two MHAC reports and uncertainties about calculating the appropriate numbers of detentions. Nevertheless, it is likely that the absolute number of suicides has risen and possible that the incidence of suicide among detained patients has risen between 1992 and 2000. Continuing and possibly increased vigilance is undoubtedly necessary. (Paragraphs 25-29).

- The need for careful monitoring of differences in gender, age and ethnicity is emphasised and any post-death audit of death from unnatural causes should pay particular attention to ethnicity and its possible effect on the cause of death. (30-32).

36   The main findings and recommendations summarised above lead to a number of more generalised recommendations. These are that:

- Efforts to identify and remove any aids to suicide should be continued as well as intensified in certain areas identified in this report;

- Risk assessment should continue to be developed and refined, with particular attention to the need for well trained and highly skilled and motivated staff;

- The resource implications of more sophisticated environmental safety and greater vigilance in observation should not be under-estimated;

- There should be a detailed post-death audit after every unexplained or unnatural death;

- The Department of Health, the National Assembly for Wales, the Mental Health Act Commission and other bodies with responsibility for the care of detained patients should co-operate to create a consistent but dynamic database. This should enable incidence and trends to be more accurately assessed and provide an ongoing means of developing better practice; and

- The Mental Health Act Commission (or its successor body) should continue to develop its own processes for reviewing deaths of detained patients and produce regular published reports on its findings.

Conclusion

37   The MHAC recognises that the figures for unnatural deaths show only the failures. The prevention of suicide generates no data. The Commission has no doubt that the dedication and care of hospital staff prevent more suicides than are not prevented. Nevertheless, if any additional life can be saved by greater awareness of the factors involved in previous suicides, emphasis on them must be worthwhile.

Mental Health Act Commission
February 2001

The National Visit 2: Key Findings

1   The National Visit 2 continued the focus on the key areas from the Commission's Equal Opportunities Policy that Commissioners had been trained in and felt were crucial to the care of Black and minority ethnic detained patients, i.e. ethnic monitoring, dealing with racial harassment of patients, staff training in race equality and anti-discriminatory practice, and the provision of, access to, and use of interpreters. Only a brief summary is provided here as the full report is now published and available.[119]

2   104 mental health and learning disability units were visited. These included acute units, medium secure units and High Security Hospitals in the NHS, and acute and medium secure facilities in the independent sector. Information was collected from 119 wards, and from the case notes of 534 Black and minority ethnic detained patients.

3   The largest minority ethnic group among the patients was Black Caribbean, comprising 42% of the total. More than two thirds of the patients were men, and the majority were aged between 25 and 44 years. The most commonly recorded religion was Christianity, with Muslims comprising the next largest group.

4   116 patients did not have English as their first language; between them they spoke 26 different languages. Fluency in English varied between nearly all of the Black Caribbean patients to only half of the Bangladeshi patients.

Conclusions from the National Visit 2

5   One immediate effect of the Visit, and of the many pilot visits which preceded it, has been to raise the awareness of many units to the specific issues in caring for this group of patients, which is a necessary precursor to any change in practice.

6   The Visit has shown that there is still a considerable development agenda. People from Black and minority ethnic communities are often not receiving care that is sensitive to their cultural backgrounds. This is reflected in the Visit's findings on recording and monitoring of ethnicity, harassment, training of staff and use of interpreters.

7   The aim of the Visit was not simply to highlight bad practice but rather to raise awareness of these key issues amongst managers and practitioners, and identify and share areas of good practice thus improving the care for detained patients from Black and minority ethnic groups. In-depth analysis of the data, as well as a thorough examination of all the written policies and

---

119   Sainsbury Centre for Mental Health (2000) **National Visit 2. Improving Care for Detained Patients from Black and Minority Ethnic Communities. Preliminary Report**. London, Sainsbury Centre.

procedures collected from the units and wards visited, will identify further examples of good practice which can be disseminated, to help those services which have been slower to develop in these areas.

Key findings of the National Visit 2

Recording and monitoring ethnicity

❑ Half the units had written policies, procedures or guidelines on recording ethnicity of patients. All units routinely recorded patients' ethnicity, but not all used the ONS categories. With a few exceptions, this data is not being put to great use.

Without knowing the language and dialect spoken by their patients, ward staff will be unable to obtain an appropriate interpreter. The interrelationship between language, dialect and religion demonstrates the importance of recording full information on all of these.

Dealing with racial harassment of Black and minority ethnic patients by other patients, or by staff

❑ Three quarters of the units had no policy on dealing with racial harassment of Black and minority ethnic patients by other patients, or by staff. Fifty nine patients (11%) whose notes were examined had reported incidents of racial harassment.

Race equality and anti-discriminatory practice

❑ Two thirds of the units had no policy on race equality and anti-discriminatory practice for staff, and a similar number did not provide training on this for their staff. However, several examples of good practice were provided, demonstrating a wide range of training and other activities aimed at raising staff's awareness and understanding of the religious and cultural needs of Black and minority ethnic patients. Many units had devised resource packs containing useful information.

Provision of, access to and use of interpreters

❑ Half the units had a policy on the provision and use of interpreters, but only three quarters used interpreters who were trained in interpreting.

❑ Two thirds of the wards had used patients' relatives or friends to interpret for them; this is of concern, as widespread use of family members as interpreters can compromise objective decision-making by staff.

Although people from Black and minority ethnic groups may be fluent in English, at times of stress, including periods of mental illness, some may prefer to use their mother tongue and would therefore require an interpreter.

Appendix D

The Commission's Regional Consultation Exercises

Background to the Regional Consultation Exercises

1   In order to meet Goal 5 of the Commission's equality statement (*To increase the number of under-represented groups amongst staff, Commission members and appointees* - see Chapter 6.14 above), we have, since our inception, been keen to appoint a breadth of Commissioners with a wide variety of skills, knowledge and experience, and like most agencies in the health and welfare field, have tried to attract those from Black and minority ethnic communities. We aimed to achieve 20% of all Commission appointments from Black and minority ethnic groups. This would be slightly higher than the Black and minority ethnic in-patient population, which is approximately 18%.

2   A number of measures were undertaken to achieve this:

❑ **Targeted advertisements** in the mainstream and the Black press with a clear message encouraging Black and minority ethnic applicants;

❑ **Flyers** distributed to over 1000 key Black and minority ethnic organisations, to ensure that:

■ the adverts received wide exposure within Black and minority ethnic communities;

■ organisations where suitable candidates were likely to be were targeted;

■ the process gave a clear message of the Commission's commitment to the implementation of equal opportunities; and

■ the recruitment process was not delayed and the cost was minimal.

❑ **Existing Commissioners** were asked to identify potential applicants. Our internal bulletins and ongoing training ensured that all Commissioners were aware of the Equality Programme and asked for their support in its implementation.

3   These short-term initiatives, coupled with the measures that we had taken over the years, produced some initial successes. However, the processes also clearly identified the constraints to achieving the targets set. These were broadly based around three areas:

❑ **The low profile of the Commission** within the targeted and wider community. Few people were aware of the existence of the Commission and fewer still understood its role and remit.

❑ **The selection and recruitment process** needed to be reviewed and the sift criteria, panel make-up and process of interview reexamined to ensure that applicants were not being discriminated against and that all applicants' views on equality were ascertained.

❑ **The geographical and professional balance of Commission Visiting Teams** was constrained by the lack of significant Black and minority ethnic communities within certain geographical areas and the requirement to have a representation of Commissioners with the different professional backgrounds.

4   It was apparent that the low profile of the Commission, the need to review the recruitment process and the requirement for geographical and professional balance would have to be addressed on an integrated basis and that more direct means of engaging local Black and minority ethnic communities would be required.

5   In order to develop an integrated response, we undertook the innovative and creative step of initiating a series of regional consultation exercises which not only identified a wide range of inequalities with respect to mental health services and Black and minority ethnic communities but also helped to:

❑ considerably raise the profile of the Commission;

❑ enable effective and meaningful consultation with community and user groups as well as service providers;

❑ provide a vehicle for people to access accurate information on the role and remit of the Commission; and

❑ encourage suitable people to apply to become members of the Commission.

The Regional Consultation Exercises

6   A summary of the methods and findings from the three regional consultation exercises follows, highlighting the five key areas which formed the focus of the survey: mental health services for Black and minority ethnic communities; detention under the Mental Health Act; race equality initiatives, including ethnic monitoring; interpreting services: and services for women. It combines the views of all those consulted and interviewed during the course of the survey along with the findings from the seminars.

7   This summary cannot cover the full range of the issues raised by participants. Greater detail can be found in the regional reports[120].

8   Three regions were selected for the consultations. Greater Manchester and the West Midlands were selected because of their substantial Black and minority ethnic populations. The North East was selected as a balance to the other two regions because of its smaller and more dispersed Black and minority ethnic populations. The Commission was under-represented by people from Black and minority ethnic groups in all three regions at the beginning of these consultations.

9   The 1991 census identified the proportion of the population as being of minority ethnic origin as 8.2% in the West Midlands, 5.9% in Greater Manchester, and 1.4% in the North East. In all three regions, the Black and minority ethnic population is concentrated in inner city areas, with the associated problems of unemployment and social deprivation. Since the 1991 census, the growth of the indigenous white population aged sixteen or under has remained stable or decreased, whilst the Black and minority ethnic population has, and continues to, increase three to fourfold.

---

120   University of Central Lancashire / Mental Health Act Commission (2000) **Mental Health Act Commission National Consultation on Mental Health Issues and Black and Minority Ethnic Communities – Greater Manchester Report**
University of Central Lancashire / Mental Health Act Commission (2000) **Mental Health Act Commission National Consultation on Mental Health Issues and Black and Minority Ethnic Communities. – West Midlands Report**
University of Central Lancashire / Mental Health Act Commission (2001) **Mental Health Act Commission National Consultation on Mental Health Issues and Black and Minority Ethnic Communities – North East Report**

10   The ethnic diversity within this section of the population must be stressed. The term 'Black and minority ethnic' encompasses a wide range of communities with different language groups, cultures, religions and geographical regions of origin and includes refugees and asylum seekers. This changing and diverse demographic profile presents many challenges to statutory providers of mental health services.

The Process

11   The methods employed to undertake the consultation exercise combined action research and community development techniques. The project was not intended as 'research', but rather the methods were designed to provide a 'snapshot' about a number of key aspects of mental health issues, from the perceptions of Black and minority ethnic communities and from those involved in providing and commissioning these services.

12   A key aim of the exercise was to listen to community groups and service providers and to raise salient issues in relation to mental health, service provision and Black and minority ethnic communities through feeding back the views of participants as part of a community event or seminar.

13   This innovative approach to community and service engagement had the further advantage of enabling the Commission to maintain its focus on the priority areas already identified i.e. ethnic monitoring, racial harassment, women, access to interpretation services and recruitment of Black and minority ethnic Commissioners.

14   This ensured that the comprehensive approach taken in the our Equality strategy involving training, guidance notes and the National Visit 2 was further developed with the introduction of the local area consultation exercises or 'roadshows', as they came to be known.

15   Interviews and focus groups involving more than approximately 50 organisations in each region took place involving Black and minority ethnic community members, mental health service professionals, local authority social services, GPs, police and probation officers, and members of relevant voluntary organisations. This part of the exercise was followed by a local seminar where the Commission had the opportunity to discuss its remit and Equal Opportunities programme, and statutory and voluntary organisations could explore mental health services through workshops facilitated by local Black and minority ethnic community groups.

16   The process enabled:

❑ the Commission to act as a catalyst in promoting greater contact and involvement between Black and minority ethnic communities and local service providers and commissioners of services;

❑ the identification of individuals from local Black and minority ethnic communities who could contribute directly to the seminars;

❑ an increase in the pool of potential of Black and minority ethnic applicants to the Commission; and

❑ an increase in awareness and knowledge about the Commission with particular emphasis on our work in the area of promoting race equality

17   The model was piloted and tested in Greater Manchester and the West Midlands by the Ethnicity & Health Unit of the Univesity of Central Lancashire, with the Unit acting as a facilitator and trainer in the North East where Commissioners themselves undertook the fieldwork activities. This ensured capacity building within the Commission: developing direct contact between the

Mental Health Act Commissioners, local service providers and commissioners of those services and local Black and minority ethnic groups and individuals.

18   Additional outcomes from the process included further local area developments as a direct consequence of the seminars and increased contact with Black and minority ethnic organisations and groups. For example, in Manchester the local authority and mental health service commissioners organised a follow-up seminar which was attended by eighty local people and led to the creation of a number of specific goals for improved partnership working in that area.

The Findings

Mental Health Service Provision for Black and Minority Ethnic Communities

19   Mental health services for Black and minority ethnic communities were found to vary greatly, both within and between the three regions. Arguably the demographic profile and the dispersal of Black and minority ethnic communities within the regions, in many instances influenced the quality and equity of service provision. For instance, within the larger conurbations of the three regions innovative and creative services that aimed to respond to the needs of Black and minority ethnic mental health service users were to be found: day care provision in the courtyard of a West Midlands Mosque; day and lunch clubs for Chinese people and Asian women in the North East; funding and facilities for voluntary organisations in Greater Manchester. However, very often, away from the inner cities, and sometimes within them, where Black and minority ethnic populations are smaller but not necessarily insignificant, services were only provided on an ad hoc and piecemeal basis. This phenomenon was most noticeable in the North East where, outside the larger cities, there had been little attempt to address the needs of Black and minority ethnic communities; it was also noticeable in many areas of Greater Manchester and in the rural areas of the West Midlands.

20   Whilst there was little demand for completely separate services targeting Black and minority ethnic communities from any of the community groups surveyed, there was a strong consensus amongst them that mainstream services should develop and deliver appropriate services to meet the multidimensional needs of communities.

21   There was a powerful perception amongst the Black and minority ethnic community groups interviewed across the three regions that the level of poor mental health is unacceptably high within many Black and minority ethnic communities. This perception was expressed alongside an acknowledgement of the difficulties faced by the statutory sector in recognising the challenges of diversity. For instance, the Greater Manchester community groups highlighted the fact that the concept of mental health differs not only from community to community, but also for some communities between generations within the communities. Many community representatives and statutory providers noted that people from Black and minority ethnic communities often only access mental health services at times of acute crisis and fundamental breakdown.

22   A complex set of factors was highlighted as influencing deteriorating mental health and lack of uptake of services, many of which were interdependent. For instance:

   ■ the stigma associated with mental ill health amongst some communities;

   ■ the shortage of people from Black and minority ethnic communities working in mental health services;

- lack of cultural awareness by service providers; and

- poverty, alienation, racism, drug and alcohol misuse.

Suggested responses from all three areas included more preventive mental health work targeted at Black and minority ethnic communities, cultural awareness training for service providers and mainstream assistance to strengthen the community mental health voice and an acceptance and provision of alternative therapies to treat mental illness.

Detention under the Mental Health Act 1983

23　There was a perception amongst Black and minority ethnic communities that the Mental Health Act is being used disproportionately in relation to their communities and that detention is on the increase. Although this view was not unanimously agreed by the statutory sector, some providers did share the view. In the Greater Manchester region women from the South Asian and Chinese communities, young African-Caribbean men, older Irish men and refugee groups were seen as particularly vulnerable. Refugee groups were also identified as being vulnerable by the voluntary sector in the West Midlands, although the statutory sector respondents in that region held a widespread view that African-Caribbean men were the group detained in numbers disproportionate to their number in the wider community.

24　In the North East the voluntary sector was more concerned with the inappropriate way the Act is initiated, particularly in relation to refugee communities, than with its disproportionate use. This view was echoed in part by the statutory sector who expressed the opinion that the small size of the Black and minority ethnic population did not make the numbers of detentions an issue, but that when detention is initiated it is sometimes done so by staff who have a lack of understanding and knowledge of the needs of the Black and minority ethnic population thereby impeding compliance with the Code of Practice.

25　In both the Greater Manchester and West Midlands regions the opinion was expressed in different ways that a reduction in the use of the Act would be an important barometer of the success of mental health services in effectively meeting need.

Race equality initiatives including ethnic monitoring

26　In all three regions a variety of issues were identified by both the statutory and voluntary sectors as crucial to providing equitable mental health services. These included increasing numbers of staff from Black and minority ethnic communities, raising awareness and understanding of the differences between white/western and other conceptions of mental health, respecting cultural differences, increasing language skills.

27　In the West Midlands and Greater Manchester regions staff recruitment and training was the most common way in which statutory services had attempted to address these issues. Targets, staff support groups, mentoring schemes, development programmes and race equality training had all been introduced. In both regions the emphasis on staffing had been supplemented by consultation with Black and minority ethnic user groups (although this consultation varied greatly within the regions) and also by the introduction of specific services (again varying greatly) to meet the linguistic, cultural and religious needs of Black and minority ethnic patients.

28　In contrast the North East with its smaller Black and minority ethnic population had few strategic initiatives in place. Although amongst many of the service providers in the North East there was a genuine will to provide equitable services, particularly amongst those who were detecting a shift in the pattern of demand on services caused by the arrival of relatively large numbers of asylum seekers in the area, the view of the voluntary sector was that there had been developments in thinking but this had not necessarily led to improvements in practice.

29   It was clear from comparing the three regions that where services were most responsive and most equitable there existed strong partnerships between the statutory and voluntary sectors. Within all three regions the surveys revealed a genuine desire from many of those who participated to forge real partnerships between the statutory and voluntary sectors. Partnership was defined in the North East consultation as having shared values, shared goals and most importantly a shared vision based on sound principles of equality. In Greater Manchester the regional consultation was followed up with a conference organised by Manchester Social Services to explore partnership working further.

Ethnic monitoring

30   Within all three regions there were major inconsistencies in the monitoring of service uptake and ethnic monitoring of workforces. Concerns were raised by respondents from both the statutory and voluntary sectors about the effectiveness of ethnic monitoring initiatives and the use made of the resultant data.

Interpreting services

31   Across all three regions, there is clearly room for improvement in interpreting services. The lack of competent, qualified interpreters trained in mental health issues was seen as a major shortfall in service provision. Many respondents from the statutory sector acknowledged this deficiency in their service and admitted using family members, telephone based language services and Black and minority ethnic staff members all of which they saw as inappropriate but sometimes necessary. A very small minority of statutory respondents claimed to offer a comprehensive interpreting service.

Services for women

32   Specific services for women in general were found to be lacking throughout the consultation with specific services for women from Black and minority ethnic communities being almost unheard of. Statutory respondents in all regions did report of a number of ad hoc initiatives which had been introduced to support women from different communities. Many inpatient service providers spoke of treating all patients holistically in terms of gender, race, culture and religion. However, particular concern was expressed by community groups in the North East for the plight of women from asylum seeking and refugee groups whose linguistic, cultural and geographical isolation would make them particularly vulnerable to stress and depression. These same factors were also reported by other regions as being an issue for many women from the Chinese and South Asian communities and in the Greater Manchester area the emergence of a number of voluntary groups with a particular focus on women's mental health is seen as evidence of a particular need which is currently not being met by statutory services.

Conclusions and future developments

33   The methods outlined above provide a model of the engagement of Black and minority ethnic communities, mental health service users, service providers and commissioners. This model can be adapted and developed for other health services and for other minority groups.

34   The high level of consultation resulted in capacity building around mental health issues and has given ownership of the project to all those who participated.

35   An indication of the success of the project is the increase in the number of people from Black and minority ethnic communities applying to become members of the Commission: the current proportion is 22%, 2% higher than our original aim.

36   The findings from this project will contribute to forging true partnerships between people from Black and minority ethnic communities and the providers of mental health services and other relevant organisations, on both local and national levels. In this way, the challenge of delivering mental health services that consistently and effectively meet the needs of diverse communities can be addressed. Developing these partnerships will require strategic thinking; commitment from all parties especially statutory authorities and other providers; and the development and cherishing of local networks.

ANNEX E

Summary of the Mental Health Act Commission's Response to the Green Paper Proposals on the Reform of the Mental Health Act 1983

The following is the summary of the Commission's full response to the Green Paper[121]. The full document is available upon request from the Commission Office. Paragraph references in parentheses refer to the text of the Green Paper itself.

GUIDING PRINCIPLES
(Consultation Point A)

1   The Commission supports the inclusion of principles in new mental health legislation. There should be a wider set of principles than those proposed in the Green Paper, which place as much emphasis on risk to health as safety as grounds for compulsion and which more strongly assert that alternatives to the use of compulsory powers should be sought.
(paragraphs 49-51)

2   The obligation to ensure that good quality care for detained patients is consistently achieved should be reinforced by the inclusion of reciprocity as one of the underlying principles.
(paragraph 53)

3   Legislation should address, as far as possible, the issue of non-discrimination in relation to areas such as employment, travel, insurance, housing, education and the public representation of mental disorder.
(paragraphs 56, 126)

DEFINITION OF MENTAL DISORDER
(Consultation Point B)

4   The Commission supports the use of a single, generic category of mental disorder to describe persons falling within the scope of a new Mental Health Act. However, there should be greater clarity about the threshold of the disorder which would justify the use of compulsion and the terms 'nature' and 'degree' should be retained in the wording of the criteria for a compulsory order.
(paragraph 57)

THE ENTRY INTO FORMAL ASSESSMENT
(Consultation Point C)

5   The Commission recommends that the applicant for admission should be an Approved Social Worker in order to ensure that there is professional distance between the applicant and recommending clinician and that full account is taken of the patient's social circumstances as well as healthcare needs. There are also benefits in securing the early involvement of social services so that consideration can be given to ensuring the continuity of care following an episode of compulsion.
(paragraph 63)

---

121   **Reform of the Mental Health Act 1983** *Proposals for Consultation. Cm.4480 Nov 1999.*
www.doh.gov.uk/mentalhealth.htm

6 The Commission would be most concerned if admission procedures resulted in a diminution of safeguards. However, if the application and recommendation are provided by mental health professionals who are specially trained with one or both having previous knowledge of the patient, a second recommendation might become superfluous. (paragraphs 65 - 66)

7 Regulations should be introduced as part of the new legislation to improve the process of approval of clinicians to make medical recommendations, thereby increasing their availability. (paragraph 67)

8 The development of large integrated health and social care trusts makes it difficult to ensure the independence of the applicant from the hospital that will be responsible for care and treatment. Furthermore, it is not helpful to retain the concept of hospital as the centre for the provision of care and treatment. (paragraph 68)

EMERGENCY DETENTION
(Consultation Point D)

9 The Commission submits that the maximum period for emergency detention for the purpose of an assessment to be completed should be reduced to 24 hours. (paragraph 69)

10 The Commission would be most concerned if two professionals were not involved in an emergency admission from outside the hospital. In the case of in-patients, the 24 holding power could be initiated by a duly trained and authorised mental health practitioner, including a registered mental health or learning disability nurse who has undertaken specific training. (paragraphs 69-70)

THE NEED FOR AN INDEPENDENT REVIEW WITHIN 7 DAYS
(Consultation point E)

11 The mechanism of a 7 day independent review could not achieve the three functions of ensuring that statutory documentation is in order, that prompt assessment and care planning has taken place and that continued compulsion is justified.

12 The primary responsibility for the scrutiny of statutory documentation must rest with the mental health unit responsible for managing the provision of compulsory care and treatment.

■ Agreed inter-disciplinary report of assessment and care planning should be completed within a time-scale of 28 days, but patients' representatives should be able to check that such a report is available and question any part of it on behalf of patients.

■ In order to avoid a disincentive for the patient to apply for an earlier hearing if the outcome might be an extension of their detention, an expedited tribunal should only have to consider whether the patient should be released from detention under the Act at that point and not make any decisions about future compulsion. (paragraphs 71 - 76)

THE TRIBUNAL
(Consultation Point F)

13 There needs to be a clearer distinction between the judicial function of deciding whether the criteria for compulsion have been met and the clinical function of determining the optimum treatment. (paragraph 77)

14 Tribunals should consist of a legal chair and two other members, not necessarily with direct experience of mental health services. The Commission is opposed to a single-person tribunal whether or not the case is contested. (paragraphs 78 - 79)

THE CRITERIA FOR COMPULSORY CARE AND TREATMENT

(Consultation Point G)

15   The Commission prefers the model without a capacity test, but strongly recommends that the criteria are more narrowly defined to ensure that patients are only made subject to compulsion when it is in their best interests.   (paragraphs 81 - 83)

16   The Commission would have major concerns about the introduction of an incapacity test as a key component among the criteria for compulsion. It doubts whether the presumption in favour of capacity and the requirement that the tribunal would have to be satisfied that capacity has been lost would be sufficient safeguards against improper application.   (paragraph 82)

COMPULSORY POWERS IN THE COMMUNITY

(Consultation Point H)

17   It is accepted that community orders might prove of practical use for some individuals with severe mental illness who regularly default on medication on discharge from hospital and then abruptly relapse. They would also allow for a smoother transition between hospital and community care, possibly reducing the length of stay. But the Commission would only support the introduction of community orders if the additional criteria recommended by the Expert Committee were adopted.   (paragraph 87)

18   There are concerns about how a patient subject to a community order might demonstrate that treatment is no longer required. Consideration should be given to the patient having the right to apply to a tribunal to have a period of time without psychotropic medication being compulsorily administered while still remaining subject to formal assessment.
(paragraphs 88, 90)

TRIBUNAL POWERS OF DISCHARGE

(Consultation Point I)

19   The Commission is strongly of the view that clinical supervisors should be left the power to discharge the patient when the criteria for imposing compulsory care and treatment are no longer met.   (paragraphs 91 - 92)

CRIMINAL JUSTICE SYSTEM

(Consultation Points J, K, L)

20   The Commission supports the proposal for the Court to have a single power to order assessment and treatment to inform its decision whether to make a mental health disposal.
(paragraph 93)

21   The Commission supports the proposal for either the Court of the clinical supervisor to grant leave of absence.   (paragraph 94)

22   The Commission supports the Expert Committee's recommendation that the tribunal's power be extended to include decisions concerning leave of absence and transfer between hospitals for patients under restriction orders.
 (paragraph 95)

23   Although not highlighted as a consultation point, the Commission agrees with the suggestion that a compulsory order made by a court should authorise that care and treatment can be given in hospital or the community on a similar basis to non-offenders.   (paragraph 96)

24   The Commission recommends that the remit of its successor body should be extended to cover both prisoners referred for and awaiting transfer to hospital and that there should be a duty to record all administration of medication said to be justified under common law.
(paragraph 97)

POLICE POWERS
(Consultation Points M, N)

25   The Commission supports the proposal that police powers to remove people from public places to a place of safety be extended to cover private premises which they have legitimately entered.
(paragraph 98)

26   The Commission supports the suggestion that arrested persons who appear to be suffering from mental disorder should, where necessary, get early access to a gate keeping assessment.
(paragraph 99)

ECT
(Consultation Point O)

27   The Commission is not convinced that a refusal of consent to ECT by a mentally capable patient necessarily should prevent that treatment being imposed. Although many patients who might be considered for ECT as a potentially life-saving treatment will not have mental capacity due to their illness, some may retain capacity. The Commission cannot see the benefit of creating a system whereby clinicians would find advantage in diagnosing their patients as lacking mental capacity.
(paragraph 103)

28   Given that ECT can be a life-saving treatment, the Commission's view is that the treatment should be available under provisions covering urgent treatment.
(paragraph 105)

SAFEGUARDS FOR SPECIFIED TREATMENTS
(Consultation Point P)

29   The Commission recommends that naso-gastric feeding for anorexia nervosa should be identified as a specific treatment that is subject to special safeguards.
(paragraph 103)

30   The Commission doubts whether it is practical to adopt criteria by which the Secretary of State can decide which treatments should be covered by special safeguards. Each treatment could be dealt with on its own merits, but if criteria are needed at all, the concept of 'invasiveness' would be relevant.
(paragraph 106)

31   The Commission agrees with the Government that depot medication should not be subject to special safeguards. It is also doubtful that it is realistic to legislate about polypharmacy or the administration of medication above BNF recommended dosages, partly because this relies on a legislative interpretation of the British National Formulary (in effect, giving it a use for which it is not designed). Good practice in the use of medication could be maintained by other means, such as guidance issued in the Code of Practice, by NICE and through clinical governance.
(paragraphs 107 -108)

SHOULD THE THREE-MONTH PERIOD BE CHANGED?
(Consultation Point Q)

32   The Commission recommends that protection of a second opinion should be offered either from the beginning of the imposition of treatment or after a shorter period than 3 months, even if such treatments are exploratory.
(paragraph 109)

EMERGENCY TREATMENT

(Consultation Point R)

33.   The Commission is strongly opposed to the proposal that patients might be detained without effective treatment that would be within their best interests for any period other than whilst being held for formal admission procedures to be completed, believing it to be unethical.

(paragraph 111)

THE NOMINATED PERSON

(Consultation Point S)

34.   The criteria for appointing a nominated person for a person who does not nominate anyone and who lacks capacity to do so should be based upon what the person concerned can do for the patient, rather than his or her relationship with the patient.

(paragraph 112)

INFORMATION SHARING

(Consultation Points T, U)

35.   The Commission believes that the further development of guidance and protocols on the sharing of information in respect of patients subject to compulsory powers is essential.

(paragraph 114)

36.   There should be a system of review available to the patient who thinks that information has been or is about to be improperly shared, including when information is to be given to victims of a restricted offender.

(paragraph 115)

MATTERS NOT INCLUDED IN THE GREEN PAPER

37.   There is no mention in the Green Paper of the need to provide more statutory guidance on control and discipline issues (seclusion; restraint; powers to search patients, withhold property, refuse leave or access to hospital activities, interfere with freedom of communication and association). The Commission urges the Government to include the regulation of the powers to exercise control and discipline, in some form, in legislation.

(paragraphs 118 -119)

38.   The Green Paper makes no reference to the Expert Committee's recommendation of a user's right to an assessment of his or her own mental health needs. The Commission urges the government to reconsider this recommendation, which would potentially reduce the risk of some individuals engaging in behaviour harmful to themselves or others before they received attention for their mental health needs.

(paragraph 121)

39.   The Commission also urges the Government to reconsider the Expert Committee recommendation concerning the introduction of a number of specific rights with corresponding duties which would apply to patients under compulsion. The Commission particularly wishes to emphasise that there should be a duty to provide information, which should extend not only to information on the legal position of patients and their rights but also on the care and treatments offered.

(paragraphs 55, 122 - 123)

40.   The gap in the provision of safeguards for compliant but incapacitated patients remains. The Commission considers that the Expert Committee recommendation that the extension of second opinion provisions to all patients without capacity to consent, whether or not they are subject to formal compulsory powers, would be a step in the right direction in ensuring that the care and treatment provided is in the best interests of such patients.

(paragraphs 124 - 125)

41. The Commission recommends that additional safeguards should be introduced to prevent patients from disadvantages that may be consequential to their having been made subject to compulsion.

(paragraph 126)

Appendix F

MANAGING DANGEROUS PEOPLE WITH SEVERE PERSONALITY DISORDERS

Response of the Mental Health Act Commission to the proposals for policy development[122]

INTRODUCTION

1   The Mental Health Act Commission (MHAC) acts as a watchdog, on behalf of the Secretary of State and the National Assembly for Wales, on the operation of the Mental Health Act 1983 (the 1983 Act) in England and Wales. During the period of the MHAC's Eighth Biennial Report, from April 1997 to March 1999, Mental Health Act Commissioners made over 1500 visits to facilities holding detained patients, had private meetings with over 15000 detained patients and made informal contact with 8000 others. Although relatively few of these patients will have been diagnosed as having a personality disorder, these visits and meetings put the Commission in a unique position to comment on the Government's proposals.

2   The 150 Commissioners are psychiatrists, psychologists, doctors, nurses, lawyers, social workers and other specialists or "lay" people with a special interest in mental disorder and many of them also have experience of either the criminal courts or the prison service or both. They therefore cover a very wide range of expertise and a correspondingly wide range of views. All Commissioners have been invited to comment individually on the Government's proposals, which have been considered in depth by the Commission's Legal and Ethical Special Interest Group. This response reflects views expressed by the Group and has been approved by the MHAC Board but cannot be regarded as reflecting a consensus of all Commissioners.

Summary of the Commission's views.

3   The Commission welcomes the consultation document as a valuable trigger for discussion of the difficult issues raised by the need to balance the safety of the public against rights of individuals who are believed likely to be dangerous. It is also a useful starting point for the development of an integrated policy for handling those who pose a real threat to the safety of the general public or of individual members within it.

4   The Commission's views are set out in some detail in the following paper but may be summarised as follows:

   i   there is not sufficient clarity about what constitutes either "dangerousness" or "severe personality disorder" to justify detention on any basis other than actual criminal behaviour or the likelihood of hospital treatment alleviating or preventing a deterioration in a mental disorder.

---

122   Department of Health and Home Office (1999) **Managing Dangerous People with Severe Personality Disorder – Proposals for Policy Development.**

ii There is not sufficient evidence to show that the risk to the public from people with a personality disorder who might be regarded as dangerous is great enough to justify significant changes to current mental health legislation.

iii If a Government believes that new indeterminate custodial disposals are needed for people who have committed criminal offences, this is a question of preventative detention under the criminal law and the issue of personality disorder only becomes relevant if a hospital disposal would provide a better chance of reducing dangerousness by alleviating or preventing a deterioration in mental disoder. In this context, we believe that "treatability" shopuld be interpreted broadly to include care and treatment which "is likely to enable the patient to cope more satisfactorily with his disorder or its symptoms, or…stops his condition becoming worse"[123].

iv The work described in Part 3, paragraph 35 onwards; Part 4; and annexes D and E in the consultation document goes a long way towards addressing problems in managing individuals who can reliably be regarded as dangerous. Disposals already available to the Courts but apparently underused would also meet some of the concerns expressed. It would be premature to make significant changes to mental health legislation before all these initiatives have had a chance to work and to be properly assessed.

v There would be advantage in having a multi-disciplinary specialist service for the assessment of dangerousness but this should be a second stage to, rather than a replacement for existing arrangements for assessment under mental health legislation and should be closely linked to funding for special provision.

vi Considerable additional benefits could be gained from changes in funding, increased and improved inter-agency training and greater multi-disciplinary co-operation in relation to people thought likely to be dangerous, regardless of whether they are diagnosed as having a severe personality disorder.

vii There are also additional preventative measures which could reduce the likelihood of danger to the public.

viii Finally, each of the three preceding points could enhance research and development which could lead, in due course, to a more empirical assessment of the need for and propriety of a new categorisation of "dangerous people with severe personality disorder".

5 All of the Commission's views are based on adherence to two fundamental principles of the centrality of the concept of justice and the need for reciprocity where people are compulsorily detained other than as a result of criminal proceedings. In our view, the concept of justice requires that the liberty of the individual should be restricted only in accordance with clearly defined legislative provisions and only when it is proved to be essential for their own protection or for that of the public. Detention on grounds other than criminal behaviour, e.g. for reasons of public health or safety whether based upon actual illness or behaviour or, even more crucially, on the likelihood of such illness or behaviour, must adhere to the principle of reciprocity, i.e. that the individaul concerned must be provided with whatever services are most likely to alleviate or prevent a deterioration in the condition which determines detention.

---

123 Mental Health Act Memorandum - paragraph 16

Dangerous people with severe personality disorder

6   The Commission found great difficulty in commenting on the analysis in the consultation document because, although it accepts the need for a generic term to describe the people to whom the Government proposals refer, we believe that the categorisation "dangerous people with severe personality disorder" is wrong and unnecessarily distorts the whole approach to the problems that the document sets out to address. Annex A to the Government document itself highlights the lack of any consensus as to what is meant by "severe personality disorder" and the summary of research in Annex C prompts the following comments:

- There are no measures to define what is meant by "severe" personality disorder, nor is there any definition of "dangerousness" which relates uniquely those with personality disorders (whether severe or not) as compared with other dangerous individuals who may show no sign of mental disorder.

- Although it is possible to identify many common developmental and behavioural indicators which may lead to behaviour attributed to personality disorder , risk assessment has to be based upon knowledge of individuals rather than on a group label because of the lack of group homogeneity or predictability.

- There is little evidence to show that particular approaches to treatment are successful except in relation to particular individuals.

7   The Commission believes that this term should be rejected because it gives the wrong impression that this is a clearly recognisable group rather than a wide spectrum of very different individuals requiring an equally wide spectrum of management.

8   The Commission has concerns about this term which are more particular to its function of monitoring the implementation of the Mental Health Act. The constant juxtaposition of the words "dangerous" and "severe" with "personality disorder" is very likely to give rise to a general belief that people with personality disorders are likely to be a danger to the public. There is no empirical basis for such an assumption. Moreover, media inaccuracy and the linkage with mental health services which is emphasised in the consultation document are likely to fuel the perception that because personality disorder is a mental disorder (and "mental disorder" and "mental illness" are not commonly distinguished from each other), the implication is that mentally ill people are more likely to be dangerous than anyone else. However unjustifiable these linkages are, we are concerned that they:

- will perpetuate the stigma attached to mental illness by implying that mentally ill people are more likely to be dangerous and that dangerous people who are mentally ill are inevitably more dangerous than those who are not;

- may increase racial prejudice because of the diproportionately high number of Black people who are detained under the Mental Health Act (even if for reasons other than personality disorder);

- will act as a disincentive to the very people who are most in need of mental health treatment but will not seek it for fear of being labelled as dangerous.

These likely outcomes are directly contrary to the Government's strongly stated support of the principle of non-discrimination and the very positive action which is already being taken to ensure that help is made available to mentally ill people as early as possible.[124]

---

124   see **Psychiatric Bulletin**, 23:12 Dec 1999 for support of these views.

The extent of the problem

9   Although the consultation document (Part 2, paragraphs 3 and 4) provides estimates of the number of people who might be regarded as falling within the DSPD group, there is little empirical basis for this estimate, nor for the assumption that greater availability of indeterminate disposals for the group referred to would lead to a reduction of 200 serious crimes a year. In 1998/99 there were only 50 court and prison disposals and 38 civil detentions for reasons of psychopathic disorder in England[125]. The consultation document records that less than 2% of those liable for indeterminate sentences under criminal legilation received such sentences. Both these figures suggest that, before assuming that new disposals are necessary, greater attention needs to be paid to the reasons for not using existing ones.

10 No information is available about how many of the 680 patients detained in hospital facilities (on 31 March 1999) with a diagnosis of psychopathic disorder might be considered to be dangerous in the sense envisaged by the proposals. There may be some whose personality disorder might not be labelled "severe" but who could be dangerous, and vice-versa. The assumption that people with a psychopathic disorders are likely to be a risk to the public seems to be based upon media hyperbole about the very small number of such people who have committed serious offences. Where there has been a public inquiry into such cases, the failure has often been in the non-use of existing services than in the absence of legislative provision. The assessment of risk which might justify compulsory detention for someone who has not already proved to be dangerous should surely be comparable with the kind of epidemiological study which supports other health initiatives.

---

125   Department of Health (October 1999) **Statistical Bulletin: In-patients formally detained in hospitals under the Mental Health Act 1983 and other legislation: 1988 -89 to 1998-99.**

APPENDIX G

MENTAL HEALTH ACT COMMISSION

Summary Financial Statements 1999/2000 & 2000/01

1998/99 £'000s	Revenue Account	1999/00 £'000s	2000/01 £'000s
	Fees and Expenses		
70	- Chairman & Non Executive Board Members	38	73
1,330	- Commissioners	1,242	1,238
1,051	- SOADs	978	1,055
	Management & Support Staff costs		
91	- Senior Management Costs	90	87
443	- Support Staff Costs	447	465
	Other Operating Costs and Expenses		
168	- Administration Expenses	194	200
146	- Accommodation & Office Equipment	226	262
0	- Cost of Capital Employed	14	22
3,299	**Gross Operating Costs**	**3,229**	**3,402**
	Funding Sources		
3,230	- Department of Health	3,047	2,998
N/A	- National Assembly of Wales	68	68
41	- Misc Fees and Recharges	73	91
3,271	**Total Resources Available**	**3,188**	**3,157**
	Analysis of Deficit(Surplus)		
0	- Cost of Capital Employed	14	22
24	- Unfunded SOAD Fees & Expenses	9	283
0	- Unfunded Costs Re Judicial Reviews	0	52
4	- Over(Under)Spend On All Other Activities	18	-112
28	**Net Deficit(Surplus)Per Accounts**	**41**	**245**
211	**Accumulated Deficit C/Fwd**	**252**	**497**
	Balance Sheet		
	Current Assets		
61	- Debtors	36	50
4	- Cash In Hand	2	2
	Current Liabilities		
-276	- Creditors due within 1 Year	-290	-549

-211	Net Current Assets(Liabilities)	-252	-497
	Funded by		
-211	General Fund at Department of Health	-252	-497
	Extract From Notes to the Accounts		
33	1 Average Staff Employed	32	31
160	2 Average Number of Commissioners	169	175
165	3 Average Number of SOADs	161	185
£55,000	4 Chief Executives' Remuneration		
	(Part year costs only 2000/01)	£51,000	£44,519
£14,204	5 Chairman's Remuneration	£12,590	18,540
	6 Remuneration of Other Non Executive Directors		
2	- £0 to £5,000 pa	5	3
1	- £5,000 to £10,000pa	1	2
1	- £10,000 to £15,000pa	0	1

Summary Directors Statement on Internal Financial Accounts

The Chief Executive, together with the other Directors, has a responsibility for reviewing the effectiveness of the organisation's system of internal financial control. In carrying out such reviews in accordance with EL97(55) directors are required to confirm that the 'minimum standards' laid down by the NHS Executive have been in existence within the organisation throughout the financial years now reported.

The directors confirm that they have undertaken such review and that the above requirements have been met with the exception that

a) there was no audit or remuneration committee. Instead, a Finance and Audit sub-committee of the Board operated throughout both years now reported.

b) the Fraud and Corruption Policy and Standing Orders were not adopted by the Board until 21 March 2001

By Order of the Board at its meeting on 16 August 2001

Dated 31 August 2001
Signed

Paul Hampshire, Chief Executive

Statutory Auditor's Report and Opinion

We have examined the summary financial statements set out on pages 157 to 158 of this report and the summary director's statements on internal financial control.

Respective Responsibilities of Directors and Auditors

The directors are responsible for preparing the Bi-ennial Report. Our responsibility is to report our opinion on the consistency of the summary financial statements and the summary director's statements on internal financial control with the statutory financial statements. We also read the other information contained within the Bi-ennial Report and consider the implications for our report if we become aware of any mis-statements or material inconsistencies with the summary financial statements.

Basis of Opinion

We conducted our work in accordance with Bulletin 1999/6 'The Auditor's statement on the summary financial statements' issued by the Auditing Practices Board for use in the United Kingdom.

Opinion

In our opinion the summary financial statements and the summary director's statement on internal financial control are consistent with the statutory financial statements of the organisation for the years ended 31 March 2000 and 2001 respectively and we have issued an unqualified statement for both years.

Signed

District Audit
1st Floor
Bridge Business Park
Bridge Park Road
Thurmaston
Leicester LE4 8BL

Chris Wilson
District Auditor

Mental Health Act Commission Members 1999 - 2001

Ms M Agar

Mr C Aggett

Mr V Alexander ~

Dr H Allen

Dr T Ananthanarayanan[W]

Ms A Anderson*

Mr A Backer-Holst

Ms C Bamber[+]

Mr R Bamlett

Dr S Banerjee

Mr M Beebe

Dr C Berry[W]

Ms K Berry

Mr A Best

Dr D Black

Mr J Blavo

Ms L Bolter

Dr D Brandford

Mr R Brown

Mr B Burke

Ms H Burke*

Ms J Burton

Ms F Cassells*

Ms M Casewell

Mr H Chapman

Ms Noelle Chesworth

Miss M A Clayton[+]

Mr F Cofie ~

Mrs A Cooney

Ms S Cragg

Mr C Curran*

Dr O Daniels

Dr C Davies

Mr H Davis[W]

Mr A Deery

Mr B Delaney ~

Mrs S Desai

Dr D Dick*

Mr M Dodds[W]

Mrs Margot DosAnjos[+W]

Mr R Dosoo

Mrs P Douglas-Hall

Mrs G Downham

Mr A Drew

Mr R Earle[TM]

Mr T Eaton

Ms P Edwards

Dr A El Khomy ~

Mr H Field

Mr P Fisher ~

Mr M Follows

Mr M Foolchand[W] ~

Miss D Frempong ~

Ms E Frost

Mr S Gannon

Ms M Garner

Ms E Gilham

Mr M Golightly

Ms J Gossage

Mr H Griffiths

Ms C Grimshaw

Mr G Halliday

Miss C Harvey

Mrs S Harvey[W~]

Miss S Hayles

Mrs J Healey

Mr S Hedges[W]

Miss A Henry

Ms P Heslop

Mrs C Hewitt

Mr D Hewitt

Mr D Hill[+]

Mr M Hill

Mr B Hoare

Dr J Holliday

Mr W Horder ~

Mr J Horne

Ms B Howard

Mr P Howes

Ms L Ingham*

Mr C Inyama

Mr M Jamil

Dr T Jerram

Ms L Jones*

Dr O Junaid

Dr A Kelly

Nr N Khan

Mr S Klein^{TM}

Dr S Knights ~

Mr G Lakes CB MC[+]

Ms A Lawrence

Mrs S Ledwith

Mr P Lee

Mr N Lees OBE [TM]

Ms P Letts

Ms H Lewis

Mrs J Lewis[W]

Mrs M Lloyd[W]

Canon F Longbottom[TM]

Ms E MacMin ~

Ms M Madden

Dr S Manjubhashini

Mr J Marlow[W]

Miss L Marriot

Mr Y Marsen-Luther [TM]

Dr R Mather

Miss M McCann

Mr C McCarthy

Mr D McCarthy[TM]

Ms S McKeever

Ms A McKenna

Dr J McKenna

Ms J McKenzie*

Mrs S McMillan

Miss N Mehta ~

Mrs J Meredith

Mr A Milligan ~

Mr J Moran

Mr B MorganTM

Mr A Morley

Mr P Moxley

Ms M Napier

Mrs A Navarro

Mr M Naylor

Ms M Nettle

Mr I Newton

Mr R Nichol

Mr L Nicholas

Inspector N North

Ms P Oglivie[W]

Mr B O'Hare

Ms J Olsen*

Mrs J Oraka ~

Ms C Parker*

Mrs E Parker

Mrs J Patel

Mr K Patel OBE [+]

Mrs J Patterson

Ms L Pavincich

Mr A Persaud

Mr R Peters

Mr S Pierre*

Mr R Plumb[TMW]

Mr E Prtak [cc]

Ms M Purcell*

Mrs S Ramprogus

Mr S Ramrecha

Ms E Rassaby[TM*]

Ms E Reid ~

Ms Marion Rickman

Dr G Roberts

Ms H Roberts

Mr N Robinson MBE JP

Mr R Robinson

Ms J Rogers [TM*]

Ms H Ross*

Dr R Ryall[TM]

Ms N Sadique ~

Dr A Sayal-Bennett

Mr J Sedgeman

Ms B Sensky

Mrs D Shaw

Mrs K Sheldon

Dr M Smith ~

Mr R Southern[W]

Mrs R Spafford

Ms J Spenser[W]

Ms S Squires[W]

Ms P Stott ~

Dr M Swann

Mr M Taylor

Mr P Taylor

Mrs H Thoma[W]

Mr P Thompson ~

Ms J Turnbull

Ms J Tweedie

Mr J Walker

Mr R Webster*

Ms M Wenham ~

Mr M Wilce

Prof R Williams⁺

Ms R Wiliams-Flew

Mr A Williamson™

Mr B Windle

Mr T Wishart

Mr J Withington*

Mr T Wrigglesworth

Mr A Wright

Mr T Wright

Dr T Zigmond

Appendix I

Second Opinion Appointed Doctors 1999 – 2001

Dr M Abdurahman

Dr R Abed

Dr P Abraham

Dr D S Addala

Dr S W Ahmad

Dr M Al-Bachari

Dr M Alexander

Dr S Ananthakopan

Dr T Ananthanarayanan

Dr R P Arya

Dr D Atapattu

Dr G Bagley

Dr S Benbow

Dr J Besson

Dr R Bloor

Dr J Bolton

Dr C Boyd

Dr A Briggs

Dr C Brook

Dr C Brown

Dr N Brown

Dr M Browne

Dr A Burke

Dr A Cade

Dr C Calvert

Dr W Charles

Dr A Chaudhary

Dr R Chitty

Dr M Cleary

Dr J Cockburn

Dr J Colgan

Dr J Conway

Dr M Conway

Dr M Courtney

Dr C Cruikshank

Dr R Davenport

Dr J Davies

Dr M Davies

Dr N Davies

Dr K Davison

Dr G Dawson

Dr V Deacon

Dr N Desai

Dr M Devakumar

Dr D Dick

Dr G Dubourg

Dr K Dudleston

Dr J Dunlop

Dr B Easby

Dr A Easton

Dr C Edwards

Dr A El-Komy

Dr V Evans

Dr G Feggetter

Dr T Fenton

Dr S Fernando

Dr E Gallagher

Dr G Gallimore

Dr N Gittleson

Dr S Goh

Dr M Goonatilleke

Dr H Gordon

Dr E Gregg

Dr G Grewal

Dr J Grimshaw

Dr K Gupta

Dr D Hambridge

Dr M Harper

Dr T Harrison

Dr F Harrop

Dr B Harwin

Dr G Hayes

Dr M Hession

Dr S Hettiaratchy

Dr P Hettiaratchy

Dr O Hill

Dr R Hill

Dr G Hughes

Dr R Hughes

Dr K Hussain

Dr M Hussain

Dr J Hutchinson

Dr G Ibrahimi

Dr S Iles

Dr J Jain

Dr H James

Dr S James

Dr P Jeffreys

Dr J Jenkins

Dr B John

Dr D Jones

Dr R Jones

Dr S Joseph

Dr F Judelson

Dr A Kaeser

Dr S H Kamlana

Dr G Kanakaratnam

Dr A Kellam

Dr J Kellett

Dr K Khan

Dr L Kremer

Dr G Langley

Dr N Lockhart

Dr M Loizou

Dr R Londhe

Dr B Lowe

Dr M Lowe

Dr G Luyombya

Dr J Lyon

Dr P Madely

Dr B Mann

Dr H Markar

Dr H Matthew

Dr F McKenzie

Dr D McVitie

Dr P Meats

Dr G Mehta

Dr I Mian

Dr G Milner

Dr A Minto

Dr N Minton

Dr B Moore

Dr K Mosleh-Uddin

Dr N Murugananthan

Dr D Myers

Dr G Nanyakkara

Dr T Nelson

Dr J Noble

Dr M O'Brien

Dr A Okoko

Dr R Oliver

Dr D Pariente

Dr J Parker

Dr G Patel

Dr I Pennell

Dr A Perini

Dr R Philpott

Dr W Prothero

Dr I Pryce

Dr E Quraishy

Dr D Rajapakse

Dr T Rajmanickam

Dr D Ramster

Dr S Rastogi

Dr N Renton

Dr E Richards

Dr J Rucinski

Dr R Sagovsky

Dr G S Sama

Dr G Sampson

Dr P Sarkar

Dr G Shetty

Dr A Silverman

Dr N Silvester

Dr I Singh

Dr S B Singhal

Dr M Smith

Dr A Soliman

Dr C Staley

Dr S Stephens

Dr N Suleman

Dr M Swan

Dr R Symonds

Dr L Tarlo

Dr T Tennent

Dr R Thavasothy

Dr R Thaya-Paran

Dr I Thompson

Dr P Urwin

Dr N Verma

Dr G Vincenti

Dr J Waite

Dr C Wallbridge

Dr A Walsh

Dr D Ward

Dr B Weerakoon

Dr M Weller

Dr A Whitehouse

Dr A Wilson

Dr S Wood

Dr A Yonance

Appendix J

Background Documents to this Report

Key Documents

Deaths of Detained Patients in England and Wales, Mental Health Act Commission, 2001

Safe enough? Inspection of Health Authority Registration and Inspection Units 2000 Social Services Inspectorate, Department of Health 2001

Mental Health National Service Framework (and the NHS Plan): Workforce Planning, Education and Training, Underpinning Programme: Adult Mental Health Services: Workforce Action Team Final Report Department of Health 2001

Detained: SSI Inspection of Compulsory Mental Health Admissions Department of Health 2001

An Audit Pack for Monitoring the Care Programme Approach, Department of Health, 2001

Mental Health Policy Implementation Guide, Department of Health, 2001

National Service Framework for Older People, Department of Health, 2001

The Vital Connection: An equalities framework for the NHS, NHSE, 2001

Valuing People: A New Strategy for Learning Disability for the 21st Century, Department of Health, 2001

Safety First: Five-Year Report of the National Confidential Inquiry into Suicide and Homicide by People with Mental Illness, National Confidential Inquiry 2000

Reform of the Mental Health Act - White Paper, Department of Health, 2000

Reform of the Mental Health Act - Summary of consultation responses, Department of Health, 2000

The NHS Plan, Department of Health, 2000

Improving Working Lives, Department of Health 2000

Finding and Keeping, Sainsbury Centre for Mental Health 2000

National Visit 2 – Improving Care for Detained Patients in Black and Minority Ethnic Communities, Sainsbury Centre for Mental Health, 2000

Women and Mental Health, Edited by Dora Kohen, 2000

A Health Service of all the talents, Department of Health, 2000

The Race Equality Agenda of the Department of Health, 2000

Provision of NHS Mental Health Services, Fourth Report, Health Select Committee, 2000. Volume I - *Report and Proceedings*; Volume II - *Minutes of Evidence and Appendices*

No secrets: Guidance on developing and implementing multi-agency policies and procedures to protect vulnerable adults from abuse Department of Health 2000

National Service Framework for Mental Health

Safer Services - National Confidential Inquiry into Suicide and Homicide by People with Mental Illness, 1999

A systematic review of research relating to the Mental Health Act (1983), Department of Health, 1999

Effective care co-ordination in mental health services, Modernising the care programme approach, 1999

Making a Difference, Department of Health, 1999

Managing Dangerous People with Severe Personality Disorder: Proposals for Policy Development, Home Office, 1999

Addressing black and ethnic minority mental health in London – a review and recommendations, London NHSE, 1999

The Mental Health Act 1983 – Explanatory Memorandum on Parts I to VI, VIII and X

The Mental Health Act 1983 – Code of Practice 1999

Statistics

In-patients formally detained in hospitals under the Mental Health Act 1983 and other legislation, England: 1999-2000 Department of Health, February 2001

Guardianship under the Mental Health Act 1983, England, 2000, Department of Health, February 2001

Statistics of Mentally Disordered Offenders in England and Wales, 1999, Home Office, Issue 21/00, issued 30th November 2000

Admission of Patients to Mental Health Facilities in Wales, 1999-00 SDB 116/2000. Available free from Viv Trew, Health Statistics and Analysis Unit, National Assembly for Wales, Cathays Park, Cardiff, CF10 3NQ (Tel: 029-2082-5016; Fax: 029-2082-5350; Email: vivien.trew@wales.gsi.gov.uk

In-patients formally detained in hospitals under the Mental Health Act 1983 and other legislation, England: 1989-1990 to 1999-2000 Department of Health, October 2000

Mental health review tribunals for England and Wales – annual report 1997 - 1998, Department of Health, May 2000

Electro Convulsive Therapy: Survey covering the period January 1999 to March 1999, England, September 1999

Government Circulars

HSC 2001/015: LAC (2001)18 - Continuing Care: NHS and Local Councils' responsibilities

HSC 2001/011 Care Standards Act 2000: transition arrangements for the creation of the National Care Standards Commission

CRIMINAL JUSTICE AND COURT SERVICES ACT 2000: AMENDMENTS TO THE SEX OFFENDERS ACT 1997. Home Office Circular 20/2001

Data Protection Act 1998: protection and use of patient information. HSC 2000/009

THE HUMAN RIGHTS ACT 1998 Health Service Circular 2000/025 & Local Authority Circular LAC (2000)17

Modernising mental health services: mental health grant 2000/2001 MISC (2000)18

After-care under the Mental Health Act 1983: section 117 after-care services LAC (2000)3

After-care under the Mental Health Act 1983: section 117 after-care services HSC 2000/003

Mental health grant (MHG): use of slippage 1999/2000 MISC (2000)1

Effective care co-ordination in mental health services Modernising the care programme approach - A policy booklet

National framework for mental health : Modern standards and service models for mental health HSC 1999/223

HSC 1999/180: LAC (99)30 - Ex parte Coughlan: Follow up Action

Commissioning in the new NHS specialised commissioning high and medium security psychiatric services HSC 1999/141

NHS modernisation fund and mental health grant for child and adolescent mental health services 1999/2002 HSC 1999/126

Mental Health Supplementary Credit Aprrovals 1999/2000 for Developing Social Care Services For People With Mental Illness HSC 1999/058

Mental Health Act 1983 revised code of practice HSC 1999/050

Modernising mental health services NHS modernisation fund for mental health services & mental health grant 1999/2002 HSC 1999/038

NHS beacon services HSC 1999/034

Mental Health Act 1983 code of practice : guidance on the visiting of psychiatric patients by children LAC (99)32

Guidance to local authority social services departments on visits by children to special hospitals LAC (99)23

NHS modernisation fund and mental health grant for child and adolescent mental health services 1999/2002 LAC (99)22

Modernising mental health services NHS modernisation fund for mental health services & mental health grant 1999/2002 LAC (99)8

Still building bridges : inspection of arrangements for the integration of care programme approach with care management CI (99)3

L v Bournewood Community and Mental Health NHS Trust decision by the House of Lords in the appeal HSC 1998/122

Joint finance and mental health HSC 1998/037

Modernising Mental Health Services: safe, sound and supportive LAC (98)25

Training support programme "Letting through light: a training pack on black people and mental health" CI (98)13

Court of Appeal judgement L v Bournewood Community and Mental Health Trust MISC (98)7 MISC (98)7

Moving into the mainstream SSI report on inspection of services for adults with learning disabilities CI (98)6

Mental Health Act Commission Publications

Patient Information Leaflets

Leaflets are available in the following languages from the Commission :- Urdu, Bengali, Gujerati, Punjabi, French, German, Somali, Vietnamese, Cantonese, Mandarin, Tamil, Spanish, English, Welsh. Copies in English and Welsh can be downloaded from the Commission website (www.mhac.trent.nhs.uk). Bulk orders of any leaflet are £12 per 50 copies +£1.50 p&p from chiefexec@mhac.trent.nhs.uk or the Commission office.

Leaflet Number 1 - *Information for Detained Patients about the Mental Health Act Commission*

Leaflet number 2 - *Information for Detained Patients about Consent to Treatment (Medication)*

Leaflet Number 3 - *Information for Detained Patients about Consent to Treatment Electroconvulsive Therapy (ECT)*

Leaflet Number 4 - *Information for Detained Patients about How to Make a Complaint*

Leaflet Number 5 - *Information for Patients about Neurosurgery for Mental Disorder (Psychosurgery) and The Mental Health Act Commission*

Practice and Guidance Notes

Available on the MHAC website www.mhac.trent.nhs.uk, or individual copies can be requested free of charge from the Commission office.

Practice Note 1   *Guidance on the administration of Clozapine and other treatments requiring blood tests* (issued June 1993, updated March 1999)

Practice Note 2   *Nurses, the administration of medicine for mental disorder and the Mental Health Act 1983* (reissued March 2001)

Guidance Note 1   *Guidance to health authorities: the Mental Health Act 1983* (issued December 1996, updated March 1999)

Guidance Note 3   *Guidance on the treatment of anorexia nervosa under the Mental Health Act 1983* (issued August 1997, updated March 1999)

Guidance Note 2/98   *Scrutinising and rectifying statutory forms under the Mental Health Act 1983* (issued November 1998, updated March 1999)

Guidance Note 1/99   *Issues surrounding Sections 17, 18 and 19 of the Mental Health Act 1983* (issued August 1999)

Guidance Note 2/99   *Issues relating to the administration of the Mental Health Act in Registered Mental Nursing Homes* (reissued December 1999)

Guidance Note 1/2000 *General Practitioners and the Mental Health Act 1983.* (reissued May 2000)

Guidance Note 1/2001 *Use of the Mental Health Act 1983 in general hospitals without a psychiatric unit* (issued August 2001)

Other publications

Deaths of Detained Patients in England and Wales; a Report by the Mental Health Act Commission on Information Collected from 1 February 1997 to January 2000.

Mental Health Act Commission publication.   44pp   February 2001   £7.95 pbk

The executive summary of this Report is at appendix X above. Copies of the full report are available from the Commission Office for £7.95 + £1 p&p (postage free for orders of more than 5 copies). Cheques should be made payable to the Department of Health.

Mental Health Act Commission Eighth Biennial Report (1997 – 1999).

Stationery Office publication ISBN 0 11 322280 7 309pp   August 1999   £14 pbk

Report available from the Stationery Office and bookshops

Contacting the Mental Health Act Commission

You can contact the Mental Health Act Commission at the following address:

Mental Health Act Commission

Maid Marion House

56 Hounds Gate

Nottingham

NG1 6BG

Tel: 0115 9437100

Fax:0115 9437101

E-mail: Chief.executive@mhac.trent.nhs.uk

Website: www.mhac.trent.nhs.uk